Multicultural Psychology

To my children, Ben, Cate, and Chloe: May the world be more just when you are grown, and may you have participated in making it so.
And for Brian, who always stands beside me.

—JTP

I dedicate this to the memory of my grandfather, Eli Williams; and to the person from whom so much of my family's identity comes—my grandmother, Lillie Williams.

—DI

Sara Miller McCune founded SAGE Publishing in 1965 to support the dissemination of usable knowledge and educate a global community. SAGE publishes more than 1000 journals and over 800 new books each year, spanning a wide range of subject areas. Our growing selection of library products includes archives, data, case studies and video. SAGE remains majority owned by our founder and after her lifetime will become owned by a charitable trust that secures the company's continued independence.

Los Angeles | London | New Delhi | Singapore | Washington DC | Melbourne

Multicultural Psychology

Self, Society, and Social Change

Jennifer Teramoto Pedrotti

California Polytechnic State University
San Luis Obispo

Denise A. Isom

California Polytechnic State University
San Luis Obispo

Los Angeles | London | New Delhi
Singapore | Washington DC | Melbourne

FOR INFORMATION:

SAGE Publications, Inc.
2455 Teller Road
Thousand Oaks, California 91320
E-mail: order@sagepub.com

SAGE Publications Ltd.
1 Oliver's Yard
55 City Road
London, EC1Y 1SP
United Kingdom

SAGE Publications India Pvt. Ltd.
B 1/I 1 Mohan Cooperative Industrial Area
Mathura Road, New Delhi 110 044
India

SAGE Publications Asia-Pacific Pte. Ltd.
18 Cross Street #10-10/11/12
China Square Central
Singapore 048423

Printed in the United States of America

Library of Congress Cataloging-in-Publication Data

Names: Pedrotti, Jennifer Teramoto, author. | Isom, Denise A., author.
Title: Multicultural psychology : self, society, and social change / Jennifer T. Pedrotti, Denise A. Isom.
Description: First edition. | Thousand Oaks, California : SAGE Publications, [2021] | Includes bibliographical references.
Identifiers: LCCN 2020017293 | ISBN 9781506375885 (paperback) | ISBN 9781506375861 (epub) | ISBN 9781506375878 (epub) | ISBN 9781506375892 (ebook)
Subjects: LCSH: Ethnopsychology—United States. | Minorities—United States—Psychology. | Ethnic groups—United States—Psychology.
Classification: LCC GN502 .P43 2021 | DDC 155.8/20973—dc23
LC record available at https://lccn.loc.gov/2020017293

This book is printed on acid-free paper.

Acquisitions Editor: Lara Parra
Content Development Editor: Emma Newsom
Editorial Assistant: Sam Diaz
Production Editor: Veronica Stapleton Hooper
Copy Editor: Cate Huisman
Typesetter: Hurix Digital
Proofreader: Sally Jaskold
Indexer: Integra
Cover Designer: Karine Hovsepian
Marketing Manager: Katherine Hepburn

20 21 22 23 24 10 9 8 7 6 5 4 3 2 1

BRIEF CONTENTS

DETAILED CONTENTS

PREFACE

When this book was still just an idea, two friends met at a luncheon on their university campus. It seems significant to note that the luncheon was to honor the African American feminist scholar bell hooks, who had come to our campus that week to give a keynote address. Dr. hooks was at a nearby table when talk of this book came up between the two authors. Maybe it was her many quotes about acting on one's beliefs, recognizing one's own power, fighting back against White supremacy, and the importance of dialogue that lingered in our ears that day, but it brought us to a place of being ready to write this book.

Though this is a book on multicultural *psychology*, and one of us is a psychologist (JTP), it is also steeped in theory and research from sociology and related cultural studies areas. We believed from the beginning that the context given by these associated fields (which are those to which DI belongs) would provide a meaningful backdrop essential to understanding this part of psychology. Though psychologists discuss environment and context in many parts of the discipline, these topics are often discussed in relation to the self. While we recognize this as important, we also understand that the self is embedded in context, and this is perhaps nowhere else so clear as in the parts of psychology related to culture, race, and other social identities.

As we began to write this text, the 2016 election occurred and brought with it a resurgence of long-lingering debates, ideas, and fears. On college campuses across the nation, students began to rise up and use their voices to call for a new culture of activism. This was the environment in which we wrote this first edition: while listening to our students begin to come alive as a new breed of activists working toward change, and needing guidance from history and scholarship as they did. These students asked different kinds of questions in the classes we were teaching at the time, including Multicultural Psychology, the Social Construction of Whiteness, Intergroup Dialogues, and Race, Culture, and Politics in the U.S. Within the midst of this, it seemed time for a different kind of book—one that would teach facts, figures, history, theory, and ideas, in addition to providing ways to channel this new knowledge toward action and social justice.

ORGANIZATION

This book is divided into sections that introduce the field, starting with the question: "What is multicultural psychology?" In breaking things into sections, we hope you can see the progression with which you are moving through the material, and organize your thoughts based on the pieces in each. In teaching these topics over the years, we have found these sections mirror the best practices we use in helping students to understand and digest the material.

Section One

This section provides history, definitions, and social context to foreground the knowledge and information necessary to both understand and apply the concepts in multicultural psychology.

- Chapter 1: "What Is Multicultural Psychology?" gives an overview of the field and its situation in the field of psychology at large. We start with a discussion of the way in which nondominant groups have been pathologized in both the field of psychology and greater society, delving into a discussion of the sometimes subjective nature of "scientific" investigations. Next, we turn to general definitions and an explanation of how we can move forward, keeping context central in thinking about theory. We finish up with some information about the way in which we hope you'll use this book and a starting assessment of where you are in your journey into multicultural psychology!

- Chapter 2: "Race: Historical Contexts and Contemporary Manifestations" begins with a discussion of contemporary racial segregation as a backdrop from which to examine the implications of our racial divide, from economic inequality to police killings of people of color. We then define race and discuss the mythology in the social narratives about race relations and racial difference. Last, the historical context for our racial divide is described for Native Americans, African Americans (including a brief description of the construction of Whiteness), Asian Americans, and Latinx.

Section Two

We next delve into a section called "Individuals and Their Contexts" that discusses worldviews, cultural identity, and racism.

- Chapter 3: "Culture and Worldview" starts this section with an overview of ways in which both cultural and unique experiences can impact the way in which we see the world. In this chapter we give you some theoretical models that help to explain the impact of self and society, as well as some specific sections that talk about distinct cultural identities.

- Chapter 4: "Cultural Identity Development" takes a step closer into your own identity and the identity of those around you by covering well-known theoretical models of identity development. In addition, a section about the importance of viewing ourselves and others with a "the whole is greater than the sum of its parts" mindset takes us into an overview of intersectionality. Finally, this chapter closes by talking about some of the research that shows the benefit of understanding one's own racial and ethnic identity.

- Chapter 5: "Our Racialized Social Context: Racism, Oppression, and Stereotyping" begins to dive deeper into the way in which race defines our experiences within social contexts. This chapter delineates the different types of racism and the impacts of racism, and it dives more deeply into how we might combat racism in our own lives.

- Chapter 6: "Whiteness" opens with a description of the ways in which Whiteness, as a racial identity, overtakes the various ethnic identities European immigrants arrived with in America. What follows is a discussion of the operational nature of Whiteness as an unraced, unseen, unspoken—invisible force. The chapter draws on conceptual essays as well as qualitative research to describe the ways that "invisibility" manifests in our racial discourse and ideology. Beginning with Bacon's rebellion, the chapter then discusses how and why Whiteness was constructed and how, through economic and political policy, it became embedded in our social structure, with a particular emphasis on residential practices from the Homestead Act to redlining. We then shift to internalization and the impacts of Whiteness on the individual, through a discussion on White privilege, anger, shame, guilt, and White identity development.

Section Three

Section Three is titled "Lived Experiences and Social Influences." It explicates some of the more powerful forces within our social world and their impacts on the development of our social selves.

- Chapter 7: "Popular Culture, Social Media, Technology, and Representation" describes the ways in which social inequality and racial representations are intertwined with current technological advancements. The chapter describes the role of representation (and absence of representation) in popular culture mediums (TV, movies, news, etc.) on social attitudes, beliefs, and sense of self. The discussion then turns to representation on new social media platforms and its implications in new technology, including algorithms, predictive analytics, and facial recognition. We then conclude with possible avenues for response (media literacy, etc.) to our technological world and the message delivery systems therein.

- Chapter 8: "Being a Person of Color" looks more deeply into experiences that many of people of color have on a daily basis. The chapter begins with an overview of some common experiences that people of color from a variety of backgrounds might encounter, and then moves into specific issues for African Americans, Asian Americans, American Indians, and Latinx individuals within the United States.

- Chapter 9: "Shades of Grey: Being a Biracial or Multiracial Person" takes a look at individuals who have racial backgrounds from more than one group. After delineating some definitions and talking about the history of experiences of biracial people in the United States, it next takes some time looking at a variety of theoretical models that focus on racial identity development when you are a person who "checks more than one box." A section on common themes in the lives of biracial and multiracial individuals concludes this section.

Section Four

Finally, the book closes with the section, "Moving Ahead: Emerging Issues and Goals," designed to take these ideas forward into multiple settings and future directions in the field and practice of psychology.

- Chapter 10: "Multicultural Psychology in Different Settings" looks at research supporting the import of talking about multiculturalism in relation to three different settings: schools, the workplace, and the therapy context.

- Chapter 11: "Looking to the Future: Becoming an Ally, Social Justice Work, and Emerging Issues" is the last chapter in this textbook. Covering topics from allyship to social justice, and talking about ways we can make change in the field and in our lives as individuals and members of different cultural groups, felt like a wonderful place to end. We also dream a bit in this chapter, talking about Afrofuturism and other theories, and submitting to you our ideas around the concept of "wholistic cultural reflexivity."

FEATURES

At the end of each chapter, you will note that we have included three sections to reinforce and inspire the further exploration of these important topics.

Assessment, Critical Thinking, and Taking Action

The end-of-chapter **A.C.T.** sections entail three important aspects of fully engaging in this work: assess your knowledge, critical thinking, and take part.

- *Assess Your Knowledge:* In these sections, you will see suggestions about how you might evaluate yourself after reading each chapter. There will be chapters that are more jarring to you or provide you with new information that may shift your thinking. Knowing where you "are" helps you to understand what is happening inside your mind.

- *Critical Thinking*: Here, we ask you to take the information you have just read in the text a step further, to push yourself beyond what you know to think of what you could become.

- *Take Part*: In these sections, we give some ideas of things to try, depending on where the first two steps of A.C.T. have led you. We make different suggestions for students at different stages of their learning about multicultural psychology.

  o **Participation**: If you are someone who is new to the concepts presented in the chapter, look to the Participation section to find things to try that suit a novice in applying some of these concepts in real life.

  o **Initiation**: Others of you will have come across some of these concepts before, though perhaps not in depth, and if you find yourself here, the section called Initiation might assist you in acting on some of these new ideas in ways that fit with your level of understanding.

  o **Activism**: Finally, if you are ready to take larger steps, the section titled Activism provides a guide to taking on new challenges, developing new behaviors, and perhaps deepening the courage to make greater change in the world.

We hope you find these sections useful in your life as you learn this material, and we entrust this book to your hands to do with what you will. Our hope is that you will take this information and allow it to forge you into a stronger and more educated individual so that you, like our own students, can begin to make the kinds of changes that you and future generations deserve.

ACKNOWLEDGMENTS

We would not have been able to complete this book without love and assistance from many, so we would like to close by each acknowledging the giants on whose shoulders we stand, those who give us inspiration, and the editors and others who made this book a reality.

Thank you to Lara Parra and Emma Newsom for their editorial work from contract to publication and the care they took with this book. I would also like to thank my mentor, Shane Lopez, for telling me I was ready to write this book and for his advice through the contractual process. Though he died shortly after I began writing, I consider his advice daily. I would also like to thank the following individuals for their work during this process and their inspiration (whether they know it or not): Will Mitchell, L. J. Lumpkin, Ashley Kaseroff, Ryan Reed, Lyndse Anderson, Elle Harris, Melissa Peters, Marcos Ramirez-Santos, Mayra Mejia, Kristen Tran, Jeremiah Hernandez, Felipe Garcia, Allison Newlee, Carrie Langner, Blanca Martinez-Navarro, and Beya Montero Makekau. This book is for all of you. Thank you to my coauthor and dear friend, Denise Isom—I could not have done this without you, and our friendship is a gift to me every day. Thank you also to my parents, Yosh and Julie, for the values that instilled in me a strong belief that I could make a difference. And finally, to those to whom this volume is dedicated: Thank you for the coffee, the midnight talks, the "quiet Tuesdays," the snuggles and comic relief when I needed it, for your love, and your enduring faith in my ability to write this book and to do anything I want to accomplish in the world.

—Dr. Jennifer Teramoto Pedrotti

With unflinching faith, love, authenticity, brilliance and strength, my grandmother has led us a mighty long way. To those who came after, carrying her legacy, and helping me do the same—my parents, Geraldine and Escoe Isom Sr., uncles Eli, James (Eddie), and Michael, and aunts Ernestine, Cheryl, and Carolyn, among so many others, I thank you. To my generation of the Isom/Williams clan, united and strengthened by the models our elders have shown us of how to live with hope and joy in the face of struggle, I thank you. To my brothers and sisters, who are my superpower, Escoe Isom Jr., Donniell Isom, Kali' Isom-Moore, Scott Moore, Dannette Isom-Norman, and Josh Norman, I thank you. To the next generation in our family, I hope we love you into yourselves, and empower you the way that those who came before us have empowered us. To Jennifer Teramoto Pedrotti, without whom none of this would have happened, I thank you for the opportunity and for the friendship, support, and laughter that grew along and marked the way. To all the friends who form my beloved community, who provide inspiration and joy, and who endured months and months of canceled engagements, limited phone calls, and too much talk of textbook writing, I thank you—Alisa Bredensteiner, Jacque Rowe Fields, Dr. Anastasia Gentles, the Ewings, the Floreses, and the Queens, thank you. I want to recognize the team at Sage too, whose invaluable efforts are greatly appreciated: Thank you.

—Dr. Denise Isom

Thanks also go to the following individuals who provided feedback on our manuscript:

Vanessa Hettinger, University of Wisconsin-Superior

Carol Huckaby, Albertus Magnus College

Chris Jazwinski, St. Cloud State University

Kerry S. Kleyman, Metropolitan State University

Shenan Kroupa, Indiana University-Purdue University at Indianapolis

Julie Lazzara, Paradise Valley Community College

Rocio Rivadeneyra, Illinois State University

ABOUT THE AUTHORS

Dr. Jennifer Teramoto Pedrotti received her doctoral and master's degrees in counseling psychology from the University of Kansas and her bachelor's degrees in psychology and English from the University of California at Davis. She is currently associate dean for diversity and curriculum in the College of Liberal Arts and professor in the Department of Psychology and Child Development at California Polytechnic State University, San Luis Obispo. Dr. Teramoto Pedrotti has taught Multicultural Psychology, Intergroup Dialogues, and other areas of psychology for over 15 years. Her research areas of specialty include the effectiveness of intergroup dialogues and other types of multicultural education, and the study of strengths within a cultural context. She is the lead editor on a volume titled *Perspectives on the Intersection of Multiculturalism and Positive Psychology* (with Lisa M. Edwards, Springer, 2014) and authored another undergraduate textbook, *Positive Psychology: The Scientific and Practical Explorations of Human Strengths* (with Shane J. Lopez and C. R. Snyder, Sage, now in its fourth edition, 2019). In addition, Dr. Teramoto Pedrotti's work has appeared in multiple books and journals, including the *Handbook of Multicultural Counseling,* the *Journal of Counseling Psychology,* the *Journal of Positive Psychology, Professional Psychology: Research and Practice,* and *Professional School Counseling.* In her current role, she encourages students, staff, and faculty daily to use their strengths to make change toward a more inclusive and culturally competent campus.

Dr. Denise A. Isom received her doctorate in sociocultural anthropology of education from Loyola University, Chicago, and is currently serving as department chair and professor in ethnic studies at California Polytechnic State University, San Luis Obispo. Her master's in curriculum and instruction with an emphasis in multicultural education, along with a BS in engineering and a BA in African American studies, were all completed at the University of California at Davis. Dr. Isom's areas of expertise include racialized gender identity, ethnic studies, Whiteness, and sociology/anthropology of education.

As a professor of ethnic studies, she teaches courses that include Race, Culture, and Politics in the U.S.; The Social Construction of Whiteness; Gender and Sexualities in the African American Community; research methods courses; and two recently codeveloped courses: Beyoncé: Race, Feminism, and Politics and Humor, Comedy, and the Politics of Identity.

Her current research agenda includes racialized gender identity and the racialized nature of congregational life. Her work has been presented at numerous national and international conferences, published in journals such as *The Urban Review* and *The Journal of Race, Equality and Teaching*, and included in chapters on boy culture, teaching race, and African American female psychology and identity.

WHAT IS MULTICULTURAL PSYCHOLOGY?

SECTION I

iStock.com/lmgorthand

1

WHAT IS MULTICULTURAL PSYCHOLOGY?

LEARNING OBJECTIVES

- Understand the importance of paying attention to cultural differences, though there is a tendency for many to avoid this in day-to-day life
- Summarize the historical treatment of race in the field of psychology
- Recognize the field's pathologizing impact of the White Standard of all non-White cultures
- Interpret research findings in multicultural psychology with regard to the four types of equivalence
- Summarize the impact of The Fourth Force on the field of psychology as a whole
- Understand important definitions in this part of the field (e.g., race, culture, etc.) and the value of using a broad definition of culture that encompasses many facets
- Assess your own level of awareness and knowledge about this part of the field
- Analyze your cultural identity (via the Culture Sketch) to determine next steps for your own learning

INTRODUCTION TO MULTICULTURAL PSYCHOLOGY

If you have already had one lecture from your instructor, you've probably started to realize that the study of multicultural psychology is not a simple one. Often people feel they should just understand the idea of **diversity** naturally: "It's all about people, and we're all people, right?" But this area of the field is much more complex than that, and studying multicultural psychology will allow you to better understand people in general, as well as the differences that exist between people from different groups. It will also help you to better understand yourself and to find new ways of explaining these ideas to others around you.

Multicultural psychology is the study of differences. The word *different* often has a negative connotation in our daily language use and therefore we sometimes form the idea that it is impolite to talk about differences, or even notice them. This often starts early in childhood. Consider stories you've heard, or maybe things you've experienced yourself that involve children noticing (and commenting on) differences. When a

White child says loudly in a grocery store, "Why is that man's skin dark?" within earshot of an African American man, a natural response of a White parent might be to say, "Shh! That's impolite." The parent in this case might simply mean that we don't call out these sorts of differences while walking through the grocery store, and of course the parent is correct about this in terms of social manners.

But without a follow-up conversation on this interaction, it is possible that the child misunderstands the exact reason the parent called attention to the behavior. This may lead to a child accidentally getting the idea that we shouldn't talk about differences, or that we should pretend not to notice them. Parents in this type of situation, particularly those who have not had much experience talking about race or other differences, may be uncomfortable starting a dialogue with the child about race at a young age, and unfortunately this allows children to instead fill in their own reasons regarding why they should not mention a different color of skin. Brown and colleagues conducted a study in 2007 in which parents of different ethnicities and races were asked if they talked to their children about race. Just 25% of White parents sampled talked to their children about race, while discussions of race in non-White homes occurred significantly more often (Brown, Tanner-Smith, Lesane-Brown, & Ezell, 2007). A parent in the scenario above might perhaps follow up later with the child, saying, "I know that you had some questions about the man's skin inside the grocery store. It was different from ours, wasn't it?" In this way a new conversation begins, and this may help a child to understand that while it is rude to yell things out about people's skin (or other features) in public places, it is OK to talk about differences.

This avoidance of discussion of differences may almost become a sort of pretending that these differences don't exist, and this can have an unintended self-perpetuating quality: If we aren't supposed to notice differences, then we can't talk about them, which leads to difficulty learning about differences in general. In the vacuum of our knowledge, stereotypes and others' opinions often fill the void, and this often leads to misunderstandings of those differences that exist between us. In the field of multicultural psychology, and in this book, difference is a main topic of discussion. While we should of course work not to discriminate against people as a result of a difference, it is beneficial to understand differences between people. James Baldwin once wrote,

"Not everything that is faced can be changed. But nothing can be changed until it is faced" (1962, p. 38). The study of multicultural psychology involves digging into differences that have to do with cultural context, identity, and experiences and trying to better understand them. As Baldwin wisely notes in his quote, we cannot make change unless we face things head on. We are hoping you are here to do just that.

A HISTORY OF PATHOLOGIZING

As a field, psychology has not always paid attention to culture and context in making efforts to understand different human behavior and experience, and it has not always been kind to those viewed as "different" in some way. Specifically, psychology, born of Western roots in Europe, has often **pathologized** those who didn't fit the cultural mold of the prominent early European theorists. In the early 1900s, H. H. Goddard, a psychologist who studied the concept of intelligence, put forth the idea that the particular shape and definition of a person's face allowed him to be able to predict the intelligence associated with that person (Gould, 1996). Individuals with "Roman noses" and "high brows" were the most intelligent, while those with lower brows were less intelligent. We have some vestiges of this notion even in our colloquial language today, where "highbrow" humor is thought to be more intellectual humor. Unsurprisingly, Goddard and colleagues' own facial features seemed to mirror the descriptions of those who were most intelligent.

Other beliefs about different groups were also held at this time, often spurred by differences from the European ideal, and these influenced psychological theories as well. For example, in the early 1800s, the idea of **polygenism** was taking hold in many areas of Europe. At the time this theory emerged, many still adhered to the religious explanations that all humans had descended from one particular line of genes (namely that of Adam and Eve from the Judeo-Christian Bible), but polygenism promoted the idea that different types of humans might have emerged from different genetic pools (Keel, 2013). Dr. Josiah Nott, an American physician, published a paper titled *Two Lectures on the Natural History of the Caucasian and Negro Races* that presented the idea that the different racial groups could not have developed such distinct features (e.g., skin color) due solely to the environment in such a short amount of evolutionary time. This was a hotly contested point of view at the time because of its dissension from biblical explanations for the genesis of human life, but it also appealed to some individuals, as it appeared to label race as a biological and genetic difference.

Around this same time, Charles Darwin and his theories regarding evolution also began to emerge. While the tenets of Darwinism are in opposition to polygenism in the sense that Darwin did not believe that the different races had completely different origins, his ideas (now the basis of **social Darwinism**) put forth the premise that different racial groups might actually be evolving differently such that they were becoming different species. These ideas, which again complemented the societal views of race at the time, quickly gained popularity in Europe. The influence of this theory led many to believe that individuals of African or Asian descent were incapable of the same type of intelligent thought as those from Europe. In making these decisions, cultural context was ignored, and behaviors were only judged from the mindset of a European cultural scholar. Though these theories and ideas are from the past, they form the basis for many stereotypes that exist about non-White groups that are held today.

IS SCIENCE ALWAYS OBJECTIVE? RESEARCH ISSUES THROUGH A MULTICULTURAL LENS

Stereotyping and Science

Even scientific experiments took on the stereotypes fueled by social Darwinism and polygenism by attempting to confirm the inferiority of certain races with physical data about brain size and weight. Today, we are aware that the size of one's brain is not the sole determinant of one's intelligence, but in the early 1900s, a physician named Robert Bennett Bean conducted studies in which he measured the brains of deceased African American and White American individuals. As a part of these experiments, Bean made claims that the African American brain was on average much smaller than White brains and thus showed intellectual deficiencies in this race (Gould, 1996; see Figure 1.1). Interestingly, Bean's mentor from Johns Hopkins, Franklin P. Mall, suspected that Bean's data too cleanly found "evidence" for his hypothesis, and so Mall

FIGURE 1.1 ● Bean's "data" was collected with the knowledge of whether the brain being studied was from a Black person or a White person and shows distinct differences between Black and White brains.

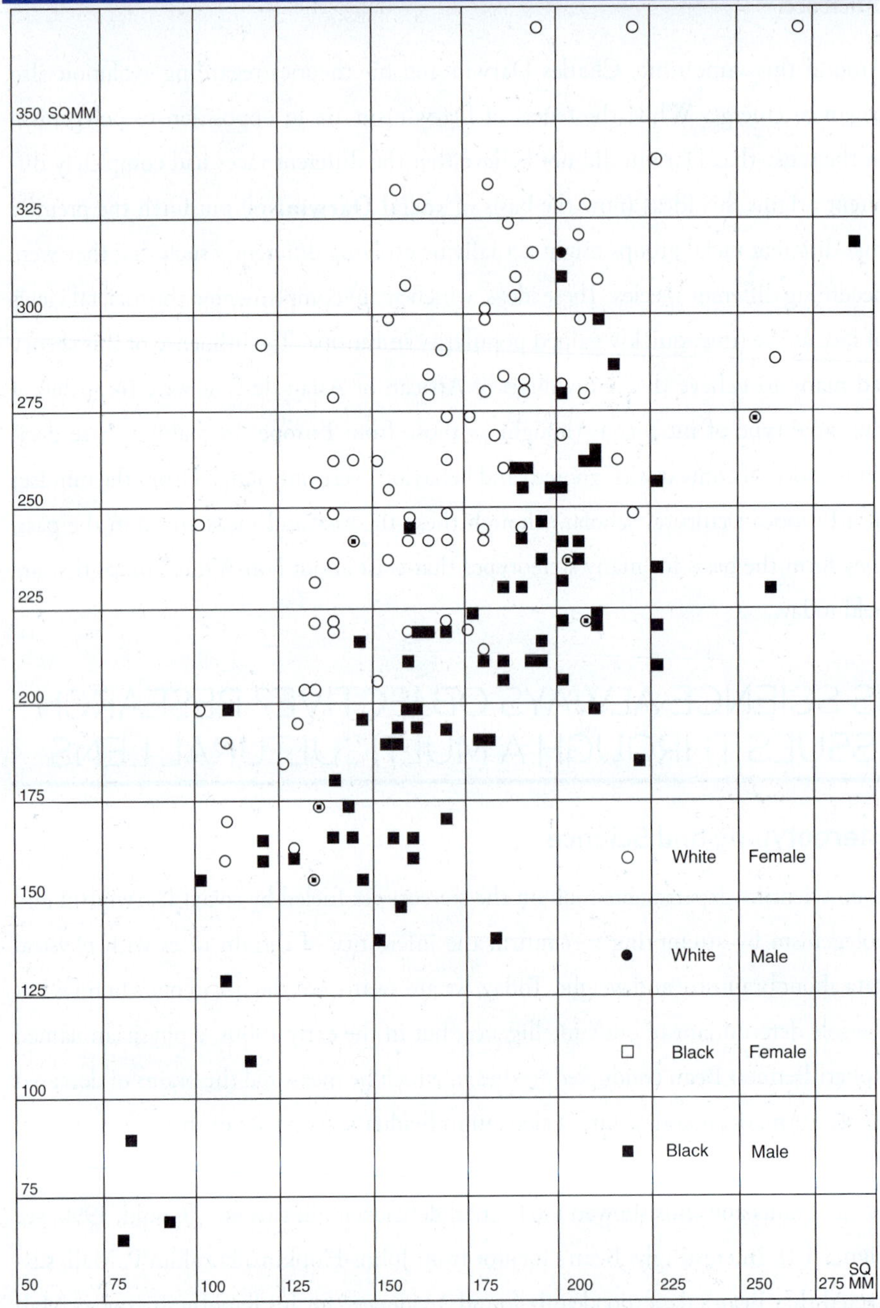

Source: Gould, S. J. (1996). *The mismeasure of man: The definitive refutation to the argument of* The Bell Curve. New York: Norton (figure is on p. 110).

remeasured the brains in Bean's experiment with one important difference: He made sure that while measuring these brains, he masked the race of the individual from which it came, making him unaware of the racial origin of the brain he was measuring. Mall's conclusions were entirely different from Bean's: There were no significant differences in average size of the African American brain versus the White brain (see Figure 1.2). Despite this counterevidence, Bean's conclusions were more widely distributed, perhaps because they confirmed the stereotype of superiority of White individuals that was prevalent at the time. Thus, Mall's findings were often dismissed, while Bean's (though incorrect) were spread.

Race and country of origin are not the only cultural facets that have influenced historically held ideas of what is healthy or positive. Adherence to the Christian religion, as the main faith of White Europeans who began to travel to the New World, influenced what was abnormal and what was not. In the United States, American Indians experienced the impact of this influence when White settlers denounced their religion as dangerous and savage, leading to the ultimate outlawing of American Indian religious practices in the late 1800s. To give a more current example within the field of psychology, same-sex orientation in individuals was given a psychological diagnosis as the pathological condition *homosexuality.* This diagnosis remained in the *Diagnostic and Statistical Manual of Mental Disorders,* from which psychologists determine diagnoses for clients, until the third edition was published in 1987 (American Psychological Association [APA], 1987).

In many of the above examples of pathologicalization, extensive research was conducted and touted as the basis for "inferiority" of particular groups based on cultural differences. For context, in traditional experimental research, differences are often studied by manipulating different variables to see how these changes impact other variables. You may remember the terms **independent variable** (the variable that is manipulated) and **dependent variable** (the outcome variable) from your statistics or research methods classes. Consider, for example, a study that seeks to determine whether a particular drug has an effect on the health of the sample of participants. Groups are set up such that one group gets the treatment drug being tested, and the other does not. The independent variable in this case is presence or absence of the drug, and the dependent

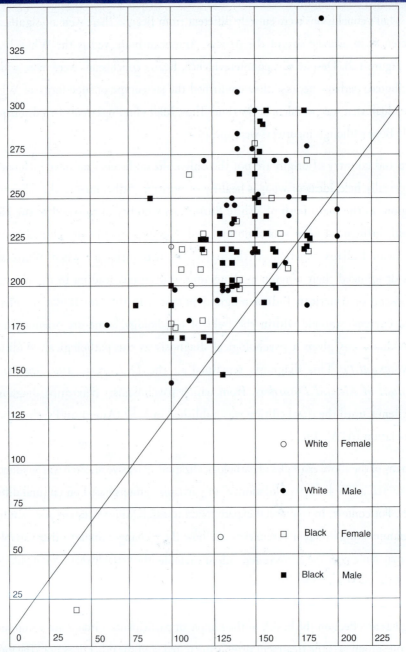

FIGURE 1.2 ⬡ Mall's data was collected *without* knowledge of whether the brain was from a Black person or a White person and shows no distinct difference between the brains.

Source: Gould, S. J. (1996). *The mismeasure of man: The definitive refutation to the argument of* The Bell Curve. New York: Norton (figure is on p. 113).

variable is a measure of the participants' health. In traditional experiments such as the one in this example, the independent variable is easy to manipulate. The research can randomly assign individual participants to group one (treatment group) or group two (control group) and administer the drug accordingly.

Research in the social sciences, particularly when we start to study social facets like race or gender, does not have the same straightforwardness. Specifically, one cannot "assign" race to someone, and so if we are curious about differences between racial groups, we must take groups that have already been formed organically. This lack of random assignment makes more room for bias to occur ("Awareness of," 2017).

Science is rather famously thought to be an objective field, when certain tenets are adhered to. Yet as noted previously, it is important to acknowledge that putting the tenets of science into practice cannot be carried out without a human idea and by a human hand in some shape or form. Humans, who are by nature often neither objective nor impartial, are the ones creating the hypotheses, designing the research studies, and choosing the measurements.

Measurement Issues Through a Multicultural Lens

Even the type of measurement used may make a difference in outcome for different races and other groups. Most surveys, scales, and diagnostic tools have been created by accessing the experiences of people in the majority culture. IQ tests, for example, were originally developed by testing boys and girls in a variety of intellectual areas. In some of the original norming studies of these tests, girls scored higher than boys in several areas. At the time, stereotypes existed that promoted male intelligence as superior, and so to combat this "obviously incorrect" result, test makers took out the questions in which girls consistently scored higher than boys. Seems fair, right? Except that these test makers did not remove the questions in which *boys* consistently scored higher than *girls*. Gender was only taken as a problematic factor when it favored girls. This was later corrected in future versions of the test, but is another example of how seemingly objective measurements have been skewed by cultural dynamics.

Another important area to consider with regard to measurement involves **equivalence** (Ho et al., 2014). There are four types of measurement equivalence that are important to our study. First, **conceptual equivalence** refers to a particular construct having the same meaning in both cultural groups. For example, the construct of wisdom is primarily thought to be a cognitive trait in the United States. Psychologists who are interested in measuring wisdom within a particular population in the United States might use a Likert scale to ask questions about flexibility of thought, creativity of ideas, and use of cognition in making decisions. However, in some other countries, such as Taiwan, wisdom is thought to also include an affective or emotional component (Yang, 2008) in addition to a cognitive component In others, such as Slovakia, wisdom has been found to be thought of as solely affective in nature (Benedikovičová & Ardelt, 2008). Imagine using a measure designed in Slovakia, with questions only about affective wisdom, to measure wisdom in the United States. What would the outcome be? Likely it would be that people in the United States are not particularly wise, but is this a fair assessment? A better way to say this is that people in the United States would not be seen as wise as defined by Slovakians; this is true for many different constructs, and therein lies the importance of making sure that we pay attention to culture when measuring various traits.

In addition to conceptual equivalence, linguistic equivalence, metric equivalence, and functional equivalence must also be assessed when measuring characteristics across cultural groups (Ho et al., 2014). **Linguistic equivalence** is more than just translating a measure from one language to another and includes the necessity of making sure that it is translated in such a way as to mean the same thing in both languages. When translating a measure in English to Spanish, for example, a psychologist must pay attention to nuances in the different languages to make sure that the same meaning is transmitted. Linguistic equivalence is assisted by **back translation** of a measure, that is, making sure a bilingual individual is able to translate the Spanish version back to English in such a way that the translated version mirrors the original English meaning.

Metric equivalence refers to equivalence in the way response items are used in different cultural groups. Consider the traditional "scale of 1 to 10" that we often use in US contexts. Some cultures are more risk averse and may not use the entirety of that scale. If one culture is using the full range to describe their experiences, while another is only comfortable using 2–9 and avoiding extremes, metric equivalence cannot be established. It is surprising to some that even when using pure numbers, we cannot guarantee equivalence culturally.

Lastly, **functional equivalence** refers to the use and function of the particular construct in daily life within the different cultural groups (Ho et al., 2014). Some constructs or traits may be viewed as positive by women, but not by men or transgender individuals, for example. As an example, the trait of gratitude has been found to be more beneficial to women as compared to men (Kashdan, Mishra, Breen, & Froh, 2009). Other cultural characteristics, such as belief in a certain religion, may be used differently in different cultural groups and may serve different functions in daily life. Forgiveness, for example, is a trait often assigned a high value in those groups who are religious, though this may not be the case in those who do not subscribe to a religion. These four different types of equivalence are summarized in Figure 1.3.

When we use our own cultural lens to make decisions about what is positive and what is negative, and how to best measure it, without considering the cultural context of others, we run the risk of setting up a deficit model. The term **deficit model** refers to the fact that when we use only our own cultural frame of reference to decide what is a positive outcome in a research study, we set all other cultural groups up to potentially perform at a deficit (Song & Pyon, 2008). An example might include a study to investigate the development of independence in children. Western cultures value strongly the constructs of independence and competition and believe them to be top strengths (Triandis, 1995). Across the world, however, there are many more cultures that believe that interdependence and cooperation should be valued over independence and competition. If a researcher from a Western cultural group asks the question, "Which cultural group has more successful parenting outcomes?" and decides to categorize independence

FIGURE 1.3 ● Measurement and Equivalence			
Conceptual Equivalence	**Linguistic Equivalence**	**Metric Equivalence**	**Functional Equivalence**
Does the construct have the same meaning in different cultures?	Does the item on a measure ask the same thing in one language as it does another?	Do different cultural groups use the same metric scale to answer items on a measure?	Does the construct have the same function in different cultures?

as a marker of this successful parenting, it is likely that the parents from Western cultural groups will score the highest, with children who are most independent. Without attention to cultural values, this research might then declare that Western children are parented more successfully toward healthy development than those other children whose parents do not appear to impart independence to their children. In looking at this finding from a multicultural standpoint, however, one might note that parents of non-Western children do not promote independence in their children because they do not value this construct as strongly. In fact, they may purposefully promote interdependence instead, believing this to be a more successful parenting outcome. In ignoring culture, the researcher is setting up a deficit model: Those who act in ways that my culture thinks are beneficial are healthy, and those that do not are thought to have a deficit. This leads, then, to potential pathologicalization of cultures that do not fit within our own cultural framework. Though this type of pathologicalization can occur in any direction (i.e., any group can think that another is less healthy than their own), it matters most when a particular social group has power or privilege behind them.

The White Standard

Within the United States, White Americans have been the main voice in the field of psychology until more recent decades, though even as late as 2013, only one fifth of those working in the field of psychology were non-White (APA, 2015). In addition, people of some races were kept out of educational experiences (some by segregation and other laws, and others by lack of resources). This means that throughout the history of psychology, many more theories and ideas have been put forward by White Americans and thus come from a Western, European American cultural framework. This is often called the **White Standard**, and we can see this in theory and in other tenets. This term comes from work done in the field of physiology and medical science, in which the physical characteristics of White individuals were used "as the standard of measurement and [scientists] judged all other race varieties as they approximated or diverged from it" (Blakeslee, 1915/2017, p. 301). As happened with the work of Goddard and Bean described earlier, reliance on White individuals as "the norm" gave many differences significance that did not actually exist. The White Standard affects the types of variables that are studied, the way they are measured, and the understanding of their functionality in daily life. For this reason, many theories and ideas put forward in the early part of the field of psychology may not be accurate depictions of psychological health for non-White individuals and groups. Thomas and Sillen (1972) called use of Whites as the standard for health **scientific racism** and listed many examples of how bias was directed at African Americans and other racial and ethnic minority groups in the form of psychological research. When we, as current or future researchers, do not attend to our own biases or the bias of our field in its origins, we run the risk of developing faulty conclusions to research. At best this can lead to mistakes, but at worst, as has been shown, this type of faulty research can portray entire populations as damaged or abnormal.

IMPACT IN EVERYDAY LIFE

We may also experience this lack of attention to cultural context in everyday life, when someone assumes that behaviors that align with various non-Western cultural norms are "wrong" when they differ from those that the majority culture believes is the "right way" of behaving. Leadership is one area in which the White Standard is often applied (Rosette, Leonardelli, & Phillips, 2008). Consider the following vignette:

> I am very good at my job and I know that my efforts were a huge part of our team succeeding in our last project. My boss knows this too. At our last large group meeting he gave me some praise and said that I was "solely" responsible for the success. I deferred a little in the meeting because I wanted to give my team credit too and talked about this as a joint effort. I'm Chinese American and was taught from a young age to share the credit whenever I can. It seems like the right thing to do as a leader. Later my boss called me into his office and said he'd like to offer me some advice. He said, "If you want to keep moving up in this business you have to take credit when it's offered to you and not give it away. That's not the style of a good leader. I'd like to promote you eventually, but you'll need to work on that weakness." I felt confused because I know he knows that I did the work, but to me it's not weak to acknowledge the others and share the credit. Instead, I think of this as the right thing to do.

> —Anna, age 30

iStock/shapecharge

Here, Anna is using a tactic that is a strength and a marker of a good leader in her cultural background (sharing the wealth), but that same trait is viewed negatively by the mainstream White culture of which her boss is a part. As a result, Anna is seen as having a deficit. This is an example of the impacts of a deficit model in everyday life.

Shaking the Pillars: Moving Forward With Theory

Though the word *theory* is really just a posited idea at its beginning, it can come to be thought of as "truth" as time goes on. As humans we tend to look for confirming evidence of things we believe (Heppner, Wampold, Owen, Wang, & Thompson, 2008), and that can leave us vulnerable to ignoring information that goes against our personal theories of life. In a field such as psychology, this **confirmation bias** continued to occur as psychology found its foothold in the United States but was still primarily a field dominated by White and European men. As time has gone by, some of these posited ideas have hardened and crystallized, carrying with them the weight of multiple studies and tests, though culture was still not often attended to. Unfortunately this scientific racism led to a number of crystallized ideas that perpetuated the deficit models. These ideas, however subjective and culturally bound, have influenced the pillars of our understandings of a variety of human behavior. As David Matsumoto and Linda Juang (2017) state,

> Understanding how cultural diversity can color the nature of truths and principles of human behavior delivered in the halls of science questions the pillars of much of our knowledge about the world and about human behavior. From time to time, we need to shake those pillars to see just how strong they are. (p. 3)

Today, one of the main goals of psychology must be to shake these pillars and to make sure that cultural context is attended to.

THE FOURTH FORCE

As a field, psychology has a history that involves several different movements or "forces." In the early days of the creation of the field of psychology, Sigmund Freud and his followers developed theories and practices based around the First Force: psychodynamics. Later, B. F. Skinner and colleagues discussed human actions in the Second Force: behaviorism. Starting with Carl Rogers, Viktor Frankl, and Rollo May, the ideas of existentialism and humanism were termed the Third Force. There is much written about these forces in terms of the way they have shaped the field of psychology, offered explanations, and given evidence for development of different behaviors, cognitions, and emotional reactions. In each of the previous forces, a particular set of theories or explanations was used to decode human behavior. In psychodynamic theory, for example, it is believed that internal drives and interactions within different parts of the mind influence our behavior. Freud's conceptualizations of the id, ego, and superego depict a constant internal battle between drive and ethics as impacting decisions, development, and emotions. This differs sharply from the theories of Skinner and Watson, who instead believed that all human traits were shaped and molded by external forces of rewards, punishments, or conditioning. Humanism and existential theorists brought forward the idea that the similarity of human conditions (e.g., loneliness, despair, desire) drives behavior. Each of these forces was deemed such after noting the deep impact each set of theories had on our understanding of human behavior, thought, and feelings.

In 1990, a psychologist named Paul Pedersen declared that a new force had emerged in the field, the Fourth Force: multiculturalism. Pedersen was pointing to the idea that culture influenced the way we think, feel, and behave on a daily basis. This is where we are in the field of psychology today. Thus, in keeping with the fourth force, culture must come into play in thinking of any type of development. Cognition, affect, and behavior can all be explained through the lens of cultural forces. Our racial backgrounds, gender identity, **socioeconomic status** groups, and other facets of our identity determine how we see the world, how we may be similar in some ways, and how we are all distinctly different. Naming multiculturalism as the Fourth Force shows the importance of each of these layers to our development and to our understandings of the world. We are not islands; we are connected to all others and able to make meaning of our surroundings and experiences primarily through our unique and culturally influenced worldview.

IMPORTANT DEFINITIONS IN MULTICULTURAL PSYCHOLOGY

Culture influences every aspect of our daily life. Even when not specifically named, culture is always in the room. Culture is in the air that we breathe.

The definition of the term **culture** has been debated by many, but psychologist Harry Triandis (1995) defines it as "a shared pattern of beliefs, attitudes, norms, role perceptions, and values" (p. 3). Kluckhohn's (1954) definition adds to this understanding of culture by using an analogy: "Culture is to society what memory is to individuals" (Triandis, 1995). That is, culture is a structural and ever-changing force that impacts our experience in the world. When researchers use the term **cross-cultural,** they are usually referring to looking at differences between two contexts, for example, comparing individuals in South America to those in North America; while the term **multicultural** is defined as looking at differences that exist within a single context, for example, those within the United States. We will use these words in this book as we define them here, but it is important to note that these words have often been used interchangeably in the past.

Culture has been described as encompassing language, ritual, ideas, customs, and history (Triandis, 1995). Each of these aspects of culture impacts the experiences of individuals and the lens they use to make sense of the world. It is impossible to accurately talk about people without attending to culture.

Though multicultural psychology encompasses many different identity facets in its study of culture, understandings of *race* and *ethnicity* are often primary areas of study. Though these are separate concepts, many use them interchangeably, and this can be confusing to individuals learning about these terms. It is also important to recognize that individuals in different fields, researchers, and lay persons disagree on definitions of words like *race.*

Psychologist Janet Helms describes this well: "Race has no consensual theoretical or scientific meaning in psychology, although it is frequently used in psychological theory, research and practice as if it has obvious meaning" (Helms, Jernigan, & Mascher, 2005, p. 27). In some fields, especially in the past, race is sometimes described as a biological construct based on physical differences and characteristics. This biological distinction has multiple issues, however, in that having a particular set of genes does not necessarily explain how one thinks, feels, or is experienced in society. In recent years several companies have arisen offering DNA testing that compares an individual's DNA with that of other individuals who have participated in their tests. Though the companies are careful to use words such as "ancestry" or "family history" as opposed to purporting to identify race, a perhaps unintended consequence of this new business venture is a misunderstanding of race as a biological construct. Consider the following story from a professor of multicultural psychology:

This DNA testing thing has had some interesting consequences in my multicultural psychology course lately. I have students who have been raised with a White cultural identity who get a result on one of these DNA company reports that says that they are a certain percentage "African" or some other cultural group that they never knew about. I have a student who has blond hair, blue eyes, and light skin. He's from an area that is predominantly White and has been having a hard time understanding concepts like White privilege. He just doesn't have any frame of reference for the experiences of racial minorities because he's met so few in his life. He took a test like this and he came to tell me about the results. He started off by saying, "So, my test says I'm 2% African. That means I'm Black! I guess no one can say I have White privilege now." We talked about what the test results actually meant and how race is more than just genes, and what White privilege actually is . . . but at the end of the conversation I'm not sure he had a better understanding. He kept thinking of race as biological because the test was of his DNA. I think it's confusing for people to understand that when we are talking about race in psychology, we're talking about racial identity and the historical experiences of one's ancestors as well as the current experiences someone has had, and those aren't just built on genes.

—Lynne, age 48

In this book, we will define **race** as a sociocultural construct that groups individuals together by both physical and social characteristics. Though there may be physical similarities among individuals within a race (e.g., eye shape, hair texture), it is not these physical similarities that link individuals to a race. For example, people of African American descent may range in skin color from light to dark, similar to those of European descent or Asian descent. Thus the idea of race "is not an intrinsic part of a human being or the environment but, rather, an identity created using symbols to establish meaning in culture or society" (Barnshaw, 2008, p. 1092). The idea that race is sociocultural as opposed to biological is difficult for many who are first entering this area of study. "People who are black share physical similarities!" is a comment we often hear from our novice students. Perhaps Barnshaw's (2008) answer to this question can assist in a better understanding: "Although physical characteristics constitute a portion of the concept of race, this is a social rather than a biological distinction. That is, human beings create categories of race based on physical characteristics rather that the physical characteristics having intrinsic biological meaning" (p. 1092). Members of any particular race have shared traditions, history, and even vernaculars at times.

Ethnicity is separate from race, though linked, and is defined as "groups that are characterized in terms of a common nationality, culture or language" (Betancourt & López, 1993, p. 631). In addition, ethnicity is often thought of as the means through which culture is transmitted. In our writings here, we will talk about groups such as African Americans, Asians, and American Indians as races; while Japanese Americans, Irish Americans, and Colombian Americans will be treated as ethnicities. As you might notice, the focus of this textbook is populations within the United States, but there are ethnic groups in all countries, of course. While race and ethnicity are two primary features of social identity and the study of multicultural psychology, there are other facets that are often included in the discussion of culture as well.

A BROAD DEFINITION OF CULTURE

The ADDRESSING Framework

Another way of thinking about culture is that there are several facets to every individual's cultural identity. Pamela Hays (2016) presents a number of these facets as a part of her ADDRESSING framework. In this model, Hays uses the word ADDRESSING as an acronym for ten different cultural identity facets. (See Table 1.1 for a description of each facet.) Each of these identity facets might impact one's view of the world on a daily basis; therefore, Hays discusses all as important to people in general. In addition, within each category, Hays notes which groups are the privileged or dominant groups in society and thus hold more power.

TABLE 1.1 ⬢ ADDRESSING Cultural Influences		
Cultural Influence	**Dominant Group**	**Nondominant or Minority Group**
Age and generational influences	Young and middle-aged adults	Children, older adults
Developmental or other **D**isability	Nondisabled people	People with cognitive, intellectual, sensory, physical, and psychiatric disabilities
Religion and spiritual orientation	Christian and secular	Muslims, Jews, Hindus, Buddhists, and other religions
Ethnic and racial identity	European Americans	Asian, Latino, Pacific Islander, African, Arab, African American, Middle Eastern, and multiracial people
Socioeconomic status	Upper and middle class	People of lower status by occupation, education, income, or inner city or rural habitat
Sexual orientation	Heterosexuals	People who identify as gay, lesbian, or bisexual
Indigenous heritage	European Americans	American Indians, Inuit, Alaska Natives, Métis, Native Hawaiians, New Zealand Māori, Aboriginal Australians
National origin	US-born Americans	Immigrants, refugees, international students
Gender	Men	Women and people who identify as transgender

Authors' Note: This table uses the categories of dominant and nondominant that Hays uses in her book; however these lists are not meant to be comprehensive. For example, we would include "nonbinary" under gender, "Asian American" under ethnic and racial identity, and anyone under the LGBTQ+ rainbow under sexual orientation.

Source: From Hays, P. A. (2016). *Addressing cultural complexities in practice.* Washington, DC: APA (p. 8).

The **A** in the framework stands for Age. Hays talks about the impact of the generation that one comes from and makes the case that this may shape beliefs and experiences. Groups that fall into the minority in this group are the aged as well as children. Both groups have less social power in our society due to their age. The **DD** in the ADDRESSING framework stands for Disability: Developmental or other Disability. This identity facet is meant to encompass any form of disability including mental, physical, or psychiatric types of disabilities, and covers both disabilities that one might be born with and those that could be acquired due to an accident or some other instance. Those who possess one of the mentioned types of disabilities are in the disenfranchised group in this category.

The **R** in Hays's ADDRESSING framework stands for Religion and spiritual orientation. This facet covers both organized religious groups and nondenominational types of spirituality. In the United States, Christian religions are the dominant group, and so all non-Christian religions (including Judaism, Islam, and Hinduism, among others) are the group lacking in power in this facet. It is important to note that within the facet of religion are also individuals who do not identify as having a religion. Hays notes that some individuals who belong to lesser-populated Christian groups (e.g., Jehovah's Witnesses) may also view themselves as religious minorities, but privileges do exist for these groups inherent in the fact that they are still part of the Christian faith.

The **E** stands for Ethnic and racial identity, and Hays makes note that non-White ethnic and racial groups are considered to be the nondominant societal group in terms of this facet in the United States. This may include individuals from Asian, Latinx, African American, and Middle Eastern backgrounds, as well as multiracial individuals that may come from a combination of racial backgrounds. This particular aspect in her model is a key feature of cultural identity. For some in the dominant White group, this facet might be one that is less salient on a personal level due to a person being a part of the majority group. Nevertheless, race and ethnicity, perhaps particularly in the United States, are distinctly important factors in worldview and daily experiences.

The first **S** in the framework is for Socioeconomic status, including social class, income, and often occupation and education. Minority groups here are those who lack social capital in the form of economics or education. Those who live below the poverty level often have no access to higher education, which in turn leads to fewer options for higher-level occupations. The second **S** is for Sexual orientation, including such cultural identities as heterosexual, lesbian, gay, and/or bisexual. Nonheterosexual groups are the minority in this facet and include anyone along the LGBTQ+ rainbow. It is important to recognize that some of the facets included in the LGBTQ+ acronym (namely transgender and sometimes queer) are really gender identities, though they have been grouped with sexual orientations in the past. In Hays's model, gender is discussed separately.

The **I** is a unique facet that is often left out of cultural discussions (Hays, 2016) and stands for Indigenous heritage in this model. Minority groups here include individuals who have native or indigenous backgrounds. Hays distinguishes this facet from ethnic and racial identity, because these facets may have different influences on life experience. As Hays states, "Many Indigenous people identify as part of a worldwide culture of Indigenous people who have concerns and issues separate from those of ethnic and racial minority groups (e.g., land, water, [or] fishing rights related to subsistence and cultural traditions) and who, in some cases, constitute sovereign nations" (p. 11). The **N** in the framework stands for National origin, and individuals who may identify as international students, immigrants, or refugees are the less powerful group in this facet. And finally, the **G** in Hays's model stands for Gender. This category has changed somewhat since the first iteration of Hays's model, as gender is viewed currently more as a fluid identity along a continuum as compared to past descriptions as a binary division. This category includes identifications such as woman, man, transgender, and androgyne, with those who identify as men being the powerful group.

All of these facets and their various combinations impact our understanding of the world and often determine our reactions, our interpretations, and our experiences in general. An example might be found in comparing the views and habits of someone who grew up during the Great Depression with those of someone who is a teenager in the current time. Differences between these two individuals might exist such that the first person is more cautious about money, or perhaps the second person is more open-minded to same-sex marriage, having been exposed to this idea from a young age. Social issues, economic conditions, or other details characteristic of the time period in which we live impact our cultural identity. Hays talks about the impact of one's ability status on one's life in general with this portion of her theory. Identifying as having a disability of any kind again impacts the way one sees the world, including factors such as safety, accessibility (both physical and in terms of feasibility), and even daily scheduling (Hays, 2016).

As shown with Hays's (2016) theory, culture can be defined in both narrow ways (e.g., only race or nation or origin) or in more broad ways (e.g., Hays's model). Today, many in the United States and worldwide are starting to realize that a broader definition might be more descriptive in coming to understandings about people in different groups. This is not to negate the power or salience of particular cultural facets in different contexts. Race and ethnicity, for example, have a very strong salience in the United States such that our history is inextricably linked to this particular identity facet. We would put forth that race, ethnicity, and the potential physical characteristics, or lack thereof, of these identities influence all of us within US society daily. Being White in our society garners different treatment than that given to individuals who are Asian American or African American. This particular facet is often used to judge other personal characteristics and to create stereotypes.

Intersectionality

Last, on this subject, though the different facets are presented as separate groups to some extent, we must also recognize that the phrase "the whole is greater than the sum of its parts" is extremely relevant here. Think of your own identity for a moment. Are you able to separate how your various identities influence how you walk in the world as a whole being? Think for a moment about your gender identity. Is this wholly separate from your racial identity, or does the combination mean something different? Instead of just belonging to one group in one facet, we all have multiple cultural identity facets, and the combinations of these also lead to different life experiences and attitudes. For example, someone who identifies as a lower-socioeconomic, White, gay man may have a very different day-to-day experience from a heterosexual, African American, wealthy woman. Consider the following excerpt from "Theresa," who is talking about her experience as an Asian American woman in a business environment.

> *Some of my colleagues expect me to be quieter than the men sometimes, and I was trying to explain this to my male friend who is also Asian. I'm not a very quiet person and so I think sometimes people look surprised when I speak up so quickly. He said, "But I've never had that reaction to me when I speak, and I hear Helen speak up fairly often and it doesn't seem like the men have the same reaction to her when she is louder. So it can't really be race or gender then, right? Maybe it's your personal issue?" I had to explain that as an Asian American woman, there are different stereotypes about me being passive or quiet in general, and that this is different from Helen who is African American, though also a woman. They seem to accept that she will be loud, and I think a lot of that is based on stereotypes. And my friend, as a man who is also Asian, gets a different reception as well. They don't seem to expect him to be as quiet. It's complicated when it's all mixed up. I have to act differently to be heard the same way.*

> —Theresa, age 43

In the vignette above, Theresa is trying to explain that it's a combination of gender and race that dictates at least in part how her colleagues are responding to her. As someone who is Asian and also female, Theresa's experience is different from the experiences of those who share just her race or just her gender. Identity is complex. Therefore, understanding the different facets and pieces of identity is also a complex process. Knowing someone's identity statuses in some of the areas Hays discusses may help us to begin to understand some parts of another person who is different from us in some way. This is by no means an exhaustive list or description, but this

iStock/Rawpixel

model helps us to identify and organize understanding of some identity facets and sets the stage for us to begin to talk about intersections between these identities as well.

It is important for us to rely on accurate information, however, in beginning to think about various identities and their intersections. Stereotyping, which has often happened to disenfranchised or historically underrepresented individuals in the past, can create **unidimensional** understandings of others who are unlike us in some way, and this can too easily lead to labeling and negative judgement about differences.

YOUR JOURNEY INTO MULTICULTURAL PSYCHOLOGY

We invite you, as you begin to read these pages, to take on what might be a different perspective for you: the realization that almost all of what you experience, think, and believe is a function of your cultural beliefs and identities. It can be daunting to realize that all you know is subjective, but it can also be exciting.

Some of you are embarking on a new journey right now—this may feel like uncharted territory for you. Perhaps you're someone who hasn't been exposed to very many people who are different from you or whose family didn't talk about race or culture much growing up. Sometimes people who have had these types of experiences have a hard time hearing about race in general or find it difficult to understand some of the experiences had by those from different cultures. Knowing this now and trying to move past these obstacles will be important for you. For others of you, you've had many experiences with people who are different from you, or maybe you've experienced some issues related to race, ethnicity, or other cultural facets yourself. The information in this book may not be as new to you, but it may provide you some different insights or some terms and theory to explain things you or people you know have experienced in the past. The study of multicultural psychology is rich, nuanced, and vast. There is something new for all of you to learn regardless of where you are now. At the end of this chapter, we'll help you to assess your current levels of awareness, knowledge, and skills and give you some ideas of where to start using the new knowledge you are accruing. This may help you to get the most out of this book.

We encourage you to open your mind wide as you read these pages. Turn the ideas presented here over (and over) in your mind. Look at them critically, and expand your understanding. This willingness to work toward true competence and understanding in this area is the key to becoming a more culturally aware individual. There are many benefits to becoming more culturally aware, as you will learn in the following chapters, but perhaps the best reason of all is that it opens your life to a broader overall experience. Being able to understand things from multiple perspectives in addition to your own vantage point, and broadening your knowledge and skills of all different groups of people, makes for a rich life.

A Brief Overview of the Book's Organization

We have broken this textbook into several sections. We've started with Section I: "What Is Multicultural Psychology?" in this chapter, and in the rest of this section we will cover where multicultural psychology is as a field and how our current climate both influences and is influenced by the study of multiculturalism. We'll also take a look backward to our history to allow us to see how we have arrived at the conclusions and ideas we support today. Section II: "Individuals and Their Contexts" will ask you to take a look at yourself and others through the lenses you use to view the world. We'll start by talking about culture and worldview and the impact these concepts can have on what we view as "normal" or "abnormal." Next we will discuss identity development with regard to race, sexuality, and other social facets. Models will be presented to help explicate the ways in which our various identity facets, and their intersections, influence our interactions, our day-to-day experiences, and our understandings of ourselves and others. Following this we will start to address the impact context has on us as individuals. Concepts such as racism, oppression, power, privilege, and stereotyping influence our lives in different ways depending on our identities and our place in the world. One strong influence on context, and how we see it, is our media, and unpacking the impact of differing images and prototypes will start out Section III: "Lived Experiences and Social Influences."

Following this contextual piece, we will detail experiences and issues commonly shared by those who identify as people of color, and those who identify as biracial or multiracial. In Section IV, "Moving Ahead: Emerging Issues and Goals," we will detail how some of the concepts learned might be utilized and experienced in different settings. Here, too, we will take some time to dream a bit, looking toward the future and encouraging you to do the same.

CONCLUSION

It is our belief, and one we share with many others in the field of psychology today, that culture counts. It must be taken into consideration in any discussion where we are talking about *people,* and as psychology is the study of people, it is particularly important in our field. In reading this book, we hope you will gain new perspectives and new understandings that will help you to shake the field's pillars and begin to see the world through different eyes.

We would now like to talk with you about how to use this book in general. Reading helps us to develop knowledge and understanding, but by itself it can only produce internal change. We are looking to help you to make actual change in your life and in the lives of others around you, to assist you in taking steps toward making your world a more socially just environment. Therefore, we finish each chapter with a series of self-reflection opportunities and make suggestions as to actions you might try to carry out each week. In the following pages you will find additional material that will help you to process some of the information you learned in this chapter. We hope you will take advantage of the media clips, self-tests, and activities we suggest.

As we said before, you are about to embark upon a journey. Thinking critically about your own experiences and how they might differ from the experiences of others will be crucial to having a greater understanding of the theories, facts, and history presented in these pages. Remember to ask questions and to consider that worldviews differ depending on our own cultural facets. Now let's begin.

ACT: Assess Your Knowledge, Critical Thinking, Take Part

Assess Your Knowledge

What did you know?

Some of the ideas you read about in this chapter may have been new, and others older. Look at the following list, and rate your level of awareness of each statement prior to reading this chapter:

	I didn't know this.	I was sort of aware of this.	I was very aware of this.
Multicultural psychology involves concepts like race and ethnicity, but also gender, sexual orientation, and social class, among others.			
Psychology has pathologized many nondominant groups with research.			
Science is not always objective, as humans are carrying out its practice.			
To avoid setting up deficit models between dominant and nondominant groups, we must make sure we are studying, and measuring, the same thing in both groups.			
Psychology and other fields, like medicine and physiology, used science to promote ideas that were racist (scientific racism).			
In the field of psychology, race is a sociocultural context, not one that is biological.			
Multicultural psychology is known in the field as the Fourth Force.			

Critical Thinking

Complete the following "Culture Sketch" from Pamela Hays's (2016) *Addressing Cultural Complexities in Practice: Assessment, Diagnosis and Therapy*

Your Cultural Self-Assessment

Age and generational influences: When you were born, what were the social expectations for a person of your identity? What are they now? Do you identify with a particular generation (e.g., baby boomers, millennials, Generation X, Y, or Z, iGen)? How have your values and worldview been shaped by the social movements of or influences on your generation (e.g., Vietnam War, women's movement, Stonewall riots,

Americans With Disabilities Act, civil rights movement, 9/11, social media, economic downturn, university costs, climate change, wars in Iraq and Afghanistan, current issues of immigration in the United States and other countries, gender fluidity, etc.)? What generational roles are core to your identity (e.g., aunt, father, adult child, grandparent)? How have these roles influenced your life?

_____

_____

_____

Developmental or other disability: Where you born with a disability, or did you acquire one later in life? If yes, is it a visible or nonvisible disability (e.g., chronic pain, psychiatric illness or cognitive impairment)? If no, have you been a caregiver for or lived with someone who has a disability? How has disability affected your life and opportunities?

_____

_____

_____

Religion and spiritual orientation: Were you brought up in a religious or spiritual tradition? Do you identify with a religion or have a spiritual practice now? How were your values and goals shaped by your religious or nonreligious upbringing? If you were not raised with a religion, how has this impacted your life?

_____

_____

_____

Ethnic and racial identity: What do you consider your ethnic or racial identity? If you were adopted, what are the identities of your biological and adoptive parents? How do other people identify you? Are these the same? Are there ethnic or racial differences within your family? If so, how are these differences perceived, and how have they affected you?

_____

_____

_____

Socioeconomic status: What social class did you grow up in, and what do you consider to be your socio-economic status now? When you were in high school, what were the educational and work opportunities available to you? Do you have peer-level relationships with people who differ from you socioeconomically (i.e., defined by education, income, and occupational levels)?

_____

_____

_____

Sexual orientation: Do you identify as gay, lesbian, bisexual, heterosexual, pansexual, or other orientation? If you are heterosexual, do you have a family member or friend whose identity lies under the LGBTQ rainbow? Is your family accepting of members of this community? How has your minority or dominant sexual orientation affected your relationships and educational and work experiences?

_____

_____

_____

Indigenous heritage: Do you have any Native heritage—for example, Native Hawaiian, First Nations, Alaska Native, American Indian, New Zealand Maori, or Aboriginal Australian? Did you grow up on or near a reservation or Native community? If so, how has this affected you? If not, how has the lack of such experience affected you? Do you belong to a culture that has a multigenerational connection to a particular land, water, or place?

_____

_____

_____

National origin: Are you a US citizen, an international student, or an immigrant? Were you born in the United States? Do you (and your parents and grandparents) speak English as a first language? How has your English-language ability affected your life and opportunities? How has your nationality affected your life and opportunities?

_____

_____

_____

Gender: What were and are the gender-related roles and expectations for you in your family of origin and current family? When you were a teenager, what were the norms, values, and gender roles supported within your family, by your peers, in your culture, and in the dominant culture? How have these expectations affected your choices in life? If your gender is non-binary, how does this fit into your family understandings and expectations?

_____

_____

_____

Source: Hays (2016, pp. 42–43). Copyright 2016 by the American Psychological Association.

Take Part

We are all at different stages with our level of comfort on topics involving multiculturalism. Look at the following list, and choose one or two things to try this week to further your knowledge in this area. Try to choose something that requires you to stretch a little—if it seems very easy to you, move up a level. When you are finished with the exercise, write a journal entry about what it was like for you and about what questions you still have.

Participation: Gather more information for yourself on the topics below. You might try a mere Google search at first, and then dive more deeply into authors who study these important concepts. Some authors who study these areas are listed next to each topic. In addition, consider doing your own PsycINFO search or look for reference books on these topics in your local library.

- Scientific racism (Stephen Jay Gould, R. M. Dennis, Frederick Douglass)

- Explaining differences to children (Rebeca Bigler, Tony Brown and colleagues)

- DNA testing issues (e.g., Sheldon Krimsky, https://now.tufts.edu/articles/pulling-back-curtain-dna-ancestry-tests)

- Conceptual equivalence (Sam M. Y. Ho, C. Harry Hui, Harry C. Triandis)

- The Fourth Force (Paul Pedersen, Derald Wing Sue)

Initiation: Think of someone you know who is different in some way from you in terms of your culture sketch. Find a time to start a conversation with this person about how her or his experience might differ from yours. You could ask the person to complete a culture sketch as well, and then talk about your differences. Which identities feel salient for this person? Which are salient for you? Why?

Activism: Choose a topic like "scientific racism" or "the White Standard" as the basis of a presentation or essay in another class, as an editorial for your campus newspaper, or as a topic of discussion in your friendship group. Prepare with statistics, terms, and details.

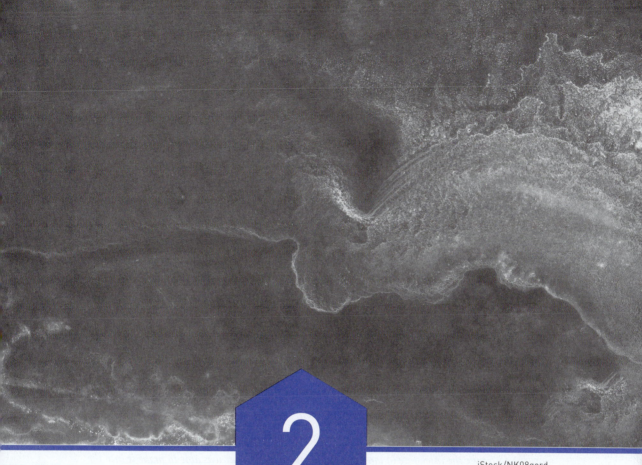

2

RACE

Historical Contexts and Contemporary Manifestations

Years ago, a White friend of mine told me the story of the day she began to see herself as White and realized that race was at work all around her. It was a surprising story, because my friend was famous for believing racism was a thing of the past, or would soon be, with people like her who treated others with fairness and respect and ignored race. Everything changed for her when her car broke down in what was considered the "bad part of town." She had been driving through the Black neighborhood of our city, despite having been taught by her parents and friends to take the interstate (a longer route) to avoid it. The car was able to make it into the parking lot of a liquor store and then just died.

Though it was in the middle of day, she had never stopped in the Black neighborhood alone before, and she found herself surprised by her growing fear. A Black store employee came out and brought her a bottle of water and offered to call someone if she needed. While she waited for help, two young Black men approached her. Afraid, she turned away from them and did not speak. Much to her surprise, they came up and said they had seen her car in distress and wondered if they could help. As they were checking out the car, the police pulled into the lot. The officers got out of the car, put their hands on their guns and ordered the men to the ground. The gentlemen were handcuffed and pushed to the sidewalk to sit on the curb. At that point, the police turned to my friend and asked if she was okay. She explained the situation and then watched as the officers gathered identifications and information from the two men and called in on their car radio before letting them go.

n 2009, historian Bill Rankin released a project called "Radical Cartography," central to which was a map of Chicago that used colored dots to represent the racial makeup of the city. Using the categories of: *White, Black, Asian, Hispanic,* and *Other,* Rankin's dot mapping revealed not only the racial segregation of the city, but the clear and stark lines that divide us.

Soon, others developed similar maps of various cities in the United States, and in 2013, Dustin Cable, of the Weldon Cooper Center for Public Service, published a map of the entire United States with a dot for every individual counted in the previous census. That work became part of a renewed national discussion on racial segregation. Despite the fact that the segregation reflected in the maps is historically entrenched, and that we have long examined the policies and social **ideologies** that created it, and that countless present-day studies reveal the various manifestations of it (from an increasing **racial wealth gap** to continued, and in some cases even worsening, school segregation (Orfield, Ee, Frankenberg, & Siegel-Hawley, 2016)—for some it felt like the maps presented new or unrealized information. The strong concentration of colors, the clear segregation, and the stark separations had a visceral impact, for some sadness and anger, for others shock and surprise.

It was as if the expanded awareness and opportunities our contemporary technology and global marketplace provided (designer patterns purported to be "Indigenous," the popularization of sushi, our love of guacamole, the commercialization of hip hop, etc.) had obscured the reality of the racial segregation that marks our social world and our day-to-day lives. It is a segregation not simply about space and place, but about how we see ourselves, others, and the world, and how and why we, individually and collectively, function as we do in society. The role of multicultural psychology is to assist in understanding those relationships between individuals and their personal, as well as social (culture, class, race, gender, etc.), structural (systems, institutions, ideologies, policies, etc.), and historical context.

The reality and implications of that psychological, social, and spatial segregation were again on display with the national coverage of the killing of Trayvon Martin in 2012. Soon, we became aware of places like Standing Rock and Ferguson, names like Michael Brown, Sandra Bland, Tanisha Anderson, Philando Castille, Melissa Ventura,

Tamir Rice, and Jason Pero; and, most recently, George Floyd, Breonna Taylor, and Ahmaud Arbery; and we became aware of movements like #ICan'tBreathe, Hands Up Don't Shoot, Say Her Name, and Black Lives Matter. Despite the expansive coverage of the deaths of people of color at the hands of police, our views on those cases often split along racial lines.

In 2014, The Pew Research Center surveyed residents of Ferguson, Missouri, following the death of Michael Brown and found that 80% of Blacks felt the grand jury made the wrong decision in the Brown case, where only 23% of Whites thought the same. Where 64% of Blacks felt that race was a major factor in that decision, only 16% of Whites saw race as a major force (Table 2.1).

TABLE 2.1 ● Blacks and Whites Divided in Views of Police Response to Ferguson Shooting

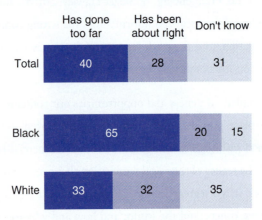

% saying police response to shooting. . .

	Has gone too far	Has been about right	Don't know
Total	40	28	31
Black	65	20	15
White	33	32	35

Survey conducted August 14–17, 2014. Whites and blacks include only those who are not Hispanic. Figures may not add to 100% because of rounding.

PEW RESEARCH CENTER

Source: Pew Research Center (2014, August 18). Stark Racial Divisions in Reactions to Ferguson Police Shootings. https://www.people-press.org/2014/08/18/stark-racial-divisions-in-reactions-to-ferguson-police-shooting/.

In analyzing these differences, Bouie (2014) argues that when you consider racial segregation, it makes sense that our views of the world around us would also break along racial lines. How and where we live impacts how we view the world. Most of us live near people of our same racial category.

Work notwithstanding, there's not much overlap between [those] worlds. "Overall," writes Robert P. Jones, of the Public Religion Research Institute, "the social networks of whites are a remarkable 93 percent white." In fact, he points out, "fully three-quarters of whites have entirely white social networks without any minority presence," a level of social homogeneity unmatched among other racial and ethnic groups. (Bouie, 2014, p. 1)

We imagine that most of us feel as if we live integrated lives, and that racial segregation is a thing of the past, but the reality is not only the pervasiveness of our residential and social segregation, but how much many of us do not even realize it is occurring.

DEFINING RACE

My brother went to a middle school that had recently begun bussing in students of color to desegregate the school's population. As an African American, he was keenly aware of the school's policy that did not allow Black and brown kids to gather in groups of more than three (a rule that was explained away as a prevention of gang activity). Nevertheless, my brother was also a big teaser, who thought he was funny. In class, one day, he took a White female classmate's Garfield pencil and was waving it around to tease her. Not amused, she told the teacher. My brother gave her back the pencil and was sent to the principal's office. My mother was called to the school that afternoon to talk about his conduct and hear the punishment. When she arrived, my brother was sitting handcuffed in the back of a police car near the school's entrance. Right before calling her, the school administrators had called the police and reported my brother for theft.

To fully understand our racial divide, our racialized social context, and their impacts on individual psyche and identity development, we must understand the term *race*, the historical context, and its contemporary manifestations. Race is, first and foremost, socially constructed. It is the meaning given to an arbitrary list of physical characteristics or phenotypes: hair texture, hair color, skin tone, bone structure, and facial features (Blumenbach in Bhopal, 2007). Creating hierarchical racial categories and projecting racial meaning onto the body worked to obscure the sociopolitical and economic intentions of the constructions, and gave these ideas a seeming scientific weight. Race is the social, disguised as the biological; it is the produced made to seem "natural." As Omi and Winant (2015) state, "Race has been understood as a sign of God's pleasure or displeasure, as an indicator of evolutionary development, as a key to intelligence, and as a signifier in human geography" (p. 4).

Though race is often thought of as a set of attitudes, beliefs, and feelings, it has always operated in structures and systems. These produced racial meanings do affect how we feel and think as individuals and thus impact our behaviors and social interactions, but they were created to impact the institutions, structures, and ideologies that form the foundation of our society. How we feel about ourselves and each other, racially, is a product of just one part of the way racism and racial inequality are at work.

Some of your parents (and one of the authors of this text) grew up in the era of the "afterschool special." It was a TV show where each episode featured a dramatization of different issues teens faced. (It was better than we're making it sound.) It, and most every other children's series we have seen, had a particular "special episode," the one where someone new comes into an established social setting or group, and the new person is different from everyone else. You have likely seen enough similarly themed shows to know how the story ends. Whether it's in a TV show or movie or book, once everyone realizes that they are more the same than different and that difference is nothing to be afraid of, social harmony is reached, the big game is won, or the play is a success or the group wins first place or everyone goes to the school dance (you get the point)—and everyone lives happily ever after. Sometimes, in TV and movies, this classic story is portrayed as a bit more complicated, and those who are different have been the victims of social inequality. In those cases, there is the cinematic hero, the lone teacher or popular kid or coach, who endures ridicule and sacrifices to make a difference, and the hero saves the day.

That story is a **social narrative**, a commonly shared belief or idea, but not necessarily a true one. In this case, it is a narrative where "difference" is a stand-in for race or another element of social inequality. The pervasiveness of that story has led many to see our problems around race as an attitude, as a natural, human response to difference. From that **narrative frame**, the solution to racial inequality is simply the need to accept differences and love one another, or for a savior to step up and fight for what's right, opening the eyes of others along the way.

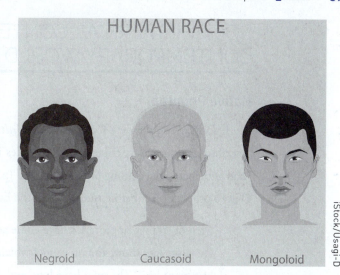

HUMAN RACE

Negroid   Caucasoid   Mongoloid

iStock/Usagi-D

Racial classifications

These stories can be inspirational, even life changing for some, but they also work to obscure the structural nature of race and racism, which can make something embedded in institutions (e.g., educational inequality) into something we think we can fix on an individual level, armed only with "good intentions," a good heart, and determination. A successful tutoring program in a low-income area can help a lot of individuals, but unless there is an understanding of, and an attempt to address or transform, the inequitable educational system that helped create the need for the tutoring, the program will never serve as an effective solution to the real problem. That purely individualized approach may also limit our ability to gain insight into the myriad impacts our inequitable system has on various groups or its broader social implications. To understand and successfully address the life and mind of an individual, we must understand the institutions, systems, and structures in and through which they were formed.

Part of the misconception of seeing race and racial inequality as natural and expected elements of the human experience is thinking they have always been around, but that story belies the actual history of the concepts of race and racial formation in the United States. The idea of race, as we know it today, is relatively new; most historians trace its emergence to the late 1600s or early 1700s. For centuries, socioeconomic class was the great social divide, but with the development of a racialized classification of humans (Caucasoid, Mongoloid, etc.), a new name and rationale for social inequality arose. Through European colonialization and the slave trade in Africa and the Americas, this notion of race would intertwine with class and gender and become woven into the fabric of our developing nation.

SOCIOHISTORICAL CONTEXT OF OUR CONTEMPORARY WORLD

Native Peoples

In *A Different Mirror: A History of Multicultural America,* Takaki (2008) described the numerous tribes whose histories include prophecies and dreams that "had anticipated the coming of the strangers" (p. 27). He recounted a dream from an Ojibwa prophet years before the arrival of the Europeans:

> Men of strange appearance have come across the great water. Their skins are white like snow, and on canoes which have great white wings like that of a giant bird. The men have long and sharp knives, and they have long black tubes which they point at birds and animals. The tubes make a smoke that rises into the air just like the smoke from our pipes. From them come fire and such terrific noise that I was frightened, even in my dream. (p. 27)

The dreams and prophesies all ended the same, with loss of native land and "death to the red man."

Numerous European settlements in what would become the United States recorded early interactions with Native peoples, encounters that saved countless European lives and were key to colony survival. Soon, European desire for more land ultimately led to the genocide (physical and cultural) of Indigenous populations.

Burial of the dead at the battlefield of Wounded Knee

Throughout the Americas it is estimated Native American population size was reduced by more than 90%, from approximately 100 million to nearly 10 million, and land holdings by more than 97% (Dunbar-Ortiz, 2015). Specific numbers for the United States are disputed, but it is estimated that a population of somewhere between 5 million and 15 million Native Americans in 1492 was down to a mere 237,000 by the 1800s. Today, the

Indigenous population in the United States is at nearly 3 million, but they are still often seen as an "invisible" people. Their representation in popular culture, when we see their images at all, is either as romanticized (mystical, spiritual, and able to speak to nature) figures or as a tragic vestige of our past.

In a time of increasing public attention to police brutality, it has gone largely unnoticed that, according to the US Centers for Disease Control, Native Americans are killed in police encounters at a higher rate than any other racial group (Hansen, 2017).

The racializing of Native peoples became the justification for slaughter, poisonings, crop destruction, war, and massacres—all for the sake of land. The same people who brought food to starving English settlers and taught them about crop rotation, fertilization, and weed management had a new identity constructed for them—"the lazy savage." Imagine the **cognitive dissonance** produced by a human being brutalizing another, especially if that person had helped or saved you. In order to justify our treatment of Native Americans, we had to dehumanize them, make them into something else, **"the other."**

Takaki records,

> As the English population increased and as their settlements expanded, the settlers needed even more land. To justify the taking of territory, the colonizers argued that the original inhabitants were not entitled to the land, for they lacked a work ethic. . . . Indian deaths were viewed as the destruction of devil worshippers . . . [and] what was forged in the violent dispossession of the original inhabitants was an ideology that demonized the "savages" (2008, pp. 41–42).

Figure 2.1 shows a timeline of Native American history.

FIGURE 2.1 ⬤ Native American Timeline	
1142	The Great Peacemaker unites the Iroquois nations, forming first democracy.
Pre-1492	Estimates of the size of the Native American population range from 12 million to over 100 million.
1492	Columbus lands in what is now the Bahamas. Thinking it is India, he calls inhabitants "Indians."

(Continued)

FIGURE 2.1	⬤ (Continued)
1600s	Native American knowledge is key to European settler survival.
	European settlers attack and destroy Native villages for food.
	Europeans increase in number and start exporting tobacco, need Indian land.
	Indians try to drive out settlers to preserve their land; violence escalates.
1610–1675	Indian population decreases sharply (due to violence and European diseases).
Mid-1700s	Iroquois democracy used as model for US Constitution and the uniting of the states.
1776	Jefferson declares Indians must be civilized or exterminated.
1830	Indian Removal Act passed.
1851	Indian reservations established.
1860–1978	Indian boarding school era.
Late 1800s	Indian religion/spirituality outlawed from this period until 1978.
1924	Indian Citizenship Act passed.
1968	Creation of AIM (American Indian Movement); Indian Civil Rights Act passed.
1969	Native Americans occupy Alcatraz.
2004	Smithsonian National Museum of the American Indian opens.
2018	Sharice Davids (Ho-Chunk) and Deb Haaland (Laguna Pueblo) are the first Native women elected to Congress,

African Americans and the Construction of Whiteness: The Intersections of Race, Class, and Gender

The increased immigration of Europeans also signaled the need for increased labor sources. In those early years, a number of ways to meet the growing labor demands were explored—enslavement of Native Americans and Africans, the indentured service of Whites and Africans, and a wage labor force of landless Whites, Native Americans, and free and freed Africans. Before 1676, landless Whites and free or freed Africans married, had children, were friends and neighbors, and worked alongside each other as laborers. Part of the story of the "naturalness" of our racial divide is that it has always been with us, that it is an expected outcome of different people coming in contact with each other. Contrary to that narrative is the reality of our history. There were interracial communities of working-class folks, people who lived and loved and worked and rebelled together. Our nation's history includes this time of racial integration. So what happened in 1676? Bacon's Rebellion. It is difficult to fully capture the impact this period in US history has had on our class, gender, and racial present and the intersecting nature of those constructs.

Increased European populations and the profitability of tobacco created a land rush, but the elite, in places like Virginia, wanted to solidify and maintain their growing wealth and political power. Among their efforts, the elite passed laws increasing the length of indentured servanthood, which limited competition for land and increased sources of labor. Landless Whites became frustrated by their economic and political limitations and, joined by free Africans, they rebelled against unfair labor practices and legislative controls. Bacon's Rebellion was born. Takaki writes, "A colonial official reported that Bacon had raised an army of soldiers 'whose fortunes and inclinations' were 'desperate.' Bacon had unleashed an armed interracial 'giddy multitude' that threatened the very foundations of social order in Virginia." Ultimately stopped, the rebellion became known as the largest to take place before the Revolution (Takaki, 2008, pp. 59–60).

Following the rebellion, the elites enacted a series of new laws designed to disempower the working class and break up the "multitude." They did so along racial lines, specifically through the deepening of the racial divide and the construction of **Whiteness**. If meaning and privilege could be given to the idea of Whiteness, then the laboring class would be divided, and thus pose less of a threat to the elite. The decision was made to concentrate on the African slave trade as the primary source of labor. "What the landed gentry systematically developed after the insurrection was a labor force based on caste" (Takaki, 2008, p. 61).

Slavery required a justification. We could not psychologically manage or ensure broader social buy-in for a system with the level of death, rape, and intentional destruction the *peculiar institution* of slavery held without making Africans *other*. Before the Constitution was written declaring that slaves would be considered three fifths human, we developed the ideas and enacted the policies that furthered the process of dehumanization. As we had seen with Native Americans before, Black maleness came to symbolize savagery and violence, and the construction of Black femaleness was formed around sexuality. Following Bacon's Rebellion, new policy helped solidify these ideas into the minds of the populace and create stereotypes and structural divides that extend into today.

Harsher slave laws were enacted, denying slaves freedom of assembly and movement. Slave militia patrols were established to monitor slave quarters and plantations to prevent runaways or unlawful assembly. It became illegal for Blacks to be educated and for Blacks to carry any kind of weapon. Expansion of the definition of who was Black led to the "one drop rule," and by 1723, "free property-owning blacks, mulattos, and native Americans . . . were denied the right to vote" (Buck, 2016, p. 22).

Simultaneously, Whiteness had to be defined and taught to Whites. (There will be more on Whiteness in Chapter 6). A 1691 law worsened the punishment for White women who married African or Indian men, and Buck writes,

> A changing panoply of specific laws molded European behavior into patterns that made slave revolt and cross-race unity more and more difficult. These laws limited, for instance, the European right to teach slaves to read. Europeans couldn't use slaves in skilled jobs, which were reserved for Europeans. Europeans had to administer prescribed punishment for slave "misbehavior" and were expected to participate in patrolling at night. They did not have the legal right to befriend Blacks. A White servant who ran away with a Black was subject to additional punishment beyond that for simply running away. European rights to free their slaves were also curtailed. (2016, p. 22)

Gender constructions and gender roles around class and race were also formed. Buck goes on to describe how, following Bacon's Rebellion, the elites developed and spread the idea of White masculinity. The underlying concept was that White superiority could be seen by how well White men were able to provide for their families. White men should work, and their wives stay home, unlike Blacks and people in Native communities, where both genders (inside and outside of the slave system) worked. The narrative of the successful White man was formed, describing men who worked and were the heads of households where women stayed home and cared for the home and children. Married White women (especially Whites who were not recent immigrants) were discouraged from wage labor with claims that "true women served only their families" (Buck, 2016, p. 24). Working-class White men became slave patrollers and plantation overseers, and were given or allowed to buy small parcels of land.

The economic benefits connected to being White helped strengthen the racial divide, but the real psychosocial work of the construction came with what W. E. B. Dubois (1935) called the "psychological wage of Whiteness," the idea that one's Whiteness had meaning and value, that it alone made one superior to other races. This "wage," along with the social, political, and economic privileges given to Whites, finally and fully disrupted the earlier interracial communities.

In 1776, the nation declared that only White male landowners could vote. By 1790, only Whites could be citizens. In 1862, the Homestead Act provided free land to anyone who improved that land within five years; the only other criterion was that one had to be a citizen, which limited this benefit to only Whites. So, whether you were from a family of wealthy plantation owners in Virginia or were a newly arrived poor immigrant, if you were White, you could own land. These race-based policies around voting, citizenship, and land ownership worked in concert to further racialize class inequality. Researchers at The Economic Policy Institute argue that the biggest factor in our increasing racial wealth gap today is housing inequality. That inequality can, in large part, be traced back to The Homestead Act as well as to the housing policies of the 1920s and 1930s (e.g., redlining—more on this in Chapter 6), and the GI Bill of World War II.

The GI Bill helped returning veterans buy homes by providing funds for down payments as well as government-backed 30-year low-cost mortgages. Of the nearly $120 billion in loans granted through the GI Bill, more than 98% went to Whites. That historically established racial wealth gap was expanded by the recent collapse of the housing market in the United States. *Harper's Magazine* published a deposition from a Wells Fargo loan officer who described how the lender targeted members of the Black and Latino communities during the housing boom (Jacobson, 2009). As new customers to the housing market, these individuals' lack of knowledge and experience with buying a home made them vulnerable. Instead of being given the 30-year flat-rate mortgages that most qualified for, they were often sold loan packages with adjustable rates and balloon payments. The selling of those loan packages meant a financial bonus for the loan officers, who knowingly increased the likelihood of foreclosure for their Black and brown clients.

FIGURE 2.2 ● African American Timeline	
1619	First African slaves arrive in what will become the United States.
1690	By 1690, there are slaves in every colony.
1691	Slaves are officially denied the rights to vote, hold office, and testify in court.
Mid-1800s	The Underground Railroad carries ~100,000 Africans to free states and Canada.
1863	Emancipation Proclamation ends legal slavery.
1865	Civil War ends. "40 acres and a mule" is offered and then rescinded.
1868	14th Amendment grants citizenship.
1870	15th Amendment grants the right to vote. The KKK forms.
1877	Reconstruction ends.
1881	First Jim Crow segregation laws are passed.
1896	*Plessy v. Ferguson* makes "separate but equal" the law of the land.
1905	W. E. B. Dubois starts the Niagara Movement, which becomes the NAACP in 1909.
1920s	Harlem Renaissance—explosion of artistic, intellectual, and political efforts.
1954	*Brown v. Board of Education* ends legal segregation in schools.
1963	March on Washington; King delivers "I Have a Dream" speech.
1964	Civil Rights Act is passed.
1965	Voting Rights Act is passed.
1989	Oprah Winfrey becomes the first African American to own her own TV and film production company.
2008	Barack Obama is elected as first Black president of the United States.
2013	#BlackLivesMatter brings new awareness to police brutality associated with African American people.
2018	*Black Panther* becomes the highest-grossing solo superhero film, refocuses emergence of Afrofuturism.

Attitudes, policies, and inequalities established in our past are still seen within today's raced and gendered homeownership levels, home values, and wage inequity. A recent Institute for Policy Studies (2019) report found that between 1983 and 2013, the median wealth of a Black household declined 75% (from $6,800 to $1,700), and that the median Latino household wealth declined 50% (from $4,000 to $2,000). At the same time, wealth for the median White household *increased* 14% from $102,000 to $116,800.

The idea of race, what it means to be Black and what it means to be White, has been constructed, enacted, and entrenched. The concepts became part of our sense of self and others; thus, our attitudes and behaviors are impacted, but more than that, race has been embedded in our laws, policies, and economic and political systems. Far from "natural," the path to race, race relations, and racial inequality in the United States was designed with purpose and intent. Understanding that sociohistorical context and the structural nature of race is key to understanding the psyches and individuals that it produces. A racial segregation timeline is given in Figure 2.2, and a table showing major events in African American history is shown in Figure 2.3.

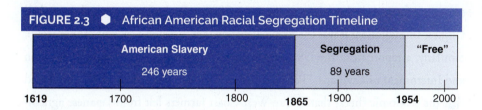

FIGURE 2.3 ● African American Racial Segregation Timeline

American Slavery	Segregation	"Free"
246 years	89 years	

1619   1700   1800   1865   1900   1954   2000

ASIAN AMERICANS

For Asian Americans, that very term raises a number of issues, from the way in which it obscures the extraordinary diversity contained within this group (more than 20 nations, cultures, histories, etc. in the United States alone) to the use of "American" for a population ironically seen as "the perpetual foreigner." Neither of the authors of this text can count the number of times Asian American students have told us the story of being praised for their command of the English language and of being asked, "Where are you from?" followed by, "Where are you really from?" when the answer of Chicago or New Orleans or Fresno isn't enough. Asian Americans are often seen as not really American; they are often betrayed in popular culture with heavy accents, but little ethnic or national specificity, they are "Asian," and thus *other*.

Early encounters, and the beginning of Asian racial constructions in the United States, began in the 1800s with the Chinese and Japanese. In *Orientals: Asian Americans in Popular Culture,* Lee (1999) argues that there are six "faces" or images that make up the racial construction of Asian Americans—the "pollutant," the "coolie," the deviant, the yellow peril, the model minority, and the "gook," each one constructed at "a specific historical moment, marked by a shift in class relations accompanied by cultural crisis" (p. 8). He goes on to write that some studies attribute hostilities towards Asian immigrants directly to economic competition and the creation of an ethnically defined segmented labor market. They provide us with an economic framework for understanding the dynamics of class and race and a map of the economic terrain on which anti-Asian hostility has been built (pp. 5–6).

In other words, the coolie representations of the Chinese were developed at a time when the Chinese laborer was seen as a threat to White labor. Politically, these representations formed the backdrop to the 1882 Chinese Exclusion Act, which barred all Chinese immigration; it was the first federal law that targeted a specific ethnic group. Similarly, a report from the US government's Commission on Wartime Relocation and Internment of Civilians, "Personal Justice Denied" (Kashima, 1997), concluded that the economic threat that White West Coast farmers felt from Japanese agricultural success formed "part of the impetus for the incarceration of the Japanese" (p. 42) during World War II. Figure 2.4 shows a timeline of Asian American history.

FIGURE 2.4 ● Asian American Timeline	
Late 1700s	First period of Asian Pacific immigration.
1820s	Cohort of Chinese men immigrate and work in railroads and mines.
1882	Chinese Exclusion Act (restricting immigration) is passed.
1908	Gentleman's Agreement brings wave of Japanese immigrants.
Early 1900s	Numerous Asian groups are brought to Hawaii for labor.
World War II	Japanese Americans are interned.
1943	Chinese Exclusion Act is repealed.
1946	Immigration opportunities for Filipinos and Asian Indians increase.
1952	McCarran-Walter Act allows Asians to become US citizens.
1979–1980s	Vietnamese, Cambodian, Laotian, and Hmong refugees come to the United States, fleeing war.
1970–1990s	500,000+ Koreans immigrate to the United States.
1982	Murder of Vincent Chin marks beginning of panethnic Asian American movement.
1989	President Bush approves reparations for Japanese American internment.
2001	Elaine Chao is first Asian American woman appointed to the president's Cabinet.
2010	Asian immigration surpasses immigration from Latin America.
2018	*Crazy Rich Asians* is the first Hollywood film in 25 years with an Asian cast.

Asian Americans may soon become the fastest growing immigrant group in the United States. According to Pew research (Lopez, Ruiz, & Patten, 2017), the Asian immigrant population grew 72% from 2000 to 2015.

LATINX

Despite the statistics for Asians, the population most of us think of when the issue of immigration is raised is Mexicans. The irony is not lost on Californians like us, who are writing about Latinx immigration on land that was once part of Mexico. As the saying goes, the story of Mexicans in the United States didn't start with Mexicans crossing the borders, but with the border crossing Mexicans.

The term *Latinx* is a gender-neutral alternative to *Latino*. It is unusual to be discussing Latinx in a chapter on race, since it is not a race. **Chicanx/Latinx** are a mestizo people: mixed—various combinations of the Indigenous peoples of the Americas, the European colonizers of those lands (Spanish, Portuguese, etc.), and the Africans who came as free and slave labor. That racial complexity is just part of a diversity that includes a myriad of nations of origin, histories, and cultures. Today, that complexity is increased by the politicization of the issues surrounding immigration, deportation policies, and economic inequity in Latinx communities in the United States. Figure 2.5 shows a timeline of Latinx history.

FIGURE 2.5 ● Latinx Timeline	
1598	New Mexico is settled by Spain.
1769	Spanish missions are established.
1821	Mexico takes over control of New Mexico and over 3,000 Mexicans in California.
1846	Mexican American War.
1848	Treaty of Guadalupe Hidalgo establishes land grants.
1851	Land grants are declared no longer valid.
1898	Spanish American War—United States colonizes Puerto Rico, mandates English as instructional language.
1902	Cuba gains independence from the United States.
1903	Mexican-Japanese farmer workers union is established.
1912	New Mexico enters the union as an official bilingual state.

(Continued)

FIGURE 2.5	⬡ (Continued)

1917	Jones Act grants citizenship to Puerto Ricans.
1942	Following mass deportations in the 1930s, the Bracero Program brings in needed Mexican laborers.
1943	Zoot suit riots are seen as the start of the Latinx civil rights movement.
1945	*Mendez v. Westminster* makes school segregation of Latinx children illegal.
1965	Dolores Huerta and Cesar Chavez start the United Farm Workers union.
2003	Latinx surpasses African Americans as largest US minority group.
2009	Sonia Sotomayor sworn in as the first Latina Supreme Court justice.
2012	President Barack Obama signs Deferred Action for Childhood Arrivals (DACA) into law.
2015	Puerto Rican American Lin-Manuel Miranda writes and stars in *Hamilton*, the winner of the 2016 Pulitzer Prize for drama and one of the all-time highest grossing productions.

CONCLUSION

Today's racial climate, our interactions within and between racial groups, and our racialized identities all emerge from our history. More than a set of attitudes and behaviors, race is embedded and operationalized in our institutions, systems, structures, and social practices. The psychologist Beverly Tatum describes race as an unavoidable smog: "Sometimes it is so thick it is visible, other times it is less apparent, but always, day in and day out, we are [all] breathing it in" (2017, p. 6). For some of us that "smog" reflects an oppressive system we must learn to navigate. For others, the smog is nearly invisible or unknown, whether from ignorance or "ignore(ance)" (not wanting to know or intentionally ignoring). Still others are finding themselves and clarity as they work through the dissonance created when reality/history reveal our internalized false social narratives.

Back to the police shootings from earlier in the chapter. To see them as a new phenomenon is to miss the long history of racial violence, from Indian wars to slave patrols to lynchings to today's racial climate. To see immigration as only a current political hot button is to miss the foundational role of economic policies and social ideologies of the past (and today), on which the current political moment is based. To see racial segregation as an issue of preference or a product of individual success is to miss the intentional policies designed to create and sustain the inequalities that are its foundation.

A few years ago, one of us (DI) team-taught a course called Global Origins of US Cultures with a colleague in the ethnic studies department who regularly utilizes community-based research as a pedagogical tool. She devised a final project for our classes that centered on that approach. From her own research, she knew that our largely White, affluent college town had a long, rich, and varied ethnic history. What we then required of students was to form groups and explore an ethnic population that used to live in the city of San Luis Obispo. They were tasked with finding out where and how the population lived, and most important, why they were no longer there.

At the end of the quarter, we put on a bike tour of San Luis Obispo's ethnic history. Campus and community members could follow our designated route through those historical neighborhoods and hear student presentations of their findings at each stop. The research alone had value, but the biggest lesson for our students, and the tour participants, was how much we could not trust our own stories, what we thought we knew, what we saw as the reality of our social world. Students, and many residents, thought of San Luis Obispo as happenstantially White and affluent. Most thought that the proximity to the ocean and the nature of the small, rural, college town simply drew a wealthier and Whiter population.

What they found among the histories was that there had been a large and vibrant Chinese community, one that was instrumental in building the roads in the area, but that was eventually seen as a threat to White labor and forced out of jobs and out of town. There was also a strong Japanese community, one of California's Japanese farming communities that were responsible for nearly 40% of the state's vegetable production before World War II. The members of this community lost their homes and farms when they were interned during the war. And the stories went on. The students found that the Whiteness they currently experience in San Luis Obispo is not "natural" and was not inevitable; it has its roots in the racialized economic, political, and social policies of the past.

Multicultural psychology draws attention to the need to understand the social context of an individual as central to understanding the individual. Insight into one's psyche does not begin and end with that person. We all come to self in a social network and milieu, and that environment is embedded within and emergent from a sociohistorical foundation. Constructions of race and gender were not simply ideas. Those concepts became shared narratives, they informed policy, institutions, and social practice. We internalized them. These constructions informed our sense of ourselves and others. It is clear, in order to effectively build relationship, counsel, assess, advise, or analyze, we must start with an understanding of the workings and operational nature of race. That understanding is the foundation for effective use of **culturally responsive counseling**.

ACT: Assess Your Knowledge, Critical Thinking, Take Part

Assess Your Knowledge

- Watch the PBS video *Race: The Power of an Illusion* (parts 1 and 2) (www.pbs.org/race), and compare the information in it to what you've heard about race and what you've learned about US history.

- Visit the Radical Cartography website (www.radicalcartography.net), and use the interactive maps to explore the nature of the racial segregation in your hometown and your college town.

Critical Thinking

- Look up a "how segregated is your city" map for your hometown, and reflect on how the demographics/race and class segregation of your city had an impact on you: schooling, community resources, cultural capital acquisition, experiences with people of other races, et cetera.

- What impact might it have had on people of other racial categories?

- Construct your own racial journal exploring the role of our racial history (immigration policy, housing segregation, slavery, etc.) on your life.

- Watch Kimberley Crenshaw's (2016) TED Talk on intersectionality.

Take Part

Participation: Replicate the class assignment described above by investigating the racial history of the town you live in right now. Which racial/ethnic groups live there, and when and why did they come, or are they indigenous to that place? Who was there before, when, and why did they leave?

Initiation: Then expose that history, start a conversation, make your findings part of a class assignment or presentation.

Activism: Identify the ways that racial inequality is most evident in the town you live in and trace its historical foundations. Locate the individuals or organizations working to address those issues, and develop ways for college students or your college itself to support their efforts.

INDIVIDUALS AND THEIR CONTEXTS

SECTION II

iStock/indianoceanimagery

CULTURE AND WORLDVIEW

The world is just so fast these days! I remember when people used to take time for each other and weren't always rushing around. Yesterday I dropped my grandchildren off at school and I saw these three mothers rushing around, wearing high heels, calling out quick greetings as they dropped off their kids—they didn't spend five minutes with each other at school. They are putting their careers and money above their families and relationships. When I was younger, the other mothers and I made time to help out in the classroom and time to chat with each other. We would often meet at each other's houses for coffee for a while after school drop off. And no one was looking at their phone all the time or texting—that's not a real relationship. It's too bad mothers don't connect anymore.

—Johanna, age 75

Yesterday, I dropped my daughters off for school, and it happened that I dropped off at the same time as two other mothers I haven't seen in a while. We were all so happy to just have a second to wave at each other and say hi for a minute as we walked to our cars. All of us had to get off to work quickly, but we told each other that we should get together soon. One texted the other two of us later that afternoon, and we made a plan pretty quickly to meet for coffee next week at a café that's pretty close to everyone's jobs. We really get each other, so it's nice to have a moment to talk about trying to balance everything. One of them just started back to work again, as she and her husband have been struggling financially a bit, so the other two of us are trying to support her while she transitions back to work. It's so great that we have the kind of technology we do today, or it would be so hard to set anything up. I don't know how mothers would have ever made plans so long ago—it would have taken forever to call all around. I'm so glad we took the time to connect with each other!

—Rachel, age 38

How we see the world depends on so many things. It seems hard to believe that two people could look at the same thing and think such different thoughts, but this is something that happens on a regular basis. You may remember in 2015 when a dress was posted on a Tumblr website and a debate began about whether the dress was white and gold, or blue and black. This debate about "the dress" had people arguing with one another all over the internet: "Are you looking at the same thing I am?" and "How can you think that it's black and blue? It's so obviously gold and white!" Though, in this case, these different views had more to do with a washed out photograph and poor lighting, worldview in general can feel like this at times. Sometimes it is hard to believe that the way you see things isn't the only way.

United States Library of Congress

Some see this as a picture of a young woman, while others see it as an older woman.

Consider the vignettes above from Johanna and Rachel. Both women recounted the same scene—three mothers dropping their kids off for school—but they had very different interpretations of what was happening. In addition, they had different opinions of many things related to this encounter, including technology (Rachel sees this as a way to connect and develop a relationship, while Johanna sees it as not actually spending time with people) and the role of women in home and work (Rachel and her friends all work outside the home, but Johanna sees this as not fulfilling their roles as women). Even the way the quick meeting with the three women was interpreted was viewed differently by the two. Rachel was thrilled to have a moment to see her friends, and the three followed up later with texts to continue their conversation to make plans to meet. Johanna viewed this as not taking time with each other and saw their phones as a distraction as opposed to a method of communication. Some of these worldview differences may have to do with age and generation. When Johanna was Rachel's age and raising young children, it was less common for women to work outside the home, and depending on the situation, a single income may have been more feasible and more common for a family. Technology in the form of smart phones and texting wasn't available, and so it may seem unfamiliar to her. Notice how Rachel can't imagine how anyone would be able to get together without this, however.

The word **worldview** is meant to encompass the way we see the world through the varying lenses of our culture, our identities, and our experiences. You may have heard the old adage, "You can't understand someone until you've walked a mile in their shoes." Understanding the heart of this message—that we all see things differently in our own lives—is critical to understanding others who are different from ourselves. Consider Figure 3.1a.

Note the caption, "Upside Down World Map." In some ways, this is an inaccurate moniker—the world is round and space is infinite, and as such there is no top or bottom in actuality. When the first cartographers began to try to make better sense out of our world, the "top" was chosen as north and became the way we look at the planet as an entity. Still, had they taken a different vantage point, the picture in Figure 3.1a could just as easily have been the "Right Side Up Map!" Take a look now at Figure 3.1b.

Does anything look different to you in this depiction? In this map, the continents are represented to scale, meaning that their actual size is represented relevant to one another. If you are from the United States, however, it is unlikely you have ever seen the continent of Africa shown in such a large and prominent way. Look at Australia, and notice that it is roughly the same size as the United States, though in many maps it looks much smaller. Finally, look closely at Figure 3.1c.

FIGURE 3.1a ⬢ Upside Down World Map

FIGURE 3.1b ⬢ Rightside Up World Map

FIGURE 3.1c ⬢ Map With Countries Represented to Scale

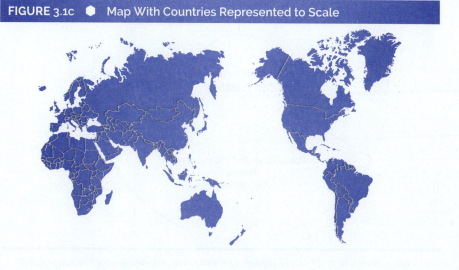

Again, this not the usual view presented on a map in the United States. We tend to place our own country in more of a place of prominence—in our culture it is often in the middle or to the top left. Maps in other countries often do not take the same vantage point, placing their country's continent front and center. Worldview helps us to determine what is "normal" or "right" from our point of view.

In a discussion of worldview, it is also important to distinguish this concept from others that are sometimes used interchangeably with it. Some may refer to worldview statements as values statements. Researcher Milton Rokeach (1973) produced a seminal book titled *The Nature of Human Values* in which he dissected the types of beliefs that humans may have and the differences that may exist between different functions and definitions of the different types. Rokeach's model posits that three types of beliefs can be seen as impacting one's overall nature: **existential beliefs**, **evaluative beliefs**, and **proscriptive/prescriptive beliefs** (which Rokeach described as values; see Table 3.1 for examples). In thinking about worldview specifically, however, Koltko-Rivera (2004) notes that all three types of Rokeach's beliefs can be influential in creating a view of the world (see Figure 3.2).

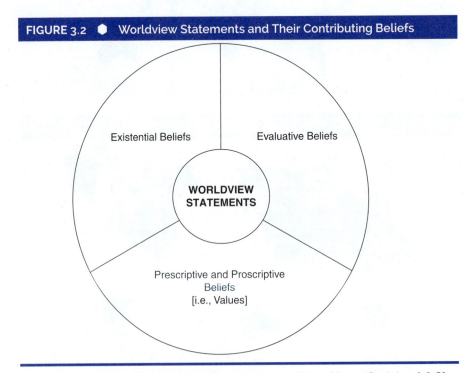

FIGURE 3.2   ●   Worldview Statements and Their Contributing Beliefs

Existential Beliefs

Evaluative Beliefs

WORLDVIEW STATEMENTS

Prescriptive and Proscriptive Beliefs
[i.e., Values]

Source: Koltko-Rivera. M. E. (2004). The psychology of worldviews, *Review of General Psychology*, 8, 3–58.

TABLE 3.1 ● Rokeach's Values Model	
Type of Belief	**Example of Worldview Statement**
Existential beliefs: What is true and what is false?	There exists a god or goddess who cares about me personally.
	Scientific research is a reliable way to establish the truth.
	There really is such a thing as free will.
Evaluative beliefs: Who is good and who is bad?	Those who fight against my nation are evil.
	Human nature is basically good.
Values beliefs: What should one do?	The thing to do in life is to live in the moment (prescriptive).
	You make your bed, you lie in it (proscriptive).

Source: Koltko-Rivera (2004, p. 5).

In this figure, Koltko-Rivera shows that any of the different types of beliefs can impact a worldview statement, but they may do so in different ways: "Worldviews thus encompass certain values but go beyond to include other kinds of beliefs as well" (2004, p. 5).

CULTURAL AND UNIQUE EXPERIENCES

Worldview can be formed by a variety of different sources, but many researchers have grouped these formative influences into two general domains: *cultural experiences* and *unique experiences* (Treviño, 1996). Culture is an important precursor to how an individual thinks, feels, and acts. As an example, different cultural societies around the world, and domestically within the United States, have been shown to use different thinking styles from one another (Nisbett, 2003). For this reason it follows, as Treviño notes, "that something about culture forms cognition; this something may include culturally transmitted worldviews" (p. 23). Some of these cultural experiences may be related to norms and values within the culture itself. Here, consider several areas in which culture may make a difference on worldview.

Value System

Whether a country is more individualistic in nature versus more collectivistic may make a difference in terms of how the world looks. **Individualism**, as denoted by

Triandis (1995), is a system adhered to by many Western cultural groups that value the individual above the group in most cases. Competition and focus on the self is common, with a high value for independence as a behavioral and personality trait. This system differs sharply from **collectivism,** which is focused on the group as a whole, and encourages cooperation and dependence. In collectivist cultures, the group is valued above the individual. The United States is probably the best example of an individualist nation with our focus on moving forward as individuals and our culture's rewarding of jobs that value this ideology (see Figure 3.3).

For example, jobs such as those of stockbrokers, CEOs, and hedge fund managers are focused on competition and personal gain and garner some of the highest salaries in this country. Compare that to more group-focused jobs such as those in the fields of social work, teaching, or nursing, and you find some of the lowest salaries. This is not to say that everyone in the United States has an individualist focus, but the value as a culture is clearly there for those who value this ideology.

Collectivist countries are myriad, as collectivism is a much more common ideology in the world. Often Asian countries such as Japan or China are used as examples for this type of value system. In these countries, a focus on the group often trumps the desires of the individual. Consider many years ago in 1980 when China began to regulate the number of children a couple might be allowed to produce. Many individuals in China may have wanted to have more than one child, but these laws were put into place to

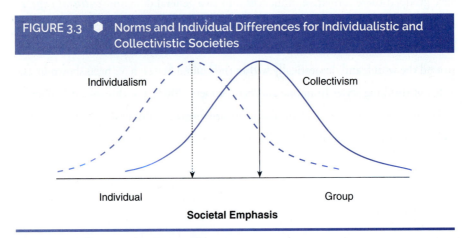

FIGURE 3.3 ● Norms and Individual Differences for Individualistic and Collectivistic Societies

Individualism

Collectivism

Individual

Group

Societal Emphasis

Source: Lopez, Pedrotti, & Snyder (2019, p. 29).

decrease population size to protect the resources for the group (Berensen, 2015). At the time many people in the United States were outraged by these laws (Hvistendahl, 2017), but it may be that many in China were as outraged by the lack of care for population overload the United States appeared to have in not adopting a law such as this.

Again, it is likely that not all in China agreed with this policy, especially in light of the fact that it is no longer a national policy, but the culture at the time dictated the most strongly valued worldview. People whose personal value systems do not mesh with their culture's value system are often called **countercultural**. An **allocentric** (or collectivist-oriented) person living in an individualist culture, or an **idiocentric** (or individualist-oriented) person living in a collectivist culture, may experience some discomfort or lack of value for their views and behaviors (Jung, McCormick, & Gross, 2012; Triandis, 2006). Finally, it is also important to note that racial groups within a country may be more or less countercultural depending on the dominant group. In the United States, for example, White Americans are the majority and dominant in terms of societal power, and the individualist nature of the European cultures their ancestors came from is strong within this cultural group. Asian Americans, however, may retain some of their ancestors' collectivist values, but as they are a minority group, these values are not given the same cultural weight as the dominant culture's values.

Time Orientation

Value system is not the only cultural trait that impacts worldview. The way a culture thinks about time is also influential. In the United States, the focus is most often on the future in terms of time, particularly in a European American mindset. Most questions are of the "where are you going" ilk, as opposed to the "where have you been." Making plans for the future, saving for retirement (often to the detriment of current life experience), and future goals often dominate our perspective. When individuals in the United States exhibits this mindset, we might call them go-getters or high achievers.

Other cultural groups may have more of a focus on the past. Asian cultures, for example, often have a stronger value for a past time orientation and may look backward to ancestors and past family events to give meaning to their present. Consider the old Chinese fable, "The Old Horse Knows the Way." In this story, a group of warriors has been to war for many years, and when at last it is time for those of them who are left to return home, they become lost. One of the soldiers realizes: "We can use the wisdom of an old horse. Release the old horses and follow them and thereby reach the right road" (Pei, 2005, p. 1). In this cultural group, looking backward and to those who know the past leads to answers and is valued.

Finally, some cultural groups are more focused on the present. Many American Indian groups, for example, take the approach to time that "something happens when it happens" as opposed to thinking of a specific starting time as important. More examples are given in our later discussion of the value of time orientation in relation to worldview models, but this basic information helps us to understand that time and the way it is valued is often dependent on culture.

High-Context Versus Low-Context Cultures

Another cultural factor that may impact worldview is the importance of context in personal and societal interactions. US anthropologist Edward T. Hall proposed the initial descriptions of cultures as high or low context in his 1978 book, *Beyond Culture.* Hall stated that high-context cultures are those in which following the social norms is crucial to the dynamics of the culture. Examples might be Asian cultures such as those of China or Japan, in which social rules are followed strictly, and conformity and hierarchy are valued strongly (Kim, Pan, & Park, 1998). On the other end of the continuum, low-context cultures, such as that of the United States, value individuality and idiographic experiences and have less focus on following a prescribed social structure (see Table 3.2). Consider your reaction to the preceding definitions. It is likely that you had a positive association with one of them and a less positive association with the other. Now think about your country's value of context. If you are from the United States, a high-context culture might sound stifling and stuffy. If you are from a non-Western culture, however, you may think that the low-context culture sounds too casual and disrespectful of status. This is yet another way in which our culture impacts our worldview.

Cultural Identity

Cultural experiences may include aspects of a person's life that are explicitly related to their cultural identity. These are individual to some extent in terms of the specific details of each experience, but may have common themes across a particular

TABLE 3.2 ⬤ High-Context and Low-Context Cultures		
Dimension	**Description**	**Example Country**
High-Context Cultures	• Strict adherence to social rules and norms • Communication is implicit (e.g., body language, tone) • Conformity and hierarchy valued	Japan China
Low-Context Cultures	• Social structure is less strict • Explicit verbal communication of rules • Individuality valued	United States Australia

cultural group. For example, an Asian American male adolescent growing up in today's society will have certain similarities with others of similar race and gender in terms of upbringing, family values, and perhaps views about safety and law enforcement in the United States. Consider this example:

I'm biracial—my dad is Asian and my mom is White—and when I was little someone in our apartment complex carved the word chink *on the back of our car. I didn't know what that meant, because I was only around 6 at the time and I had never heard that slur for Chinese people. When my parents explained what had happened and what that meant, I remember being confused at first—we're Asian, but we're actually Japanese, not Chinese. But then I remember having a new understanding that some people might think my dad was different in some way and also lump him together with others who looked like him. To me at that time in my life, he was just "Dad" but when I started thinking about it more, I realized that there weren't many other people who looked like him in our apartment complex. This was the first time I realized people might make decisions about you based on how you looked or what color your skin was. And sometimes people might get mad at you or call you names for that.*

—Morgan, age 43

In the above example, Morgan is learning to view the world in a certain way. His worldview might now incorporate ideas such as "non-White is different" or "sometimes people treat you differently because of your race" into the rest of his understanding of the world.

These types of experiences are cumulative in terms of a developing worldview, which then in turn might influence what future understandings, experiences, and interactions one has in the world. Consider the rest of Morgan's story:

> *I think [the experience with my dad being called a name] helped me later to understand what some of my other friends of color experienced in life. When I was a teenager, I remember a Latino friend telling our group that he had been pulled over by a cop for no reason and asked if his car was really his own, and he shared his frustration that he felt he was pulled over because he was dark skinned. Our White friends had a lot of reasons besides this that they thought could be the case, but I already knew things like this happened, and so it was easier for me to just attend to his frustration. We became closer than either of us were with our White friends because of that.*

—Morgan, age 43

Much research shows that experiencing invalidation from their White peers is one of the most common causes of decrease in interracial friendships as individuals of color grow into adolescence (McCormick, Cappella, Hughes, & Gallagher, 2014; White et al., 2009). You can see here that some of Morgan's earlier experiences with race and discrimination led him to have as a part of his worldview an acceptance and belief that situations like that above do happen. White individuals may have many fewer interactions with this type of discrimination, and therefore may have a harder time integrating them into their worldview.

Even when racism is viewed once or twice, the tendency may be to try to paint these experiences as one-offs or unique and situationally based experiences. In recent years, the Black Lives Matter movement has been hotly debated by many different cultural groups, and one of the points of disagreement between African American and non–African American groups has centered around beliefs about the value of Black lives in the United States. In a Pew Research poll regarding the violence that took place after a Black Lives Matter rally in Ferguson, Missouri, 50% of Black people surveyed responded that the police had gone too far in their attempts to quell the demonstration, in comparison to only 27% of White people. Relatedly, 38% of African Americans in this same Pew Research poll stated that the protestors in Ferguson acted reasonably, while only 15% of Whites felt the same.

Finally, respondents were also asked about their view of the Michael Brown case as raising racial issues. While 80% of African Americans polled endorsed the statement, "This case raises important issues about race," 47% of White Americans polled endorsed the statement, "Race is getting more attention than it deserves [in the Michael Brown case]" (Pew Research Center, 2014). Here two groups with different cultural worldviews are looking at an event and are starkly divided by their viewpoints (see Figures 3.4 and 3.5).

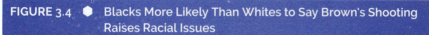

FIGURE 3.4 ● **Blacks More Likely Than Whites to Say Brown's Shooting Raises Racial Issues**

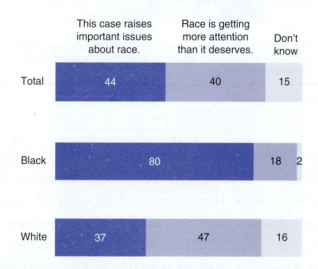

Thinking about the police shooting of an African American teen in Ferguson, Missouri, percent saying. . .

	This case raises important issues about race.	Race is getting more attention than it deserves.	Don't know
Total	44	40	15
Black	80	18	2
White	37	47	16

Survey conducted August 14–17, 2014. Whites and Blacks include only those who are not Hispanic. Figures may not add to 100% because of rounding.

Source: Pew Research Center (2014).

One reason for some of the differences here may be to the point above regarding personal knowledge of discrimination in different racial groups. In a study of children done with over 17,000 kindergarteners, researchers found that 75% of the White parents in this sample had "never" or "almost never" spoken of race to their children. In contrast, many parents of color find themselves in situations like

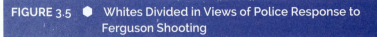

FIGURE 3.5 ◆ Whites Divided in Views of Police Response to Ferguson Shooting

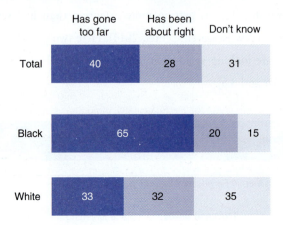

% saying police response to shooting. . .

	Has gone too far	Has been about right	Don't know
Total	40	28	31
Black	65	20	15
White	33	32	35

Survey conducted August 14–17, 2014. Whites and Blacks include only those who are not Hispanic. Figures may not add to 100% because of rounding.

Source: Pew Research Center (2014).

Morgan's parents above, where due to some experience with racial discrimination, they are in the position of having to talk to their children about race from an early age (Brown, Tanner-Smith, Lesane-Brown, & Ezell, 2007). In fact, in the study by Brown and colleagues, non-White parents were more than three times more likely to have already discussed race in some way with their children. In addition, many parents of color have a necessity to tell their children about certain discrimination and racism that the children may encounter in order to help their children to stay safe. See Spotlight Feature 3.1 for a discussion of "The Talk" that may provide many African American children with their first information about racial relations. More of us can give this "talk" to our children about race in general as well. We will come back to #BlackLivesMatter and other examples of worldview in this and other circumstances in another chapter, but for now it is important to understand that worldview may impact our future relationships with those who are different from us in some way.

The Opposite of Colorblind: Why It's Essential to Talk to Children About Race
By Stacy Whitman

Many African American parents already know what "the talk" is. It's not the talk that many white parents might expect—we're not talking about the birds and the bees. No, this "talk" is the one where black parents have to sit with their children and discuss how they might be perceived by the world around them: particularly police, but also teachers, neighbors, and friends who are not from their racial background.

Though the burden often falls on parents of color alone to discuss these issues with their children, in reality all parents should address race with their kids in a conscious and meaningful way. Communities are also seeking ways to address interpersonal racial issues, particularly in schools. Having the tools to know how to discuss racial matters is essential for children from all backgrounds.

Research has shown that the "colorblind" approach—teaching children that it is racist to acknowledge racial and ethnic differences—is doing no one any favors, and in fact can reinforce racist attitudes and assumptions, and especially reify systemic racism. "Black children know irrefutably that they're black by the time they're about 6 years old and probably earlier," one article noted in our research. Do white children know they're white? If not, how do they think of themselves?

At Lee & Low, we've always believed that even the youngest readers have the capacity to understand and appreciate difference—that's why many of our children's books address issues like racism and discrimination. But you don't have to take our word for it: many experts, educators, and academics have done work on this topic as well and their recommendations can help point parents and teachers in the right direction.

"Young children are hard-wired in their brains to notice difference and to categorize it. So it is vital during early childhood to put some context around making sense of differences," said Shannon Nagy, preschool director in 2011 at Lincoln Park Cooperative Nursery School in Chicago.

Studies have also shown that not addressing difference does not make children colorblind—it only encourages them to absorb the implicit racial messages of American society. Children learn that race is a category even when parents try to teach them not to recognize race. Much like children learn to perform regional accents even when their parents are from another location, children learn. Young children are hard-wired to notice difference—how the larger society around them views race, via inference and transductive reasoning. "In other words, children pick upon the ways in which whiteness is normalized and privileged in U.S. society."

Teaching children to be "colorblind" has led children (and adults) to believe that it's rude or racist to even point out racial differences—even kids of color. This makes it

(Continued)

(Continued)

exponentially harder to have frank discussions about racial issues when they need to be had.

"Nonwhite parents are about three times more likely to discuss race than white parents," said a 2007 study. "It's the children whose parents do directly address race—and directly means far more than vaguely declaring everyone to be equal—who are less likely to make assumptions about people based on the color of our skin."

One study even had white parents dropping out of the project when the researchers asked them to discuss racial attitudes with their children, even when they went into the study knowing that it was intended to measure children's racial attitudes.

Many argue that "the talk" should happen far more often than once, and that parents shouldn't bear the sole burden to teach their kids about race—that it is a community-wide issue.

Erin Winkler provides several ways for parents and teachers to address the biases that children might pick up, including discussing ("the talk" should happen far more often than once) the issue in an age-appropriate way, with accurate information that doesn't shame or silence children for having questions. They also suggest encouraging complex thinking and taking children's questions and biased statements seriously—"When children are taught to pay attention to multiple attributes of a person at once (e.g., not just race), reduced levels of bias are shown," the author notes, and suggests that the most important thing parents and teachers can do is to give children information that empowers them to be anti-racist.

One New York City–area school asked, "Can racism be stopped in the third grade?" They began a "racial affinity program," in which elementary-age kids were sorted by racial groups for discussions of questions that "might seem impolite otherwise," and to then come together as a school community to discuss these questions and experiences in a way that fosters greater communication. Parents and students are mixed on whether this program succeeded, with Asian students noting that the discussions of race still focused on the dichotomy of black and white, and some parents uncomfortable with the idea of discussing race at all. The administration notes, however, that many of their students of color needed this program—mandatory for all students—to combat microaggressions between students.

Allie Jane Bruce, the librarian at Bank Street School in New York City, has been discussing race, biases, and stereotypes with the students in her school for three years, using children's book covers as a launching point. "I'm constantly delighted by the new discoveries kids make, and by the wisdom and insight already present in 11- and 12-year-olds," Bruce noted in her most recent series of blog posts about the curriculum, which she has named "Loudness in the Library." She notes especially that kids at this age tend to feel very uncomfortable with discussing race at first. "The fact that race-related conversations are so very fraught is a huge part of the problem. We must be able to communicate in order to solve problems that exist at interpersonal, institutional, and societal levels. If kids in 6th grade already have the inclination to stay silent in conversations on race, how much stronger will that inclination be in adults? And if we can't talk about race and racism, how will things ever get better?"

Parents, what does "the talk" look like in your home? Teachers and librarians, how do you approach discussions about race with your students and patrons?

Source: Whitman, S. (n.d.). The Opposite of Colorblind: Why It's Essential to Talk to Children about Race. https://www.leeandlow.com/imprints/tu-books/articles/the-opposite-of-colorblind-why-it-s-essential-to-talk-to-children-about-race.

Unique Experiences

It is also important to consider the impact of unique situations and experiences on the development of individual worldview. Growing up in a home in which violence is commonplace, for example, may lead one to feel less safe or less trusting of others. In addition, it may be that particular events—both positive and negative—may impact a change in worldview, though negative events may be slightly more impactful (Gutierrez & Park, 2015). Influences of unique experiences may be moderated, however, by pre-event worldviews. In a study by Gutierrez and Park (2015), college students who had worldviews that included strong senses of self-worth had greater increases in their self-worth following positive individual events, as compared to those who had lower self-worth at the beginning of the study. Thus, personal psychological health may be important in maximizing positive events and potentially also in buffering against negative events (Lopez, Pedrotti, & Snyder, 2019). Think for a moment about different life events that have happened to you specifically as an individual. Some have likely influenced beliefs you have about the world and the way in which you see things. Our own worldviews are woven together by the cultural and unique experiences that fill our lives.

We next turn to a discussion of several models that flesh out some of the influences we've described here.

MODELS OF WORLDVIEW AND VALUES

Kluckhohn and Strodtbeck's Value Orientation Model

One of the best known models of worldview is that of Kluckhohn and Strodtbeck (1961), which includes descriptions of several different value orientations that may impact the way in which one sees the world. As we have already noted, different cultural groups

TABLE 3.3 ⬡ Value Orientations and Potential Variations					
Orientation	Human Nature	Person-Nature	Time	Activity	Relational
Range of Variations	Evil	Subjugation of nature	Past	Being	Linearity
	Neutral	Harmony with nature	Present	Being-in-becoming	Collaterality
	Good	Mastery over nature	Future	Doing	Individualism

Source: Adapted from Kluckhohn, F. R., & Strodtbeck, F. I. (1961). *Variations in value orientations.* Evanston, IL: Row, Patterson, & Co.

often have different orientations, and those endorsed by the group explain the dimensions that a particular culture finds beneficial and positive (Carter, 1991). Kluckhohn and Strodtbeck distinguished five main dimensions and asked the question "How might different groups respond to these different dimensions?" Each dimension and its range of variations are listed in Table 3.3.

The first dimension described by Kluckhohn and Strodtbeck (1961) has to do with *human nature.* The researchers give options of evil, neutral (mixture of good and evil), and good for this particular dimension; these refer to one's inherent nature (Zaharna, 2000). For this orientation only, there are also qualifiers given to the variations; Kluckhohn and Strodtbeck note that some groups may allow for this dimension to be mutable (i.e., a group belief that human nature can change) while others view it as immutable (i.e., the belief that human nature is set, and thus unchangeable). Dimensions 2 through 5 do not have such qualifiers.

The second orientation is listed by Kluckhohn and Strodtbeck (1961) as *man-nature,* though more recent authors have changed this title to person-nature to be more gender inclusive (Mio, Barker, & Domenech-Rodriguez, 2015). This dimension describes the relationship groups of people might have with nature in terms of their tendency to live in harmony with nature, or to have a relationship that dictates either person or nature as dominant.

The third orientation, *time,* refers to the orientation a particular group may have with the past, present, and future. The United States, for example, is very future oriented. If you are a student in college right now, you probably get many more questions about what you *will* be doing with your degree, than what you are doing right *now*.

The fourth orientation, *activity,* describes the value one has for different types of activity and lists the variations being, being-in-becoming, and doing. These variations are less self-explanatory, and so we will delve into their meanings a bit more here. Groups who value *being* believe that what one is currently doing is the positive state and might involve less focus on self-development or change. *Being-in-becoming* instead emphasizes the value of "working on" oneself from where one currently is and striving toward self-development, while *doing* is more self-explanatory in that groups that value this appreciate what someone *does* more than who the person *is*.

Finally, the fifth orientation described by Kluckhohn and Strodtbeck (1961) is *relational* and focuses on the types of interpersonal dynamics that are valued by different groups. For some that relationship is valued most if it is *linear*, meaning that a hierarchy involving a wide social circle (including family, friends, leaders of the community, etc.) is valued most, and groups that have this orientation may also have specific rules in terms of how to interact with others. *Collateral* relationships involve those that value input and respect for family members, often including extended family and friends, while groups that value *individualism* emphasize the individual person in making decisions and in determining how one interacts with others (Carter, 1991; Kluckhohn & Strodtbeck, 1961; Zaharna, 2000).

The values such as those described above greatly influence worldview and thus many have made efforts to categorize various groups on Kluckhohn and Strodtbeck's (1961) dimensions. Some distinctions have been found with regard to cultures that embrace more individualist ideals in comparison to those that are more collectivist in orientation. Cheung, Maio, Rees, Kamble, and Mane (2016) conducted a study in which they investigated the connection between individuals and their culture's values in participants from Britain and the United States (individualist nations), and compared these connections with those of participants from India (a collectivist nation). In this study it was found that individualist nations have stronger connections to the value orientations that refer to *self* as opposed to community. Specifically, participants from these countries valued their own personal values (which may also be tied to their cultural values, but did not have to be) more than those that they understood they were "supposed to" value based on their culture. The opposite was true for the participants from India, with results showing a strong value for those values set forth by their culture as things they should do and value (Cheung et al., 2016). This provides evidence for the notion that collectivist cultures ask individuals to **assimilate** (i.e., adhere closely to cultural norms) more often than those in individualist cultures.

Other studies have linked Kluckhohn and Strodtbeck's (1961) framework to particular cultural groups. See Table 3.4 for Ho's (1987) helpful description of five different cultural groups and their value orientations based on common cultural norms for each group. Note that there are many similarities among Asian Americans, American Indians, African Americans, and Latinx Americans in many of the different value orientations, though some variations are noted. These similarities are in contrast to what is valued as a norm among middle-class White Americans in most cases (Ho, 1987; Sue & Sue, 2016). This type of multicultural comparison is important and may explain some tensions in communication and other factors between racial and ethnic majority and minority cultures.

TABLE 3.4 ⬡ Value Orientations in Different Ethnic Group					
	People to Nature/ Environment	**Time Orientation**	**People Relationships**	**Preferred Mode of Activity**	**Nature of Humans**
African Americans	In harmony with	Present	Collateral	Doing	Good and bad
American Indians	In harmony with	Present	Collateral	Being-in-becoming	Good
Asian Americans	In harmony with	Past-present	Collateral	Doing	Good
Latinx Americans	In harmony with	Past-present	Collateral	Being-in-becoming	Good
Middle-class White Americans	Mastery over	Future	Individual	Doing	Good and bad

Source: Ho, M. K. (1987). *Family therapy with ethnic minorities*. Newbury Park, CA: SAGE.

Derald Wing Sue's Worldview Model

A second very well-known model of worldview was created by psychologist Derald Wing Sue (1978) and is used in many contexts. Sue discusses two main dimensions as a part of his model: **locus of control** and **locus of responsibility**. As shown in Figure 3.6, Sue places these two dimensions perpendicular to one another and gives options for more internal or external locus of control and locus of responsibility.

Take a look at the four quadrants in this model. Quadrant I is labeled to be high in both locus of control and responsibility (IC-IR). People who fit into this particular quadrant believe that they have much control over the way in which their life unfolds, and that they thus have a high amount of personal responsibility in terms of successes and failures. This is a very traditional worldview for someone who believes in the **American Dream**, which explains personal success with personal attributes and hard work, as opposed to luck or privilege. Quadrant II describes people who have a high level of personal responsibility and hold themselves accountable for success and failure, but who also believe that they do not have as much control over their lives and how they are situated within them. (EC-IR). This worldview may lead to some despair in individuals

FIGURE 3.6 ⬡ Sue's Worldview Model

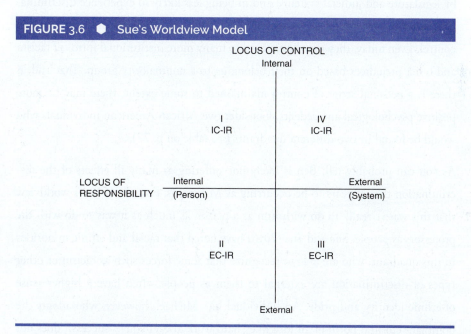

Source: Adapted from Sue, D. W. (1978). Eliminating cultural oppression in counseling: Toward a general theory. *Journal of Counseling Psychology*, 25, 419–428.

who hold it, as they may feel responsible for their lot in life, and yet recognize that much of it is out of their control. Similarly, those in Quadrant III feel out of control of their lot in life, but they also feel they are not responsible for this fact. This group is a particularly problematic group to be a part of, as individuals who fit into this group may give up trying to improve their lives. In their worldview, the system is against them, and there is nothing they can do about it. Finally, those in Quadrant IV have a high level of internal control, but they also have determined that there are some external forces for which they are not responsible (IC-ER). Individuals who fall into this quadrant are more balanced to some extent in terms of their view of the world, as they see that they lack responsibility for some external circumstances, but they also feel that they have some control over the ways in which they move through their lives.

As you have probably already noticed, social identity facets such as race, ethnicity, gender, sexual orientation, socioeconomic status, and other facets may impact the quadrant by which a particular individual can be described. White Americans, for example, have historically had much more control over their own lives than non-White Americans, both in terms of physical freedom (e.g., not enslaved, represented by legislature and judicial systems) and in being less likely to experience discrimination, while racial and ethnic minorities have not always enjoyed this same level of control. Even today, they may be exposed to many more institutional forms of racism and other prejudices based on their belonging to a nonmajority group. That said, if there is a personal sense of control maintained to some extent, there may be more positive psychological antecedents. Consider two African American individuals who would be found in two different quadrants (see table on p. 77).

As you can probably tell, Ben is likely not suffering as many ill effects of the discrimination that appears to be occurring as Michael is, because of Ben's worldview that this wasn't really to do with him as a person as much as it was to do with the professors as people. Sue and Sue (2016) have noted that racial and ethnic minorities in this quadrant, who are able to recognize that some forces such as racism or other types of discrimination are external to them as people, often have a higher sense of ethnic identity and pride. An individual like Michael, however, who adopts the dominant cultural norm of an idea like "hard work always equals success," does not allow himself to consider the fact that his supervisor may be operating based on some

EC-IR	IC-ER
Michael was raised by parents who instilled the value of hard work as being a blueprint for success. Michael's father worked for everything he'd ever gotten, and was often heard to criticize other African Americans for not doing the same thing or for "complaining" about discrimination or prejudice. "You just have to work harder!" he would often say, and Michael believes this as well. He hasn't progressed much in his career as a computer scientist, as he doesn't seem to catch the attention of his supervisor, who is White. Michael works long hours but has been passed over for a promotion twice, though his evaluations were higher than those of the White colleague who was chosen. When he talks to his supervisor about this, he is told, "You're more of a worker bee, I think. It might not come to you naturally to be a leader—you don't look like one." Michael leaves this conversation disappointed with himself. "I'll just have to work harder, I guess," he thinks.	Ben is a graduate student in psychology, in a department with few racial or ethnic minority professors. He has tried to connect with some of them to seek some mentoring about his future, but he finds that these conversations often lead to these professors mentioning that he should seek out help from African American professors at his institution, but outside his profession. Many of them seem uncomfortable when he asks if they might mentor him. The last professor he asked said, "I mean, I can, but I'm not sure I could be of much help since we aren't very similar." After hearing that his African American classmates across the field have had similar experiences, he decides instead to join the student membership of the Association of Black Psychologists (ABPsi). Here he finds many potential mentors and many individuals who have had the same types of experiences before finding the ABPsi. He is glad to have found some mentors and recognizes that not being able to connect with the non-Black professors was likely because of some aspect of discomfort on their part, not his.

biases, however implicit, regarding who "looks like a leader." Of course, these scenarios are very simplistic—many factors may be at play in both of these situations—but one can still see that a particular type of worldview may impact the psychological health of those in nondominant cultural groups who are experiencing some type of discrimination.

WORLDVIEWS IN DAY-TO-DAY LIFE

In this section, we offer you several vignettes that detail worldviews from many different social identity groups. In most, we offer the perspective as coming from one prominent identity (e.g., gender, race, etc.), but it is important to remember that as individuals we are often coming from multiple identity points at the same time. As mentioned in Chapter 1, intersectionality is an important part of our experiences as individuals, and so nuances exist between the different facets that make us who we are. In thinking about the impact of worldview in the field of multicultural psychology, it becomes important to clarify differences in the way different cultural groups see the world. Depending on our level of exposure to people who differ from us culturally, these different worldviews can be the source of disagreements or tensions when first encountered. There are many pieces of cultural identity that shape our worldview, and the intersection of these identities is influential as well.

Worldview Related to Gender Identity

I know that as a woman, I make many choices in my day that focus on making sure that I am safe in my day-to-day routine. For example, it's important to me to be able to get some exercise each week, and my favorite way to do this is to take a run outside. There are a lot of great trails in my area, but because of my work schedule I usually need to be working out pretty early in the morning, and there aren't very many people out at that time. As a young woman, I don't feel comfortable being all alone on my own out there, just in case someone with bad intentions was out there too, so I paid to join a gym instead. Another example is after work. Sometimes I'll have to park pretty far away from my office downtown, and so on those days I know I need to leave before it gets dark, because my office isn't in a very well-lit area. It's frustrating sometimes to have to stop working on something because of that—I'd rather stay and get my work done, but I know I'm taking a risk walking by myself as a woman after dark. Sometimes when I think of all the changes I make in my daily life just to keep myself safe from risk of sexual assault, it boggles my mind. I know my male friends don't worry so much about physical safety.

—Janie, age 28

Gender is one identity facet that shapes our worldview. In the vignette above, it's easy to see that Janie's worldview includes the idea that because of her gender, she might not be safe physically from sexual assault. Many women might make changes in their daily schedule, plans to walk together after dark to avoid being caught alone, or other changes to their daily schedules because they perceive the world as less safe through their lens as a woman. In large-scale studies conducted within the United States, stark differences are often found in many everyday practices of women and transgender individuals as compared to those of male identified individuals. Gallup polls regularly find that women worry more than men about sexual assault, with 36% of female participants in 2018 reporting "frequent or occasional worry about sexual assault" in comparison to just 4% of men surveyed responding in this way (McCarthy, 2018). In another study, 50% of men in the study stated that they "do not worry about safety" as compared with only 26.9% of women (Logan & Walker, 2017). Transgender individuals are also at risk in terms of safety, with one in four trans individuals reporting being assaulted because of their gender identity (James et al., 2016).

In addition to safety, gender identity may also impact other pieces of worldview. Gender may impact the amount of choices one sees available in terms of career, for example. In our current workplace landscape, only 5% of CEOs on the 2018 Fortune 500 list in the United States are female, and zero are transgender. Seeing so few examples of themselves in these types of high-power occupations may cause young girls to rule out positions such as these (Rios, Stewart, & Winter, 2010).

Worldview Related to Socioeconomic Status

I'm a hard worker and I always have been. There wasn't much money growing up, and so I had to work a lot on our family's farm just to make sure we made ends meet. No time to play sports or sit around reading a bunch of books. I worked from the time I was 8 years old to help my parents out, and I was glad to do it. There were a few times when I was growing up that we almost lost the farm because of taxes and poor crops. We all had to pitch in double during that time, and sometimes that meant skipping school or sleep, but we made it work. I'm raising my kids this same way, and so when my son turned 14 this last year, I told him that he needed to start putting in more time on the farm so that he can start contributing to the family. I told him he couldn't try out for the track team because practice is every day, and there's way too much to do on the farm to be able to adhere to that kind of schedule. His teacher called me and said that his homework is slipping, but I told her that he is lucky to be learning in school—after school he needs to do real work that adds up and prepares him for the real world too. She didn't get it. Books can't help you lift bales of hay or drive equipment, and we don't have money for college anyway—what's the point?

—Steve, age 58

If you are a student in college right now, the worldview above might be one to which you have a strong reaction. A common response from someone who feels college has value might view Steve's comments above as shortsighted and even as problematic parenting. Others of you might have heard Steve's ideas from some of your own family members as you began your journey as a first-generation college student. Regardless of your potential agreement or disagreement with Steve's ideas above, consider some of the reasons he may have adopted this worldview. First, it seems clear that hard work as a positive activity was ingrained early on in Steve's worldview from his parents. In addition, "work" appears to be defined for him more as manual labor than as studying or other activities. In Steve's view, this type of work is what will help his son the most to prepare for life. In addition, Steve's view doesn't include the option of a college education because of his limited socioeconomic status. In our country, approximately 30% of adults are college graduates (US Census Bureau, 2017). The price of tuition and fees for a four-year, in-state, public college education rose approximately 3.2% beyond inflation every year from the 2007–08 academic year to the 2017–18 academic year (College Board, 2017). Therefore, many families may not be able to see a way to put their children through college. Thus, worldviews such as Steve's may be supported by many who do not have the experience of college themselves. It is important to be able to understand the potential origins for this type of worldview even if one does not hold the same ideas.

Worldview Related to Race and Ethnicity

I'm in college right now and I go to a private college—my dad went to the same one years ago and I've always dreamed of coming here—but there aren't very many African American students like me here, and almost no professors who aren't White. Sometimes other students think I'm here on scholarship or that I got in because of my race, but I actually come from a pretty affluent area, and went to a high school that had a lot of AP classes available. I have always been a good student, and so my grade point average is as high or higher than that of a lot of the students here. Whenever I start a class with a new professor, especially if the professor is White, I have a few things that I do so that I get off on the right foot. I'm a big guy, and my skin is very dark. I know sometimes this makes people feel afraid of me before they know me—I see this in their eyes sometimes. So, I always go up on the first day and introduce myself, especially if there is another Black student in the class, so they don't mix us up. Sometimes I try to get it in the conversation that my dad is an alumnus, so they know I belong here. Then I try to work twice as hard as everyone else, go into office hours whenever I can, and make sure that the professor knows I'm a good student. I'm not sure if it's annoying to them sometimes, but I want to make sure that they know me for me, instead of via some stereotype about Black people that they may have. It takes a lot of extra time to do all of this, but I feel like I have to if I'm going to be treated fairly. White students still ask me if I'm on an athletic scholarship, or if I'm a first-generation college student, or if I'm from a bad neighborhood, but at least I make sure my professors know my real story. Who knows—this might help me in other ways too. It seems like lately there are so many news stories out there where people call the police because they think an African American person is not supposed to be in a particular place. Having so many professors to be able to verify that I'm a real student and also a good person might help me out if that ever happens to me.

—Alex, age 19

The story above shows that Alex does some things on a regular basis based on his worldview of what he experiences as a "normal" reaction from White people. His worldview impacts his daily activities and the way in which he carries himself, and it also involves some expectations he has for others who may be different from him in some way. Given what we have already discussed about different models of worldview, Alex appears to embody a IC-ER type of worldview as described by Sue (1978). This is clearly illustrated in the high level of control he has over his behaviors in terms of the structure and specificity he provides in this vignette. It is also clear, however, from this description that Alex understands that there are forces here that are out of his control in terms of stereotyping and racism. Alex is attempting to modify others' initial and implicit impressions of him by behaving in a way that potentially counteracts these types of stereotypes. In addition, he recognizes that even though he makes these efforts, there may still be factors and experiences linked to stereotyping (e.g., someone thinking he doesn't belong on campus as an African American man) that he cannot control and are thus outside of his responsibility.

Worldview Related to Sexual Orientation

I'm just starting a new job right now and I'm still getting to know my coworkers and my boss. I live in the Midwest in a pretty small town, where a lot of the community is pretty religious and also pretty conservative. I'm used to this because I grew up in a similar kind of town, but as an adult it's been a little more difficult for me. I've been out as a gay man for several years, and my partner and I have been together for quite some time, but until recently we were living in a larger city and it was less conservative as well. We have a long-distance relationship right now, so no one knows us as a couple here. I'll have to see how things go as I get to know my coworkers a bit more, but for right now I don't feel comfortable disclosing to anyone that I'm gay. I had a picture on my desk of the two of us when I first started working, and I got several questions about it. One coworker seemed to stare at it for a while and then said, "Oh, that must be your brother, I guess," and another asked if my partner was a college roommate. I started realizing that this might be a situation in which I have to hide my sexual orientation for a while before I decide if it's safe to let anyone know. I know in this state there isn't a law protecting sexual minorities from being fired from their jobs, and I need this job, so I think I'll keep quiet for a while. I took the picture off my desk too.

—Lou, age 30

Similar to the vignette describing gender and worldview, this scenario also concerns safety, though of a somewhat different type. At the time this book was published, only 22 of the 50 states (and Washington, DC) included protections for sexual orientation in terms of prohibiting discrimination, including being protected from being fired from one's job for this reason (Williams Institute, UCLA 2019). Though the Equality Act (which offers protection from firing for both sexual orientation and gender identity in addition to other protections) passed the House of Representatives in May of 2019, it remains to be seen currently whether the act will pass the Senate. In addition, only 19 states prohibited discrimination against individuals related to gender identity. (Note: Though being transgender is related to gender—not sexual orientation, as transgender people may be of any sexual orientation—these laws are noted here because transgender individuals' status is often discussed with respect to laws related to LGBTQ status.) Talking about family and friends, and perhaps especially partners or spouses, is a very common part of one's ordinary life in both work and personal domains. Lou, however, based on the worldview he describes above, is clearly nervous that exercising this everyday right might not only impact his employment status but likely raise other potential issues for him as well. Thus, Lou's worldview is that the world is not always safe. Physical safety, or lack thereof, might also be a prominent feature in the worldviews of LGBTQ individuals across the country. The Anti-Defamation League (2020) reports that approximately 16% of hate crimes are recorded as being related to sexual orientation, and many of these crimes victimize personal safety for LGBTQ individuals. Though federal laws have been changed in recent times to give rights to LGBTQ individuals for same-sex marriage, it is important to note that states may not all offer the same protections within this community.

Worldview Related to Nation of Origin

I can't understand how marriage works in the United States. In my country of India, I am so grateful to my parents that they'll be able to guide me in making a good decision about my marriage when I am old enough. In the United States, I know that they think that arranged marriages are archaic, but there are so many features to them that I appreciate. For one, I don't have to look all over the place to find girls my age to date. I know that if I met someone reasonable that my parents liked, I could still make a suggestion that they could talk to her parents, but at least I don't have to count on this. For several reasons, I want to marry when I'm ready, as opposed to waiting to see if I meet someone. At work, I notice that the boss seems to favor the married guys a little—he might go over to their house for dinner a bit more often, and some of their wives know his wife, so it's a bit more social. I'm looking forward to having a stronger relationship with him. Also, I want to be a father and I want to do that while I'm younger so I can play sports with my kids and be more active with them as well. My parents know whose families are ones that would make a good match for me, and though I know people in the United States think it's a forced marriage, I do have some choices. I can say no if I really don't like their choice, as long as I don't embarrass her family or mine. To me, there's no better way to keep families close together and strong.

—Chandra, age 25

Different nations of origin also shape worldview. If a statement about marriage were being written by a 25-year-old man in the United States, you might imagine that it would be pretty different. Chandra's worldview clearly shows value for his elders and their decision-making process and also shows a strong value for family (within his respect for parents and his desire to start his own family) as well. In addition, there is little emphasis on personal choice, though a bit is noted. There may also be some value for improved social relationships with his boss at work. This example highlights the fact that different worldviews encompassing social behaviors and norms may be impacted by the country in which one is raised, but there may be many other examples of impact on worldview surrounding ideas of safety (e.g., worldviews in a country with political stability versus one in the midst of war), materialism (e.g., comparing worldviews from those in a developing nation to one that is prosperous), and education (e.g., comparing worldviews between countries that have different ideas about the value of education for different groups of people).

Worldview Related to Disability Status

I just got my class schedule for my junior year at college, and this is the first time I haven't been thrown off by a bunch of new classrooms and buildings. My campus is pretty large, and it's not too wheelchair friendly in some parts, and because I am a paraplegic, I have to plan my day out pretty carefully. My first year this meant I had to visit all of the buildings ahead of time to find out where the elevator was and where the ramps I could use were. Some of the older buildings have stairs in the front, but the ramp has been added to the back or somewhere else when the Americans With Disabilities Act (ADA) requirements were put into place—you can't always see it unless you know where that entrance is. One year, I thought I had the whole thing mapped out, but then my class was moved to another building at the last minute. I was really stressed out because I knew I'd be late. Most teachers are pretty nice about that, but I know that I might have some other illnesses or issues associated with my health at a different time in the quarter, so I don't like to ask for very much in the beginning to save a little good faith for later. Anyway, it's surprising to others sometimes how many times a day I have to think about my disability to just make everyday plans.

—Luisa, age 22

As is made clear here, disability and one's interaction and status with this particular identity facet can impact daily life rather strongly. In the example here, Luisa has many different pieces to consider each day that surround her experience with her identity. These impact her choices, her ability to succeed in college, and the types of communication and navigation skills she has had to develop in order to cope with these daily experiences. Though Luisa has a physical disability, there might be a similar impact for those who are dealing with a mental disability, such as learning disability or mental illness, as well. Regardless, the world may look very different to someone who is coming from the worldview of an individual dealing with a disability.

Worldview Related to Age or Generation

The vignette at the very beginning of this chapter provides some great examples of differences that can occur due to generation with regard to worldview. Recall that Johanna was frustrated by what she interpreted as the younger women she was watching spending less time with children and family, and more on themselves and career pursuits. At the same time, the younger women showed some disdain for lack of technology in times past. As we have noted several times in this chapter, our worldviews are shaped by our experiences, and growing up in a particular generation has an enormous impact on the types of views we develop.

IMPLICATIONS OF DIFFERENT WORLDVIEWS

There are many examples throughout history of the impact of different worldviews on entire groups of people. Perhaps one of the greatest examples is provided by the experiences between White settlers and American Indians and other Indigenous peoples in the beginnings of immigration from Europe to the Americas. In the National Museum of the American Indian in the Smithsonian Institution in Washington, DC, there is a full collection (see Spotlight Feature 3.2) that depicts different transcripts, letters, and ideas recording the worldviews of Andrew Jackson and other White officers and those of the leaders of a variety of Native American tribes. Woven throughout these records are fundamental differences in worldview in many different areas, including land and ownership, religious ideals, and social interactions. One of the starkest surrounds a depiction of the different beliefs about oral versus written agreements.

SPOTLIGHT FEATURE 3.2

Native and US Viewpoints

On language	Viewpoint: Native Nations	Viewpoint: United States
	To Native people, oral speech was more trustworthy than written words.	**Europeans** regarded written language as more authentic and trustworthy than memory.
	"We . . . have Methods of transmitting from Father to Son an account of all these things, whereby you will find the Remembrance of them faithfully preserved," Kanickhungo (Seneca) assured some Pennsylvanians in 1736.	"The doing of business with beads might . . . do among Indians but not in their transactions with white people," said U.S. Indian Agent Benjamin Hawkins in 1808. "The beads may be forgotten, but an agreement written by a faithful agent could never be forgotten."
	You could say things in Indian languages that weren't translatable into European tongues, and vice versa. (p. 5)	But writing could not make language more truthful, or promises more binding. (p. 5)
On land ownership and use	Viewpoint: Native Nations	Viewpoint: United States
	The Northern Plains Nations had traded with Europeans for more than a century. . . Now eastern tribes, pushed out of their homelands, were moving to the Plains. Non-Indian immigrants traveling to Oregon and California poached buffalo, cut down trees, and spread diseases. "We used to own all this country and went where we pleased," said Big Yankton (Sioux). "Now we are surrounded by other Indians, and the whites pass through our country." (p. 34)	**The United States** wanted safe passage for trappers, miners, and immigrants traveling west, and a railroad to the West Coast. Only peace with the Native Nations would allow that. To keep the peace, the federal government wanted a right of way, permission to build forts, and a definition of each nation's territory to make it easier to determine who was at fault when attacks occurred. (p. 34)
On negotiations	Viewpoint: Native Nations	Viewpoint: United States
	Native Nations arrived from all across the plains: Lakota,	**The United States** negotiators were two men from the

Cheyenne, Arapaho, Crow, Assiniboine, Arikara, Hidatsa, Mandan, Shoshone. They made grand entries dressed in their finest regalia. They had no central leader, no one negotiator. Each delegation spoke a different language, so they needed interpreters to speak to one another. They were not all at peace, but they set aside differences while the council was in session.

Though they did not speak one language, the nations had common goals: security from invasion and guarantees of their land rights. (p. 35)

Office of Indian Affairs, David D. Mitchell and Thomas Fitzpatrick. A detachment of soldiers, fur traders, frontiersmen, missionaries, a journalist, and a lawyer provided support.

Mitchell asked each Native delegation to name one "chief of the whole nation" for the United States to deal with, instructing them to "respect, obey, and maintain him in the exercise of his just authority." The Indians politely humored Mitchell, but the demand was so contrary to their existing political system that they did it just for show. (p. 35)

Viewpoint: Potawatomi

The Potawatomi chiefs were not united. So they used a strategy of giving up the land but reserving many small plots for individuals and villages to live on. The Indians could not keep newcomers out, but at least they would be able to remain on reserved lands.

In 1832 the Potawatomi gave up their last large piece of tribal land in Indiana. The treaty provided more than 120 small reservations for them. They thought they would be safe. (p. 52)

Viewpoint: United States

U.S. treaty commissioners used ruthless tactics. Whiskey flowed freely. Influential chiefs and interpreters got bribes. When one chief refused to sign, the commissioners found another who would. Trivial clashes with non-Indians were exaggerated into "Indian uprisings," giving U.S. agents excuses to threaten punishment and demand land in compensation.

To persuade the Potawatomi to move west, the government offered payments, transportation, and millions of acres of new land. Every year from 1833 to 1837, hundreds of Potawatomi gave in and moved. (p. 52)

(Continued)

(Continued)

On confiscation of Indian land	**Viewpoint: Native Nations** **Most Native Peoples** entered the nineteenth century thinking the United States recognized their inalienable rights to their lands, sovereignty, languages, and cultures. But the young republic's imperial expansion alarmed them. In the War of 1812, many sided with Britain in hopes of stopping U.S. growth. After the war, Britain withdrew support for its Indian allies. Native Nations realized they needed new strategies. They were weary of war. Their population was dropping as epidemics of European diseases swept through. They pinned their hopes on treaties of friendship, hoping to live peaceably with their new neighbors. (p. 45)	**Viewpoint: United States** **The United States** was becoming an expanding power with continental ambitions, but it lacked the power or will to control its own citizens. The European population boom was overflowing onto U.S. shores. Americans moving west squatted illegally on Indian lands while speculators sold rights to Indian lands even before they were ceded by treaty. Pressure for new land for a growing population made the acquisition of Indian lands by treaties a national priority. (p. 45)
On removal of the American Indians	**Viewpoint: Native Nations** **Native people** east of the Mississippi knew their right to choose their own path was under attack. Some withdrew, some resisted, others adapted. By 1830, many Indians in the East had become farmers who raised livestock and crops for market and practiced Christianity. It made no difference. The most prosperous tribes were the first to be deported to western lands. They objected strenuously and fought removal as long as they could. (p. 46)	**Viewpoint: United States** **Among non-Indians**, removal was also controversial. Public figures like Congressman Davy Crockett argued that it violated the law and honor of the United States. Advocates of removal had to make it look voluntary. They used a new kind of treaty: the removal treaty. To pressure Native leaders into signing, they tried persuasion, promises, bribes, threats, fraud, and coercion. The United States promised new land, education, economic help, and relocation aid in return for the Indians' ancestral land. When nothing convinced tribes to consent, soldiers forced them out. (p. 46)

	Viewpoint: Navajo	Viewpoint: United States
	The Navajo leaders were Manuelito and Barboncito, both warriors. "In Navajo, a warrior says what is in the people's hearts," said Bighorse, who rode with Manuelito. He "talks about what the land means to them. Brings them together to fight for it." The tall, powerful Manuelito had held out longer than any other Navajo leader. "I will shed my blood on my own land," he said. Barboncito was small and tough, with spiritual power. Before the treaty, he performed a ceremony called the *Ma'ií Bizéé'nast'á* (Put Bead in Coyote's Mouth). Afterward, he predicted, "We'll be set free." (p. 70)	**The main U.S. negotiator** was General William Tecumseh Sherman, famous for his ruthlessness in the Civil War. After Appomattox he was put in charge of the western army. Sherman's stated policy was that all Indians not on reservations "are hostile and will remain so till killed off." Sick of war but skeptical of peace, he wanted the Navajo to move to Oklahoma to avoid further conflict with non-Indian newcomers. He was authorized to offer them cattle, seed, schools, and other inducements. If those failed, he had soldiers. (p. 70–71)
On civilization	Viewpoint: Native Nations **Indian Peoples** never thought of themselves as uncivilized. They had governments, religions, and social systems, and they wanted to stay civilized in their own way. Some defied U.S. policies. Many more showed outward compliance but preserved their cultures in secret. Others sought to blend in but felt inauthentic. Luther Standing Bear (Lakota) said he felt like "an imitation of a white man." Nevertheless, by 1900 whole tribes, languages, and cultures had been wiped out. The Indian population sank to a low of 250,000. (p. 75)	Viewpoint: United States **The United States** summarized its pragmatic new Indian policy: "It costs less to civilize than to kill." Even well-meaning advocates of American Indians believed that the modern world had no room for Native Nations. The rights of Indian sovereignty could scarcely be imagined by policy makers of the time. They believed that Native Nations had to be absorbed into an American notion of civilization at whatever cost. To break down Indian resistance, officials used ruthless methods. (p. 75)

Source: Smithsonian National Museum of the American Indian (2014).

Whereas in the European worldview at the time, a written agreement stood as law, there was less value in an oral agreement made without writing. The exact opposite worldview was held by the American Indian groups—oral agreements were binding and important, while writing something down had less value. Just this one difference alone led to many circumstances that ended in violence and distrust between these nations.

As we have noted thus far, there are many implications of interacting with people who come from different worldviews. It is often the case that differences in these views can be a source of tension between groups, and this may be particularly true for those who have not had exposure to many people who are different from themselves. When we are young, we interact most often within our family structure, and during our childhood, our parents' views often become ours as well. We learn what is "normal," and what is "right" at this time, and as our families are often our biggest influence at this time, we may subscribe to our family's worldview simply because it is the only one we have ever heard. In many cases this may extend to friends' and community ideas, if one's community network is homogenous.

When individuals who have had this experience first encounter a view that is different from their own, they may experience a kind of cognitive dissonance, or a shaking of the foundation of their beliefs. This dissonance may be greater if they have a strong relationship with the person who has the different worldview. As individuals grow into adolescence, they begin to enter new spaces without their families (e.g., via friends, others' houses, etc.). This also commonly occurs during the college years, as you may have already experienced, as it is sometimes the first true move away from family that an older adolescent experiences. In a positive outcome of this type of scenario, individuals learn that not everyone sees the world the same way, and they start to become aware that other worldviews may also be viable. In other cases, however, they might double down on their worldview and reject that another could be true. It is in this type of scenario that tensions may arise between people with different worldviews. Recall the previously discussed vignette involving Alex, the African American college student. If you recall, Alex had many behaviors that he engaged in based on his expectation that he might experience stereotyping and potential discrimination without them. Consider this response to Alex from one of his White classmates:

I don't get why Alex thinks he has to do all of that stuff with professors. I never do any of those types of things (like going up and introducing myself), and I only go to office hours if I really need to—I just don't have the time. Regardless, I've never had an experience where my professors think ill of me for doing that. I just let them find out what I'm like naturally instead of being so forced like Alex. They always learn my name pretty quickly, and I've never been mixed up with others in the class. Also, I know Alex worries sometimes that someone might think he doesn't belong on campus if he's somewhere by himself. I think that's being way too paranoid. Just because that has happened to a couple people on the news doesn't mean that it will happen to him. Besides, if someone called the police on me and said I didn't belong somewhere, I wouldn't sweat it. I would just explain that I did belong there. I never think about my race, and as a result I don't get bothered about it very much. He should take a lesson from me.

—Connor, age 19

Think for a moment about the impact that these different worldviews might have on the friendship between Alex and Connor. What tensions could these different views lead to in their relationship? One thing that is important to consider here is the fact that many researchers say that most racial and ethnic minorities have a greater knowledge and understanding of worldviews within the dominant culture than the average White person has about racial and ethnic minority worldviews (LaFromboise, Coleman, & Gerton, 1983). One major reason for this difference is that nondominant groups have had less power in society and thus must have this knowledge in order to get by in a society that is largely supportive of endorsement of this worldview. Alex likely understands some of the arguments that Connor makes, and Alex may find some of Connor's answers naïve due to Connor's lack of experience with people of color. Connor holds the viewpoint that Alex is thinking about his race too much, and yet many in our country understand that for Black men in particular, being unaware that your race may impact your daily life may have dire consequences (Hadden, Tolliver, Snowden, & Brown-Manning, 2016; Patton & Snyder-Yuly, 2007).

It is possible that if the two remain friends, Connor might witness some of the experiences that Alex has that deal with racial discrimination in his life, and this may allow

Connor to make room for the possibility that Alex's worldview is linked to concrete experience and evidence in his life. Though this might first lead to cognitive dissonance in Connor, he may be able to start to open his worldview to include the idea that race may impact people on a daily basis. This type of **ethnocultural empathy** is often developed when we interact with individuals who are different from ourselves. For a current example, you might look up the story of John Lewis (a former Freedom Rider who is now a US senator) and Elwin Wilson (a former member of the Ku Klux Klan that confronted Lewis at a rally long ago). When Wilson actually spoke to Lewis, he had a different sense of him as a man, and Wilson changed his life because of this interaction.

One final note in this section: Ignoring the fact that worldviews of others can be different can lead to members of one group assuming that their ideals, beliefs, and characteristics might be viewed in the same way by another group. Researchers in the field of psychology often call the concept of this practice **imposed ethics**, which refers to putting one's worldviews onto others as "right," "normal," or "healthy" (Berry, 1990; Leong, Leach, Marsella, & Pickren, 2012). This may be intensified by the fact brought up earlier that invalidating the worldviews of nondominant groups by dominant groups may also result in fewer friendships between these two groups, thus making groups more homogenous. Going back to our discussion of the differences between White settlers and American Indian and Indigenous populations in the Americas, the White settlers brought with them a host of customs and practices that were based on their own worldview and insisted that the native populations adhere to these. Any dissensions from this norm were seen as "savage" and "primitive," among other descriptors. The nondominant group, in this case the native peoples, suffered greatly under these imposed ethics. It is a lesson that our country should not forget in thinking about how to integrate more worldviews into our current social milieu.

CONCLUSION

In this chapter we have explained a number of different factors that may impact the development of worldview in groups and in individuals. We have used more vignettes than we used in any of our other chapters to help provide you with a variety of voices from all different groups. Some of you have heard many of these worldviews before, or have more intimate knowledge of people that may hold similar beliefs, while others of you may be hearing about some of them for the first time. One of the most effective ways to learn about those who are different from you in some way is to develop a level of **multicultural competence** that allows you to have a level of awareness of your beliefs and others' beliefs, knowledge of different groups, and skills for working and interacting with many different kinds of people (American Psychological Association, 2008). As you develop this multicultural competence, you may see your friendship and social circles expanding naturally to include a more diverse array of individuals. Note that we use the word *diverse* here to mean a group that has many different types of identities and worldviews present— some from majority cultures, and others from more underrepresented or historically disenfranchised groups. Consider some of the activities in the ACT section below to help you learn about other worldviews this week and to expand your knowledge of other groups.

We close by asking you to work toward distinguishing between *the* path and *your* path. There is no one path that works for us all, and we would all do well to remember that (Coelho, 1993).

ACT: Assess Your Knowledge, Critical Thinking, Take Part

Assess Your Knowledge

Think back to Chapter 1 when you first created your culture sketch. Look over your answers, and choose several identities that feel salient or prominent in your daily life; then complete the following questions for each. (See the example of Jonas below for some ideas.)

- Does your status on this identity facet hold power in the United States? (For example, if you identify as a man, your gender is a group that holds power in the United States today.)

- What messages do you get about this identity facet in the media or from other information readily available? Do you agree or disagree with these messages?

- What values, strengths, or beliefs do you think come along with your identity in this area?

Example: Jonas on the facet of ethnicity and race

1. My status does not hold power in the United States. As a Latinx man, I have less social power than White men and women today.

2. The media often depicts my group as non-English-speaking, undocumented, poor, and uneducated. These aren't things that are true about me, so I don't agree with the messages, but I fight them all the time. I do feel like people often stereotype me in this way and are surprised that I'm a college student in engineering and that I speak both Spanish and English fluently and without an accent. I try to make sure I correct people if I feel like they are stereotyping me.

3. I think family is very important, and I know this comes from my Latinx heritage. I think men should be strong and care for their family. I'm not super religious, but I believe in God, and I think that comes from my grandmothers talking about this so much. I also believe in standing up for myself, and I think that comes from my family being in a position of having had to do that for many generations because of racism and other discrimination.

Critical Thinking

In looking at the answers to the above questions, can you begin to see your own worldview? Does the world feel safe to you? Does it feel fair? Does it feel open or closed? How do the intersections of your various identities manifest in everyday life for you?

Now take one of your salient identities and try to answer the above questions as if you held a different identity on that facet. If you are a man, for example, try to answer those questions as though you were a woman or a nonbinary individual. How are your answers different? Is the worldview different as well?

Take Part

Participation: If you are imagining the answers of someone who is different from you in race, gender, or some other facet, now is your chance to do a little research. Choose an identity that is different from yours, and find some literature about that population. This might be a novel or short story narrating another's experience, or a series of articles that talk about views of this group. See Appendix for a list of novels about different racial groups.

Initiation: Find a person who shares several of your identity facets, and conduct an interview with this person on these facets by asking the questions in the preceding Assess Your Knowledge section. As you begin to see the shape of this person's worldview, note where you are similar and where you are not. You may find some diversity in worldviews because of the intersections of their other facets as well.

Activism: Find a person that you know is different from you in ways that might mean your worldviews are incredibly different. Sometimes this is a person who is older than you (of a different generation) or of a different racial or sexual orientation group. Make some time to conduct an interview asking the person the questions in the Assess Your Knowledge section. Though you may not agree with this person's viewpoints, try hard not to disagree and to just record the answers. Plot these into a worldview sketch of the person based on the answers. Does this help you to better understand where this person comes from? What is your reaction to the different worldview? How might you still interact with a person whose worldview is incredibly different from yours?

iStock/Victor_Tongdee

4

CULTURAL IDENTITY DEVELOPMENT

LEARNING OBJECTIVES

- Know of the major theories in the field related to racial identity development.
- Understand that additional models of identity (e.g., LGBTQ+, gender, disability, etc.) exist and interact with the development of racial identity.
- Critique the major issues related to models that use stages to explain identity development.
- Recognize the benefit of development of a healthy racial or ethnic identity for people of color.
- Analyze the impact of personal racial identity development on multicultural social interactions.
- Analyze your own current racial identity status and interpret its manifestation in your daily life.

Who are you? This is a question that you may not have considered lately. If you ask a child this question, you are likely to get a variety of answers: "I am Chloe!" "I am her sister!" "I am a ballerina!" "I am a goalie!" "I am a Laker fan!" All of these answers will depend on context and age and development of the child, as well as their understanding of themselves. In this chapter we will explore this question in greater detail, delving into who we are racially, ethnically, and in terms of gender identity and social class, along with many other cultural facets.

AN ECOLOGICAL APPROACH

There are many factors that might both influence identity development and impact how people experience their identities in the world. Urie Bronfenbrenner was a well-known United States–based developmental psychologist who proposed the ecological systems theory (Bronfenbrenner, 1979).

In this model, Bronfenbrenner highlighted different spheres of influence including the **microsystem** (a child's experience in their personal environment), the **mesosystem** (composed of connections such as neighborhood, school, and parents' workplace that interact with the child's personal environment), the **exosystem** (including surrounding institutions that impact the child indirectly, such as the legal system or media), and the **macrosystem** (the societal and cultural values that impact the child; see Figure 4.1).

Derald Wing Sue (2001), another United States–based psychologist who has been influential in many areas of multicultural psychology, modeled his tripartite model of personal identity after Bronfenbrenner's (1979) systems model, including three layers: individual level—uniqueness, group level—similarities and differences, and universal

FIGURE 4.1 ⬡ The Ecological Systems Model

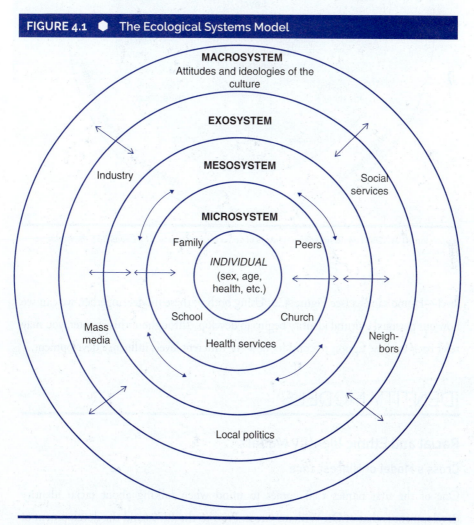

Source: Adapted from Bronfenbrenner and Morris (2006).

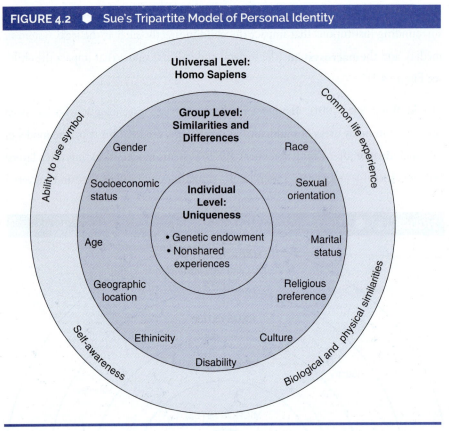

FIGURE 4.2 ⬡ Sue's Tripartite Model of Personal Identity

Source: Sue, D. W. (2001). Multidimensional facets of cultural competence. *The Counseling Psychologist,* 29, 790–821.

level—Homo sapiens (see Figure 4.2). Using both of these models together, we can see how our personal cultural identity begins to develop. Throughout this chapter, you may refer back to these figures to consider how the different levels influence development.

IDENTITY MODELS

Racial and Ethnic Identity Models

Cross's Model of Nigrescence

One of the first names that comes to mind when talking about racial identity development is that of Dr. William Cross. Prior to the 1970s and the development of Cross's model of nigrescence, Black identity had not been explored in a positive light.

As we have already covered in other chapters, African Americans and other racial and ethnic minorities had often been pathologized when being compared to White populations. Cross's model (1971), however, offered a window into how individuals could be Black or African American and also have a positive view of themselves and their place in the world.

The model has four different stages: Pre-encounter, Encounter, Immersion-Emersion, and Internalization (see Table 4.1). Pre-encounter describes the first stage of African American identity and is characterized by a lack of understanding about race beyond basic skin color. Often someone in this particular stage may embrace more White ideals in terms of identity and positive attributes. The term *Pre-encounter* makes additional sense when one understands the second stage, Encounter, which begins when an event occurs in an African American person's life upon which they begin to realize that being Black makes their life different in some way. Many throughout history have described a moment such as this as occurring when they first saw John Lewis and the Freedom Riders beaten in the streets during the 1960s in Alabama and Mississippi. Others may have had this "aha moment" when they heard about the first Black Lives Matter posts or during televised accounts of the police riots in Ferguson. Consider the story of one of our authors, Dr. Isom, an African American woman, as she recalls her experience with her own "encounter."

> *There are two moments that mark my initial encounters with my Blackness, one from elementary school and the other from my junior year of college. When I was in the first grade, a group of students told me I couldn't play with them, because I was "chocolate milk" and they were "regular." As a big fan of chocolate milk, I was initially amused at the description, because I believed I was delicious. But the clear rejection it embodied—the rejection of my very self—left me self-conscious: aware of my skin, my racial identity, and the negative meaning it held for others. I understood what it meant to be Black like never before.*
>
> *As an engineering major in college, I only had eight unrestricted electives, so it wasn't until my junior year that I was able to take an African American studies course. The readings, material, and discussions of Black racial and cultural identity provided a profound sense of belonging. I had always thought my family was unique—a singular mix of wit and resilience, struggle and joy, faith and social*

activism—but what I found out in that class was that we were Black. We, I, were part of a deep tradition and history. Who we were reflected African American culture and the way that culture, my people, had responded to the long racial history of America. I felt a personal largesse, a newly articulated responsibility to a community. That sense of belonging empowered me, changed me, gave a new meaning to being Black and a new purpose to my life.

—Denise, age 54

As you can see, prior to this experience Dr. Isom had a different frame of reference about her family as a whole and a different understanding of their common practices and traditions. The two events noted here propelled her into a different understanding of who she was as an African American person and gave her a broader perspective on her place in the world.

The third stage, Immersion-Emersion, is more of a continuum than a single stage. Persons experiencing the immersion side of the continuum are very embedded in their racial identity as African American persons during the time they spend in this stage. They may choose to associate with an all–African American group as much as possible, and have an idealized view of Blackness coupled with a negative association with Whiteness. As they move closer to the emersion side of the continuum, this idealized view becomes a bit more realistic. Persons on this side of the continuum are able to realize that in any race there may be good and bad, and that a person of one's own race, or another race, may be good or bad.

This more nuanced view of Blackness helps many move into the final stage of Cross's model: Internalization. Individuals who are in this stage have a positive but also realistic view of Blackness in general. This was revolutionary at the time that Cross first proposed his model, as African Americans could for the first time see themselves for themselves, as opposed to in comparison to White identity as a whole (de Walt, 2013). In 1991 Cross released a revision to his 1971 model that included a sixth stage: internalization-commitment. In this final stage, African Americans are comfortable with themselves and with both Black and non-Black groups and individuals, and may begin to work as agents for social justice for African American people. Though Cross's model reads like a stage-by-stage, linear model, it should be noted that not all

TABLE 4.1 ● Cross's Model of Black Racial Identity Development	
Pre-encounter	World is non-Black or anti-Black; internalization of White superiority
Encounter	Significant event forces reevaluation of the process (e.g., assassination of Dr. King)
Immersion-Emersion	Idealization of Blackness and immersion in culture; rejection of all that is not Black
Internalization	Positive and secure feelings about Black identity; increased comfort with other cultures

Source: Adapted from: Cross, W. E. (1971). The Negro-to-Black conversion experience. *Black World*, 20, 13-27.

individuals experience it in this way. Changes of environment, new encounters, and other factors may capitulate African Americans who have been in one or another stage back to another immersion-emersion experience, for example. New encounters can also occur throughout a person's life.

Helm's White Racial Identity Development Model

A second model that is important to note here is Janet Helms's (1990) White racial identity model. Developed almost 20 years after Cross's original model, it follows some of the same ideas of stages of this model. One might ask, Why did so much time elapse before this particular model was created? The most likely reason is that even as Cross (1971) was attempting to find a positive place for African American people in mental health research, there was still an overwhelming presence of Whiteness both in the United States as a whole and within the field of psychology (Helms, 1990). This acceptance of White as the norm made it difficult for people to see that there was a unique White experience and White identity. In Chapter 6, we go deeper into the construction of Whiteness, but here we will touch on the identity aspect of this racial group.

Helms (1990) uses the term *status* or *schema* instead of *stage* to describe each step a White person might take in their journey toward better understanding their racial identity. This is partially because Helms believes that a White person could be in more than one status at the same time. The first status is called Contact, and a person in this status is described by Helms as being "timid" and uncertain about race (see

Table 4.2). A White person in this status may not have interacted with many people who are non-White in any close relationship, or may have interacted only in limited ways. This status is similar to Pre-encounter in Cross's model in some ways—race is a nonexistent concept in many ways for a White person in this initial status. Following this stage is Disintegration. Similar to the Encounter stage, White persons are often propelled into this status when some sort of event or circumstance occurs that begins to open their eyes to the fact that people who are non-White may experience the world in a different way. This often happens in our classes for White students who enter college in the Contact stage. Reflect on our student Lindsay's words:

> I grew up in an all-White neighborhood and went to an almost all-White school. I didn't have any non-White friends until I got to college. When I think about this now, I don't even remember thinking about this as different or strange, even though it seems strange to me now. I go to college at a university that is also mostly White, but my roommate is African American. I wasn't sure we'd be friends when I first met her. She seemed so different to me. But as I got to know her, we began to get close. We have a lot in common—we're both the only girls in our families, we love sports, we're good students, and we have close-knit families at home.
>
> But she has really different experiences with professors and other students sometimes. I've been with her when I have heard people whisper the n-word under their breath or make a racist joke about Black people in front of her and then pretend like they are kidding. At first I brushed this off because she seemed to also, but the closer we get, the more I'm realizing that people treat her differently because she's Black, and the people who most often do this are White like me. It's hard for me to know just how I feel about this. I want to feel ok about my racial group too, and I know I'm not saying those types of things to her, but it feels like White people are so often on the wrong side of race relations. I would be so upset if someone said things to me like that. We've started to talk about this a little bit, but it's hard because I feel so guilty about my race treating hers so badly.
>
> —Lindsay, age 18

You can likely hear in Lindsay's voice the conflict she feels about wanting to feel proud of her group, but at the same time realizing that some people who are part of her racial group are not doing things she can feel proud of. Helms describes this conflict as a dissonance that comes between two thoughts: *I want to be proud of my group,* and *People in my group at times benefit from racism* (Helms, 1992/2008). Disintegration is an uncomfortable status for many White people, as they begin to discover that they may be treated better than non-White people at times.

Likely, at least in part because Disintegration is often so uncomfortable, many White people move quickly into the next status, Reintegration. In Reintegration, the White person tries to think of other reasons besides race or racism that may be at the root of why the types of things Lindsay is describing above happen to people of color. In this status, White people try to *reintegrate* this new information (that sometimes non-Whites are treated differently) into their old schemas or thought processes. A common result is that people in this status begin to explore the idea that maybe there is something about non-White persons that makes them deserving of this behavior. When reading this in black and white, that may be hard to imagine, but there are many ways in which White people in this status may do this. A primary way it occurs is via **scapegoating**. You have probably heard some White people say about non-White groups: "Well, it's their own fault—if they would just stop talking about race so much, there wouldn't be such racism!" or "Of course they don't fit in—learn to speak English!" or other such comments. Statements like these come from a desire for a White person in Reintegration to avoid confronting the fact that racism and discrimination lie at the heart of the reason why White people have been treated better in the United States throughout history. Reintegration may bring a feeling of comfort for White persons in this status—they may feel they have "made sense" of a problem that seemed like it was about unfairness.

Because White people are in the majority in terms of power and point of view, there are likely many people supporting the viewpoint that people of color are to blame for their own predicament (Helms, 1992/2008). As a result, it usually takes time and some very purposeful steps to exit this status and move on to the next. To this point, Helms (1992/2008) states,

> Ceasing to rely on [the reintegration] schema probably requires a catastrophic event or a series of personal encounters that the person can no longer ignore. That is, [their] moral conscience, abandoned during Disintegration, must be re-awakened. This moral re-awakening both ends the racism phase and begins the nonracist or antiracist White identity phase. (p. 32)

TABLE 4.2 ● Helms's White Racial Identity Development Model	
Contact	Innocence and ignorance about race and racial issues Not consciously White Curious or timid about other races

Disintegration	Awareness that racism exists produces confusion and a dilemma:
	
	    "I am part of a group that at times benefits from racism."
	
	    "I want to be proud of my group."

Reintegration	Distortion of reality to deal with the dilemma of scapegoating (e.g., "They must do something to deserve it.")
Pseudo-Independence	Scaling of positive view of Whiteness to realistic intellectual understanding of existence of racism Denial of responsibility of majority for maintaining institutional racism
Immersion/Emersion	Efforts to look at "unsanitized" White history Exploration of racism and White culture Realistic awareness of assets/deficits of being White
Autonomy	Active confrontation of racism and oppression Seeking of within-race and cross-racial interactions Equalitarian attitude regardless of race

Source: Adapted from Helms, J. E. (1990). *Black and white racial identity: Theory, research, and practice* (J. E. Helms, Ed.). New York: Greenwood Press.

The next status is Pseudo-Independence, and according to Helms it is at this point that White individuals begin to resolve some of the cognitive dissonance they may have felt in the past. In this status, an intellectual understanding of race and its impact on everyday life is starting to form, and many White individuals may begin to seek ways to decrease discrimination or to raise awareness in others about racism and prejudice. During this period, however, White individuals may still not feel particularly comfortable talking about their Whiteness and may avoid being close with other White people, instead seeking out friends of color. At the same time, White persons in this status may not be able to think about themselves as a part of the group that has maintained racism over many years and instead may think of themselves as separate from "bad White people" in some way.

The reality is that people of any race have good and bad traits, and one can be a "good White person" and still benefit from, or be blind to, racism against people of color at times. This is a very difficult concept to understand and will be elucidated further in Chapter 6 of this volume, which details the concept of Whiteness and being White in general. If you identify as a White person and are reading this section, it may be hard for you to think of yourself as part of a group that has perpetuated racism in our country, depending on your stage of development. This limited understanding may also lead you to feel attacked if someone discusses Whiteness in a way that feels as though it does not describe you personally. To move past this stage, however, White persons must be able to look at their group as a whole, as opposed to trying to distance themselves from it. Pseudo-Independence is a more comfortable stage for White people than Disintegration, as they are better able to cope with some of the realities of their racial history, but many in this stage still might not recognize that by not "actively working to dismantle racism" (Helms, 1992/2008, p. 33) they are still in some ways perpetuating it.

As White people move through this stage, they may find themselves entering Immersion/Emersion, the next status in Helms's (1990) model. This status has the same name as Cross's third stage in his theory of Black identity development and has a similar continuum structure. In this stage, a White person begins to work hard to better understand the history of race relations in our country in a way that Helms (1992/2008) calls "unsanitized" (p. 33), meaning that it is looked at closely without making excuses or glossing over parts that involve negative things about White historical figures. This is starting to occur in some states as elementary school curriculums involve more truths about figures like Columbus, or the function of the California missions. Though some of these historical incidents recount mistakes and also atrocities committed by European and European American individuals at the time, White people in Helms's Immersion/Emersion status are not denying the real experiences that happened to people of color. Helms (1992/2008) states, "When using [the Immersion/Emersion] schema, the [White] person assumes personal responsibility for racism and develops a realistic awareness of the assets and deficits of being White" (p. 33).

This phrase, "assumes personal responsibility for racism," is often misunderstood by folks that are just beginning to think about race and racism. Many may believe that this means that they are personally dishing out racism to people of color on a regular basis, and they become defensive about this "accusation." Contrary to this misunderstanding, Helms uses the word "responsibility" to mean that persons in this stage of White racial identity development accept that they too, not just people of color, have a responsibility to act against racism, to stand up for justice, and to help promote equity. When thinking about "personal responsibility" in this way, one might better understand the stance White persons in this status are beginning to develop. They are making a decision that they as White persons are responsible for relearning some of the sanitized history they may have been taught in the past, and for paying attention to an unsanitized view of how non-White racial groups have been treated historically in our country. White persons in this status are starting to better understand how their identity can be utilized to make change, and they are becoming more comfortable with being White *and* being non-racist.

The final status of Helms's (1990) identity model is called Autonomy. This term is meant to sum up how White persons may be able to feel once they have reached this point in the model. Instead of being trapped in a colorblind world that does not acknowledge that Whiteness means something (and that was developed to ignore and deny racism), White persons in Autonomy can acknowledge that racism exists and that their ancestors may have perpetuated it, while at the same time working themselves (or alongside people of color) to correct this wrong. This provides a new view of what it can mean to be White. Being antiracist and White is the final step toward achieving a healthy White identity and allows White people to be more authentic in their relationships with other White people and with people of color. Consider the following statement from Nora, a White woman who has some experience now with the Autonomy status:

> It gave me some relief to be honest, to admit that I knew that racism still existed and that I knew I benefitted from it at some level every time a person of color was discriminated against. And I felt like I could admit that because I was finally doing something to change it! Some of my White friends have said to me, "Why are you so involved with this? They [people of color] must think of you as the bad guy—doesn't that feel uncomfortable?" The reality is that if I was not involved, I really would be the bad guy—my Black friends, my Asian friends, and others, know that I am being real. They know I might not understand some of their

experiences right off the bat, but they also know that I am willing to listen to them and believe them, and that develops our friendships much more deeply than if I was still pretending that I couldn't get it. I like that I can interact with people as people now, while at the same time acknowledging that we have differences because of our races and what we experience. I don't worry anymore that they think I'm racist, and when I make mistakes, they know I'm still coming from a good place, even though they might still call me on it, just like I would if they did something similar. That's because we are friends, that's what friends do—we know each other authentically.

—Nora, age 50

One final point on Helms's theory before we move forward. Helms is clear in stating that this model is not intended to be linear in terms of a White person's progression between the statuses or schemas. Different environmental influences (including national climate) may lead to some White individuals moving backward or forward in their understanding of White identity. Figure 4.3 depicts Helms's statuses the way

---

FIGURE 4.3 ⬡ **A White Individual May Have Different Amounts of Different Statuses**

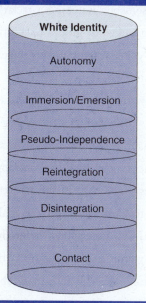

White Identity

Autonomy

Immersion/Emersion

Pseudo-Independence

Reintegration

Disintegration

Contact

Source: Adapted from Helms, J. E. (1992/2008). *A race is a nice thing to have: A guide to being a White person or understanding the White persons in your life.* Alexandria, VA: Microtraining Associates, Inc. p. 39.

that she thinks is most helpful. Imagine this cylinder as filled with varying amounts of liquid. A White individual may have a touch of Autonomy, a bit of Reintegration, a lot of Immersion/Emersion, and so on. Thinking of identity development in this way as a process, and as dynamically interacting with our experiences and the environment around us, may help in recognizing that identity is not something with which we can be "done." It is a continuous process of learning, revising, and growing.

Sue and Sue's Racial/Cultural Identity Development Model

A third major racial identity development model was created in the 1990s by Derald Wing Sue and David Sue; it charts racial identity development for racial and ethnic minorities as groups. Table 4.3 delineates this model. As you may be able to tell from the names of the various stages, this model is also based on Cross's (1971) original model of Black racial identity development, and Helms's (1990) subsequent model of White racial identity development. Stage 1 in this model, Conformity, is generally characterized by the racial or ethnic minority individual having a preference for and assimilation to the dominant White view. Individuals in this stage are effectively less appreciative of themselves and their own cultural group, and more appreciative of the dominant White group. Though this acting in opposition to self-interest may be somewhat confusing to someone watching a racial minority in this stage, it is this assimilation that is often lauded by groups attempting to deny racism. You may have experienced persons of color who are in this stage and been surprised by their reaction to racism or discrimination. Individuals in this stage are often the ones cited when someone says, "But my friend is African American, and he thought my racist joke about Black people was really funny!" Other researchers talk about this process of preferring the dominant group over one's own as internalized racism, which refers to an acceptance of racist views such that one applies them to oneself (Jones, 2000). Examples of practices of someone in this particular group might include an Asian woman who decides to have eye surgery to make her eyes more round, an African American individual who uses whitening products to lighten their skin, or an American Indian person who is a strong supporter of the Cleveland Indians and Washington Redskins mascots. We will talk more about how and why someone might feel comfortable in this stage in future chapters, but as Sue and Sue say, it is the "most damning indictment of White racism and because it has such a profound negative impact on persons of color, understanding its sociopolitical dynamics is of utmost importance" (2016, p. 367).

The second stage in Sue and Sue's model is termed Dissonance and represents a stage in which something occurs in a person's life to make them question their preference for White culture over their own. Similar to Disintegration in White racial identity development, this event or experience brings new evidence to light for racial or ethnic minority individuals that causes them to think there may be other perspectives to consider. A common experience might be interacting with a person of color who is more involved with their own culture, or meeting someone from a particular racial or ethnic group who seems to make it clear that the stereotypes previously believed about that group may have exceptions (Sue & Sue, 2016). Persons going through this stage may feel a sense of conflict and tension as they wrestle with this new information and discovery.

Stage 3 in Sue and Sue's model is called Resistance and Immersion and is similar to the first half of the continuum in the Immersion-Emersion stage in Cross's model. Individuals in this stage at first almost completely reject the White culture they have been so accepting of prior to this process and may surround themselves with other racial and ethnic minorities exclusively. This stage may be characterized by some anger that they have been subjected so strongly to the dominant culture in the past, and an attempt to push it away as far as possible. As Sue and Sue state, "The most common active types of affective feelings [in this stage] are *guilt, shame*, and *anger*" (2016, p. 372). The intensity of this particular stage is what often leads individuals to move into the next stage in the model, Introspection. In this stage, individuals attempt to look at things from both sides, and they start to come closer to an authentic understanding of themselves and their place in society. Friendships with fair-minded, nondominating White individuals may help this stage to begin and may allow racial and ethnic minorities to scale back their feelings about Whiteness to a less emotionally charged view that takes differences, both within a group and between groups, into account.

Finally, Stage 5 in this model is called Integrative Awareness and is characterized by a more realistic view of Whiteness coupled with a more realistic awareness of one's own group as well. Individuals in this stage may be similar to those in both Helms's and Cross's models' final stages, in that they are able to interact comfortably in many

TABLE 4.3 ● The Racial/Cultural Identity Development Model					
	Conformity	Dissonance	Resistance and Immersion	Introspection	Integrative Awareness
Attitude Toward Self	Self-depreciating or neutral (low race salience)	Conflict between depreciating *self* and appreciating *group*	Self-appreciating	Concern with basis of self-appreciation	Self-appreciating
Attitude Toward Others of the Same Group	Group-depreciating or neutral (low race salience)	Conflict between feeling some shared experiences while depreciating group views of minority hierarchy	Group-appreciating experiences and feelings of culturocentrism	Concern with nature of unequivocal appreciation	Group-appreciating
Attitude Toward Others of Different Disenfranchised Racial Group	Discriminatory or neutral	Conflict between dominant held beliefs and group-depreciating	Conflict due to feelings of empathy toward other minority groups	Concern with nature of ethnocentric basis for judging others	Group-appreciating
Attitude Toward Dominant Group (White)	Group-appreciating	Conflict between group-appreciating and group-depreciating	Group-depreciating	Concern with the basis of group depreciation	Selective appreciation

Source: Author adapted from: Sue, D. W., & Sue, D. (2016), *Counseling the culturally diverse: Theory and practice*, (p. 367) Hoboken, NJ: Wiley.

situations with both people from their own cultural group and those from the White cultural group. Progressing to this stage allows for a diverse friendship group and provides freedom to engage with people from all different groups.

Other Racial Identity Development Models

Sue and Sue (2016), in the seventh edition of their seminal work *Counseling the Culturally Diverse,* cover several other models of racial and ethnic identity development, each specific to a particular racial group. These have been summarized for you in

Table 4.4. One thing to note—the process of moving through the stages in any of the models discussed here is not the same for all individuals within a particular cultural group. Some individuals may move quickly to a state of Integrative Awareness or Autonomy, and others may remain stuck in Reintegration or Immersion and stay there for the entirety

TABLE 4.4 ● Models of Racial Identity Development for Asian and Latinx Americans			
Asian Americans (Kim, 1981)		**Latinx Americans (Ruiz, 1990)**	
Ethnic Awareness	Positive or neutral attitudes toward one's own ethnic group are formed, directed by parents/family (childhood stage).	Casual Stage	Affirmation is lacking about ethnic identity due to denigration, ignoring, or negation of ethnic heritage in one's environment or among significant others.
White Identification	As child enters school, peer attitudes toward Asian Americans impact self-esteem and identity; recognition of "differentness" leads to desire to escape by identifying with White society.	Cognitive Stage	Negative and distorted messages lead to three mental sets: Poverty and prejudice are associated with Latinx identity. Assimilation to White culture is only escape. Assimilation in only road to success.
Awakening to Social Political Consciousness (age varies)	Significant events (e.g., civil rights demonstrations) lead to an awakening and adoption of new perspective; individuals abandon identification with White society and begin to better understand oppression and oppressed groups.	Consequence Stage	Unwanted self-image (as defined in previous stage) leads to embarrassment and shame about cultural identifiers and markers (accent, name, etc.); individuals reject Latinx heritage.
Redirection to Asian American Consciousness	Individuals renew connections to and develop pride in Asian American heritage and culture; anger against White racism (in part due to experiences in youth) becomes a defining theme.	Working-Through stage	Psychological distress at fragmented identity becomes too great, and move begins toward reclaiming disowned pieces of ethnic heritage.
Incorporation	Individuals have positive and comfortable identities as Asian Americans as well as respect for other cultural/racial groups.	Successful Resolution stage	Greater acceptance of one's culture and ethnicity occurs; improvements in self-esteem and positive ethnic identity provide a source of drive toward success.

Source: Adapted from Sue, D. W., & Sue, D. *Counseling the culturally diverse: Theory and practice.* Hoboken, NJ: Wiley.

of their life. The catalysts for change are often environmental and may span many different systems within a person's life. Family, friends, personal physiognomy (i.e., what a person looks like physically in terms of hair color and texture, skin color, and other factors), region or area in which one lives, and national climate may all impact individuals' understanding of their race and their relations to other races. Finally, multiracial individuals may go through an entirely different process of racial and ethnic identity development. Models for multiracial individuals differ sharply from models that describe monoracial individuals and will be discussed in Chapter 9 on multiracial individuals.

Nation of Origin: Immigrant Identity and Acculturation

We turn now briefly to a discussion of identity based on nation of origin, via the lens of immigration to a new national context. This area of research is well studied, but we will provide a few highlights for you here, particularly as immigration and documentation statuses have been so oft discussed in our national news in recent times. The United States is a tremendously diverse nation in comparison to most others, and its diversity and independent spirit are often touted as hallmarks of being an American. The term *American* often evokes certain images, and so we ask you to engage in a

FIGURE 4.4 ● Images That Come to Mind With the Word *American*

iStock/LightFieldStudios

iStock/Sophia_Apkalikov

iStock/shironosov

small exercise before moving forward. Think for a minute about the term *American,* and try to pay careful attention to the images that spring to light in your mind. Take a look at

Figure 4.4: Did your mind immediately jump to an image that looked similar to any of these? What do you notice about the people in these images in terms of their skin color? It is common that when people think about the word *American,* they imagine White people. These images may occur to you even if you are someone who fits the description of American and is not White! These images, however unbidden, may not fit what we actually *know* to be the definition of American. When allowed to take more time to think about the concept of this identity, other images such as those in Figure 4.5 may also enter your mind. Regardless, unless persons are of Native American descent, they are descendants of persons who at some point were immigrants. Therefore, models of acculturation—that is, how one adjusts to a new home culture—must be included in a discussion of national identity.

Perhaps one of the most well-known acculturation models is from psychologist Teresa LaFromboise (LaFromboise, Coleman, & Gerton, 1983). In her work with colleagues, LaFromboise identifies five potential statuses that individuals might adopt upon attempting to integrate themselves into a new culture.

FIGURE 4.5 ● **These Pictures Also Show** *Americans*

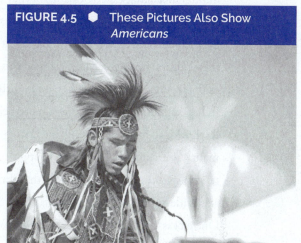

The first of these is Assimilation, and in this status, individuals completely absorb themselves into the dominant culture. Perhaps you have heard stories of European immigrants doing exactly this when they first set foot on American soil. When Irish, Italian, and other non-English immigrants came to the United States generations ago, they experienced much discrimination at first due to stereotypes and beliefs about their cultural heritages. Many escaped this type of discrimination by assimilating. For example, some made small changes to their last names to sound "less ethnic." (A more Italian sounding *Rossi* became a more neutral, English-sounding *Ross* for example.) As those who hailed from England during colonial times were thought to be the dominant culture, many assimilated to appear more like them. Efforts to lose an accent or to stop speaking a language other than English became a way to increase one's social status (de Souza, Pereira, Camino, Lima, & Torres, 2016; Gluszek & Dovidio, 2010). One fact is important to note: This type of assimilation could not be complete if one was not White. Though sometimes immigrants or descendants of immigrants from non-European home cultures attempt also to assimilate (e.g., survivors of the Japanese American internment camps who dropped their language, modern-day immigrants from other countries who take on American-sounding names in order to better fit in), complete assimilation to the dominant (i.e., White) culture is impossible for all those who are not White, even though they may try to fit into the dominant culture in this way. Thus even as some call for any non-White culture to assimilate to the majority, it is not possible for all.

In addition to the Assimilation status, LaFromboise and colleagues (1983) depict other statuses. Acculturated individuals are those who are able to get along in their new culture, though they may still keep much of their own culture. Many immigrants who have been in the United States for more than a few years may be completely competent in moving through White America and living within this system, but may also still hold fast to cultural traditions, language, and other aspects of their family's original home culture. Fusion is a third status described by these researchers, and individuals who can be described by this have combined pieces of their family's original home culture with pieces of the dominant culture in the context in which they currently reside to create some new culture. In some examples of this status, people may operate from a colorblind perspective and attempt to ignore other differences. LaFromboise and colleagues point out that a good example of this type of acculturation is the experience of American Indians as they came to be seen as one group, belying their many tribal and regional ethnic differences. There is a loss here to the fusion status, similar in some ways to the assimilation status. Though American Indians are obviously not immigrants, they are often treated as strangers in their own land, and so their status is relevant to this type of identity here.

The last two statuses are Alternation and Multicultural statuses. Alternation refers to a what we might call "code-switching" today, that is, the tendency for individuals in this identity status to alternate between their own home culture and the dominant culture based on the context in which they find themselves. Here is Rosa's description of her experience with this status:

> At home with my family, I think I'm much more Mexican. I speak more Spanish, I am very deferent to my elders, especially my parents; even the food I eat is different at home. But when I go back to college all that changes again. I am more assertive with my professors, especially if they are not Mexican, and would feel comfortable questioning them—I would never do that to my elders at home! I don't even think about speaking in Spanish most days when I'm at school. I'm not even really conscious of this switch, but I am almost a different person with my Mexican family than I am in my mostly non-Mexican life at college.

—Rosa, age 20

As Rosa describes so clearly, someone who uses an Alternation model can move back and forth between these cultural contexts.

Lastly, Multicultural in LaFromboise and colleagues' (1983) model of acculturation describes individuals who are able to keep both their home culture and their host culture within a single context. In a true Multicultural society, LaFromboise and colleagues state that four conditions are encouraged: "[All people should] (a) maintain and develop their group identities, (b) develop other-group acceptance and tolerance, (c) engage in intergroup contact and sharing, and (d) learn each other's language" (p. 401). In many ways this type of cultural society sounds idyllic; people can feel at home in their adopted culture while still maintaining respect for their own cultural group and those of others. Though this is at times touted as the goal of the United States as a whole, we believe we are still quite far from this dream.

One important point to note with regard to acculturation is the idea that some circumstances of immigration may make this process more traumatizing. Compare, for example, a planned move to a new nation versus a suddenly necessary move due to violence, war, or other atrocities in one's home country. Refugees may have a very different sort of transition to a new country (or count*ries*, as the first country of settlement is often not the final destination) and are much more at the mercy of the new nation in terms of acceptance. In addition, refugees may often leave their home country with little more than the clothes on their back and may suffer mental health issues due to the driving reason for leaving, including posttraumatic stress disorder (PTSD) and other such diagnoses. In many situations, families may be split up by this process as well, for example in the cases where only some are able to withstand the rigors of what often amounts to an escape from their home country.

Other Cultural Identity Models

LGBTQ+ Identity Development

Models of other types of cultural facets have also been developed in the field of psychology. Vivienne Cass (1979), a clinical psychologist, developed the Cass Identity Model for individuals who fall along the LGBTQ+ continuum. This model, created originally in 1979, has been used widely by clinicians and researchers to help clients and others better understand this identity facet. It is important to note that, at the time this theory was formed, the only terms used in this field were *gay* and *lesbian,* and thus this model doesn't reflect the more nuanced understanding of multiple nonheterosexual identities that the LGBTQ+ spectrum does today. In addition, this model offers experiences of genders within a binary, though study of LGBTQ+ individuals has now gone beyond this dichotomous understanding of gender. Cass's (1979) model is presented here in its original form, but it would be appropriate to add these other identities in discussion of this framework.

Stage 1 is termed Identity Confusion and is described as being the time in which an individual might first begin to ask the question, "Could I be gay?" During this stage, individuals are not certain of the answer to this question, and their responses to it may range from trying to deny their same-sex attraction or encounters as a one-time thing to developing same-sex relationships that are emotionally involved, though not explicitly sexual.

In Stage 2, Identity Comparison, individuals begin to seriously consider that they are gay or lesbian, and Cass states that they may go through a sort of grieving process in this new transition. This will of course depend on the type of understanding the LGBTQ+ individual has of this identity.

Stage 3 is called Identity Tolerance and involves the LGBTQ+ individual in seeking out others who are also LGBTQ+. This may include more exploration of LGBTQ+ culture as well, and the individual may be more immersed in this culture as opposed to being a part of LGBTQ+ and heterosexual culture. You likely can see some of the obvious connections to the Immersion stages in other models (e.g., Cross, 1971; Helms, 1990; Sue & Sue, 1998).

Stage 4 is termed Identity Acceptance and represents a turning point of sorts for an LGBTQ+ individual in Cass's (1979) model. In this stage, the main task being accomplished is pulling the public self and the private self closer to one another. As opposed to trying to deny that being gay could be a possibility (Stage 1), or keeping to oneself in order to keep one's private self more of a secret (Stage 2), the LGBTQ+ individual is starting to have the sense, "I will be OK." Though there may still be some experience of grief over past ideas of what life might have been like, there is new acceptance and support seeking.

Stage 5 (Identity Pride) and Stage 6 (Identity Synthesis) represent the positive end of the continuum of Cass's model. In Identity Pride, LGBTQ+ individuals begin to share themselves with the world as gay or lesbian persons. Similar to individuals in the Immersion-Emersion stage of Cross's (1971) model, LGBTQ+ individuals divide the world into gay (i.e., gay = good) and straight (i.e., straight = bad). Anger may arise as a primary emotion during this stage, as individuals begin to be themselves authentically, and this may cause difficulty with friends who have known the person as straight or nongay prior to this time. Invalidations and lack of acceptance from others may drive this anger.

Finally, in the Identity Synthesis stage, the LGBTQ+ individual integrates sexual identity with all other aspects of self. Cass (1979) states, "Instead of being seen as *the* identity [sexual orientation], it is not given the status of being merely one aspect of self" (p. 235). Though some anger at heterosexism (that is, discrimination leveled at LGBTQ+ persons because they are not heterosexual) may still exist, the intensity of this emotion begins to decrease as more trust begins to build with nongay others. In this final stage, LGBTQ+ individuals are "whole" in the sense that they experience the world as a complete person, not only as a person of an LGBTQ+ sexual orientation (Cass, 1979).

One caveat—this model was originally developed in the late 1970s, and at that time being gay or lesbian had different implications, and there was a different understanding surrounding it based on many different factors. Importantly, in the early 1970s "homosexuality" was still a viable diagnosis in the second edition of the *Diagnostic and Statistical Manual of Mental Disorders* or the *DSM-II* (American Psychiatric Association, 1968). The *DSM* is the definitive diagnostic guide for the field of psychology, and its current iteration (*DSM-5*; American Psychiatric Association, 2013) remains so today. Homosexuality was taken out of the *DSM* in 1973, and so the third edition (*DSM-III*; American Psychiatric Association, 1980) and following editions do not consider being same-sex oriented to be a disorder of any kind (Drescher, 2015).

However, the stigma associated with a nonheterosexual sexual orientation remained as a part of the zeitgeist of the time. This is evident to some extent in the wording used to describe the various stages of this model. Though it is true that individuals may still struggle as they make the decision to come out as gay or lesbian or another queer identity, the process is likely different in many areas of the country. In some states, voters took to the polls to support the rights of same-sex couples to marry, showing public support for these groups. This is a likely barometer for the stigma or lack thereof associated with LGBTQ+ populations in these areas. In others, the stigma of being part of the queer community is still high, and therefore some individuals from this group may have a different experience with their identity development as a result.

Regardless of different regions' views, today the American Psychological Association and the American Psychiatric Association stand together against heterosexism and against so-called "**reparative therapies**" that still exist in some fringe groups and are aimed at "curing" people of being gay. The field of psychology as a whole decries these "treatments" and has made a definitive statement that psychologists do not treat things that are not mental disorders, and being gay is not a mental disorder. In 2009, the American Psychological Association Task Force on Appropriate Therapeutic Responses to Sexual Orientation released a report including a resolution that in part stated that same-sex orientation was not a mental disorder, and since therapists only provide treatments for mental disorders, it followed that "reparative therapies" or "conversion therapies" designed to change one's sexual orientation had no place in the field. The resolution from the APA (2009) includes (among others) the following points:

> **Therefore be it resolved** that the American Psychological Association affirms that same-sex sexual and romantic attractions, feelings, and behaviors are normal and positive variations of human sexuality regardless of sexual orientation identity;

> **Be it further resolved** that the American Psychological Association reaffirms its position that homosexuality per se is not a mental disorder and opposes portrayals of sexual minority youths and adults as mentally ill due to their sexual orientation.

You can see the entire resolution that resulted from the task force in Spotlight Feature 4.1.

In summary, it is important to note that sexual orientation and the field's view of what constitutes a healthy sexual orientation has changed greatly since Cass's original publication. Nevertheless, the Cass theory is still very much used in thinking about LGBTQ+ groups in today's field of psychology (Cass, 2015). In addition, there is a better general understanding within cultural psychology that other sexual orientation identity statuses exist beyond gay and lesbian, including bisexual (being sexually attracted to both opposite-sex and same-sex partners), pansexual (being sexually attracted to a variety of gender

The rainbow flag represents pride in the LGBTQ+ community.

iStock/FG Trade

identities), asexual (being interested in intimate relationships that do not involve sexual activity), and others. For more details on the "LGBTQ+ rainbow," see the website of the Gay and Lesbian Alliance Against Defamation (GLAAD, www.glaad.org/).

SPOTLIGHT FEATURE 4.1

American Psychological Association Resolution on Appropriate Affirmative Responses to Sexual Orientation Distress Change Efforts

Resolution

Whereas the American Psychological Association expressly opposes prejudice (defined broadly) and discrimination based on age, gender, gender identity, race, ethnicity, culture, national origin, religion, sexual orientation, disability, language, or socioeconomic status (American Psychological Association, 1998, 2000, 2002, 2003, 2005, 2006, 2008b);

Whereas the American Psychological Association takes a leadership role in opposing prejudice and discrimination (APA, 2008b, 2008c), including prejudice based on or derived from religion or spirituality, and encourages commensurate consideration of religion and spirituality as diversity variables (APA, 2008b);

Whereas psychologists respect human diversity including age, gender, gender identity, race, ethnicity, culture, national origin, religion, sexual orientation, disability, language, and socioeconomic status (APA, 2002) and psychologists strive to prevent bias from their own spiritual, religious, or non-religious beliefs from taking precedence over professional practice and standards or scientific findings in their work as psychologists (APA, 2008b);

Whereas psychologists are encouraged to recognize that it is outside the role and expertise of psychologists, as psychologists, to adjudicate religious or spiritual tenets, while also recognizing that psychologists can appropriately speak to the psychological implications of religious/spiritual beliefs or practices when relevant psychological findings about those implications exist (APA, 2008b);

Whereas those operating from religious/spiritual traditions are encouraged to recognize that it is outside their role and expertise to adjudicate empirical scientific issues in psychology, while also recognizing they can appropriately speak to theological implications of psychological science (APA, 2008b);

Whereas the American Psychological Association encourages collaborative activities in pursuit of shared prosocial goals between psychologists and religious communities when such collaboration can be done in a mutually respectful manner that is consistent with psychologists' professional and scientific roles (APA, 2008b);

Whereas societal ignorance and prejudice about a same-sex sexual orientation places some sexual minorities 2 at risk for seeking sexual orientation change due to personal, family, or religious conflicts, or lack of information (Beckstead & Morrow, 2004; Haldeman, 1994; Ponticelli, 1999; Shidlo & Schroeder, 2002; Wolkomir, 2001);

Whereas some mental health professionals advocate treatments based on the premise that homosexuality is a mental disorder (e.g., Nicolosi, 1991; Socarides, 1968);

Whereas sexual minority children and youth are especially vulnerable populations with unique developmental tasks (Perrin, 2002; Ryan & Futterman, 1997), who lack adequate legal protection from involuntary or coercive treatment (Arriola, 1998; Burack & Josephson, 2005; Molnar, 1997) and whose parents and guardians need accurate information to make informed decisions regarding their development and well-being (Cianciotto & Cahill, 2006; Ryan & Futterman, 1997); and

Whereas research has shown that family rejection is a predictor of negative outcomes (Remafedi, Farrow, & Deisher, 1991; Ryan, Huebner, Diaz, & Sanchez, 2009; Savin-Williams, 1994; Wilber, Ryan, & Marksamer, 2006) and that parental acceptance and school support are protective factors (D'Augelli, 2003; D'Augelli, Hershberger & Pilkington, 1998; Goodenow, Szalacha, & Westheimer, 2006; Savin-Williams, 1989) for sexual minority youth;

Therefore be it resolved that the American Psychological Association affirms that same-sex sexual and romantic attractions, feelings, and behaviors are normal and positive variations of human sexuality regardless of sexual orientation identity;

Be it further resolved that the American Psychological Association reaffirms its position that homosexuality per se is not a mental disorder and opposes portrayals of sexual minority youths and adults as mentally ill due to their sexual orientation;

Be it further resolved that the American Psychological Association concludes that there is insufficient evidence to support the use of psychological interventions to change sexual orientation;

Be it further resolved that the American Psychological Association encourages mental health professionals to avoid misrepresenting the efficacy of sexual orientation change efforts by promoting or promising change in sexual orientation when providing assistance to individuals distressed by their own or others' sexual orientation;

Be it further resolved that the American Psychological Association concludes that the benefits reported by participants in sexual orientation change efforts can be gained through approaches that do not attempt to change sexual orientation;

Be it further resolved that the American Psychological Association concludes that the emerging knowledge on affirmative multiculturally competent treatment provides a foundation for an appropriate evidence-based practice with children, adolescents and adults who are distressed by or seek to change their sexual orientation (Bartoli & Gillem, 2008; Brown, 2006; Martell, Safren & Prince, 2004; Ryan & Futterman, 1997; Norcross, 2002);

Be it further resolved that the American Psychological Association advises parents, guardians, young people, and their families to avoid sexual orientation change efforts that portray homosexuality as a mental illness or developmental disorder and to seek psychotherapy, social support and educational services that provide accurate information on sexual orientation and sexuality, increase family and school support, and reduce rejection of sexual minority youth;

(Continued)

(Continued)

Be it further resolved that the American Psychological Association encourages practitioners to consider the ethical concerns outlined in the 1997 APA Resolution on Appropriate Therapeutic Response to Sexual Orientation (American Psychological Association, 1998), in particular the following standards and principles: scientific bases for professional judgments, benefit and harm, justice, and respect for people's rights and dignity;

Be it further resolved that the American Psychological Association encourages practitioners to be aware that age, gender, gender identity, race, ethnicity, culture, national origin, religion, disability, language, and socioeconomic status may interact with sexual stigma, and contribute to variations in sexual orientation identity development, expression, and experience;

Be it further resolved that the American Psychological Association opposes the distortion and selective use of scientific data about homosexuality by individuals and organizations seeking to influence public policy and public opinion and will take a leadership role in responding to such distortions;

Be it further resolved that the American Psychological Association supports the dissemination of accurate scientific and professional information about sexual orientation in order to counteract bias that is based in lack of knowledge about sexual orientation; and

Be it further resolved that the American Psychological Association encourages advocacy groups, elected officials, mental health professionals, policy makers, religious professionals and organizations, and other organizations to seek areas of collaboration that may promote the wellbeing of sexual minorities.

Source: American Psychological Association (2009).

Socioeconomic Status/Social Class Identity Development

Some researchers have posited that identity associated with social class can have a profound impact on many other factors in an individual's life. Though no identity development model with regard to social class per se currently exists, there may be a tendency for people to take on the identity of the level of class in which they grew up (Mossakowski, 2008; Pedrotti, 2013). You may have heard of "poverty mentality," for example, in which an individual who grew up with little gains wealth later on but still lives as though this change in socioeconomic status (SES) had not occurred. In addition, some individuals who grew up with money, but later on lost that money and shifted down in their economic level, may still have higher levels of well-being and mental health despite this environmental shift. Though SES can change (for the better or worse) throughout one's lifetime based on a number of different factors, some state that the way in which one thinks of oneself is the important piece. Palomar-Lever found in a 2007 study that lower-SES students who did not classify themselves as "poor" in terms of their identity (though they objectively could be described this way based on SES) had higher levels of well-being than those who did define themselves in this way (Pedrotti, 2013).

In addition, and related to the idea that SES changes may bring other changes during one's lifetime, some researchers are investigating what happens in terms of identity when this type of upward (or downward) mobility occurs. Though some research shows that benefits in areas like health may occur when SES changes for the better (e.g., better health access, nutrition, etc.; Gruenewald et al., 2012), and more risks to health when SES decreases (Collins, Rankin, & David, 2015), others have found that any type of change can "yield unique physical and mental health risks, especially among individuals from particularly disadvantaged backgrounds" (Destin, Rheinschmidt-Same, & Richeson, 2017, p. 276; see Brody, Yu, Miller, Ehrlich, & Chen, 2018). This leads us as a field toward more exploration of what might be difficult about changes to SES. In cultural theories of SES identity, some researchers have suggested that an upward change in SES might lead to alienation from old contacts, including perhaps family or other close friends from earlier periods in one's life (Destin et al., 2017). In addition, Destin and colleagues have noted that there appears to exist a phenomenon called **status-based identity uncertainty** that may bring about psychological distress for those who experience a change in SES status during their lifetime. Destin and colleagues call for more research in this area of SES identity and changes to status that may shift when SES changes by saying, "The status-based identity concept provides the opportunity to ask new questions with a unique emphasis on how people understand the meaning and nature of their own status within the socioeconomic hierarchy" (p. 285).

Gender Identity Development

Though the idea of gender identity is of course not new, there is new research in this area at present that is starting to investigate gender in a more fluid way than has previously been considered. Harken back to your first developmental psychology course, in which the instructor likely told you about Lawrence Kohlberg (1966) and his definitions of **gender constancy** based on work by famed developmental psychologist Jean Piaget. Many children believe that certain outside characteristics (e.g., long hair, certain clothing) determine a person's gender, and up to a certain age, children believe that this is changeable from moment to moment. In the original studies from Kohlberg, children were asked to look at a child described as a boy, with short hair and gender-stereotypic clothing. When asked what would happen to the gender of this child if they put a dress on him, however, children under the age of 6 or 7 said he would then be a girl. Kohlberg's theory states that at around first or second grade, children begin to understand that their gender does not change based on these types of outside appearances. Today, however, theories and models are being utilized to explain transgender identity development in different ways. Bilodeau (2005) has written about a six-stage model that involves moving from leaving one's connection to a **cisgender** identity behind to developing personal and social **transgender** identities and eventually becoming involved in the transgender community both socially and politically. At some point in the near future, perhaps models that are inclusive of the many ways one can identify with regard to gender may be developed.

Disability Identity Development

Few models exist in this area of identity development, but one that we will highlight here has been developed by researchers Forber-Pratt and Zape (2017). In their model, these researchers emphasize four different developmental statuses, which we will describe briefly here. The term *status* is used specifically here, as it is used in Helms's (1990) model, to denote the fact that individuals may move in and out of various statuses during their lifetime. In addition, each status might be viewed as a sort of continuum, as variation occurs in the experience of each. Finally, this model is inclusive of people who were born with a disability and those who have acquired one during their lifetimes.

The first status noted by Forber-Pratt and Zape (2017) is Acceptance, and this is described as something each of the participants in their qualitative study experienced. This status deals with the level of acceptance and the process of moving toward this as related to their disability. Next is the Relationship status, which focuses on the networks that are built between the individual dealing with a disability and others with disabilities. Forber-Pratt and Zape report that many participants stated that there was "a sense of comfort around health-related and disability-related issues by having these connections and relationships with others" (p. 353). The third status in this model is called Adoption and describes the process of adopting core values regarding disability culture. The researchers describe this as a transition status of sorts, in which an individual dealing with a disability moves from just knowing and interacting with a few others who have disabilities to interacting with the culture in general in a more community-oriented way. Finally, individuals with disabilities may go through the fourth status, Engagement, in which they may offer themselves as role models in the disability community as a part of giving back.

Overall Critique of Stage Models

One thing we would like to note before we leave this section is that many have raised viable criticism about the way in which many identity models employ a stage-by-stage approach to development (Pedrotti, Edwards, & Lopez, 2008). Though this may be the way in which some experience development of identity, it is likely much more "messy" than neatly jumping from stage to stage. An African American in Cross's stage of Identity Acceptance may be catapulted backward when a new Encounter is experienced. A White individual in Helms's model who feels they have achieved Autonomy may not be in this status at all times, but might experience new Disintegration or Reintegration as they encounter new experiences in which racism and their racial identity are brought up.

In addition, as you may have already noted, many of the models end in some sort of ideal "acceptance" stage, in which the individual is depicted as having "resolved" identity conflict. It is unlikely that any of us completely resolve our identity, as new situations and contexts may open our minds to new people, ideas, and relationships to them (Pedrotti et al., 2008). Thus, many today call for a more fluid approach to talking about identity that is neither linear nor ending in a "final" stage. Using the term "statuses" instead of "stages" is one way that several theorists have begun to signify that their models are not meant to be a set of tasks to check off (e.g., Forber-Pratt & Zape, 2017; Helms, 1990). Nevertheless, the stage models presented here can still be viable and helpful in understanding identity if we are not too rigid in the way that we think of people traversing through the stages. Thinking of identity as a dynamic, nonlinear, and continuous process is likely the best way for us to understand what others (and ourselves) are going through with regard to identity development.

INTERSECTIONALITY OF IDENTITY

In 1989 Kimberlé Crenshaw, a Black feminist legal scholar and thinker, coined the term **intersectionality** to describe the fact that looking at the influence of racial identity or gender identity to the exclusion of other facets of identity ignored the combined impact of their intersection. Crenshaw started her now famous paper by quoting from a title used for Black women's studies writings by Gloria Tull (Tull, Scott, & Smith, 1982): "All the Women Are White, All the Blacks Are Men, But Some of Us are Brave." Using this title as an example, Crenshaw (1989) stated, "I have chosen this title as a point of departure in my efforts to develop a Black feminist criticism because it sets forth a problematic consequence of the tendency to treat race and gender as mutually exclusive categories of experience and analysis" (p. 139). In later writings, Crenshaw (1994) and others who engaged in writing about this idea discussed violence toward women and noted that other identities, such as race and class, impacted the type of violence perpetrated and its potential frequency and likelihood. In viewing only one identity of any particular person, we miss a host of other pieces that contribute to that person's experience in the world.

Tibrina Hobson/Contributor/Getty Images

Kimberlé Crenshaw

Beyond the simple fact that we cannot have a close relationship with someone when only thinking of one facet of their personhood, we may also miss the types of experiences that individual may have had in terms of safety, discrimination and oppression. Patricia Collins (2000) speaks to this fact by discussing the multiple forces of oppression that Black women may experience in terms of being subjected to both racial and gender oppression. Today, many other writers have called for more intersectional analysis in terms of multicultural psychology and sociology, among other fields (Moradi & Grzanka, 2017). Efforts to compartmentalize are sometimes levied by individuals who are not as grounded in their personal understanding and awareness of the intersection of their own identities. Consider below, for example, the words of a White woman who is focused on her gender identity but has spent less time thinking about her Whiteness and how she experiences the world:

I was at a women's group at my university the other day. Some of us had organized a time to meet in community to talk about what it was like to be women on our campus. I had envisioned that we could find ways to support one another toward certain types of discrimination that women face, including having a harder time getting promoted and facing issues of sexual harassment and safety. We were very inclusive about who we called together—professors, administrative assistants, people in leadership, custodial workers—the thought was that all of us could be united in our identities as women.

We started by asking some questions of the group, like "What are your experiences as a woman on this campus?" but some of the women started adding in things about how being a woman of color impacted them. Others talked about how being a woman who was in a lower-status role (like that of the custodians) was different. I kept thinking, "No—we're all experiencing sexism. I'm White and the chair of a department, and I still experience sexism just like they do." Finally, one of my colleagues said, "I think we're here to talk about gender, not race." But then I noticed that none of the women of color seemed to contribute after that.

The next meeting, almost no women of color came, and I started to think maybe we were wrong about thinking we could just talk about one piece of our identity. Being White doesn't come up for me very much, so I didn't think race really mattered in this conversation. I'm really grateful that another woman who is also a department chair and who is a person of color asked me out for coffee in the coming weeks and gave me some feedback. She explained that though we may all be experiencing sexism, she also experiences racism at times, and that some of the women who worked in jobs that had less status than ours probably dealt with classism and other discrimination and stereotypes as well. I wasn't thinking about my race because I don't usually have to, but she does. My race actually does impact me, though, in terms of the lack of racism I have to deal with—it's a part of my experience too. I need to think more about that.

—Liz, age 55

As the speaker above notes, if some of our identities are not marginalized (e.g., we come from a high socioeconomic status or a nondisabled status), we may not think much about them in terms of their impact on our daily lives and with regard to things like discrimination or safety concerns we might experience. They do still impact us, as Liz above is starting to realize. Think for a moment about any identities you have that are nonmarginalized. In what ways do they impact your life? How might that be different for someone who has more marginalized identities than you do? In addition, might some marginalized identities be compounded to some extent by other marginalized identities? Take for example the difference in experience between someone who has a disability but is from a high SES versus another person with a disability who struggles more financially. Both may have times when their disabilities (or others' reactions to them) put them in situations that are more difficult for them than for those who do not deal with disabilities. The low-SES person, however, may have a few more obstacles in terms of ability to afford accessibility devices, medical care, or accessible transportation.

Before we leave this topic, we would like to also comment on the way that some people from marginalized groups may experience additional marginalization within their cultural communities. Jordan, who is gay and African American, may experience some racism from non-Black members of his gay community, while also experiencing **heterosexism** from people in his African American community who are not LGBTQ+. We have heard students in our classes voice confusion when someone from a marginalized community marginalizes someone else. "But don't they understand they shouldn't be sexist because they know what racism feels like?" is a common type of question. It is important to understand a few different pieces with regard to this question. First, we can all work to be more culturally competent with individuals and groups who differ from ourselves in some way. Second, no one group has *more* responsibility to understand discrimination. Even if many White people do not experience racism and so may not know what that feels like, it does not give them more leeway to be discriminatory in other ways. And finally, the whole of the experience is greater than the sum of its parts.

BENEFITS OF DEVELOPING A HEALTHY ETHNIC AND RACIAL IDENTITY

Ethnic and racial identity (ERI) development has been studied by many researchers in ethnic and racial minority groups and to some extent in White individuals (often in comparison to minority groups). Several findings point to the fact that developing a strong ERI is a positive developmental stage, particularly in racial and ethnic minority youth. See Table 4.5 for a brief summary of some recent studies in this area.

TABLE 4.5 ⬡ Evidence for Positive Impacts of Healthy ERI	
Latinx Populations	
Piña-Watson, Cruz, Llamas, & López (2018)	Feeling good about one's own ERI is related to positive psychological functioning and positive academic outcomes in youth of Mexican descent.
Williams, Anderson, Francois, Hussain, & Tolan (2014)	ERI is related to lower levels of externalized symptoms (e.g., anger, aggression, delinquent behavior) in Black and Latinx populations.
Bonifacio, Gushue, & Mejia-Smith (2018)	Higher levels of ERI are related to better self-efficacy with regard to career outcomes.
Diaz & Bui (2017)	Positive ERI is related to higher satisfaction with life in Mexican and Mexican American women.
African Americans	
Moses, Villodas, & Villodas (2020)	For Black (but not White) adolescents, ERI is positively correlated with more positive occupational and educational outcomes.
Kyere & Huguley (2018)	ERI predicts positive academic performance.
Mushonga & Henneburger (2019)	ERI is positively correlated with positive mental health.
Ajibade, Hook, Utsey, Davis, & Von Tongeren (2016)	Having a stronger ERI is related to higher satisfaction with life.
Asian Americans	
Kiang, Supple, & Stein (2018)	Higher ERI is related to decreased negative emotions.
Yoo & Lee (2008)	Stronger connection with ERI is related to coping style with regard to single versus multiple racist or discriminatory acts.

Thus ERI may be described as a positive coping strategy for dealing with many different stressors in life, including educational and occupational expectations (Moses et al., 2020) and coping with microaggressions and day-to-day racism (Forrest-Bank & Cuellar, 2018), and in overall positive mental health (Huguley, Wang, Vasquez, & Guo, 2019). This is at times a complicated process to understand. Many studies find that having a higher sense of ERI actually increases one's negative reactions to discrimination or prejudice, particularly if that discrimination occurs multiple times (Yoo & Lee, 2008). This makes sense if we think about it logically: If people do not identify strongly with an ethnic group, they may not feel much of anything when negative associations or prejudice are directed at that group. On the flip side, if people are highly connected to their own ethnic or racial group (i.e., high ERI), they may react strongly and in a negative way to others denigrating their group. This said, there are also many studies that show that in the face of being forced to deal with racism, individuals with strong ERIs are much better able to cope with it. There is even some evidence to say that discrimination leads to stronger coping responses and resilience in some racial and ethnic minority individuals (Fingerhut & Maisel, 2010; Romero, Edwards, Fryberg, & Orduña, 2014). In summary, helping ethnic and racial minority youth to develop a strong and healthy ERI can be beneficial in numerous ways.

Impact of Identity Development on Developing a Diverse Social Circle

Throughout this chapter we have provided you with different models of identity and have explored what it may be like to be at one particular stage or another. For the most part, this discussion has been held from the view of the individual. In this last section we want to talk more about the way identity, and the particular stage in which one resides, may also impact social relationships. Consider, for example, the interaction that might occur between James, who is African American and in the Immersion side of Cross's (1977) Immersion-Emersion continuum, and Scott, who is White American and dealing with the Pseudo-Independence status of Helms's (1990) model:

> ***Scenario:*** Scott wants to be an ally for students of color after a racist incident occurs on their college campus in which the N-word is scrawled

on a university building. He is part of a diverse group of students that wants the president of the university to make some changes. He and James have an altercation about who should be involved in these efforts.

James	Scott
I can't believe these White boys who act like we need their help all of a sudden when something like this happens. We don't need anything from them! They're half the reason things like this happen in this country, and I don't need to spend my time explaining to them what it is like to be Black in the United States. The Black Student Union is working together to take care of this, and we will demand a meeting with the president *now*. We don't need White people getting in our way during that meeting. They can't understand anyway, and I don't want their help. They can never understand what it's like to be me, and we can't trust any of them.	I was trying to help! I can't believe James is so adamant that it should only be the African American students that go to the meeting with the president. They might need people like me there too—I'm not the kind of White person who is going to try to take their power away or anything, but I care about racism too, and I want things to change at this university also! This feels to me like *he* is being racist. He doesn't want me there just because I'm White, and I'm not like other White people—I'm not racist! He shouldn't tell me not to help—he should be thankful for my involvement in this process. Maybe next time I won't volunteer to help at all.

You can see in the above points of view that both men are angry in this scenario, and this anger is coming from their distinct stages within their racial identity development. James, in his stage of Immersion, is idealizing Black identity and at the same time is somewhat negative about interacting with White individuals. This desire to only be in the company of other African Americans is fueling his discomfort and anger with Scott trying to become involved in a process that James feels Scott has no right to. On the other hand, Scott is depicting definitive characteristics in terms of his own Pseudo-Independence identity status. Recall that in this White identity status, White persons do not yet fully connect their own Whiteness with institutional effects of racism and discrimination aimed at non-White individuals. Scott is placing his own desire to help over James's desire for him not to participate. The clear reference Scott makes about James being "racist" shows Scott's lack of understanding of his connection to Whiteness in the United States, regardless of his intention. Consider the different interaction (in the same situation) that might occur between Will, an African American student in Cross's (1971) Internalization stage, and Ben, a White student who understands his identity according to Helms's (1992) Autonomy status at present.

Will	Ben
I've been listening to James and Scott fight about this issue, and I can tell they are in stages where it's really hard to hear each other. I don't want the White students to come to the meeting with the president either, but it's not for the same reasons as James is expressing. I think it's important that the president hears from just the BSU first, before we bring others in. I talked about this with Ben, who is White. Before I explained to him why I wanted it to just be Black students in the first meeting, he just said, "OK—my guess is you have some good reasons. Are there other things that you think would be helpful for someone like me to work on? I have a couple ideas of things I could do in the meantime to keep moving forward, and I can share those first if you want." I really appreciated that trust that he gave me in that moment. I know Ben knows that my experience and his are different, but I am also really glad to have someone like that as a part of the fight against this type of thing. He's willing to use his White privilege to help out where he can, and he doesn't make me come up with a bunch of ideas for him. James wasn't very fair to him, and I'm going to talk with James about that later, but Ben took it in stride. He understands that James is really mad right now, and part of that is making James act like a jerk in some ways, but Ben's willing to give him some leeway while James figures things out, and I would bet that might change James's ideas about him, and maybe other White people, in the future.	I feel for James when I hear some of the things Scott is saying to him, and I'm going to try to talk with Scott later. James isn't being racist the way Scott means it; he just doesn't trust many White people yet, because he hasn't known too many he can trust. I don't think it will always be like that, but that's where he is right now. Sometimes that's hard to be around, but I want James to be able to feel in control in this situation. When Will told me that they wanted it to just be the Black students in the meeting first, I was a little disappointed, because I thought it would be great to share my views with the president too, but I understand that the Black students should have the first choice of how the meeting is worked out. What I want as a White person needs to come second to that for the time being. When I heard Scott was complaining about James being "ungrateful," I cringed—no one needs to be "grateful" for someone doing the right thing. I don't think Scott understands that we don't have less of a responsibility to work against discrimination just because we are White. James said something similar to me about my not "having a place" in this fight—that's because he thinks all White people are the same and most are racist. I know that's not right, but I can see how he might feel like that given his experience. He hasn't been treated well by White people—I know I'm not being racist in this scenario, but I want to let Will and James and all the Black students to know I'm there to back them no matter what they might think of people who look like me.

In this second depiction of points of view, we hope you can see more depth to each side of the picture. Will and Ben are working together, but they are able to better do that than James and Scott because of where they are in their current racial identity development. As noted above, people in these final stages of the model are better able to interact with and get close to people, even when they are different from them.

CONCLUSION

In this chapter we took you through many different models of identity development. Some may resonate for you more than others, and some may be a new way of looking at the question we used at the beginning of this chapter: Who are you? In the following ACT section we offer you some opportunities to think more about your own identity development in a number of different ways and to ask others to tell you more about theirs as well. In thinking more comprehensively about various identities, the products of their intersections, and their impact on people's daily lives, you gain more chances to really *know* those around you and to better *understand* yourself.

ACT: Assess Your Knowledge, Critical Thinking, Take Part

Assess Your Knowledge

In this chapter we learned about racial and other cultural identities using several models and frameworks. First, identify which of the models listed makes the most sense for you racially. If you are White, for example, looking at Helms's model will be appropriate. If you are African American, then Cross's model will make the most sense for you. Sue and Sue's racial/cultural identity development model will work if you are not Black, but still a person of color. (If you are biracial, peek ahead to Chapter 9 for a model that fits you.) Take some time to journal or write your thoughts on the following questions:

- Where are you in your own racial identity development? Think about the various models. Does one resonate for you? How can you tell that you are in this stage?

- What other identities (e.g., gender, sexual orientation, social class, etc.) feel relevant and salient for you at this time in your development? Why is this so? How do you know this about yourself?

- In what stages do you think that others close to you are in terms of their racial identity development? Why do you think this? What does this mean for your own understandings of race in your social circle?

Critical Thinking

Take some time to look over your assessment. How do you think this impacts you in your daily life? Try jotting down some examples of ideas or values you hold about race and ethnicity, or other cultural identity facets. Next, try to trace them to your identity status. Finally, think a bit about where you would like to be in the future. If you are a traditional-aged college student, keep in mind that very few people are at the most advanced stages of racial identity development at your current age. In addition, changes in environment might cause someone to move between stages in a nonlinear fashion. Where were you last year? Where would you like to be next year?

Take Part

Consider taking the following actions based on your current circumstances and feelings.

Participation: This week, pay explicit attention to how your stage of racial identity manifests itself in everyday life. Use a chart or journal to keep track of instances in which this identity comes up for you and is experienced.

Initiation: Have a conversation with someone else you know well about their racial identity development. Utilize dialogue (as opposed to debate) strategies to talk about your perspectives while gaining insight into theirs. Think about ways in which this conversation could be broadened in sphere to have more influence. Are there are other groups you could talk to? Organizations in which you have influence in which the conversation could be raised with a larger purpose?

Activism: Think of your sphere of influence broadly, and work to make change in this group. Move beyond conversation to actual action, which could include changing policies at your internship or work site, or volunteering to present on topics related to race and other social identities that are left out of classes in which you are enrolled. Work to identify other stakeholders and constituents in any groups to which you belong, and ask them to assist you in your efforts. Record or institutionalize your efforts in a meaningful way for others to follow.

iStock/Justinreznick

5

OUR RACIALIZED SOCIAL CONTEXT

Racism, Oppression, and Stereotyping

LEARNING OBJECTIVES

- Articulate impacts of bias in the experience of discrimination of non-White groups in the United States
- Connect historical issues to current issues regarding racism in the United States
- Distinguish between institutional, personally mediated, aversive, and internalized types of racism
- Infer the differential impacts of institutional, personally mediated, and internalized racism
- Explain the different types of microaggressions and their cumulative impact on individuals who experience them
- Distinguish and articulate the impacts of racism on non-White and White people in the United States
- Recognize the importance of talking about race and racism to children and the results of avoiding this conversation
- Assess your own implicit bias and how this might impact your interactions with others and follow up on gaining more awareness, knowledge, and/or skills to decrease these biases

This chapter was perhaps the most difficult one to write in the entire book. One of the reasons the authors felt this is because of the sheer amount of material that must be covered here. Too, talking about stereotypes, racism, oppression, prejudice, and similar concepts is emotionally difficult. You may find it emotionally difficult to read as well. In the following pages we will outline for you some of the major concepts we believe you should learn in regard to this important topic. That said, there is still more to be learned. Dr. Keeanga-Yamahtta Taylor, a Black scholar and author who wrote *From #BlackLivesMatter to Black Liberation,* wrote, "We live in a thoroughly racist society, so it should not be surprising that people have racist ideas. The more important question is under what circumstances those ideas can change" (2016, pp. 212–213). We will begin by discussing stereotypes and bias, leading into how these concepts may often impact people through discrimination, oppression, and prejudice. Next, a thorough discussion of what racism *is* will follow. We finish with a section on how racism is maintained in our society when we ignore its impact or its import, and some suggestions that attempt to answer Dr. Taylor's question in her quote above regarding how changes to our historical silence on racism might through dialogue lead to changes in ideas as well.

STEREOTYPES

A simple definition of the term **stereotype** is this: a belief that one holds and applies to all members of a group. This usually occurs in characterizing groups that one does not belong to, though some common beliefs that are positive may also be held about one's own ingroup (Bigler & Liben, 2007). Nevertheless, much research to date shows that individuals can see much more variation within their own group than they see in other groups (Park & Hastie, 1987; Young, Hugenberg, Bernstein, & Sacco, 2012). Put plainly, we each have a tendency to think, "I am unique, as are many in my group despite some similarities amongst us, but you and your group are all the same." Many studies have been conducted on what stereotypes are and what purposes they serve. McGarty, Yzerbyt and Spears (2002) have organized the findings from these many theoretical thoughts and empirical findings to fall into three categories.

First, stereotypes may help with explaining why groups should be catalogued as different from one another. In this category, researchers have pointed to the fact that groups may look for reasons to show why someone is not a part of their group, or why someone is. Stereotypes, which rely on beliefs that apply to all members, attempt to make solid distinctions to establish easy reasons for differences. In the second category of findings, stereotypes are thought to exist because of the time- and energy-saving benefits they bring to those that use them. Gordon Allport (1954) was a strong proponent of this explanation for stereotypes, noting that being able to categorize people reduces effort needed to be taken on the part of the person survey-ing the situation. Perhaps particularly in our current time and culture, where things move fast and busyness is almost a requirement, we may use stereotypes in part to categorize people efficiently. As Allport noted, this may even have some evolutionary benefit for us. (Taking time to make sure your view of a hungry saber tooth tiger isn't based on bias might not be the smartest plan!) Third, McGarty and colleagues (2002) note that stereotypes may be similar to norms in that they generally fall in line with the beliefs of the group. Thus endorsement of stereotypes might galvanize a group to some extent (Allport, 1954).

Stereotypes can take many forms and may be held with regard to what seem to be positive traits. For example, you may have heard others say, "African Americans are better athletes than White Americans," or "Asian Americans are the best at math." Though these statements appear to affirm a positive trait in an underrepresented group, the use of such stereotypes is nevertheless negative overall, as it reduces the group's heterogeneity in possessing a particular trait (Schneider, Major, Luhtanen, & Crocker, 1996). Too, we must realize that to say a particular skill or ability is inherent in a racial group removes any hard work the person has done to achieve that ability. Consider the following vignette:

> I spent most of my elementary school years struggling with math. I was much more in my element writing or analyzing literature, but math just didn't make much sense to me. What made it worse is that while no one explicitly said, "Why aren't you *good* at this—you're Asian?!" I knew others thought that sometimes. When almost every Asian actor on TV is playing a scientist or math whiz of some kind, people get the idea that we're just good at that kind of thing. Well, I worked hard and my parents found me tutors in junior high, and by the time I had gotten to high school, I understood most of the concepts I needed to get decent grades in math classes. I remember one time being in a group of students in a math class, and all of us were struggling over a particular problem, and the teacher came over to praise our group for working hard. He said to our group, "I know this is hard for you, but it speaks well for you that you're working so hard to get the answer! Well, except you, Chase—this is probably easy for you, right?" The teacher and everyone else in the group was White. I felt like he took all my hard work away with that statement. I was trying just as hard as everyone else, but he thought it just came naturally to me.

—Chase, age 17

If we believe, for example, the stereotype that math comes easily to Asian people, we may rank a White person who is talented at math as more impressive than an Asian person who is also talented at math, as was shown in this vignette. Or we may hold

Asian people to a higher standard, because we believe they should be better at that subject. In either case, the stereotype causes an inaccurate perception of Asian people and diminishes them to a single trait.

Though we may not even realize it, we may make many decisions about others based on stereotypes on a regular basis, unless we are consciously making efforts to reject them. That said, this form of simplification obviously does not always lead us to a correct decision. As McGarty and colleagues (2002) state, "Stereotypes are not so much aids to understanding, but aids to misunderstanding" (p. 4). As with anything, such oversimplification often leads to making more errors than correct judgments. In some ways, one might think that the types of mistakes that stereotyping leads to might turn us from using them. There are, however, other powerful reasons at play that may keep them in use. Some research has shown that stereotyping other groups in a negative way can make us feel better about the group to which we belong (Allport, 1954; Bigler & Liben, 2007; McGarty et al., 2002). This self-enhancement function of stereotyping may lead us toward using stereotypes when they are available. Second, and perhaps most relevant to our discussion in this chapter, stereotypes can also help us to justify systems that are already in place in order to maintain the status quo (Crandall, Bahns, Warner, & Schaller, 2011; McGarty et al., 2002). As Crandall and colleagues note, "As knowledge, stereotypes represent the world; as justifications stereotypes *explain* the world" (p. 1488). Stereotypes in this way can fill in the blanks for individuals as to why certain people are treated the way they are without having to challenge the system. In sum, stereotypes are often kept in place by all of these different purposes: They make things easier for an observer, they help us to feel better about our own group, and they remove the need for change (Crandall et al., 2011). Thus, we are often motivated to, however unconsciously, work to maintain them.

Think for a moment of a potentially familiar scene that you may encounter while driving that may trigger the use of stereotypes. You are driving behind someone who is driving slower than the traffic around them, stops often, and seems unsure of where they are going. After a few minutes of frustration, you may start to make some assumptions about who the driver might be. Soon, you are able to pull past them and take a look at the driver before you drive on, expecting perhaps to see an elderly driver. "I thought so," you say to yourself when indeed the driver is elderly,

"Older people shouldn't be driving after a certain age!" Many who are reading these words have made this assumption. After all, a well-known stereotype of older drivers is that they are not as competent behind the wheel. Compounding this stereotype is the "data" you collected when passing the driver: They were indeed elderly and so fit your stereotype. Sometimes this type of data collection causes people to make the statement that "some stereotypes are true."

Now, let's take a step back from this situation for a minute. As you likely have some knowledge of psychology if you are reading this book, an assumption might be made that you are also familiar with the scientific method and have some understanding of research as well. Think back to what you know about hypotheses and data collection. If you only "collect data" (i.e., check to see if the driver is older) when there is a poor driver in front of you, you are not collecting this data in an unbiased way. Unless you check every good driver to see if they are elderly as well, there is no way to make a statement like, "Most elderly people are poor drivers." This phenomenon of only paying attention to a result if it fits a stereotype you already hold is called **confirmatory bias** (Heppner, Wampold, Tao, Wang, & Thompson, 2015). This type of bias may also drive us to have less memory of data that does not fit our original hypothesis, further compounding the maintenance of stereotypes. Though it may be tempting to give in to the belief that stereotypes are "true," this idea is not reached with any scientific backing; it seems merely to stem from our desire to continue reliance on stereotypes like this.

We would like to take this space to also introduce a few more concepts that are important to understanding stereotypes and their impacts. **Bias** is one such concept that is important to this discussion. There are many types of bias, but in relation to our discussion here, this term might be best defined as a preference for (or an avoidance of) a particular group based on a belief. In thinking of how bias may impact our daily lives and our potential interactions with other cultural groups, we might consider it to be "a tendency to think, act, or feel in a particular way" (Hays, 2017, p. 23). Bias is not always something overt; instead it may manifest as an **implicit bias** resulting in favoritism or avoidance of something in a seemingly more unconscious way. Though many people may not overtly report having bias toward or against a particular group, they may still act or feel in ways that are related to biases they hold (Lee,

Lindquist, & Payne, 2018). In several studies, participants who report no negative feelings toward other groups may give biased answers on measures that elicit more automatic responses about these groups (Dovidio, Kawakami, & Gaertner, 2002; Lee et al., 2018). Both explicit and implicit bias can lead to **discrimination,** or treatment that stems from prejudice or bias about another group.

One way in which discrimination has impacted people of color in our country is via the laws and limits put upon non-White groups throughout history that have led to **oppression** of these groups. Oppression is defined in sociological terms as occurring when a group in power exerts that

iStock/pzAxe

Marilyn Frye describes oppression as a birdcage

power over another group in such a way as to benefit themselves and exploit and abuse the other (Cudd, 2013). Marilyn Frye, feminist theorist and philosophy professor from Michigan State University, describes oppression as a birdcage:

> The experience of oppressed people is that the living of one's life is confined and shaped by forces and barriers which are not accidental or occasional and hence avoidable, but which are systemically related to one another in such a way as to catch one between and among them and restrict or penalize motion in any direction. It is the experience of being caged in.

Consider a birdcage. If you look very closely at just one wire in the cage, you cannot see the other wires. If your conception of what is before you is determined by this myopic focus, you could look at that one wire, up and down the length of it, and be unable to see why a bird would not just fly around

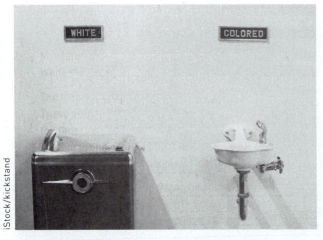

iStock/kickstand

Jim Crow era signs for water fountains

the wire any time it wanted to go somewhere. . . . It is only when you step back, stop looking at the wires one by one . . . and take a macroscopic view of the whole cage, that you can see why the bird does not go anywhere; and then you will see it in a moment. . . . It is perfectly *obvious* that the bird is surrounded by a network of systematically related barriers, no one of which would be the least hindrance to its flight, but which, by their relations to each other, are as confining as the solid walls of a dungeon. (Frye, 1983, p. 12)

A historical example of oppression that is easy to recognize is that of the enslavement of Africans brought to the United States and physically kept captive against their will. But even as this type of slavery waned, oppression still existed via Jim Crow laws preventing African Americans from using public bathrooms, taking public transit, or sitting at a lunch counter in a way that was equal to that of White Americans. Today, we may feel that this oppression has gone away, but it exists still in the way African American and other people of color are treated by the media, by the police at times, and by their own neighbors. Many of these topics will be discussed in more detail in future chapters, but we note them here to make clear the ways that discrimination and prejudice have oppressed people of color throughout our country's history.

RACISM

We now turn to the concept of racism, and we will focus on this topic in its many forms for the rest of this chapter. *Racism* is a difficult word for many people to use or hear. You can tell this when this word is brought up in conversation and debate often ensues regarding "Was it *really* racism?" One reason that this word is difficult for many people is likely due to the fact that it evokes such a negative feeling—we know that *racism* is a "bad word." Another reason for this difficulty is likely that people use this word in different ways and to mean different things. To combat this confusion, we will spend some time here talking about the different ways racism might be mediated in today's environment, and we will talk next about different types of racism. One final thought: The word *racism* is one of the most emotionally charged words used in society. For some, hearing the word makes them think of ways that they or members of their group have been treated either now or in the past. For others the word brings embarrassment or anger that they are part of a group who has enacted racism upon other groups now and throughout history. We would ask you to try to read this section carefully and to note the research and experiences detailed here. At the end of the chapter, we'll finish with some ways to combat some of these feelings and to use them to fuel your own self-development.

Racism in Action: Definitions

Put simply to be **racist** means to take race into account and to use it to make decisions about people that may result in different outcomes for different racial groups. This is a general description; however, Dr. Camara Phyllis Jones (2000) presents a framework with three levels for understanding the implications of racism in its different forms. At the highest level of impact is **institutionalized racism**, described by Jones as "differential access to the goods, services, and opportunities of society by race" (p. 1212). Institutionalized racism occurs within the structure of society and is maintained by social norms and also by legalized practices at times.

A very clear example of institutionalized racism is found in the fact that laws existed that prevented African American men from voting until the Fifteenth Amendment was ratified in 1870. (Women were still not allowed to vote until the Nineteenth Amendment was passed in 1920.) In this way, African Americans were forcibly prevented from having a voice in all decisions, from choosing the leaders of our country to deciding which schools their children were allowed to attend. This occurred from the time the first slave ships landed on North American soil in 1619 and they were disenfranchised for over two centuries in this way. Some might think that with the signing of the Fifteenth Amendment, this racism ended; however, institutionalized racism continued to prevent many African Americans from voting for decades after this time. Because of tactics that ranged from making specific requirements of Black voters (e.g., requiring proof of the ability to read and understand the Constitution before being allowed to vote, though this was not a requirement of White individuals), to preventing them from registering to vote through violence and scare tactics, a majority of African Americans were not registered to vote, particularly within the southern states. This continued until the passage of the Voting Rights Act in 1965 outlawed the reading tests and poll taxes that often kept African American would-be voters away from polling locations.

Even today, there are practices that make it more difficult for individuals from certain racial groups to vote. One of the original provisions of the Voting Rights Act included requirement of federal oversight before any changes were made in voting areas in which less than 50% of the non-White population was not registered to vote. This provision was to make sure that race was not a determinant of ability to register. In 2013, however, this part of the Voting Rights Act was struck down, which allowed changes to be made that might impact non-White voters, such as moving polling locations far away from neighborhoods that have many African American residents. Today Black voters, on average, wait twice as long to vote at the polls in comparison to their White counterparts (Overton & Sotto, 2016). Thus, though the laws that explicitly prevented Black Americans from voting are gone, institutionalized practices and racism keep this type of differential access to voting alive and well.

The next level of racism discussed by Jones (2000) is **personally mediated racism**, which is also sometimes called **personal racism**. This type of racism occurs as prejudice and discrimination are enacted on the basis of race. Examples of personally mediated racism include incidences in which people are unwilling to hire people of a different race from their own because of their belief that other races are not as intelligent as they are or are lacking in some other way. Personally mediated racism can be either intentional (as in the example above) or unintentional. Jones gives many examples of ways in which

iStock/adamkaz

Black voters

personally mediated racism manifests itself, including people with brown skin being watched more closely by shopkeepers in stores, or everyday avoidance such as crossing the street or holding one's purse or wallet more tightly when seeing a Black person coming one's way. Of course there are more obvious ways, such as the commission of hate crimes against racial and ethnic minorities. Other ways that personally mediated racism manifests might be less overt, as is described in the vignette that follows:

> *I'm a guidance counselor at the high school, and sometimes I feel like certain students just don't have what it takes to follow particular careers even if they want to, for example, when the Hispanic kids come in and want to be doctors or engineers or something. I mean realistically they probably don't even have enough money to go to college, much less to get the type of education they'd need for those types of jobs. I mean how many Hispanic engineers do you even see out there? I try to steer them toward jobs that are more reasonable for them or talk them into the vocational schools. Maybe they want to work as a social worker—they might have experience with that job growing up because of home situations, or just forget college all together and learn a trade. I think it's kind of cruel to set them up to fail, so I just try to steer them away from those more difficult jobs.*
>
> —Bill, age 55

The above example is clearly based on beliefs about what can be accomplished based on one's racial background, and it confounds race with socioeconomic status and other factors (e.g., negative family situation), but it is being framed by the perpetrator as a kindness. Omitting options for some but not all based on assumptions about a racial group is also personally mediated racism.

Sometimes personally mediated racism can lead to institutionalized racism. Considering the scenario above, if this guidance counselor does this to all of his Latinx students, he may effectively keep information from a larger percentage of them that may impact their ability to get into college in the first place, much less to pursue the types of degrees being discussed, which may require more information prior to application. Though some of these Latinx students may be able to recognize this as racism or be able to gain this information elsewhere, a percentage may not recognize that this is happening due to race, and they may follow the guidance counselor's advice or have decreased self-confidence in their ability to succeed. If many people have these ideas about Latinx students, and at least some of those people are counselors or teachers or others who might influence these decisions about college, what starts out as personally mediated racism may effectively prevent more Latinx individuals from attending college in the long run, and thus may prevent more of this population from getting high-level jobs. The reality is that this type of personally mediated racism is still occurring all across our country and is a part of the maintenance of institutionalized racism. As institutionalized racism is structural and thus is often not able to be seen as clearly as other types of discrimination (Jones, 2000), it is both insidious and far reaching.

We would like to make one other final point on these two types of racism before moving on to other types in Jones's (2000) model. This point addresses the populations that can be affected by both personally mediated and institutionalized racism. Because personally mediated racism can be applied at many different levels, some have posited that this type of racism can be conducted and felt by people of any race. An African American business owner, for example, may decide not to hire any White workers in her organization. Though this may impact individual White workers who could otherwise work for her, it is much less impactful on the White race as a whole than having a White business owner decide not to hire any African Americans. Even if all Black business owners in the United States used this type of personally mediated racism to keep Whites out of their organizations, they would likely still have very little impact overall on White economic progress or unemployment in any meaningful way. First of all, there are not enough Black business owners to impact a very large number of White workers. In 2016, the percentage of businesses in the United States that were owned by Whites was approximately 81% (Kenney, 2016). In addition to this being a large majority of the businesses, it also means that White workers could just apply to any of these businesses and avoid this personally mediated racism. There would of course not be the same level of accessibility to a Black worker in the same situation.

Thus, personally mediated racism may be perpetrated by people other than White individuals, may impact White people individually from time to time, and may *feel* the same to the individual when it occurs, but it does not lead to institutionalized racism when conducted by non-White individuals, and thus has less of an impact at the macro level. Consider the scenario above in reverse, however. If even some of the White business owners adopt this same personally mediated racist practice against African Americans, this could impact a very large portion of the African American population, as there would be relatively few businesses who would hire them. This could then have the potential to affect both unemployment rates and socioeconomic status of the African American population as a whole, and thus it has more potential to lead to institutionalized and structural damage.

Some might argue that this could have impact in areas that are heavily African American, but again, due to the fact that the African American population within the United States is only 13.4% (US Census Bureau, 2020), White individuals could likely always find a way around this type of personally mediated racism before it turned institutional in any way. Thus, institutionalized racism must be backed by the institution, and in the United States the controlling members of the institution (e.g., the government) are overwhelmingly White, meaning institutionalized racism may only be perpetrated against non-White individuals. Sometimes perceived discrimination against people who are White is referred to as **reverse racism**. This is actually a misnomer, however. If White people are discriminated against because of race in a personal interaction, this is still just plain old racism. Again, this is not racism on an institutional level but could be termed personally mediated racism in some cases.

Finally, in Jones's (2000) model is the concept of **internalized racism**. This type of racism is described by Jones as

> the acceptance by members of the stigmatized [non-White] races of negative messages about their own abilities and intrinsic worth. It is characterized by their not believing in others who look like them. . . . It involves accepting limitations to one's own full humanity. (p. 1213)

Common examples of internalized racism include practices such as African American women straightening their hair to look more like the hair of White women, or the use of bleaching creams by many dark-skinned races to lighten their skin. Others might include Asian persons changing their non-English names in favor of names that are "easier to say," or not speaking a heritage language so as not to stick out. Sue and Sue (2016) describe internalized racism as "racial self-hatred, in which people dislike themselves for being Asian, Black, Hispanic, or Native American" (p. 369). When one is surrounded by messages from the media, from stereotyping, and pseudoscience telling them that their race is inferior in some way, one might feel they have little choice but to believe it. This is the reason that Sue and Sue (2016) call this type of racism "the most damning indictment of White racism" (p. 367).

One of the more famous studies detailing the impact of internalized racism is that of Clark and Clark (1947), which was instrumental in ending segregation in schools in the landmark court case *Brown v. Board of Education, Topeka* (347 U.S. 483, 1954). Mamie and Kenneth Clark were a married, African American couple who worked as a team of psychologists to investigate racial identity development in African American children. In their groundbreaking 1947 study, the Clarks tested 253 African American children ages 3 to 7 by asking them a series of questions regarding two dolls. The dolls were identical to one another except for skin color. One had black hair and brown skin, and the other had yellow hair and white skin, and both were clothed only in a cloth diaper. The questions asked of the children are presented in Table 5.1.

The results were shocking to many people at the time, and yet they were reflective of the way African Americans were treated at this time in our country. The majority of the African American participants at every age level chose the White doll as the one with which they would prefer to play, as the nice doll, and the nice color, and this was true regardless of age and regardless of skin color (light, medium, or dark) of the child (Clark & Clark, 1947). To see if these preferences for Whiteness existed in both northern and southern regions of the country, Clark and Clark separated the results this way as well, but found that the preference for the White doll existed in both regions. Clark and Clark asked Questions 5 to 8 (see Table 5.1) to see if children chose based on the racial category of the dolls, as opposed to choosing based on something else. They found that almost all children correctly labeled the dolls as "White," "Colored," and "Negro" in all age groups, with increasing percentages labeling correctly from three years old (77% correctly labeled the doll as White or Colored) to seven years old (100% correctly labeled the doll as White or Colored). The label of "Negro" was slightly less known to the children, though a similar pattern was found (correct label of doll as Negro ranged from 55% in the three-year-olds to 85% in the seven-year-olds). Last, most children correctly identified themselves as looking like the brown

TABLE 5.1 ● Questions Asked of African American Children in the Famous Clark and Clark (1947) "Doll Test"	
1	Give me the doll that you like to play with.
2	Give me the doll that is a nice doll.
3	Give me the doll that looks bad.
4	Give me the doll that is a nice color.
5	Give me the doll that looks like a White child.
6	Give me the doll that looks like a Colored child.
7	Give me the doll that looks like a Negro child.
8	Give me the doll that looks like you.

Source: Author created. Info from: Clark, K. B., & Clark, M. P. (1947). Racial identification and preference in Negro children. In E. L. Hartley (Ed.) *Readings in Social Psychology.* New York: Holt, Rinehart, and Winston.

doll (Question 8), though some variation existed with regard to the skin tone of the individual child. (Those with light skin tone were more likely to choose the white doll.)

We want to remind you that all of the children in this study were African American, so it was not a choice of children choosing their own race as nice or good. Instead, it was African American children choosing White as better in several ways in comparison to their own race. These results provide a number of implications for African American children in the United States. As young as age three, the children in this study showed preference for White skin in terms of who they would like to play with and in terms of internal characteristics of the child (e.g., who looks bad, who looks nice). Let that sink in for a minute. What might it be like for a child with brown skin to "know" that White skin is better and to prefer it in terms of making decisions about internal characteristics? How might that impact one's own self-esteem and identification? And how might that impact relationships within the African American community as a whole? Note, these children were not asked, "Which do *others* think is nice (or bad, or a nice color)?"

These studies were a linchpin in the case against school segregation, *Brown v. Board of Education,* that took place in 1953. In this case, proponents of desegregation of schools argued that keeping races apart was causing feelings of inferiority to be lodged in the minds of African American children. Chief Justice Earl Warren, a Supreme Court justice who was part of the case, noted that desegregation must occur, because to separate [African American children] from others of similar age and qualifications solely because of their race generates a feeling of inferiority as to their status in the community that may affect their hearts and minds in a way unlikely to ever be undone. (Order of Argument, 2016, para. 6)

You may be thinking that these results would not be found today, based on different norms that likely exist in the country today as compared to 1947. However, recent studies have been conducted that appear to mirror the responses of these original African American participants. In 2005, Kiri Davis, an African American high school student from Harlem, created a documentary titled "A Girl Like Me," in which she recreated the original Clark and Clark (1947) study with preschoolers living in Harlem. Of the 21 African American children she surveyed, 15 preferred the white doll over the brown doll. In addition, a professor at the University of Chicago, Margaret Beale Spencer ("Study: White and Black Children Biased," 2010), conducted a pilot study with early- and middle-childhood-aged participants (some African American and some White) in 2010 as a part of a CNN series on race in the United States and recreated parts of the Clark and Clark study, using a series of pictures of children with six skin tones that varied from light to dark. Spencer and her team and found that 50% of her sample of African American children, and just over 75% of her sample of White children, chose the two darkest skin tones in response to the directive, "Show me the dumb child." Similarly, 37.5% of Black children and 62.5% of White children in the study chose the two lightest skin tones in response to the question, "Show me the nice child," while approximately 57% of Black children and 65.5% of White children chose the two darkest skin tones for the directive "Show me the mean child." Thus, some variations occurred in this study in comparison to the original Clark and Clark study, but these results provide evidence for the idea that there are still many African American children who prefer Whiteness over their own skin color and associate more positive characteristics with White children in general.

Choosing white skin over one's own brown skin is the epitome of internalized racism and may lead to a myriad of other problems with regard to racial identity, as detailed more clearly in Chapter 4. The fact that this preference still exists for many African American children today shows that we may not have come as far as we would like to think since the original study was conducted over 70 years ago. This type of racism, as well as institutionalized and personally mediated racism, continues to pose a threat to African American children (as well as to people from other non-White groups) in the United States. (See Figure 5.1 for definitions of racism.)

Types of Racism: Overt, Covert, and Aversive Racism

Different types of racism also exist in terms of the way they are enacted, and this is potentially part of the reason that different people disagree on what racism actually "is." **Overt racism** may be the category with which most are most familiar. This type of racism can be illustrated with examples such as the Ku Klux Klan, use of racial slurs, and other overt discrimination that is done intentionally. In the past, this type of racism was both visible and rampant in our country. Perhaps one of the best examples of this type of racism is told by the story of Emmett Till. Emmett was a 14-year-old African American boy who was murdered by a lynch mob in 1955 after Carolyn Bryant, a White woman, told her husband that Emmett had offended her in some way. Some reports say that Emmett whistled at Carolyn, others state that he squeezed her hand or groped her in some way, while some allege "attempted rape."

FIGURE 5.1 ◗ Examples of Institutionalized, Personally Mediated, and Internalized Racism		
Institutionalized Racism	**Personally Mediated Racism**	**Internalized Racism**
• Redlining practices of banks and mortgages lenders, in which loans are given only to White applicants	• A shopkeeper watching people of color more closely in their store because of suspicion of potential stealing	• A person of color supporting colorblindness as a reasonable position
• Internment of Japanese Americans during World War II	• A parent not wanting their children to marry someone of a different race	• A Japanese American person explaining the internment camps as a necessary evil
• Using standardized tests as the primary way to enter higher education, despite issues related to stereotype threat	• A teacher not offering opportunities to all students because of their beliefs about the abilities of some	• People of color expecting other people of color to act in ways that assimilate to White culture
• Enacting laws or practices against some groups that prevent them from realizing their civil rights, including slavery and the lack of voting rights, but also the policing of Black and brown people at different rates than White people)	• Telling (or laughing at) racist jokes	• A person of color ascribing to the American Dream worldview that all have equal chances at success in the United States

Recently, some 60 years later, Carolyn Bryant (now Carolyn Bryant Donham) who is still alive, has recanted her testimony in this case, saying, "Nothing that boy did could ever justify what happened to him" (Tyson, 2017, p. 7). Today, it is clear that no assault ever occurred (Tyson, 2017). This is, of course, but one story of many that occurred at this time, but it makes the murder of this child no less horrifying.

Some have said that overt racism is no longer as common in today's society within the United States; however, many would argue that this is not the case. The White nationalist riot in Charlottesville, Virginia, in 2017, and the racially motivated shooting of nine African American people at a church in Charleston in 2016, are both examples of overt racism. It is not particularly useful to think of overt racism as in the past, as it may make invalidation of accounts of racism occur. Though it is difficult for all of us to think of the pain this type of racism causes those that bear its brunt, bearing witness and listening to those who recount it is part of the solution to ending overt racism in our nation.

A second type of racism often discussed is **covert racism**. Covert racism involves actions, beliefs, or emotions that are predicated on stereotypes or other types of discrimination, but covert racism is at times harder to define upfront as racism. Often there are other potential explanations for the behaviors labeled as racism, and thus defining them as racism is sometimes called into question. Covert racism can be intentional or unintentional (Ridley, 1989). Intentional covert racism is racism that occurs in scenarios in which the persons perpetrating racist acts know they are doing it because of race, but are trying to pretend that it is not due to racism. An example of this type of racism might be one in which parents try to prevent their children from dating people of other races by making excuses about other characteristics of the potential mates ("they just seem different from us"), when they are really opposed to the interracial nature of the union. In short, *intentional* covert racism is purely overt racism kept under wraps, often because of fear of revealing racist viewpoints.

Examples of *unintentional* covert racism are also still very common in today's society and are often rejected as "actual racism" by those called out on these acts. As one example, consider two news reports from 2015 regarding the arrest of three White men for burglary compared with the arrest of four Black men for the same type of crime. In each news story, pictures of the arrested men in the two different burglaries were included. Though the stories were about the same crime, and reported by the same news source posted on the same day, the pictures and headlines differ sharply. In the report about the White burglary charges, the three suspects were pictured with their school yearbook photos, dressed nicely in suits and ties. In addition, the headline refers to their status as student athletes, reading "Three University of Iowa Wrestlers Arrested. Burglary Charges Pending." In the article about the burglary in which Black suspects were arrested, the men are shown with their mugshots with the headline "Coralville Police Arrest Four in Burglary Investigation." Viewers complained about the differential treatment of the reports, saying that race had been a factor in the way the suspects were pictured and the way the headlines were written. Some argued back that this was not racism, because it was likely the African American men were not in college and so did not have readily available college pictures. Regardless of this potential explanation, since all seven men had already been arrested, one type of picture did exist for all seven of them: mug shots. The station released a statement saying that the men were processed at different jails and that mug shots were not easily available from the jail at which the White men were processed. The question remains, "Does this matter?" Reporting in such a way as to make Black men appear dangerous and criminal, while White men accused of the same crime are made to look adolescent and respectable, furthers racial stereotypes in our country whether intentional or not.

One type of covert racism that has been studied extensively by social psychologist Dr. John Dovidio from Yale University is termed **aversive racism**. This type of racism was first defined by Kovel in 1970 and is described by Dovidio and colleagues as "a subtle, often unintentional form of bias that characterizes many White Americans who possess strong egalitarian views and believe they are nonprejudiced" (Dovidio, Gaertner, Kawakami, & Hodson, 2002, p. 90). Dovidio and his colleagues note that this type of racism is difficult for individuals to accept, because it conflicts so strongly with their view of themselves. As Dovidio et al. (2002) note, "In contrast to the feelings of open hostility and clear dislike of Blacks, the negative feelings that aversive racists experience are typically more diffuse such as feelings of anxiety or unease" (p. 90). This type of racism most often occurs when aversive racists can convince themselves that there is another reason that they are acting in a way that can be perceived as racist.

In one study conducted by Dovidio (1999), White college students were paired with Black partners and asked to complete a task that required teamwork. Prior to being paired up, the White college students were administered a self-report inventory regarding their racial attitudes. Response sets were divided into three groups: (1) Nonprejudiced Whites: those who were low in racial prejudice attitudes and found to be unbiased on an implicit bias measure; (2) White aversive racists: those who reported low prejudice on the self-report scale but exhibited racially biased attitudes on the implicit bias scale; and (3) prejudiced Whites: those who endorsed prejudicial attitudes on the self-report scale and were also found to be racially biased on the implicit bias scale. Results showed that when the teamwork task was timed, the White individuals in the pairs that finished the task first were from Group 1, with an average completion time of 4 minutes and 35 seconds. The pairs with White members from this group also reported the most satisfaction in completing the task as compared to those with White partners from Groups 2 and 3. Interestingly, the pairs that finished second quickest were those with White members from Group 3, the group described as prejudiced Whites, who finished in an average of 5 minutes and 45 seconds. The pairs who had White partners from Group 2 (those described as White aversive racists), however, took a full 6 minutes and 10 seconds, on average, to complete the task.

In other measures given as a part of this study, Black partners also rated these aversive racist Whites as less trustworthy than either the nonprejudiced Whites or the prejudiced Whites (Dovidio, 2001). Thus, even when the racism harbored by White persons might be denied overtly, their implicit and covert racism may impact their relationships with non-White individuals, such that it makes them seem less trustworthy than a White person who is openly prejudiced. To make implications even more broad, Dovidio (1999) posits that it is likely that there are many more aversively racist Whites than there are members of either of the other two groups. This was borne out in his sample (40% of the sample was defined by the measures as aversively racist), and these figures may be indicative of the population at large.

Think for a moment what this might mean. In another article about the topic of aversive racism, Dovidio et al. (2002) asks the reader to imagine a company that employs 100 people. For simplicity's sake, this company is described as having 15% Black workers (close to the percentage of African Americans in the United States today), and 85% White workers. The tasks at this imaginary company are completed by pairs of workers and timed for efficiency. Dovidio then asks a series of questions.

First, if a worker is White, what race is their partner most likely to be? The answer, based on probability, would be White. Second, if a worker is Black, what race is their partner likely to be? Again, based on the numbers in the company, the answer is White. In thinking about Dovidio's hypothesis of the most common type of White person (nonprejudiced, prejudiced, or aversive racist), what type of White person is most likely to be the partner of a worker of any race? The answer would be an aversive racist White person, again based on probability due to numbers.

Now Dovidio makes his point. If a worker is Black, the worker is most commonly paired with a White aversively racist partner, and it follows from the study above that this pairing results in the least efficient work. When it comes time to assess work, it may thus appear that when a Black worker joins a partnership, the efficiency goes down. In this example, it is not the fault of the Black person that the efficiency goes down; instead it is a result of the aversive racism of the White person. But this is hidden in the depths of this situation, and other more stereotype-confirming answers are available. So it is likely that the Black workers will unfairly pay the price for this lack of efficiency. When promotions are given, who is most likely to get one? Likely those in the most efficient partnerships (those that are White/White, or non–aversive racist White/Black). Thus, fewer chances exist for Black workers to have these promotions, because they have fewer chances to be in productive partnerships. What's more, the boss handing out these promotions has "hard data" to show that efficiency is lacking when Black members join the group, but that when they are not present, the efficiency likely goes back to normal. In this way, Dovidio describes the most insidious nature of aversive racism.

Microaggressions

Microaggressions are an example of racism that is often covert and unintentional, though they can also be overt and intentional. In 2008, psychologist Derald Wing Sue built a theory upon Chester Pierce's (1978) notion of microaggressions, which are defined by Sue and colleagues as "brief and commonplace daily verbal and behavioral indignities . . . that communicate hostile, derogatory, or negative racial slights and insults" (Sue, Capodilupo, & Holder, 2007 p. 329). Microaggressions will be discussed in more detail in Chapter 8, but we would like to introduce the idea here briefly. There are three types of microaggressions in Sue's theory: microassaults (intentional acts of racism aimed at a particular group), microinsults (comments, actions, and behaviors that are generally not intended as insults but appear to rely on stereotypes, communicate surprise at the accomplishments of people who are not part of the dominant culture, or exhibit rudeness in discussing these groups), and microinvalidations (situations in which a dominant culture person invalidates the experience of another involving a microinsult or other action) (see Figure 5.2).

We will revisit this topic more in a subsequent chapter and give more examples, but one final point must be made here. Often someone who engages in either microinsults or microinvalidations is surprised when someone responds negatively to them in these scenarios, and that is usually because it is not their intention to insult or invalidate the person to whom they are speaking. One reaction is to become defensive, because they didn't mean to upset the person they are offending. While it is understandable that someone might feel frustrated that their intention is not appreciated, it is also important to recognize that intent may be different from impact. One of the authors (JTP) is a mother to three young children, and she often hears statements from them such as "But I didn't *mean* to hit him!" in response to

FIGURE 5.2 ● Types of Microaggressions		
	Microassault	**Microinsult**	**Microinvalidation**
Definition:	An intentional act of racism (or other –ism) aimed at a particular group.	Comments, actions, and behaviors that are generally unintentional but communicate surprise at positive attributes of nonmajority groups and/or exhibit rudeness or exclusion in discussing nonmajority groups.	Comments and actions that appear to doubt the validity of accounts of racism (and other –isms) and/or reduce the recipient's reaction to these as unreasonable or too emotional.
Example:	A decision made not to hire Latinx people in a company because of a belief that they are not as intelligent as Whites.	To an Asian American: "Well, of course *you're* good at math!" To an African American: "I'm sure you must be the first in your family to move out of the ghetto."	Comments such as, "I'm sure the store owner wasn't following you around the store to see if you'd steal something. She probably wanted to help you." "I've gotten pulled over by the police when I wasn't really speeding too. They do that to everyone. I think you're being too sensitive."

one sibling accidentally hurting another. Her response is often, "But it *still* hurt." This is an analogy we can use in thinking about microaggressions and intent and impact. Even if one is not intending to cause harm or to offend, the impact may be that they did just that.

RACISM: IMPACTS, MAINTENANCE, AND EDUCATION

In this next section, we would like to cover several topics about racism in terms of how it is learned and maintained, how it impacts others, and how we can educate others about this. You have made a decision to learn more about this topic via your choosing to pick up this book, and we hope you will in turn think about ways you can share with others some of these basic ideas. The question "What is the impact of racism?" is complex, because there are many answers, and these differ for different people. Racism against people of color has led to their oppression, and this may be a somewhat simple answer, but unpacking the many ways racism toward people of color impacts both people of color themselves and White people is important to understanding this concept more fully.

Impacts of Racism on People of Color

The layperson can likely think of many impacts of racism on people of color, both in daily experience and over the course of a lifetime or even generations in terms of the significant harm that is a result of racism. Many, many studies have also documented the impact of racism on people of color as well, however, and we will list a few for you here. Racism can directly impact both the mental and physical health of people of color in myriad ways (Alvarez, Liang, & Neville, 2016; Tao, Owen, & Drinane, 2017).

With regard to mental health, some studies have found that chronic exposure to racism is similar to the impact of trauma in general. In his race-based traumatic stress model (RBTSM), Robert T. Carter (2007) detailed the way in which this comparison can be made. Carter likened trauma due to fear for one's life to race-based traumatic stress, which he notes "occurs from events that are experienced as sudden, out of one's control, and emotionally painful (negative)" (Carter et al., 2013, p. 2). Some of the antecedents for this type of event might include anger, low self-esteem, shame, anxiety, depression, and guilt, all of which have also been found to be linked to poor overall well-being (Carter et al., 2013; Harrell, 2000). Other studies show that racist experiences such as microaggressions have impacts that range from increased depression (Nadal, Wong, Griffin, Davidoff, & Sriken, 2014; Tao et al., 2017) and increased stress (Harrell, 2000; Mercer, Zeigler-Hill, Wallace, & Hayes, 2011), to decreased self-esteem (Wong-Padoongpatt, Zane, Okazaki, & Saw, 2017) and poorer overall mental health (Alvarez et al., 2016; Miehls, 2010). Finally, some studies have also shown that increased alcohol use and anxiety are found in samples of ethnic minorities who report experiencing frequent microaggressions (Blume, Lovato, Thyken, & Denny, 2012).

Of course, many of the mental health concerns noted previously can also lead to physical health issues. Excessive alcohol use, for example, can lead to many health complications (Blume et al., 2012). In addition, Kaholokula (2016) found an overall decrease in physical health for people of color who experience racism often. Some studies have also looked at physical impacts in terms of effects of racism on mothers of color and their babies. Slaughter-Acey, Talley, Stevenson, and Misra (2018) conducted a study as members of the New York Academy for Medicine and found that maternal experiences with racism were associated with a higher probability of delivering infants who were small for their gestational age in African American mothers. In addition, higher infant mortality in African American births (as compared to White births) was found in relation to the effects of structural racism (also referred to above as institutionalized racism) that impacted access to housing, imprisonment, educational attainment, income, and other factors in which racial inequality is present within the United States (Wallace, Green, Richards, Theall, & Crear-Perry, 2017). These results have been replicated in many other studies.

In sum, racism has a multitude of dangerous effects for people of color today, and the results listed here are merely in regard to experiences with racism that are not life threatening in the moment. Too often, we know, racism can also result in death via intentional violence, mistakes made with regard to the threat a person of color presents, and hate crimes of other sorts. Racism is deadly both in its acute sense and in its long-term impact.

Impacts of Racism Against People of Color for White People

Often when we think of the impact of racism, we think only of the effects it may have on the victims of racism or those who are overtly racist in their daily lives. Psychologists Lisa Spanierman, of Arizona State University, and Mary Heppner, of the University of Missouri, assert that "racism also affects the 'silent' and 'blind' White majority in both 'positive' and negative ways" (2004, p. 249). We have spent much of this chapter discussing the "positive" ways racism against people of color can create opportunity and normalcy for White people in the United States, but Spanierman and Heppner (2004) also discuss what they term the "psychosocial costs of racism" to White people (p. 249). These costs fall into three different categories: **affective costs of racism, cognitive costs of racism,** and **behavioral costs of racism.**

Affective Costs of Racism

Spanierman and Heppner (2004) list many costs of racism that fall in the category of negative experiences of emotion for White people. Some of these include emotions such as anxiety or fear, that is, fear that members of other races will harm them in some way physically or through some crime. As Spanierman and Heppner note, "[This] cost reflects an irrational sense of danger and safety" (2004, p. 251). Other emotions may be related to feeling as though racism toward people of color is overwhelming and may be experienced as helplessness or sadness and anger. Finally, guilt and shame may be experienced by White people in hearing or talking about racism that exists toward people of color (Spanierman & Heppner 2004).

If you are a White person reading this chapter, you may have experienced some of the above feelings and know their cost. Some of these costs can be mitigated by exposure to more multicultural training experiences. In a study by Paone, Malott, and Barr (2015), for example, those with four to six of these experiences with multicultural education scored significantly lower in White fear than those with fewer experiences of this sort. White guilt, in the study by Paone and colleagues (2015), was increased by learning more about race, and this is a troubling finding, as other studies have found that guilt can block empathy for other groups (Spanierman & Heppner, 2004). That said, perhaps knowing this might help to change its impact. If you are a White person taking a course that discusses race and feel guilt begin to settle upon you, you might remember that guilt implies that one has done something wrong personally. One way to make sure you are doing something right is to try to make change toward decreasing racism as a whole. (See Chapter 11 for more details here.)

Cognitive Costs of Racism

Cognitive costs in this area refer mainly to the distortion that occurs for White people when they think about themselves and their experiences versus those of people who are not White (Spanierman & Heppner, 2004). Depending on White persons' own racial self-awareness, they may have no sense of themselves as racial beings, and so they cannot be connected to this part of their identity. In addition, they may rate race as unimportant in the lives of non-White people as well, and in this way distort its importance and impact to many in society.

One way in which this type of distortion may occur is through an inaccurate perception of the way in which work against racism might impact White people. Michael Norton from Harvard University and Samuel Sommers from Tufts University (2011) asked both White and Black participants to estimate the amount of bias they perceived to occur against White and Black groups over a variety of decades. Figure 5.3 depicts the results of this study. In looking at this figure, one can note that both Black and White participants noted that bias against Black people has decreased since the 1950s. Black people reported that they still experience bias more often than White people reported they think this type of bias occurs, but the same general pattern is found. Other findings, however, differ between races more sharply. Whereas Black participants noted that anti-White bias was relatively low in the 1950s and has not increased much if at all over the decades, White participants rated anti-White bias as increasing quite a bit over the decades. But notice where the lines in Figure 5.3 cross. This finding was made in conjunction with anti-Black bias decreasing, such that results showed that Whites in this study rated anti-White bias as *more* problematic than anti-Black bias in recent times in the United States. The researchers who conducted this study note that both groups noted rather little anti-White bias in the 1950–1970 range, showing that these differing results in later decades were not due to different reference-points with regard to race. Instead, the levels of anti-Black and anti-White bias were correlated within each decade rated by the White participants, indicating that Whites were linking the trends in bias to one another. Norton and Sommers (2011) surmise that it is possible

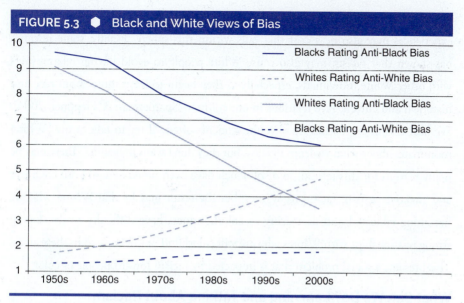

FIGURE 5.3   ●   Black and White Views of Bias

- Blacks Rating Anti-Black Bias
- Whites Rating Anti-White Bias
- Whites Rating Anti-Black Bias
- Blacks Rating Anti-White Bias

Source: Norton, M. I., & Sommers, S. R. (2011). Whites see racism as a zero-sum game that they are now losing. *Perspectives on Psychological Science, 6,* 215.

that Whites "may fear that minorities' imposition of their cultural values represent an attack on White cultural values and norms" (p. 217), which has been supported in other studies as well (Norton, Sommers, Apfelbaum, Pura, & Ariely, 2006).

This study shows a good example of cognitive distortion, brought on by racism toward people of color, such that White people fear something that is not occurring the way they may feel it is. All one must do to see that anti-White bias is not stronger than anti-Black bias is to look to who holds power in the United States (see Chapter 2). At time of publication, 91 of the 100 senators in our country identified as White American (US Senate, 2018), only three CEOs in Fortune 500 companies were Black (McGirt, 2018), and we had had only one non-White president since 1776. If bias truly existed in the way that the data in the Norton and Sommers (2011) study exhibits the White participants felt it had, none of the above would be possible in such strong numbers. And yet this fear exists. This is one of the cognitive costs White people may deal with as long as racism against people of color exists.

Behavioral Costs of Racism

One final way that racism against people of color can impact White people is that they may feel a desire to avoid situations in which they will come into contact with people of another race, and this may limit their actions or abilities to develop a variety of social relationships (Spanierman & Heppner, 2004). Missing out on multicultural experiences may also be a cost that falls within this sphere. Finally, some research has shown that racism may also cause White people to avoid having relationships with other White individuals, especially as they begin to learn more about race and historical and current race relations in our country (Spanierman & Heppner, 2004). We hear this in our classes from White students often: "I try to talk to my [White] roommates about what we learn in class, but they don't want to hear it." There may be many reasons for this refusal, some of which have been noted here in both cognitive and affective costs of racism to Whites, but the result may be that Whites who are becoming educated and decreasing in colorblindness have difficulty in developing strong relationships with Whites who are still colorblind or uneducated in these areas. This presents a social problem that is impacted by racism toward people of color.

What Can We Do? Learning and Talking About Racism

Clinical psychologist Beverly Daniels Tatum (1997/2017) has written,

> Cultural racism—the cultural images and messages that affirm the assumed superiority of Whites and the assumed inferiority of people of color—is like smog in the air. Sometimes it is so thick it is visible, other times it is less apparent, but always, day in and day out, we are breathing it in. (p. 6)

Tatum goes on to explain that we may not want to breathe the smog, and we may not describe ourselves as intentional breathers of it—and yet it goes into our lungs on a daily basis. Tatum uses this analogy to describe the way in which we are exposed to stereotypes and negative images of racial and ethnic minorities through the media, through casual comments and "jokes," and through the omission of discussion of positive accomplishments and contributions of people of color. Our country has a long history of discrimination based on race, and so it is no wonder that we might still be dealing with its effects.

But what can be done about this? Sometimes when speaking about racism, we see our students, of all races, become overwhelmed. How can we deal with such a large problem if it is everywhere? The short answer to this question is this: We can talk about it. We can explain it. And through this process, we can demystify it and remove some of its power.

Some of you may not have talked about race much growing up. For others of you, namely people of color or those of you who grew up in more diverse areas, you may remember the exact moment that you learned about race for the first time. Research shows that African American children usually learn about race before other children and that this is particularly true for those who live in very diverse areas (Root, 1992). What reasons can you think of for this? See this vignette from James, who is African American:

> *I remember this little girl in first grade who was White who wouldn't sit next to me or play with me. She told the teacher she wouldn't, and when the teacher asked her why, she said, "Because he's bad. He's Black." The teacher didn't tell my parents this happened, but I guess I mentioned it to them after school, and they were very upset. They went and talked to the teacher and the principal of the school too, and I remember my mom sitting me down after they got back. She said to me, "James, sometimes people will say things like that about you, and I want to make sure you know that that is wrong. You are Black and you are wonderful, and if people ever tell you those things can't go together, they are wrong." I remember being a little confused at the time and kind of embarrassed and sad, but glad that my parents said something to the teacher. When I think about it now, I realize that the teacher didn't even say anything in that moment when the little girl said that. The teacher was White too, and maybe she thought she didn't know what to say. I thought it was funny to think of later that she was a grown up and didn't know what to say, but that I was only a kid, and I did know what she should have said. She should have just said to that little girl, "You're wrong."*

—James, age 30

In this case, and in many cases in families who have some members who are not White, it becomes necessary to talk about race and racism at an earlier age, as certain situations may bring this construct into the family dynamic or experiences of some or all of the members of the family (Brown, Tanner-Smith, Lesane-Brown, & Ezell, 2007). Talking about racism with small children may sound daunting to some, but it may be unavoidable in a non-White family. For families that are White, however, the choice may be there to ignore race, or to decide not to bring it up, as it may not work its way into the family dynamic in the same way that it does in non-White families.

Instead, White families may choose to wait until the child is older as they may think they'll be better able to understand the concepts then (Vittrup, 2018).

The way in which families teach their children about race and its social meaning and consequences is termed **familial ethnic/race socialization** (Brown et al., 2007), and this socialization is a process. As a part of this process, a variety of topics may come up depending on the experiences of the individual, including history or heritage, prejudice or discrimination against the group, and other pieces of cultural norms, ideology, and practices. As noted above, conversations about race and ethnicity may seem more appropriate to have with older children. You may have heard people say, "Children don't see race!" or other such comments that imply that understanding racial differences or topics such as prejudice may be too difficult cognitively and emotionally for young children. Research, however, shows that children do see race and other types of differences at much younger ages than you might imagine.

Psychologist Phyllis Katz led a series of studies as part of a six-year longitudinal project to better investigate 100 Black and 100 White children's ability to notice and form meaning about different racial groups. In one of the first studies in the series, Katz and Kofkin (1997) showed the then six-month-old infants photos of faces of people who were the same race as their parents and of people from different races from their parents. The babies spent significantly more time looking at photographs of people who were of a race different from that of their parents, showing that they noticed a difference in these pictures. Katz (2003) was careful to point out that at this age, race may not hold a social meaning, but babies are certainly not colorblind—they see differences in skin color, and as they do with any new object, they begin trying to assign meaning to this difference as well.

Other research has shown that just slightly older children begin to categorize and form ideas about differences when they are presented to them. In a study giving evidence of this, psychologist Rebecca Bigler (1997) randomly gave school-aged children either a blue or a red shirt upon their entry into a summer school class. No comments were made about the meaning of the shirt, but in some classes the colors were used to divide the group into activities or to organize seating; in others, teachers did not use colors in this way. Results showed that in the classrooms in which the differences were used to label, greater ingroup biases developed (e.g., "All Reds like me are good, but some Blues are mean"). This result might lead one to think that not noting race, or pretending to ignore it, might be a good strategy. Yet in other studies, Bigler (1995) noted that ingroup preferences were found to flourish in children as young as age three or four without any noting of these differences. These preferences were particularly highlighted in studies in which the difference was more strongly attached to the person (e.g., having the child wear a red shirt, versus just noting that the child was part of the red group).

In another study, Bigler (1995) asked teachers in one experimental classroom to use gender to organize activities, and the classroom seating, and to use gender as a label often (e.g., "Girls, please stand up. Boys, please sit down"). In other classrooms, children were instead divided into color groups randomly, and this label was used to organize and discuss a variety of things in the classroom. (For example, "Go with your blue group, John." Or "The green group is working well together") Teachers in both groups were instructed not to treat one group better than the other or to make overt comments about one group being more positive. Results in the development of ingroup favoritism and bias differed in these two conditions, however. Bigler (1995) found that in the gender-based groups, biases and favoritism were found more often than in the color-based groups. Bigler hypothesized that the fact that gender was a perceptual marker, that is, a physical difference, while the red/green/blue distinction was made verbally, but the color was not physically placed on the children, may have been the reason for this difference.

In another of Bigler's (1997) studies, when children were asked to wear different colored t-shirts, the bias and favoritism was more pronounced. For example, in this t-shirt study, when asked how many of the Blues were "mean" or "dumb," those with red t-shirts noted that "some" were mean, though "none" of the Reds were. Much more variability in traits (e.g., children were more willing to say some Reds were nice and some mean, as opposed to "most" or "all" Reds being mean) was found in the study in which the colors were not physically used (Bigler & Liben, 2007).

Let us pause for a minute to summarize what these findings tell us. First, though many people believe that children "do not see race," the studies above have shown that babies as young as six months notice racial differences. Second, when differences are connected more strongly as a part of the person (e.g., gender, color, etc.), children are more likely to develop hypotheses about what "red/blue/green people" are like and show both bias against the outgroup and preference or favoritism for the ingroup. Third, when differences are labeled and emphasized, the ingroup favoritism grows stronger. And last, this type of bias and favoritism occurred even when teachers were neutral about what the labels and differences meant. Importantly, differences such as skin color are able to be perceived and physically reside with people, and so even when these differences are not mentioned, they are likely to be perceived and used for categorization. Within society it is unlikely that children would not hear a label assigned to people from different races. The bottom line of this research is this: Children notice differences, they make hypotheses about these differences, and these hypotheses are most often biased against the outgroup and favorable toward their own group.

Now let us take this information to the next step. If the above points are true, children are forming their own hypotheses when they are left to fill in the blanks about why differences exist. But what if we, as adults, parents and teachers, were not silent about what these differences mean? What if instead of remaining neutral, we were positive about differences in a way that might counteract the hypotheses that children are creating in the absence of our intervention?

Brigitte Vittrup, former graduate student and mentee of Dr. Bigler and now an academic at Texas Woman's University, asked this exact question. In a study designed to investigate the effects of talking with children about race, Vittrup created three different conditions. This study was conducted in the notably progressive and liberal area surrounding The University of Texas, Health Science Center at Houston, and involved 93 White families and their children ages five through seven (Vittrup & Holden, 2010). A majority of the parents of the children in this study held college degrees. The three experimental conditions created for this study were meant to test whether watching television with diverse characters (such as those on Sesame Street) improved children's racial attitudes, and whether parental discussions about race accompanying this type of television watching enhanced these gains. In Group 1, children only watched the racially diverse videos, which depicted interracial friendships. Group 2 added a parent-child discussion component to the activity of watching the racially diverse videos. Finally, children in Group 3 did not watch the videos but still had discussions with their parents about race. (A control group that involved no watching of videos or discussion was also included in this study.) In the groups involving discussion, parents were given instructions on the topics to discuss with their children, ranging from the importance of showing respect for others regardless of skin color, to making positive comments about interracial friendships and similarities between different friends, to discussing real or hypothetical interracial friendships in more of a real-life scenario with their children. Parents in the groups involving discussion were to keep a diary of the discussions in which they engaged. Vittrup and Holden hypothesized (1) that White children in the study who had discussions with their parents about the racially diverse television programs would have more positive attitudes about African Americans, and (2) that the children in this group would also be better able to accurately predict their parents' attitudes about African Americans.

Upon first looking at the results, Vittrup and Holden (2010) found something surprising. In posttests, results did not vary among the different groups of children on their attitudes toward African Americans nor on their ability to predict their parents' views of African Americans. When looking more closely at the data, however, the researchers found that a large number of parents who were involved in the discussion sections of the study did not in fact have these discussions with their children; only 10% engaged in discussions that were substantive in nature about the topics at hand. In addition, two families withdrew from the study, giving the reason that they did not want to have such conversations with their children. In the small group that did have the discussions with their children, improvements in racial attitudes toward African Americans were observed.

In addition to findings noted above, Vittrup and Holden (2010) also found that children were rather inaccurate about their parents' having African American friends. (Among the parents, 75% reported having African American friends, but children's reports showed only about 50% were aware of these friendships; the researchers hypothesized that some might exist outside of the home, such as in the workplace.) The researchers reported, "Children who were aware that their parents had Black friends evaluated Blacks more positively . . . than children who reported that their parents did not have Black friends . . . or that they were unaware" (Vittrup & Holden, 2010, p. 92). Other research has shown that when White children can observe interracial friendships between their parents and others, they generally have more positive attitudes about these types of friendships (Castelli, De Dea, & Nesdale, 2008). In addition, parents overall reported rather positive views of African Americans, but when asked point blank as a part of the study, "Do your parents like Black people?" only 44% of children answered "Yes" in the pretest, and a whopping 44% said "I don't know"; 12% said "No."

Let's unpack these results a bit here. First of all, it becomes clear that many of the White parents in this study did not choose to have discussions about race with their children, even when asked to as a part of the study. When Vittrup and Holden (2010) asked for examples from those who did discuss these topics with their children in the study, a majority (53%) used colorblind statements (e.g., "skin color doesn't matter" or "God loves everyone"), and only 8% of parents discussed any historical issues or other pieces of discrimination. The most likely reason for this is because these parents were uncomfortable talking about race in this way with their children. If you are White, think back to your own childhood—there are likely many of you for whom race was not brought up by your parents until it was a necessity. In fact, in another study of over 17,000 parents of kindergarteners, non-White parents were more than three times more likely to discuss race with their children than White parents, and 75% of White parents reported "never" or "almost never" talking about race with their children (Brown et al., 2007). It seems clear from these studies that, at least in White families, many parents are not discussing these issues with their children.

When combined with the studies from Katz (2003) and Bigler (1995, 1997; Bigler & Liben, 2007), and with what we know about natural tendencies toward ingroup favoritism and bias, it is no surprise that White children form their own, often negative, conclusions about people of different races from their own. When parents don't correct the potentially incorrect assumptions children make about race, and about what their parents think about race, the results are most often negative. In addition, if these parents are also not visibly interacting with people from these other racial groups, children again may form their own conclusions. The worst part of this is that in the study detailed by Vittrup and Holden (2010), the assumption that their parents did not like Black people seemed to be mostly false. Parents of these children overwhelmingly reported positive attitudes about Black people, and yet their children formed incorrect conclusions about their parents' attitudes, likely because they weren't aware of them. This underscores the importance of White families having friends of different racial groups and involving their children in these friendships in visible ways. Even in cases where children do not see these interactions, parents can still talk about them with their children and reinforce the idea that people of different races can be friends and can have both similarities and differences.

One of the authors of this book (DI) is fond of satirically saying to her class, "Right. Don't talk about race. Because not talking about problems in society always makes them go away. When any big problem exists, in what alternate universe do we say that not talking about it is sure to solve the problem?" The antidote to racism: Don't let children fill in their own blanks—there is likely no other topic that we keep so off limits under the faulty guise of protecting them. We tell children about drugs, how to manage their sex lives (whether through birth control or abstinence), how to deal with bullying, and about body image issues. And the main reason we talk about these often very difficult topics is that we want our children to know how to think about these things—to know that drugs can harm them, or that there are resources to deal with bullying. Why then do we think it would be best to allow them to come to their own conclusions about a complicated issue like differences and race? If parents want their children to have positive ideas about race from an early age, it is essential that they explain race along with other important lessons.

The *way* in which we talk about race, racism, skin color, and the like to children is also important. As noted by Brown and colleagues (2007).

> Although these topics may seem appropriate only to considerably older children, research suggests that young children must learn to manage racialized interactions, often in the kindergarten/elementary school setting and in response to performed acts of racism or questions about their ethnic/racial identification. (p. 14)

In another study conducted by Vittrup (2018), she asked White mothers the ways in which they discussed race with their children. Within her sample, 70% of the mothers reported using a **colorblind** (e.g., "race is not an issue," or "treat everyone the same") or **color mute** (remaining silent about race) approach in discussing race. The

White mothers in Vittrup's study gave a variety of reasons for addressing race in this way, but the three primary reasons given were: (1) "My child is already colorblind" (usually determined because her child played with children of other races willingly), (2) "She is too young" (with the caveat that the discussion would occur later if the child asked about it or if the child made an inappropriate comment), and (3) "Pointing out differences would be problematic" (linked to the idea that we should treat everyone the same instead of paying attention to differences) (pp. 678–679).

Colorblindness with regard to race is often a well-meaning strategy that parents and teachers use to teach children about race. Some of you reading this chapter may have been told things like, "Skin color doesn't matter" and been given other messages such as this designed to keep you from harboring negative feelings about different skin colors. There is one problem with this—skin color does matter, and we are not blind to it when we meet someone. When adults tell children to ignore skin color, they are likely really saying that skin color shouldn't be a basis for discrimination. But when parents are not explicit, children may instead learn the lesson that talking about skin color is wrong and that they should therefore pretend that they do not see it.

Similar to colorblindness, color muteness (i.e., staying silent about skin color and often about race) can also be problematic. As described previously,

> When parents and other important adults remain silent about race and other topics surrounding diversity, children form their own conclusions based on their limited experiences. . . . This often leads to misattributions of the parents' actual attitudes. (Vittrup, 2018, p. 671)

In keeping silent about race and pretending that it does not matter, parents and teachers may actually allow their children to form much more negative views of other races than they would hope the children have.

Finally, directing children to stay silent about race and culture also denies children of color the opportunity to talk about their race in a variety of ways. First of all, children of color may be proud of their race and want to talk about their cultural background. Acting as though this important part of a child "does not matter" may be both invalidating and limiting to children of color. In addition, it may form a

TABLE 5.2 ● Colorblindness, Color Muteness, Color Consciousness			
Scenario	**Colorblindness**	**Color Muteness**	**Color Consciousness**
A White child points out the darker skin of an African American man.	"That's not important. We don't see color."	No comment, or redirection to a different topic.	"Yes, that man is African American. You're right—his skin is darker than yours."

narrative that does not allow children of color to report experiences with discrimination and other forms of prejudice. If children believe the narrative "race does not matter," it may be difficult for them later to understand why race matters very much in situations involving discrimination, interactions with the police, and stereotypes developed about different groups. Table 5.2 summarizes these different approaches to discussing race with children.

So what should parents and teachers do? In Vittrup's (2018) study, a small portion of her sample (30%), used what can be termed a **color conscious** approach in talking about race and differences in skin color. White mothers in this portion of the sample talked about the importance of talking about inequality and discrimination to their children and reported that they made efforts to do so directly. One mother in this study commented,

> Children are curious. I think . . . the more they understand another culture, the more they can understand how to appropriately interact with others. . . . I do not want my children to grow up and focus on skin color. I want them to grow beyond that and learn to appreciate people for who they are, not what they look like. (Vittrup, 2018, p. 681)

In addition, the color conscious mothers also took care to make references to skin color (including conversations about physical differences) and promoted the idea that exposure to different cultures was a way to break down stereotypes and to give their children experiences that would help them to make their own decisions about people of all races based on personal characteristics.

In closing to this section, we would summarize the above by making a few recommendations. First: Talking about race is a good thing. Leaving children to make their own assumptions about race and racism does them a disservice, particularly in the absence of experiencing diversity themselves. We talk to children about all sorts of things that seem hard to handle: drugs, body image issues, death, and others. Talking about race is just as important. Second: Children notice when adults who are important to them do not interact with races different from their own and may make their own conclusions about this. Taking time to get to know families that are different from our own broadens our children's understandings of race and of differences overall. This does not mean "collecting" people who are different from you in order to show these relationships to your children. Instead, it is a conscious choice to put yourself in situations where you will naturally meet others who are different from you. And finally: Education should be given to children about the historical significance of race and other facts early in their elementary school years. If children could start to understand that race has always mattered in our country, and evaluate the impacts of the discrimination some racial groups have dealt with for decades, they might better be able to make decisions to make race matter for the right reasons (e.g., to get to know more about other persons and to understand some of their experiences) rather than to discriminate in their own lives.

CONCLUSION

In this chapter, we have covered many difficult topics, and it is likely that there have been concepts discussed that different students will view or react to in different ways. Before making your decisions, we would ask you to go back to Chapter 4 to review the racial identity model that is most appropriate for you. If you are White and have found yourself reacting negatively to some of the topics here, you might look carefully at Helms's model and see if you can't gain more insight into your beliefs by thinking about the various stages. Might you be in Reintegration, for example, and be pointing blame toward people of color for asking you to change behavior? Or might you be in Pseudo-Independence and feeling that you as a White person have nothing to do with racism, as you do not knowingly perpetuate it? If you are a person of color and you find yourself reacting negatively to the idea that understanding racism may be avoided by White people because it is hard for them to think of the amount of hurt that occurs at the hands of those who look like them, look back to the models for people of color in Chapter 4. Might you be dealing with some Immersion at present? The reality is that we can all work to better understand race in our daily lives. Even if reading this textbook is required for you as a part of a class, it is unlikely that you would be reading this book unless you cared to better your understanding of this topic. That is the first step. Education leads to more understanding, and this is something that can only benefit us all.

We hope that you now understand that racism is something that must be dealt with as a day-to-day reality in our country. Denying its existence or pretending that it is no longer a threat contributes, however inadvertently, to maintaining its existence. One thing that is important to know is that someone could be a very good person and also be influenced by racism or do racist things. This is hard to understand for many people, as the word *racist* certainly means "a bad person," right? None of us would likely want to be called racists, but until we acknowledge that good people are not immune to racism creeping into their daily actions, thoughts, and beliefs, it may be difficult to see racism within ourselves.

This folds into our final point in this chapter. All of us will make mistakes about race from time to time, and sometimes those mistakes may result in one of us being called "racist" or "discriminatory." This is part of life when we interact in circles where differences exist. In our classes, we often hear our White students report the fear they have about saying the wrong thing. We often respond by asking these White students what it is they fear. Many say they fear being labeled a racist, or that someone will think they are doing something discriminatory or based on prejudice, even though they do not intend this. The bottom line here is that we are not able to control others' perceptions of us all the time. And because of some of the ways that people of color are treated now, and have been treated in the past in our country, sometimes a good intention is not enough to keep someone from feeling the impact of racism. Recall from our early discussion of racism and its effects that an act being born of "true racism" is not the only act that can cause harm to a person of color. Instead the *perception* of racism can cause equal harm (Clark, Anderson, Clark, & Williams, 1999). It is important, however, to understand that if someone attributes something we say to racism, we *do* have control over our own response to this accusation. See the following vignette for a way one person decided to do this:

I was in a meeting a few weeks ago, and one of the participants was a new person on campus—an African American man, John. After hearing about his position and his goals during the meeting, I was hoping we could work together on a few projects in the future. On my college campus, there are very few African American students and even fewer staff. So when I saw an African American man at a forum on diversity a few weeks later, I thought to myself that I might check in with John to see how he was moving forward with his plans. I went up to this man and said, "I met you in a meeting a few weeks back—John, right?" The man looked at me for a minute and said, "I think you might be confusing me with John who works in the advising center, but I'm actually Samuel—I work in financial aid."

I couldn't believe I had done that—mixed up two African American men on my campus, when there are so few of them, and because I work in diversity areas myself I knew what he must be thinking. My face was bright red as I said, "Wow. I can't believe I just did that. That's terrible and I'm really sorry. My name is Mei Chi," and I held out my hand.

Samuel took it in stride. He said, "No problem. It's nice to meet you," but I felt just awful. I thought to myself that maybe I should explain that I had only met John once and that maybe I should talk about what my position on campus was regarding diversity or something, so he would know I didn't have a bad intention. And then I thought that my intention didn't really matter. For someone like Samuel, this kind of thing probably happens pretty regularly, and it often is because of racism or because people don't take the time to get to know him. Regardless of my intention, the impact was that he potentially thought I was doing the same thing.

I know where I am in my journey toward eliminating racism in my life, and I also know that I made an honest mistake based on a quick first meeting with John. But I also know that Samuel could have taken that very differently and that he has a right to, based on how people usually treat him in society and on campus. In the end, Samuel and I became friends and he got to know me, and we've joked about my mistake a few times since. He knows my intent now because he knows me now, and I'm really glad I didn't try to make excuses for myself when I made that mistake. I think if I had we might not have gotten to be friends in the end.

—Mei Chi, age 42

As you see in the vignette, acknowledging the impact we have on others is important, as is being aware that our intention is separate from that impact. If you are ever in a position where someone believes that something you do is motivated by race, it is a good thing to acknowledge that you can understand why they might think that based on other experiences they may have had, and then try to move forward. Something you might say is, "I didn't intend that to be a racist statement, but I can see how you might have taken it that way. I'm sorry." We have all heard celebrity "apologies" that start with the dreaded "I'm sorry if you felt offended. . . ." Acknowledging that you may have hurt someone even if you didn't intend to is an important part of being a good person.

One way to make intention and impact more closely related is to get to know people who are different from ourselves. In establishing a more intimate or close relationship with a person who is different from you racially or in terms of gender, sexual orientation, or other cultural identity, you begin to see ways in which the two of you might better understand each other as would occur in any relationship. For example, knowing that it bothers your friend Sophie when people make light of her religious views as a Christian might cause you to try to better understand them and to get closer to Sophie in the process. Understanding that your friend Jeff is self-conscious about his lisp might lead you to avoid certain comments that might exacerbate that for him. After developing enough trust with your friend Zayne for him to explain to you about his experience living in a community that treated people from his racial group very poorly, you might better understand when he is reminded of those stereotypes by various comments and is upset by them.

Sometimes we hear people saying that changing your behaviors or language to change the impact you might have on another is just being "PC" (politically correct). This may be true if you are only changing these things to avoid having the person call you on that behavior or comment. In the scenarios above, however, perhaps you would make that type of change not because it is *politically correct*, because it is actually just *correct* with no politics involved. You are choosing not to hurt your friends because you care about them and wouldn't do so on purpose. The bottom line is this: It is true that we cannot control how others take the things we say, but we can work to try to alter our behavior if it is apparent our actions have hurt another regardless of intention. Instead of becoming defensive, we can acknowledge that person's hurt and continue to build a relationship with them. On the flip side, of course, if you never make friends with people who are different from you in any way, you may not know what kinds of things hurt them. Only through actual relationships can we potentially begin to build bridges toward understanding.

We hope you will take some time to explore the ACT section at the end of this chapter and to think more about ways that you can continue to work toward the eradication of racism. Whether it be teaching children in your job or in your family that race does matter, or if it instead involves trying to diversify your own friendship group, we know that talking about race and racism and working hard to understand your own identity are key components to this important work. Only in this way can we begin to clear Tatum's (1997/2017) "smog" from the air we breathe.

ACT: Assess Your Knowledge, Critical Thinking, Take Part

Assess Your Knowledge

First, spend some time looking back to Chapter 4 regarding racial identity development for the group of which you are a part. Pay careful attention to the stages that you think best represent you, as some of this may influence your understanding of and your resonating with the material in this chapter. Second, go back through Chapter 5, and find the parts that you thought were hardest. Do a little additional research on these areas. Try hard to go to nonpartisan sites if you are looking online. Remember that the material presented to you in this chapter is science based—spend some time looking for additional sources to bolster your understanding. Some keywords to search: *institutionalized racism, structural racism, internalized racism, aversive racism, implicit bias*. Last, go to this website, and take Dr. John Dovidio's Implicit Association Test (IAT) for Race: https://implicit.harvard.edu/implicit/takeatest.html. You may take the time to take some of the other IATs as well. Print out your results or view them on your device.

Critical Thinking

Review your results from your Implicit Association Test carefully. What patterns surprise you? What thoughts are running through your head about this test and your scores? Take five minutes to jot down some of these thoughts on a piece of paper. Often, our students will look at their results and begin to complain about the "fairness" or accurateness of the IAT. Here are some things to be aware of regarding the IAT and this reaction:

1. The IAT is *counterbalanced*, meaning that different items are given first to some participants and later to others.

2. The IAT has been *validated*, meaning that it has been shown to be psychometrically sound over many, many participants and their scores.

3. Many people do not like their results, and the most common reason is that they have been previously unaware of the *implicit biases* they hold.

To this last point—implicit biases are biases that people are unaware of in any sort of conscious way. Because of this, if you scored as "Preference for Whites" or "Preference for Blacks," this means that you may hold some biases in this direction. Biases are not a positive thing; however it is important to know that we all hold them. Denying or resisting analysis of your results is a common reaction to getting results that you do not like; however, we urge you to try to sit with your results. Take another few minutes to reflect on *why* the results feel incorrect to you or feel upsetting. Last, sometimes our White students will report excitedly, "I have a preference *for* Blacks!" and may feel relieved that they have "proved" themselves nonracist. This is not accurate. Showing a preference for any race over another is still bias, and decreasing bias should be a goal for us all.

Take Part

Participation: One of the main parts of this chapter focused on what you can do to increase your knowledge of race in general. Make a list of your friends, and label them by closeness. (Try to be very honest in this part.) Then list their races next to their names. What patterns exist for you? If you find that you have less diversity in your friendship group than you would like, in what ways can you seek out a more diverse group of people? If you are a student, there may be clubs you can join and organizations of which you can be a part. Even if you are not a student, there are groups within your community or national organizations that you can join. Often, joining groups that are focused on diversity in general can increase diversity of membership. Remember that it is not about "collecting" friends of different racial groups but about putting yourself into social circles that include more diversity than you usually encounter.

Initiation: As you learned in this chapter, getting rid of racism is aided by talking about it more. Many times, we hear students saying, "I'm not ready to talk about it. I just need a little more training." If this is you, put your money where your mouth is, and make some plans to get extra training on how to talk about race, racism, and other types of discrimination. You might seek out an opportunity to learn more about the Intergroup Dialogues programs that exist across the country. These trainings go by many other names as well, including "Difficult Dialogues" and "Intergroup Relations." Look into investing some time in learning more specific skills designed to help you talk to people with different views from those you hold or from different cultural backgrounds.

Activism: Try some of these skills out. Taking the knowledge you have from this chapter and other things you have read, attempt to talk to someone whom you know has different beliefs than you do about race and discrimination. Plan out your talk, being careful to select an appropriate time and location, and think a bit about some of your goals. How can you make change with this conversation? Set a goal for yourself with respect to the number of people you will talk to about these topics this month. How can you keep these conversations going with those who are also invested in promoting equity? Starting a book circle, having a regular discussion group, or taking trainings together may be another way you can keep things moving forward. Keep pushing yourself.

iStock/Mimadeo

6

WHITENESS

LEARNING OBJECTIVES

- Describe the invisibility of Whiteness and its operations in today's context
- Outline the historical, political, economic, and social contexts for the construction of Whiteness, and analyze the way those structures intersect and inform each other
- Identify and analyze the impact of White privilege on one's lived experiences and psychological well-being
- Analyze the social and psychosocial sources of anger, guilt, and shame for White Americans
- Define racial identity development stages and evaluate one's own developmental stage as well as the stages of others

If you know Chicago, you know that it still reflects the rich ethnic history of it's past. All over the city there are markers of the Ukrainian, Polish, and Italian (to name a few) neighborhoods that thrived in the city. In an area of Chicago known for its Swedish American roots, there is a small liberal arts college that draws a significant number of its students from Swedish American ethnic enclaves from around the United States. That ethnic linkage led to an exchange program with Sweden. Every year, it seemed, the same set of cultural misunderstandings occurred.

Students in Chicago were always eager to take the newly arrived exchange students to local Swedish American restaurants and stores. They were then surprised by how much the exchange students did not recognize the food. Our students were unaware of how much the menu items reflected what farmers ate in the 1800s. Many in Sweden do not eat those foods anymore, and most had never heard of many of those dated and regionally specific dishes.

In conversations, the exchange students were often frustrated by the US students' lack of engagement with global affairs and what appeared to them as vague and allusive discussions of controversial issues, and the US students were often put off by what seemed to them as the brazen, overly political, opinionated speech of the Swedish students. The US students presumed they shared a common set of values and common culture with the exchange students, but that was not the case. The Swedish American students were ethnically Swedish (marked by the red wooden horses and love of Swedish pancakes they grew up with), but in terms of how they saw themselves and functioned in the world, they were culturally American, and more specifically, White American. The ethnic and cultural identity that their ancestors came to the United States with had been largely supplanted by a new national, cultural, and racial identity.

They came as British, Dutch, French, German, Italian, Irish, Polish, and then they became White and American. It wasn't an inevitable or "natural" transition. As described in previous chapters, it was the work of intentional identity constructs and racialized social, political, and economic policy. Over time, the distinctive cultures and ethnicities that arrived with the European immigrants were largely overtaken by a racial identity. As we've seen, the idea of Whiteness (moral, intellectual, and economic superiority) did not simply exist as an ideology, but was manifested in structure and deepened and maintained through policy and social practice. Ironically, one of the most powerful characteristics of this construct is its ability to operate as an unspoken, unseen, unraced "invisible" force.

We do not commonly think of White when we think of race, and most conversations about race focus on people of color. For many Whites then, what is one of the most powerful features of a person's identity, race, can go unknown, unrecognized, and unexamined in themselves. Socially, we rarely talk about Whiteness, even in all-White spaces. As a result, Whites can operate as unraced people and draw (often unconsciously) on the power of the "invisible" nature of their race. The Whiteness scholar Richard Dyer wrote,

> As long as white people are not seen and named [as White], they/we function as a human norm. Other people are raced, we are just people [and there] is no more powerful position than that of being 'just' human. The claim to power is the claim to speak for the commonality of humanity. Raced people can't do that—they can only speak for their race. (2016, p. 10)

As a result, it feels natural to talk about a movie with a largely Asian cast as an "Asian movie" and see it as about an aspect of the "Asian experience," targeting an Asian audience. But a film with a largely White cast is commonly seen as a film with universal appeal and displaying an exploration of an aspect of the human experience. Similarly, we may hear the ideas of people of color as impacted by their racial experiences, perspective, or interests, but see Whites as simply stating their opinions. An unraced opinion carries the benefit of potentially being seen as an unbiased, individual, personal opinion. When people have that lack of racial awareness, it can make understanding how race works in themselves, in others, or in our society difficult to fully comprehend and easy to misunderstand or even deny.

People of color, as well as their actions and artifacts, are readily raced (my Asian professor, that Mexican neighborhood, Black music, etc.). where there is often an absence of reference to Whiteness in comparable unraced descriptions. For example, a research study on high school girls, whose participants were largely White, might simply be called something like "Gender and Schooling," but if participants were largely African American, it would likely have a title along the lines of, "Black Girls and Schooling: Race and Gender on High School Campuses." This is so common, in fact, that it may even seem odd to hear Whiteness addressed as we do other races. During the 2008 presidential election, then-candidate Obama was asked several times whether he would be the president for just Black people, or for all people.

Not only was his opponent not asked the parallel question, it would likely have been jarring, and sound almost comical to us, if then-candidate McCain were asked, "Do you intend to be the president for just White people, or for all people?" The invisibility of Whiteness in these examples isn't simply about language but reveals the way in which Whiteness is situated as the presumed status, the norm. It can stand in for universal humanity, unencumbered by the perceived limitations of a racialized identity, set of experiences, or agenda.

In numerous qualitative studies of race among White college students by researchers such as Bonilla-Silva (2018)

Pool/Pool/Getty Images

Obama and McCain on campaign trail

and Feagin (2013) as well as among the students the two of us encounter in our classrooms, we regularly hear White students report that they do not think about their race, that race makes little difference in their lives, and that they know little about Whiteness particularly. Tim Wise states,

> Being a member of the majority, the dominant group, allows one to ignore how race shapes one's life. For those of us called White, whiteness simply is. Whiteness becomes, for us, the unspoken, uninterrogated norm, taken for granted, much as water can be taken for granted by a fish. (Wise, 2011, p. 2)

So how did this racial project of Whiteness become internalized, then operationalized through structure and policy, and end up unknown by most of those who are directly connected to it? To understand the unraced/invisible nature of Whiteness and how it functions in our current society, lived experiences, and personal psyches, we must look to history.

THE HISTORICAL CONTEXT FOR THE CONSTRUCTION OF WHITENESS

In Chapter 2, we described Bacon's Rebellion and the economic impetus for the creation of the idea of Whiteness, the social mechanisms for its spread, and the policies (voting rights, citizenship, the Homestead Act, etc.) that were central to ingraining Whiteness into our social structures. That time period was the first of a series of pivotal moments in the construction of Whiteness, followed soon after (both in time and import) by the New Deal era and the period surrounding World War II.

Following the Great Depression, the **New Deal** brought about federal policy designed to stabilize the economy, protect workers, and establish a social safety net. That set of policies included the Wagner Act (legalizing unions and protecting workers' rights) and the Social Security Act (providing retirement income and care for retired workers). Those federal policies gave workers access to better wages, health care, and protections, and worked to greatly reduce the financial strain a family might face in caring for an aging relative. That history is fairly familiar to us—the intent of the New Deal, the creation of the social safety net, and the impact they had on our economic health

Redlining map with legend

as individuals, families, and as a nation. What is less known is the way those policies were racialized, in other words, who was not included. The Wagner and Social Security Acts excluded domestic and agricultural labor, significant employment sectors for people of color. Limitations in employment opportunities and protections have obvious economic and social implications, but arguably the most powerful forces in the creation of Whiteness, segregation, and our racialized wealth gap of that era were the raced-based government policies and practices around housing.

In 1934, the Federal Housing Authority (FHA) was created and, in an effort to expand the housing market, it guaranteed private mortgage loans. With those government secured loans, banks lowered interest rates and greatly reduced required down payments for mortgages (which at that time were commonly 50%), making home ownership possible for millions of US citizens, but not for everyone. The FHA determined where banks should give mortgages through a color-coded, raced-based system, which became known as "redlining."

Redlining was a rating system that identified which neighborhoods were a good investment, and thus would accrue high property values, and which ones were bad investments, where banks should not lend. The highest rating, "Green," was given to all-White neighborhoods, and the lowest rating, "Red," to non-White or heavily mixed areas. For example, in 1939, the FHA denied guaranteed loans in the racially mixed Los Angeles neighborhood of Boyle Heights, because, as they described it, it was a "'melting pot' area literally honeycombed with diverse and subversive racial elements" (Rothenberg, 2016, p. 100).

In 1939, we entered World War II. The construction of Whiteness was greatly abetted by several aspects of the World War II era, two chief elements being racial identity development and the GI Bill. By the early 1900s, the United States had already experienced waves of European immigration, and many of those immigrants lived in **ethnic enclaves** and, like most of the people in the United States, struggled economically following the Great Depression. For those immigrants, joining the armed forces meant not only employment but also a move away from their ethnic roots and into an American identity. Many European immigrants lived in areas where they spoke their native language, in and outside of the home (school, church, etc.), and were surrounded by neighbors and traditions reflective of their country of origin. Many of those who went to war entered with an ethnic identity but emerged with a newly formed American one. They had fought for our country, our national ideals; they had fought alongside soldiers from all over of the United States, and they had come together through a shared experience, shared goals, and a shared language, but all within a racially segregated environment. The United States fought World War II with a **Jim Crow** army, racially segregated—Native Americans in Native American units, Japanese Americans in Japanese American units, African Americans in Black units.

European immigrants were becoming White Americans in a segregated world. That segregation deepened following their service through the use of the residential benefits of the GI Bill. In 1944, to assist our veterans returning from war in their transition back to civilian life, and to continue the work of the New Deal, congress passed the GI Bill. It provided educational, occupational, and residential assistance and opportunities for GIs. The housing assistance meant low-interest-rate mortgages with little or no money down, but tragically the GI Bill used all of the FHA's race-based practices. The FHA, beyond providing a federal guarantee

Bettmann/Contributor/Getty Images

WWII segregated unit

for mortgage loans and rating neighborhoods, also subsidized mass production of housing developments—suburbs, but with the requirement that the homes not be sold to African Americans. That restriction was written into deeds and resale contract language that became known as restrictive covenants. As an example, in the 1930s and 1940s, 85% of the subdivision housing developments in New York had restrictive covenants (Rothstein, 2017). Through government policies, suburbs were developed for, and restricted to, Whites. The government's use of the FHA's policies in distributing the GI Bill's housing benefits meant that almost exclusively, White soldiers were the beneficiaries of the over $120 billion in government-backed loans the GI Bill sponsored. Less than 2% of this benefit went to non-Whites. White soldiers used them to live in intentionally segregated White neighborhoods. GIs and their families who formerly lived in rural or urban ethnic enclaves now lived in suburbs, where it was their Whiteness, not an ethnic identity, that marked the space and unified the residents.

Without having to know, or even agree with, the racial discrimination embedded in those policies, Whites came to possess a set of economic and social privileges (worker protections, retirement, home ownership, etc.), benefits connected to their Whiteness, benefits that would help establish the racial wealth gap we still experience today. Those policies also resulted in **racial segregation**, the creation of **White space** (suburbs), and a White racial identity. Absent this historical context, it is easy to see how, today, a White person might feel like, "My family came to America with little money, worked hard, and saved, and that is how we got where we are today," and never see how that story likely also relied on Whiteness and racial discrimination. There is no doubt that families have worked hard, saved, and tried to make the best decisions for their future, but, for some, Whiteness meant access to benefits others were denied. Our history books tell us a bit about the discrimination against people of color in the past, but rarely do they discuss the creation of Whiteness and the accompanying structural benefits to Whites or how those policies live on and impact our lives today.

From an ahistorical vantage point, one might look out at the racial inequality that exists today and mistakenly think the explanation for it lies in problems in the communities of people of color or in people of color themselves: "There must be something wrong with them." Eduardo Bonilla-Silva (2018), in *Racism Without*

Racists, calls this reasoning **cultural racism** (p. 56), the idea that racial inequality can be explained exclusively by the behavior of people of color. In his study of how White college students think and talk about race, he argues that cultural racism is one way Whites make sense of the world when they are unaware of how inequities came to be and how race works in our society. Without the historical context and understanding of race, there is little way to know that what one is witnessing in the present was intentionally created, and is embedded, in a racialized past.

Our inability to see Whiteness, it's "invisibility" in our nation's history, our family story, or our individual identity, can, in part, be ascribed to its operational position as norm. Whiteness can go unseen because it is the presumed status, the norm, the position to which everything else is compared. When people use their identity as the norm against which everyone else is measured, it is called ethnocentrism. When that is done with Whiteness at that center, it is Eurocentrism—assessing others through a presumed White norm.

Over the years, students of color have come to our offices to talk through the ways in which they are not presumed to be the "typical" student or where the presumption of Whiteness has made them feel invisible. Some of the most common ones have included these:

- At orientation, students are told which businesses are most welcoming to students, the best places to eat and shop, and the parts of town that are safe to traverse at night, as well as which should be avoided. Yet, the culturally specific needs, interests, or desires of student of color around food, hair care, et cetera, are not described. Often, the described "unsafe" neighborhoods are ones marked by race and/or class, while there are no mentions of the places where students of color may not be welcome or should be careful, nor are they given advice on how to respond to or report acts of discrimination they may encounter.

- Being mistaken for janitorial staff members.

- Classrooms developing standards through consensus for appropriate class conduct and discussion, in predominately White institutions, and presuming everyone's values and standards are the same.

WHITE PRIVILEGE

In 1988 and 1989, respectively, Peggy McIntosh wrote the essays "White Privilege and Male Privilege: A Personal Account of Coming to See Correspondences through Work in Women's Studies" and "White Privilege: Unpacking the Invisible Knapsack," and they have since become foundational pieces in Whiteness studies, particularly in the area of **White privilege**. Though she was not the first to use the phrase *White privilege*, the lists (46 items in the first essay and 26 in the second) that both essays included of the race-based privileges she encountered in her life have become starting points for discussions of the idea of privilege.

White privilege is made up of the peculiar set of inherent/unearned advantages ascribed to those seen as racially White. As a race-based notion, White privilege operates as a concept vested in systems, structures, and ideologies. The idea of White privilege is not about undermining or ignoring the lived history or accomplishments of any individual, family, or group. It is not intended to minimize the impact of personal hardships or disadvantages from other identity constructs (class, sexual orientation, gender identity, etc.). It does not try to make Whites living today responsible for our nation's history, but it is intended to show how Whites today benefit from that racial history and our current racial inequality. The idea of White privilege is not about making anyone feel guilty for being White, but it is intended to articulate the ways Whiteness is at work in the lives of Whites and how it manifests in all of our lived experiences, social relationships, and social structures. Tim Wise makes the point that part of the issue with White privilege is simply grammatical—advantage is a relational term; for one to have an advantage is for someone else to have a disadvantage, so the obverse of White privilege is discrimination against people of color. To effectively counter racial inequality and understand how to address it in our lives and psyches, we must engage both sides of the relationship, the role and work of disadvantages, discriminations, systematic racism, and the role and work of the advantages, privileges, and power.

We have likely had far more conversations about the negative effects of racism on people of color than we have had about the "positive" impacts of racism on Whites. The overtness of racial discrimination is easy to identify: income inequality across racial lines (Manduca, 2018), people of color being stopped more by police despite having no greater a level of infractions, teacher perceptions of race and student achievement (Cherng, 2017; Ochoa, 2013), differences in callback rates for job interviews where resumes were identical except for "ethnic sounding" names—on average White applicants received 36% more callbacks than Blacks and 24% more than Latinx applicants (Quillian, Pager, Midtboen, & Hexel, 2017).

The opposite of these disadvantages is the advantages they afford to those not targeted—not simply the tangible advantages, but the benefit of not having to think about or endure the psychic weight of race. DiAngelo (2018) beautifully conveys the psychological benefit of being free of that weight, the advantage of being part of the presumed status of "normal," and the privilege of Whiteness in her description of racial belonging:

> In virtually every situation or context deemed normal, neutral or prestigious in society, I belong racially. This belonging is a deep and ever-present feeling that has always been with me. Belonging has settled deep into my consciousness. . . . The experience of belonging is so natural that I do not have to think about it. The rare moments in which I don't belong racially come as a surprise—a surprise that I can either enjoy for its novelty or easily avoid if I find it unsettling. (p. 53).

This is not an advantage or privilege that can be measured easily with statistics and data, but it reflects a clear psychological benefit; having a racial identity that fosters a sense of belonging is an antecedent to confidence, personal security, and comfort.

In describing the development of her list of White privileges, McIntosh (2017) wrote,

> My schooling gave me no training in seeing myself as an oppressor, as an unfairly advantaged person. . . . I was taught to see myself as an individual whose moral state depended on her individual moral will. . . . I began to

count the ways in which I enjoy unearned skin privilege and have been conditioned into oblivion about its existence." [That list includes the following:]

- I can if I wish arrange to be in the company of people of my race most of the time.

- [If I move], I can be pretty sure that my neighbors . . . will be neutral or pleasant to me.

- I can go shopping alone most of the time, pretty well assured that I will not be followed or harassed.

- I can turn on the television or open to the front page of the paper and see people of my race widely represented.

- When I am told about our national heritage or about "civilization," I am shown that people of my color made it what it is.

- I can go into a music shop and count on finding the music of my race represented, into a supermarket and find the staple foods that fit with my cultural traditions, into a hairdresser's shop and find someone who can cut my hair.

- Whether I use checks, credit cards, or cash, I can count on my skin color not to work against the appearance of financial reliability.

- I can arrange to protect my children most of the time from people who might not like them.

- I can swear, or dress in second-hand clothes, or not answer letters, without having people attribute these choices to the bad morals, the poverty, or the illiteracy of my race.

- I can do well in a challenging situation without being called a credit to my race.

- I am never asked to speak for all the people of my racial group.

- I can criticize our government and talk about how much I fear its policies and behavior without being seen as a cultural outsider.

- I can be pretty sure that if I ask to talk to "the person in charge," I will be facing a person of my race.

- If a traffic cop pulls me over or if the IRS audits my tax return, I can be sure I haven't been singled out because of my race.

- I can easily buy posters, postcards, picture books, greeting cards, dolls, toys, and children's magazines featuring people of my race.

- I can go home from most meetings of organizations I belong to feeling somewhat tied in, rather than isolated, out-of-place, outnumbered, unheard, held at a distance, or feared.

- I can take a job with an affirmative action employer without having coworkers on the job suspect that I got it because of race.

- I can choose public accommodations without fearing that people of my race cannot get in or will be mistreated in the places I have chosen.

- I can be sure that if I need legal or medical help, my race will not work against me.

- If my day, week, or year is going badly, I need not ask of each negative episode or situation whether it has racial overtones.

- I can choose blemish cover or bandages in "flesh" color and have them more-or-less match my skin. (McIntosh, 2017, pp. 2–3)

She goes on to write,

> For me, white privilege has turned out to be an elusive and fugitive subject. The pressure to avoid it is great, for in facing it I must give up the myth of meritocracy. If these things are true, this is not such a free country; one's life is not what one makes it; many doors open for certain people through no virtues of their own. (McIntosh, 2017, p. 3)

We often have the students in our classes update this list (removing those items that no longer seem true, adjusting and updating those where they think there have been changes, and adding new ones they have experienced or learned of) and speak to the ones that surprise or resonate with them. The results always split along racial lines. Many White students have never thought about, and are surprised by, the advantages their race affords them in their daily lives. They are also often saddened by the realization that the vast majority of the privileges she describes are still privileges they have, and how easy it is for students of color to add even more to the list. It is also rare for us to have these kinds of discussions and not need to address the emotions they evoke. For many of our White students, the topic of race, and Whiteness in particular, raises the questions of how we respond to the dissonance, how we reconcile what we thought we knew to be true with reality.

ANGER, GUILT, AND SHAME

As we know, one of the primary responses to cognitive dissonance is to resolve the psychoemotional discomfort it creates. With Whiteness, that means there is a need to address anger, guilt, and shame; this is the pathway to fostering a healthy racial identity, not despite our historical and contemporary racialized context, but within it. As Tim Wise (2011) asks, "What does it mean to be White in a nation created for the benefit of people like you" (p. 2)? For some, coming to understand the power of race and the construction of Whiteness leads to anger at our history and the systems of inequity and oppression we now live in. For others, the dissonance manifests as a denial of that reality. In describing her work as a diversity trainer, Robin DiAngelo (2018) wrote,

> I was taken aback by how angry and defensive so many white people became at the suggestion they were connected to racism in any way. The very idea that they would be required to attend a workshop on racism enraged them. They entered the room angry and made that feeling clear to us throughout the day as they slammed their notebooks down on the table, refused to participate in exercises, and argued against any and all points. (p. 2)

This anger seems, at least in part, to be connected to a desire to distance oneself from what we know to be the horrors of racism, the genocide of Indigenous populations, slavery, lynchings, internment camps, et cetera. As we have described in previous chapters, many of us know little about the intentionally constructed nature of race, we are not well versed in the racialized history of our country's institutions and structures, we commonly frame that history as firmly in the past with limited awareness of its impact today, and we're surrounded by a narrative of racism that situates it in individuals (their attitudes, beliefs and behaviors), obscuring its systematic nature. In other words, we may be socializing people who feel like, "I don't see race, racism is in the past, racists are bad, and as a good person, I am not responsible for, or connected to, any of that." Discussions of race, for people with that frame of mind, might lead to anger when they are pushed to address the realities of racial inequality and our racial identities. In examining her own Whiteness, and the anger she saw in other Whites, DiAngelo goes on to say that she "saw our investment in a system that serves us. I also saw how hard we worked to deny all this and how defensive we became when these dynamics were named. In turn, I saw how our defensiveness maintained the racial status quo" (2018, pp. 3–4).

For some Whites, the feelings of anger are related to feelings of guilt and shame: guilt about our racist past, guilt over the privileges that past affords, and ultimately shame over being White. Those feelings have the capacity to cripple one with inaction or, conversely, to propel one into a process of identity development. Guilt can cause some to seek easy solutions as an escape from examining more deeply the problems of race in our society and ourselves. For others, guilt can become a psychological tool for avoidance. As Dyer (1997) describes,

> One wants to acknowledge so much how awful white people have been that one may never get around to examining what exactly they have been. . . . This problem . . . is a special temptation for white people. We may lacerate ourselves with admissions of our guilt, but that bears witness to the fineness of our moral spirit that can feel such guilt—the display of our guilt is our Calvary. (p. 11).

Here, the feeling of guilt itself becomes the proof that we are good, and if racists are bad, then our guilt helps us convince ourselves and others that we are innocent.

In *White Like Me*, Wise (2011) describes workshops on race where he asks participants to break off into racial groups to write on boards what they love about their racial/cultural category. He says the lists from the groups of Whites are always different from the others. The Whites seem to have the hardest time constructing the list, and often end up with a list largely comprising what is good about not being a person of color. Part of that, he argues, comes both from the invisibility of Whiteness and from the fear and dis-ease of feeling good about being White and the shame in Whiteness. Additionally, he goes on to describe how difficult it is for Whites to name White racial heroes—other Whites who are role models for social justice activism and antiracism. How does one come to a healthy sense of self and agency without models to follow?

USING WHITE RACIAL IDENTITY TO DECONSTRUCT WHITENESS

Drawing on the work of psychologist William E. Cross (1971) and his nigrescence Black racial identity development model, Janet Helms (1984, 1995) proposed a White racial identity development model that you were introduced to in Chapter 4. You may recall that the Helms model's six identity statuses are divided into a two-segment process—Phase 1: abandoning of racism, and Phase 2: defining a nonracist White identity (see Figure 6.1).

Each phase is made up of three statuses that operate in relationship to one another, with individuals cycling through the process following new discoveries, relationships, or experiences. Though we think of progress and development as moving in a linear fashion (one is ever improving; each new encounter moves us further along our path), the reality is rarely that clean. We have an experience or take a class or watch a documentary, and it starts a process that leads to identity development and growth, but we also regress—have times where we default back to old ways of thinking, or where an experience fills us with overwhelming emotions and we shut down, or when our strides in one area mask how much we still don't know or understand. The following vignette provides an example of this nonlinear development:

A Latinx student described the day she felt betrayed by a White faculty member who she had seen as an ally. The student was weeks from graduating from college and had a job offer from a company near her college town, when she received a call from home informing her that her undocumented father, who was the primary

FIGURE 6.1 ● The Two Phases and Six Statuses of Helms's Model

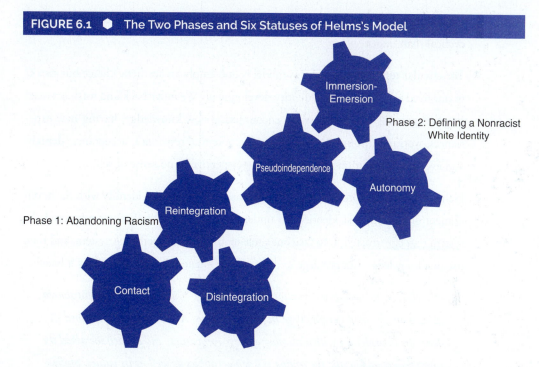

economic provider for the family, would not be able to return to his job due to the discovery of his status. Overwhelmed by fear, sadness, anger, and uncertainty, she went to talk with the faculty member who had been a great support in the past. She talked with him about the impact of this news and the imperative she felt to financially support her family. He was unaware of the cultural value placed on family responsibility in Latinx communities, and his advice was for her to think of herself and her promising future and let her family care for themselves and their issues. The student left his office in tears, and the faculty member was confused about what had happened.

Later, when he shared the story with a colleague who told him about Latinx culture and the complicated role of children with undocumented parents, he felt defensive and angry, he avoided contact with the student and withdrew. It was months before he pursued another conversation with his colleague and started reading articles about labor and the Latinx community. He then realized what he really felt had been embarrassment over his lack of knowledge and the centering of his identity and experience as the norm she should follow.

Helms argues that our movement through healthy identity development is more cyclical than linear.

The circular representation of this model is not simply an aesthetic choice but speaks to our lived experiences with identity development. We move back and forth between stages, regressing and progressing, encountering new knowledge, having new experiences, working through the emotions, the potential resistance, acceptance, denials, and eventual integration into our beliefs, perspectives, and sense of self.

Helms's model also connects the development of a White racial identity with the development of an antiracist identity. To understand one's racial self is to understand the system that constructed it, to face one's role in and benefits from that system, and then use that knowledge and privilege to dismantle Whiteness and the inequality it breeds.

> *In a class on the social construction of Whiteness, a White business student shared about how she used her privilege in job interviews. As a highly accomplished student, she interviewed with a number of large companies, and at each she asked the interviewers to describe the company's demographics as well as its values, philosophies, and efforts/programs around diversity, equity, and inclusion. She knew that by doing so, she would be amplifying and expanding the validity of the voice of those with marginalized identities who were likely concerned with and working on those issues within the company already. She would also be establishing the fact that these are not just issues for folks with marginalized identities, that all companies should be thinking about this. Asking these questions as a person of color comes with the risk of being seen as someone who may not fit in or who could be demanding, but she knew that asking as a White woman might actually work in her favor, positioning her as someone who thinks about others, company values, and social relations. She could then share what she learned from what and how they answered with others.*

In 2017, Helms called for us in the field of counseling psychology to use our growing awareness of the operational nature of Whiteness to deconstruct it, or what Whiteness scholars describe as "making Whiteness strange," making Whiteness and the White lived experience the subject of study and analysis. To that end, Helms offered the following strategies:

- Suppose White psychologists were to make conscientious efforts to replace their virtually exclusive focus on race and racism, defined as experiences of others, with self-exploration of Whiteness and self-disclosure about race and racism as they affect themselves and the White people they love and respect who benefit from it. For example, they could provide a window into Whiteness by revealing their own feelings when some tragic incident happens in society (e.g., White police shooting unarmed Black teenagers).

- If psychologists practiced ongoing self-diagnosis of their own racial identity schemas, recognizing that some moments, days, or weeks will be more progressive than other times, they could structure their own roles in their racial interactions better instead of being at the mercy of others.

- Considering that White people's reactions (e.g., students in classes) to counter normative discussions about racism are well known and predictable, teachers and researchers could develop and study inductions by which students, for example, are forewarned about their likely reactions to explicit racial content.

- Alternatively, imagine class activities with deconstructing Whiteness as their theme. . . . Such strategies would be an alternative to asking the student(s) of color to share their experiences of racism.

- Rather than collaborating with People of Color to study psychological issues in their communities, White researchers should collaborate with them to operationally define and study Whiteness explicitly.

- Instead of disregarding theories of Whiteness contributed by scholars of color, White theorists, researchers, and practitioners should recognize such exclusion as another form of othering that prevents them from learning as much about themselves as they otherwise could. (Helms, 2017, p. 725)

ACT: Assess Your Knowledge, Critical Thinking, Take Part

Assess Your Knowledge

- Watch Part 3 of Race: *The Power of an Illusion*, "The House We Live In" (Adelman, 2003), and think about how the information in it adds to or changes your understanding of the social context of your family's story and our nation's racial history.

- White students, take Helms's White Racial Identity Attitude Scale (WRIAS) (Helms, 1990, pp. 67–69 & 249–251). Students of color, assess the WRIAS as an instrument.

- As a way to begin some self-assessment around race, work through these two prompts augmented from "Autoethnography as a Method" (Chang, 2008):

  1. Considering your knowledge of race, select and chronologically list major events or experiences from your life that built that knowledge base. Include the date and a brief account of each item. Select one event/experience from your timeline that led to significant racial/cultural self-discovery. Describe its circumstances, and explain why it is important in your life.

  2. List five artifacts, in order of importance, that represent your race/culture, and briefly describe what each artifact represents. Select one, and expound on the meaning of this article to your life.

Critical Thinking

- Work through this modified autoethnographic prompt (Chang, 2008): Using race as a behavioral and cognitive topic on which to observe yourself, select a manageable time frame for self-observation, and identify a recording method (narrative, structured format, or hybrid). Conduct systematic self-observation and record your observation, including context information such as time, duration, location, people, occasion, and mood.

- Review Peggy McIntosh's list of White privileges (2017) and contemporize it. White students, make note of the ones you have experienced. Students of color, denote how you have observed those privileges at work for Whites, and make note of privileges you may possess.

- Read Tim Wise's *White Like Me* and/or Robin DiAngelo's *White Fragility*, write your own racial awareness timeline, and begin to chronicle your own racial identity journey.

Take Part

Participation: Begin to "make Whiteness strange" by noticing and naming it in discussions with friends and family.

Initiation: Read one of the studies on race and college students referenced in this chapter (e.g. Bonilla-Silva, Feagin), conduct that same study among your peers, and then analyze and discuss your results.

Keep a racial journal of your day-to-day life on your college campus. Journal about discussions of race, acts of discrimination, racial jokes, et cetera, and then look for patterns and meaning in your entries to share, discuss, and explore further.

Activism: Bring up Whiteness in your classes; make it a source of conversation and study in your academic program. If a course on Whiteness does not already exist on your campus, start asking why, and start a movement to begin one.

Form a White identity affinity group to study more about Whiteness and White identity development and to strategize ways White students can serve as allies to students of color and other marginalized students.

LIVED EXPERIENCES AND SOCIAL INFLUENCES

iStock/mediaphotos

7

POPULAR CULTURE, SOCIAL MEDIA, TECHNOLOGY, AND REPRESENTATION

LEARNING OBJECTIVES

- Describe, and give examples of, the role of popular culture in the distribution and maintenance of social narratives and stereotypes
- Outline the links among stereotypes, social practice, and public policy
- Characterize the impact of social media on social attitudes, psychosocial health, and ideas about race
- Extract and analyze the, at times unseen, ways that social inequality and White privilege can be embedded in technology

I believe that artificial intelligence will become a major human rights issue in the twenty-first century. We are only beginning to understand the long-term consequences of these decision-making tools on both masking and deepening social inequality. . . . While we often think of terms such as "big data" and "algorithms" as being benign, neutral, or objective, they are anything but. The people who make these decisions hold all types of values, many of which openly promote racism, sexism, and false notions of meritocracy. (Noble, 2018, p. 1)

Black fishing . . . cultural appropriation . . . racial limitations on facial recognition . . . predictive analytics . . . news coverage of "looting": Though seemingly an unrelated list of items, they are all linked by racial representation—the ideas we have of others. In the case of these issues of representation, they are also linked by their presence in popular culture, social media, and digital technologies. In Chapter 2 we discussed racial projects; in Chapter 5 you read about stereotyping. So you are likely well aware of common social constructions and inaccurate media representations—poor people are lazy and have dysfunctional families (a.nd in terms of news and media representation, are largely people of color), while middle-class folks have strong family values (and are often represented as White and suburban); women are overly emotional and dependent, while men are more rational and independent; homosexuals are flamboyant (and in popular culture, largely White and middle/upper-middle class);

Asians are quiet exotic foreigners, Muslims are terrorists, and Black and brown folks are overly sexual and criminal. Not merely stereotypes, these ideas have become social narratives. These images, stories, and popular culture representations inform how we view these populations, how we explain social phenomena, and they become the ways in which we see individuals.

The media has long been seen as the primary vehicles for the transmission and reifying of these representations, television and film chief amongst its instruments. In recent years, the media for social narrative construction and distribution have expanded to include social media and digital technologies, all available to us on devices we carry with us and screens we access for, according to a Nielsen study ("Time Flies," 2018), on average, about 11 hours a day. We are consuming images, ideas, and advertising messages all day long on various social media platforms. The representations, and our internalization of them, are almost inescapable.

POP CULTURE, THE NEWS, AND THE IMPLICATIONS OF REPRESENTATIONS

We are likely most familiar with the images on television and in films. There are the classic stereotypes—the dumb blonde, the Mexican drug dealer, the sassy Black friend, and the oft-used character tropes—the brunette (especially if she wears glasses) is the smart one, the villain looks and sounds different from the other central characters (darker skin tone, and in cartoons sometimes a different color, an ill-proportioned body, and/or foreign accent) (Dobrow & Gidney, 1998), the hero is often a lone wolf tough guy, White and male (sidekick and love interest often included) (Vera & Gordon, 2003), et cetera. Those images do more than draw us into a fictional story. As we have discussed, when it comes to people with marginalized identities, limited individual contact means that those images can shape our sense of reality; in other words, they feel true. When these representations become shared narratives, they shape ideologies, social practice, and even policy.

Part of the power of these constructions is that they exist almost everywhere we look. Television and movies aren't the only places where men are portrayed as strong,

smart, and natural leaders, while women are imaged as nurturing, kind, and dependent. For example, in many churches, men are leaders, and women organize the food
and work in the nursery. We have likely witnessed a teacher needing help with tech
and how often they ask a boy to assist, but if they need someone to show around
the new student or model appropriate behavior, a girl is the likely choice. If we were
thinking of an elementary school teacher in that last example, we probably imagined
a woman, but if we were talking principals, we'd likely think of a male. So entrenched
are these representations that they have become normalized and expected. A former
male colleague of mine recounted this story:

> A new female faculty member struggled when she first began teaching in
> the education department at our small liberal arts college. She had previ-
> ously taught online classes in a large, research-based institution and had
> gained a reputation as a strong teacher and researcher, but at this school,
> her evaluations were uncharacteristically low. Students reported find-
> ing her "unapproachable" and "rigid," the material difficult and "poorly
> explained," and the expectations "too high."
>
> I gave her some advice. I thought, now that she was teaching in-person classes,
> that students were likely seeing her through a gendered lens. I suspected that
> what was seen from me, a male professor, as intellectual rigor and seriousness
> could be viewed as cold sternness and dispassion from a female faculty
> member. So, sadly, I advised her to periodically use upspeak, vary her tone of
> voice—sporadically raising it an octave or two, smile more, and gently touch
> students on their arms from time to time. As she tried out these suggestions,
> she changed nothing in the syllabus, not the number or kinds of readings,
> and not her assessments, yet her evaluation numbers rose significantly.
> Students began to see her as a strong teacher who had "high expectations" but
> "explained concepts well" and helped students reach their goals. She was now
> seen as "relatable," "available," and "helpful." Seemingly, her previous affect
> and approach did not reflect how students expected a female faculty member
> to behave. (Those characteristics had worked well for me; my evaluations
> are always good.) When she operated in the ways her students expected

of a female—kind, friendly, approachable, relational—suddenly how they saw her, her teaching, and the class changed. Course assignments were no longer "too difficult," and concepts were easier to understand. I hated that it worked.

Since 2007, the Geena Davis Institute on Gender in the Media has studied gender and racial representation in popular culture, focusing on family films, prime time television shows, and children's shows, and they have recently added LGBTQ+ and disabilities representations to their areas of analysis. Their most recent research (2018) on the top 100 highest-grossing family films of 2017 revealed many of the same trends they have reported over the past decade: Male characters outnumber female ones two to one. (In the films they studied, 59% of the characters were male, and 26% of the characters were female—surprisingly, in previous studies, they have found the worst gender ratios occurring in children's shows.) Men take up 60.9% of the screen time and 63.7% of speaking time, despite findings that family films with a female lead grossed 38% more revenue than films with a male leads in 2017.

Regarding race, White lead actors were present at a four-to-one ratio to actors of color (73% vs. 17%), despite findings that family films with racially diverse coleads earned 60.5% more revenue than films with only White lead actors. Less than 1% of family films had an LGBTQ+ lead, and similarly, less than 1% had a lead with disabilities, an underrepresentation that they found unchanged over the last decade.

The overrepresentation of men is not simply inaccurate but reflects social values and ideas about gender; it speaks to whose voices we value, who we see as leaders, who we expect to act, and who we expect to be passive. These messages, delivered to children during a key developmental stage, have the added effect of impacting identity development as well as internalized expectations for social behavior.

iStock/metamorworks

Constructed, then projected, these representations inform social practice, the lens through which we see the world, and how we function therein. Consider this story:

> A White friend of mine was driving her high school son and his friends home from school, when she became curious about the whispering and laughter from the back. After dropping off the friends, she asked her son about that conversation. Eventually, her son described to her a "game" many of his friends were playing. Students would go to local stores after school, shoplift, and then display what they had stolen the next day in a kind of contest—who had stolen the best, biggest, and most stuff. Recovering from her initial shock and disgust, the mom first condemned their actions, asked about her son's involvement, asked how long it had been going on, and warned him of the trouble they would be in if this was discovered. Her son then told her some of the schemes they used to avoid getting caught—they selected stores with Blacks in them; then they could likely avoid being watched, knowing that the Blacks would draw more attention; and then they wouldn't exit until they could do so at the same time as a Black person, so that if an alarm went off, they knew security would stop the Black person, and they'd be able to walk away undetected.

Ideas become behaviors, behaviors impact social practice, social practice influences policy. You may recall the news coverage that followed the aftermath of Hurricane Katrina in 2005. One infamous image from that coverage showed side-by-side pictures of a young Black man and a White couple carrying goods from a local store. The Black man was described as carrying goods he had looted, while the White couple was described as having "found" goods at a local store. The same behavior is characterized in very different ways. The Whites were seen as doing what they needed to in order to care for their families in a crisis, while Blacks, doing the same thing, were seen as committing a crime.

More recently, a similar comparison was done with mug shots. Black and brown bodies are commonly represented as criminal, violent, and aggressive throughout popular culture, from news coverage to television and film images, but what may be less obvious is the counter construction of Whites. In the use of senior portrait pictures, cap-and-gown pictures, or pictures of men in suits as the way we depict White criminals, we afford to Whites the privilege of being more fully human. They become persons with a back story who have a broader set of factors to consider, who are possibly more innocent. In contrast, Black and brown bodies are often represented with mug shots. It is possible that the folks making the decisions about which pictures to use are not fully conscious of why they've made those choices. They are likely operating out of their unconscious bias—out of ideas of Whiteness and of people of color they may not even be aware of possessing. Whether the choice is made consciously or not, the images impact social beliefs, and those beliefs can impact actions and policies in and out of the judicial system.

Research on medical doctors has revealed racial disparities in care, access, and outcomes between patients of color and White patients (Brewer & Cooper, 2014). In many of these cases, the doctors weren't conscious of their discriminatory actions; they thought they were merely assessing patients, drawing on their experience and training to evaluate and develop the right treatment plan for each one. But what was also at work in the doctors' assessments were the representations the doctors had seen of who people are and what their lives are like, as well as the doctors' ill-informed assumptions about their patients' behaviors, values, and intelligence levels, based on the representations the doctors had seen. Imagine how these representations might impact therapeutic work as well: which emotions, intensions, and behaviors, we may be more apt to see in one client than another. Consider how those views might impact treatment plans, relational engagements, or even our affect and approach in sessions, et cetera.

Simultaneously, think about the mental and physical impacts on people with marginalized identities of dealing with and fearing these representations, stereotypes, and biases on a daily basis. Recently, medical and psychological research has shown the linkages between health and racism, discrimination, and other intersecting oppressions:

> Racial and ethnic discrimination has been postulated as a multidimensional environmental stressor at the societal and individual levels. That is, there are physiological consequences of chronic exposure to fluctuating or heightened neural or neuroendocrine response that results from repeated or chronic stress. Over time, these stressful life experiences can have detrimental effects on the health of people in historically marginalized groups. (Brewer & Cooper, 2014, p. 455)

Drawing on the known link between sleep and mental and physical health, Ong, Lee, Cerrada, and Williams (2017) conducted a study called "Stigma Consciousness, Racial Microaggressions, and Sleep Disturbance Among Asian Americans." Their findings included the following:

> As participants' levels of stigma consciousness increased, so did their tendency to experience diminished sleep quality and shorter sleep on nights after they reported more racial microaggressions. These results remained robust after adjustments for age, gender, nativity, socioeconomic status, and individual differences in the average level of daily racial microaggressions reported. . . . In addition to actual exposure to discrimination, evidence suggests that individual differences in stigma consciousness or the extent to which one expects to be stereotyped by others is associated with poor mental and psychological health outcomes. . . . (p. 1)

> More generally, this study adds to a growing body of data suggesting that daily discrimination may impact mental health via its influence on sleep disturbance. (p. 6)

SOCIAL MEDIA

My (DI) 13-year-old niece told me about the social networking site she was allowed to use, as her mother deemed her too young for Facebook. She boasted of having over 100 friends on the site. I asked how many of them were people she knew, and she said, "all of them." I then realized that words that I thought were commonly understood now had variant meanings. By "knew" I meant folks she had face-to-face contact with, but she felt as if being identified as a "friend" on her site was the same thing as "knowing" someone. The *Daily Telegraph* (Chester, 2017) referenced three studies that each reported that 15% of people admit to interrupting a sexual encounter to answer the phone. Our students talk about their preferences for texting because of the vulnerability they feel in making a phone call, even for important conversations.

Our near constant engagement with social media has changed our notions of intimacy, the construction and projection of our identity, our sense of reality, and even how our brain works and processes information (Vannucci & Ohannessian, 2019):

> Social media appears to be a pervasive and salient developmental context in the daily lives of early adolescents. . . . (p. 14)

> Yet, little is known about social media use patterns and their longitudinal impact on social development and psychopathology during early adolescence, which are crucial years during which social media use begins, peer acceptance and friendships become paramount, and risk for psychopathology increases. (p. 20)

Social media use has been linked to social anxiety, depression, and addiction (Vannucci & Ohannessian, 2019). Beyond social networking, we have seen its ability to empower social movements (the **Arab Spring**, #BlackLivesMatter, #MeToo, etc.), influence behavior (planking, the cinnamon challenge, etc.), and sway opinion (Russian efforts to impact the presidential election of 2016). As a tool for messaging and advertising, it is unparalleled. Pew Research Center (2019) reported that in 2005, 5% of the those surveyed used at least one social media site/app, by 2011 that number was 50%, and today it is 72% (97% for adolescents), with most visiting a site at least once a day and spending an average of 142 minutes on social media. Salim (2019) indicated that this figure grew to more than three hours for those age 16–24). Like other forms of popular culture, social media platforms are effective message creation and delivery systems, and given our level of consumption, one of the most invasive.

Representations are commonplace in memes, gifs, posts, and advertising as well as in our interactions with the messages we receive. In "When Memes Are Mean," Duchscherer and Dovidio (2016) write,

> Internet memes may not only represent an individual's expression of bias, but also may perpetuate bias online. Situations on the Internet that prioritize humor and allow for the expression of negative attitudes toward outgroups can lead to communication that reflects disparagement humor—remarks

that derogate a target for amusement (Ford, 2015). Such attitudes are present in many Internet settings, such as communities that share memes whose messages make light of holding objectionable views (Vickery, 2014) or perpetuate stereotypes, which may trivialize the stereotypes' impacts on low-status groups (Penney, 2015). Consistent with this observation is the finding that stereotypical jokes and statements are generally considered to be more socially acceptable in Internet contexts than elsewhere (Shifman & Lemish, 2011). (p. 1)

We both create and re-create representations and are simultaneously influenced and changed by them.

In 2011, following the devastating tsunami in Japan, a student sent me a snapshot of one of her social media feeds. The post included statements such as the following:

"Apparently God hasn't forgotten about Pearl Harbor either. . . ."

"It's been almost a full day of tsunami coverage. Time to move on. At first, I really did kinda feel bad for Japan. But then, I Googled 'Pearl Harbor Death Toll" There. All better."

"So I was watching videos of the earthquake and tsunami in Japan and I was thinking, this is the worlds payback for pearl harbor!"

"Japan comes to America to attack pearl harbor. America goes to Japan to help. Well, at least we haven't forgotten 9/11."

"those damn krauts deserve to be hit by a earthquake tsunami for nuking pearl harbor."

It is likely that the primary contributors to this wall are not themselves veterans of World War II, and given some of the statements posted here and the silence in our classrooms when we ask questions about US history, we also imagine that few of those posting have much knowledge of Pearl Harbor. So why the vitriol? Beyond messaging, social media operates as an informal community-building feedback loop.

Social media algorithms take in data about which pages we visit, which videos we watch, and how long we hover over images, and from that data, these media determine what we are likely to be drawn to, and we are then given more of that. We feel connected to others who comment on or "like" the things we do, those ideas get projected and repeated back to us, and we feel affirmed by voices that agree with us and more distant from those that don't. In the tsunami posts, Pearl Harbor and the Japanese operate like a straw man—a stand in for other ideas, a representation of a threat and the construction of an "other." The contributors to these posts are expressing their views but also gaining a sense of community with others, both of which appear to heighten their emotional response. This response feeds and reifies itself, making it harder for us to differentiate our ideas and thoughts from those of others or to identify how much the feedback loop has enhanced or manipulated the veracity of our emotions.

Social scientists now regularly track and analyze the presence of hate speech on social media and its implications for how we view ourselves and others. In 2013, Dr. Monica Stephens introduced what she called a "Geography of Hate," a map of the United States that indicated the places of origin and concentrations of "hate tweets" posted during and following major events.

The Southern Poverty Law Center now monitors not simply the physical presence of hate groups throughout the United States but also their digital presence and actions as well. Websites, blogs, fan fiction sites, and invitation-only social media circles have become the primary recruitment and communications mechanisms for these organizations, allowing for the development of a feeling of community and acceptance well before users might know the nature of the organization they are engaged with.

TECHNOLOGY

We cannot count the number of times we say, "We are living in the future." Technological advancements occur at a spectacular pace, bringing constant changes to the ways in which we live. That includes robots, artificial intelligence, and **predictive algorithms** that used to function largely in the terrain of science fiction. Today, they are changing the way we operate in the world, from the mundane elements of daily living to changes to our labor market and economy. With devices in our homes, cars, and hands, we can listen to almost any song, get information, or communicate with others, simply by requesting it aloud. We likely are able (or will soon be able) to make a dinner or hotel reservation over the phone with a robot, be driven by an autonomous vehicle, and have coupons delivered to us based on a program's awareness of our current location and documented interests. On social media, we can create and project whichever version of ourselves or our lives we wish, but in virtual reality, we can experience a whole world of our making.

As the quotation from Noble (2018) states in the opening of this chapter, we tend to think of the tech behind these advancements as "benign" or "neutral," but because these advancements have come from our minds and out of our unequitable social context, we bring our biases, attitudes, and history into their development. In "Biased by Design" (2016), Y-Vonne Hutchinson wrote about Snapchat's inability to read her dark skin. Tom Simonite, of *Wired* (2017) reported on Gfycat's facial recognition system's difficulty in distinguishing Asian faces, and that research had found that "Microsoft and IBM were at least 95 percent accurate at recognizing the gender of lighter-skinned women, but erred at least 10 times more frequently when examining photos of dark-skinned women." He also reported on the various measures taken by their and other companies to address and improve their systems. Even some automatic soap dispensers were reported to have difficulty reading darker skin because of light sensors' settings (Plenke, 2015). In each of these cases, the lack of diversity, equity, and inclusion in tech companies and the general default to Whiteness, as a stand-in for all of humanity, led to technological developments that replicated our social inequalities and hierarchies.

When Henry Gan, a software engineer at Gfycat, began working on their facial recognition issue,

> He first tried to fix the problem by gathering more examples of the kinds of faces where his software stumbled. . . . Adding in Asian and Black celebrity faces from Gfycat's own image collection helped only a little. (Simonite, 2017)

In response, Gan built what he called an "Asian-detector," which, when it reads an Asian face,

> flips into a more sensitive mode, applying a stricter threshold before declaring a match. . . . "[That] was the only way to get it to not mark every Asian person as Jackie Chan or something," Gan said. The company says the system is now 98 percent accurate for white people, and 93 percent accurate for Asians. (Simonite, 2017)

Our histories of racial segregation and isolation as well as the primacy of Whiteness are present in these technologies, and just as it is with tackling those problems in society, the answer is not simply numbers based. Adding more diversity (in the content of our data, in tech company personnel ranks, engineering teams, marketing/testing teams, etc.) along with the inclusion of their voices and ideas was a start, but real gains came from specificity of understanding.

Imagine if one's presumption as a therapist was that bias could be overcome by simply treating everyone the same and trying to avoid bias by avoiding the stereotypical ideas associated with a marginalized identity. That approach blinds one to the many ways representations of race are always at work in us as well as to the specificity of experience a client may be facing, how a client's particular and complex identity, within our broader social context, impacts their life. Imagine the feelings of invisibility, the lack of belonging, the lack of value one experiences in a world where their presence in technological developments has either been marked by racial constructions or not existed or been considered at all, where people—along with sensors to open doors, take a picture, wash your hands, et cetera—don't "see" you.

When it comes to race and technology, lack of representation is too often accompanied by misrepresentation. "In 2015, U.S. News and World Report reported that a 'glitch' in Google's algorithm led to a number of problems through auto-tagging and facial recognition software . . . its photo application had automatically tagged African Americans as 'apes' and 'animals'" (Noble, 2017, p. 6). Noble also chronicles the changes to Google software after it was reported in 2012 that amongst the first results for searches of "Asian girls," "Latinas," and "Black girls" were porn sites (a glitch that has since been corrected). Similarly, Otterbacher (2016) reported that image results depicting "doctors" retrieved significantly more images of men than would be expected given the number of men who actually work in the profession. The reverse was true for "nurses." In other words, the researchers showed that image search engines exaggerate gender stereotypes concerning professions. (p. 1)

We bring our biases and social inequality with us. In this case, our use of the internet, the sites we search, the gendered connections we make in the digital world, became the data that software programs used. They are now reflecting those constructions back to us, creating another feedback loop, making a gender construction seem like factual reality.

OUR RESPONSE

These narratives, representations, and constructions are pervasive and powerful, and a good deal of their impact comes from our lack of recognition of them. When we passively consume these messages, they are easier to internalize and more readily obscure reality. The Center for Media Literacy has long argued that our best tool to disengage the power of media messaging is media literacy—our ability to recognize and assess media images, their meanings, and their potential implications. The center's staff has recently updated their definition of *media literacy* to capture the changing landscape of popular culture. They now contend that

Media Literacy is a 21st century approach to education. It provides a framework to access, analyze, evaluate, create and participate with messages in a variety of forms—from print to video to the internet. Media literacy builds an understanding of the role of media in society as well as essential skills of inquiry and self-expression necessary for citizens of a democracy. (2019)

Tim Wise (2011) used a kind of media literacy to engage race and gendered messages, with the goal of enabling his children to become "conversant with the dominant culture and [to] develop a way to eventually critique it" (p. 255). In a discussion he described having with his four-year-old daughter, Ashton, about a Disney film, he wrote,

Something about the way that Hollywood . . . had managed to characterize Matoaka (Pocahontas's real name)—as an intensely spiritual stereotype—struck me as deeply troubling. Not to mention, Matoaka's story is quite a bit less romantic than the Disney version, involving as it does her forced abduction by Englishmen, from which abduction she was only able to obtain release if she agreed to marry John Rolfe. . . . That in the wake of Matoaka's capture the English would come to decimate the Powhatan people calls into question such a sanguine account. . . . After the movie ended we watched some of the special features and one in particular stood out. . . . The chief illustrator . . . displayed an image of his Pocahontas and then contrasted it with the actual image of Matoaka. . . . Needless to say, she looked nothing like the image he had created—a fact about which he proceeded to joke. . . . I saw it as my opportunity.

So he asked his daughter,

"How do you think you'd feel if someone wanted to make a movie about your life and decided they didn't like your red hair, or the color of your skin, or something like that, and decided to change it?"

"I think that would hurt my feelings," she replied.

"Yeah, I bet it would," I said. "So how do you think Native Americans might feel, seeing him joke like that about how much prettier his version is, compared to the actual Pocahontas?"

"I think it would hurt their feelings. I don't see why they couldn't just make her look the way she really looked." (2011, pp. 256–259)

Not only does Wise use the opportunity to deconstruct the sexualized and gendered issues of beauty for women in popular culture, he links that

Pocahontas wood engraving, 1884

iStock/ZU_09

discussion to race and power. He takes his daughter through a discussion where she comes to this new idea and is then given the space to begin expressing her voice and thoughts on the topic. As Vittrup (2018) writes, "Parents cannot shield their children from all the biased messages and examples of inequality that surround their children. However, they may have an opportunity to disrupt the development of biased scripts" (p. 2).

Engaging media representation is not always about countering messages, but also should amplify affirming ones:

> *My five- and seven-year-old nieces love watching YouTube videos, so I used a clip on "Black Girl Magic" to introduce them to that phrase, to amazing Black girls and women, and to talk about the power of their racial identity, their cultural tradition, and activated self-love. We watched the video featuring Black female athletes, artists, mothers and daughters, politicians, ballerinas, scientists, writers, warriors, and little girls, all moving and speaking with pride, joy, determination, and confidence. When it was done, I asked them, What did you see? They named people they recognized and asked about some they didn't, and we talked about all the poses, styles, and facial expressions as well as the girls that looked like them. We watched it again, and I asked them, What is Black Girl Magic? They thought about it and then began to say—one after another—"dancing," "power," "pride." After a bit the five-year-old said, "Wait, you're making me cry, this is making me cry, Auntie." I said, "I know, me too. This is amazing—what it means to know and love who you are, and to have that be the source of your ability to change the world." I then asked them what their magic is, what about who they are makes the world a better place and makes them happy to be who they are. . . . I loved their answers.*

Beyond the opportunities and tools to deconstruct and thus disempower negative representations, some argue that we should rethink our usage of and reliance on some of the sources of these messages, our personal devices and social media use. As we have seen in this chapter, there is growing evidence of the link between social media consumption and issues such as anxiety and depression. Lessening how much we use social media may seem an easy solution, but it doesn't address the reasons those issues arose—the sources of one's feelings of inadequacy or fear of missing out (FOMO). Along with analyzing the representations we are taking in, we should also analyze our engagement with them—when do we use our devices? Why? How are we feeling while doing so? et cetera. Assessing ourselves and our use of digital technologies, social media, and the internet lessens the power of the narratives therein and assists us in gaining a more accurate view of ourselves and reality. Becoming conscious of how and why we use social media is part of what Cal Newport (2019) calls "digital minimalism," where he emphasizes the import of using digital media with purposeful intentionality, having a philosophy about our use and needs that allows us to decide what to use and how, and thus minimizing external manipulation.

The rise of the internet and social media sites has also shown us the potential for communication, connectedness, and activism. We have seen movements like the Arab Spring use social media as a covert communication mechanism, we've witnessed #BlackLivesMatter move from a Twitter discussion to a physical movement and organization with branches across the country, we've seen hashtags used to intentionally start a movement, as with #MeToo. The use of social media as a location for the articulation of digital **counter narratives** and community building is evident with the rise of collectives like "Black Twitter" and the social media campaign of "It Gets Better." In a 2018 study on activism and social media, researchers at Pew Research Center found that people in the Black and Latinx communities see social media

> platforms as an especially important tool for their own political engagement. For example, roughly half of black social media users say these platforms are . . . important to them as a venue for expressing their political views or for getting involved with issues that are important to them. Those shares fall to around a third among white social media users. (Anderson, Toor, Rainie, & Smith, 2018)

Table 7.1 shows the use of different kinds of social media by people in various demographic groups.

TABLE 7.1 ● Demographics of Internet Usage

Percentage of US adults who say they ever use the following online platforms or messaging apps

	YouTube	Facebook	Instagram	Pinterest	LinkedIn	Snapchat	Twitter	WhatsApp	Reddit
US adults	73%	69%	37%	28%	27%	24%	22%	20%	11%
Men	78	63	31	15	29	24	24	21	15
Women	68	75	43	42	24	24	21	19	8
White	71	70	33	33	28	22	21	13	12
Black	77	70	40	27	24	28	24	24	4
Hispanic	78	69	51	22	16	29	25	42	14
Ages 18–29	91	79	67	34	28	62	38	23	22
18–24	90	76	75	38	17	73	44	20	21
25–29	93	84	57	28	44	47	31	28	23
30–49	87	79	47	35	37	25	26	31	14
50–64	70	68	23	27	24	9	17	16	6
65+	38	46	8	15	11	3	7	3	1
<$30,000	68	69	35	18	10	27	20	19	9
$30,000–$74,999	75	72	39	27	26	26	20	16	10

	YouTube	Facebook	Instagram	Pinterest	LinkedIn	Snapchat	Twitter	WhatsApp	Reddit
$75,000+	83	74	42	41	49	22	31	25	15
High school or less	64	61	33	19	9	22	13	18	6
Some college	79	75	37	32	26	29	24	14	14
College+	80	74	43	38	51	20	32	28	15
Urban	77	73	46	30	33	29	26	24	11
Suburban	74	69	35	30	30	20	22	19	13
Rural	64	66	21	26	10	20	13	10	8

Note: Respondents who did not give an answer are not shown. Whites and Blacks include only non-Hispanics. Hispanics are of any race. Survey conducted Jan. 8–Feb. 7, 2019.

Source: Pew Research Center (2019).

CONCLUSION

There is no inherent evil in the technological advancements we are experiencing, other than what we bring to their use and development. We have infused popular culture with the stereotypical representations of folks from marginalized communities; our biases have become embedded in the digital programs and technologies we create. Technology's benefits of access and convenience come with the costs of loss of privacy and personal information manipulation. The images and narratives they produce and project can reify existing social inequalities and, in response, we can become equipped to deconstruct, dismantle, and disrupt those messages and use the potency of these technologies to reaffirm our identities and operate in our agency to restructure the world.

ACT: Assess Your Knowledge, Critical Thinking, Take Part

Assessing Your Knowledge

- Visit the Geena Davis Institute on Gender in Media online, and review the collection of studies.

- Read and employ the suggestions for media usage offered by the Center for Media Literacy.

- Watch documentaries on media representation (e.g. *Mickey Mouse Monopoly, Codes of Gender, Dream World 3, Beyond Beats and Rhymes, Latinos Beyond Reel, The Slanted Screen, Reel Injuns, Ethnic Notions, Tough Guise 2, Miss-Representation,* etc.)

Critical Thinking

- Rewatch some of your favorite childhood shows and movies, and apply the questions of representation reflected in the research posted on the website of the Geena Davis Institute on Gender in the Media (number of characters, screen time, speaking time, occupations, sexualization, etc.), focusing on various social identities (LGBTQ+, immigrants, men, etc.).

- Apply those same criteria to some of your favorite current popular culture elements.

Take Part

Participation: Keep a journal of your social media usage: when you use, amount of time, duration, sites visited, et cetera. Then do a self-analysis of your use and its impact on you. Think about how you want to use digital media and what media you want to use, and make that change.

Initiation: Consider the representation that you have internalized, and think about ways to explore and produce a counter narrative (e.g., join or start a community through a Facebook group, hashtag, or set of posts) and to augment your speech in your face-to-face social circle to reflect that counter narrative.

Activism: Watch the YouTube video of the 2018 Infinity Award winner, Alexandra Bell. She researches the stories behind the images, headlines, and text in newspaper coverage; edits them; turns her efforts into printed posters; and posts them around New York City. Follow her pattern with a news story of your choosing. Then challenge your local and/or school news outlets to expand their approach to news coverage.

iStock/stock_colors

8

BEING A PERSON OF COLOR

LEARNING OBJECTIVES

- Understand the significance of microaggressions in the lives of people of color, and be able to critique the arguments against their impact

- Analyze the complexity of the concept of cultural appropriation and its impact on people of color in the United States

- Summarize the specific issues detailed for African Americans, Asian Americans, American Indians, and Latinx individuals in the United States

- Contrast and compare the issues of acculturation and assimilation that occur for people of color in the United States

- Interpret the significance of terms such as *psychological invisibility* and *perpetual foreigner* that keep some groups from feeling a sense of belonging to the United States

- Understand that though some issues are commonly experienced by members of racial groups, it is still important to treat everyone first as an individual and second as a member of a cultural group

- Select and enact a next step in learning more about one of the topics in this chapter

We titled this chapter "Being a Person of Color" because we wanted to focus some time on some of the experiences of many non-White individuals in the United States. We begin with some overarching issues and then move to individual sections for African American, American Indian, Asian American, and Latinx populations. These sections offer some common experiences that these groups might find relevant in their daily lives. It is important to note that not all people of a particular cultural group agree on what experiences are "common"; some may not experience these regularly or may never have experienced them in their lives. Remember too that depending on one's stage of racial identity development, one might acknowledge or understand different experiences in different ways. Regardless, there are some experiences that many within a racial group have experienced, and we lay out a few of these for your consideration here. First,

iStock/SDI Productions

however, we will cover two main areas that many experience in being a person of color.

MICROAGGRESSIONS

In the late 1990s, psychologist Derald Wing Sue built an expanded theory upon Charles Pierce's (1970) notion of **microaggressions**, which he defines as "brief and commonplace daily verbal, behavioral, and environmental indignities, whether intentional or unintentional, that communicate hostile, derogatory, or negative racial slights and insults toward people of color" (Sue, Capodilupo, & Holder, 2007, p. 271). As you might recall, we spent a brief amount of time in Chapter 5 talking about the three types of microaggressions in Sue's theory. Here we will go into greater detail. The first is **microassaults,** which are intentional acts of racism aimed at a particular group. Sue gives several examples of these types of microaggressions that include telling racist jokes, using racial slurs, or not hiring people of a particular race intentionally. These microassaults might be similar to either overt racism or intentional covert racism as described previously in this book. The second type of microaggression is the most commonly discussed in society today: **microinsults**. There are many examples of this type of behavior, but the gist of these are comments, actions, and behaviors that are generally not meant to be insults but that communicate surprise at the accomplishments of people who are not a part of the dominant cultural group, or rudeness with respect to discussing them. We are focusing on the racial aspects of microaggressions in this chapter, as it is focused on people of color. Nevertheless, members of any historically disenfranchised group may be impacted by them. Table 8.1 gives multiple examples of microinsults compiled by Sue and colleagues in their 2007 *Professional Psychology* article.

Consider an experience of a graduate student in the Midwest:

> One time right after I moved to the Midwest, I was in the elevator at my university, and a White man got on. We started to ride up to the top of the building, and all at once he asked me, "What country are you from, honey?" No one had ever asked me that before, probably especially because I am biracial White and Asian. Coming from California, I think people just know what that combo looks like. So I thought maybe I didn't hear him correctly, and I said, "What?" He started speaking very

slowly and loudly and he said again, "What . . . country . . . are . . . you . . . from?" like he thought I didn't understand what he said the first time because I didn't speak English. I couldn't believe it! I got mad and said loudly back, "I'm from this one. What country are you from?" He got very embarrassed and stopped talking.

I fumed the entire way up to the sixth floor to my class. I couldn't understand why it bothered me so much—I don't think there's anything wrong with being from another country! But later I thought it seemed like just one more thing telling me I didn't belong. This wasn't my place.

This was one of many experiences with microaggressions I had while in my non-diverse graduate school town. Sometimes people would "compliment" me on my nonaccented English (I don't speak any other languages) or make assumptions, such as when people seemed surprised that I was married to my White husband, and I always felt the same: confused and uncomfortable or angry when these things happened. I lived there for five years, and then we moved back to California, where there are more people like me and I am less "foreign." I can't imagine what it would be like to deal with that every day of my life.

—Jen, age 45

As you hear in this account, feelings of confusion are often present when microaggressions occur, and at the same time it may feel awkward to call someone on this type of behavior. Sometimes this type of comment is meant as a compliment, or someone, like the man in the elevator, is trying to make small talk or be friendly. Nevertheless, the impact on the person experiencing the microaggression is generally negative. A second example of a microaggression is this:

When we go shopping for a big item like a car or a computer or something that requires talking to a salesperson, we are used to how the salesperson is probably going to respond to us. They'll speak to me first because they're not 100% sure if my husband speaks English. I'm White and my husband is Mexican American, but he is third generation in the United States. He doesn't even speak Spanish. It's interesting how it trumps gender in a lot of ways. Usually there would be a stereotype that you might talk to the man in a couple about the specs on a car, for example, but without fail, if the salesperson is White, they start with me. We've gotten to the point where we can laugh about it now. I try to stay in the background sometimes or behind him if it's a purchase my husband wants to make. But it happens all the time still.

—Julie, age 70

The third type of microaggression detailed by Sue (2007) is **microinvalidation**. This type of microaggression occurs when a person labels an incident as racist, sexist, heterosexist, or the like and is told by another person that the label is not valid. Consider the vignette below.

I'm African American and I have pretty dark skin. I was dating a White girl at the time this incident took place, and we were having a fight after class on my college campus. She was yelling at me and waving her arms around because of something she thought I had done, and I was getting pretty annoyed back and started raising my voice a little. All at once these two police officers came running up and told me to put my hands up, and one had his hand on his gun. They handcuffed me real quick and asked my girlfriend if she was OK and if I was bothering her or had I hurt her or anything. She said "No! We're just having a fight—he's my boyfriend," and tried to explain what was happening, but they just kept asking her if she was OK and moving her away from me.

She realized what was happening pretty quickly, because she's seen this type of thing happen to me before, and she tried to diffuse the situation as quickly as she could by moving back over closer to me, but they wouldn't let her. They kept saying, "Do you want to press charges? Did he touch you?" and things like that.

Later I told that story to a friend of mine who is White, and he said, "Well, that would probably happen to any guy who was in that situation. They always believe the girl. I don't think that was racism." I didn't try very hard to explain it to him, but I knew that wasn't the case, and my girlfriend knew it too. It would have been different for him than it was for me, and the fact that he didn't believe me hurt our friendship a bit as well. I felt like he thought I was making too big a deal out of it or something. It was a big deal, and he should have believed me, his friend.

—Rob, age 24

One of the consequences of microinvalidations, as you can see in this vignette, is that sometimes interracial friendships decrease during adolescence (Aboud, Mendelson, & Purdy, 2003; Schachner, Brenick, Noack, Van de Vijver, & Heizmann, 2015) when more racial incidents begin to occur for Black and brown men in particular. You have likely heard others invalidate stories of racism or other discrimination before, or perhaps you have experienced this yourself when something has happened to you. You may even be realizing right now that you have perpetrated this type of invalidation yourself. The motive behind this invalidation is likely to assure the person that racism isn't the cause to help them to feel better about the situation. Unfortunately, the result of this behavior is often more frustration on the part of the person who has experienced the situation. Below is the rest of the story about Jen's experience with the man in the elevator (which was detailed above as an example of a microinsult):

The worst part of this situation is that when I got off the elevator after that encounter, I walked into my classroom, and some of my classmates (all of whom were White) were in there already. I was still pretty upset, and I said, "Listen to what just happened to me!" and detailed the story. I felt pretty good that I had stood my ground with that man and asked him what country he was from as well, and I expected my friends would respond positively to my comment to him, but when I told that part of the story, everyone looked uncomfortable. I was confused, but finally one girl said, "I don't think it was very nice of you to yell at him like that. He was probably just trying to find out about your culture." The rest of them all nodded and started to agree with her. I felt shocked. These were my friends, but they felt more empathy for this guy they didn't even know than for me—someone they knew and liked.

I told one of my friends in the program later who was also a person of color, and she understood what I was talking about. She also helped me understand their reaction a little, saying "I think it's so hard for White people to believe that things like that happen all the time, maybe partly because they wish they wouldn't happen. And maybe some of them have said things like that before and were trying to defend themselves." I think that's probably right. It doesn't come from a place of

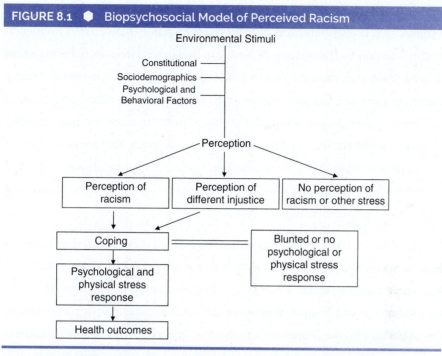

FIGURE 8.1 ● **Biopsychosocial Model of Perceived Racism**

Source: Clark, R., Anderson, N. B., Clark, V. R., & Williams, D. R. (1999). Racism as a stressor for African Americans: A biopsychosocial model. *American Psychologist*, 54, 805–816.

it might be nice to be so clear about intent at times, the idea that negative impact of microaggressions must be proven before accepted is naïve at best, and incredibly invalidating to many people of color and other marginalized groups at worst.

CULTURAL APPROPRIATION

Another racial and cultural issue that many racial and ethnic minority individuals face is the concept of **cultural appropriation**. A succinct definition of cultural appropriation is this: the adoption of various objects, cultural content, and/or the voice of a culture to which one does not belong (Crayton, 2018; Rogers, 2006). Examples might include adopting a pattern of speech, music, dress, or the rituals of one cultural group by another cultural group, but this adoption does not necessarily connote understanding or correct usage of these cultural markers. In addition, cultural appropriation should be understood within the context of power structure, and it is most problematic when a person from the dominant or privileged cultural group appropriates from a culture that is disenfranchised or holds minority status (Biolsi, 2007; Rodriguez, 2006). Behaviors such as wearing an American Indian headdress when the wearer has no connection with the symbolism behind it, or, as some have commented, "taking the pretty parts of a culture" without truly standing for the values, livelihood, or well-being of the culture from which the objects are being taken, are good examples of cultural appropriation. In addition, in a country in which media representation of any group other than White Americans is still rather scarce (see Chapter 7), putting forward images of stereotypic dress or features of non-White Americans is damaging to the way others see them in their daily lives.

We would like to take a moment to address some of the comments and questions we hear when talking to our students about cultural appropriation. Some of the things below may have been said to you before, and others you may recognize as things you have thought or said yourself. Remember that all of us make mistakes from time to time, but that does not exempt us from their consequences. Making mistakes doesn't make you a bad person, but failing to acknowledge and address their impact often leads to problems in a relationship.

"I love Japanese culture—I'm honoring it by dressing in this beautiful kimono!"
This comment is a common one by many and may be a true intent with regard to dressing in a particular way. The fact of the matter is, however, if you are not Japanese, you may not understand the significance of some of the pieces of that culture. In the 2013 American Music Awards, singer Katy Perry dressed in a kimono and painted her face like a Japanese geisha in her act. Many Asian Americans called her out on this outfit, but Perry responded by saying, "All I was trying to do is just give a very beautiful performance about a place that I have so much love for and find so much beauty in, and that was exactly where I was coming from, with no other thought besides it" (Klein, 2014). Geishas were actually entertainers in wealthy Japanese society, and they were lauded for their beauty and traditional femininity. Regardless of the fact that traditional geishas were not actually prostitutes, many Westerners have the belief that they were, and so the representation of this figure sexualizes Asian women as well. In addition, Perry's outfit wasn't even completely Japanese, but instead had Chinese features as well, and the song she sang while wearing it was instead about Madagascar.

Many comments were made on both sides of the issue. While some asked for Perry to make a better apology, others said she should not apologize, because she hadn't intended to offend. (See previous section for difference between intent and impact.) Though Perry and the dancers mimicked the stereotypical palms together and bowing accents that one often sees as a part of mocking Asian culture, others said, "Frankly, Perry's performance could have been a lot worse. There was no eyelid tugging. There were no grating fake accents and cries of ching-chong" (Park, 2013, para 15). We are left with the question: "Is 'could have been worse' all we can expect?" Yes, it's true that Perry didn't commit the most outrageous racism that we've seen in popular culture, but the bottom line here is that if you aren't from a particular culture, you probably shouldn't adopt its traditions, unless you have full understanding of what they mean.

As another blogger notes about appropriation, "Whether people 'should' be offended by it or not doesn't matter; the fact that some people *are* offended by it does" (Feeney, 2013). Herein lies the crux for us: If someone says something hurts, is it better to say, "It shouldn't hurt you; I didn't mean it to," or "I didn't know; I'm sorry"? Katy Perry herself talked more fully about the American Music Awards and other cultural gaffes she has made in various performances in 2017 after learning more about cultural appropriation herself. In an interview with Black Lives Matter leader DeRay Meckesson, Perry noted, "I didn't know I did [the geisha performance] wrong until I heard people saying I did it wrong. . . . And sometimes that's what it takes, is it takes someone to say, out of compassion, out of love, 'This is where the origin is, and do you understand?'" (Chasmar, 2017, para 6). One final point here: A better way of honoring a culture is to stand up for it in times of discrimination. If that idea makes you feel uncomfortable, you may be, as noted above, just taking the pretty parts of the culture.

"You're being too sensitive. I didn't mean to hurt anyone with this outfit." Intentionality of this type of appropriating is not the issue in this particular concept. You may hear celebrities from time to time who have made the mistake of appropriating a piece of someone's culture making comments such as "I'm sorry *if* you were offended!" as opposed to taking responsibility for making this type of mistake. You may have had friends apologize to you in the past using the phrase "if you were offended" and may have experienced that this comment doesn't always feel like a "real" apology. The impact is the issue here, and so noting how racial and ethnic minorities experience this type of slight is more important to acknowledge than the intent.

"If Black people wear their hair like that, I don't understand why I can't too!"
This argument is often used to defend a hairstyle such as cornrows or braids. Again, we see these hairstyles on many non–African American music stars and other celebrities. In 2015, African American 16-year-old actress Amandla Stenberg created a You Tube video titled "Don't Cashcrop on My Cornrows," in which she talked about the purpose of cornrows for African American women (to keep their hair neat and healthy). In the video, Stenberg noted, "Braids and corn rows are not merely stylistic," and commented, "Appropriation occurs when a style leads to racist generalizations or stereotypes where it originated, but is deemed as high fashion, cool, or funny when the privileged take it for themselves." In addition, Stenberg recounted hip hop musician Azealia Banks's comments on White musicians adopting black culture but not supporting it, "As Azealia Banks observed in her tweets, musicians who partook in hip-hop culture and adopted blackness, Iggy Azalea in particular, failed to speak on the racism that comes along with black identity [during the beginning of the recognition of police killings of African American children like Trayvon Martin and Tamir Rice]." Thus, "borrowing" accessories, clothing, or hairstyles that originate in Black culture or any other racial or ethnic minority group without truly supporting that group in any meaningful way is often viewed as appropriation.

"What about Notre Dame's Fighting Irish mascot or the Patriots football team? Isn't that appropriation of White culture?" The short answer to this is "No, see above." As noted in the beginning of this section, cultural appropriation is most harmful when the act includes a person from a *privileged* culture taking something from a *nonprivileged* culture. Since White Americans are the privileged group, taking things from that culture is more likely to be seen as assimilation than appropriation. In fact, many non-White cultural groups have been forced to take on White or European culture to survive. In trying to "civilize" American Indian people, White missionary groups often kidnapped American Indian children and used the phrase "Kill the Indian, save the child" (a variation on a speech given by R. H. Pratt at the Carlisle Indian School in 1892 ("Kill the Indian," n.d.). These children were forced to cut their hair into Western styles, forbidden to follow any religion except for

Christianity, and kept from visiting their parents for the first four years they attended White schools to fortify their cultural transformation. In addition, however, there are so many different images of White people and White culture shown in the media and everyday life in the United States, it would be almost impossible to stereotype them in any visible way with clothes or manner. Seeing the Fighting Irish mascot doesn't make people believe that all Irish people fight, for example, even if they are able to recognize that someone's heritage is Irish. The mascot would not keep people of Irish descent from getting a job, nor deem them as less human or of the past (as some American Indian mascots do, for example). Thus, this is not appropriation.

"The Redskins did a poll, and 70% of American Indians thought their mascot was fine." This comment is akin to saying, "My black friend thinks that racist joke is funny." The bottom line on this comment is that just because one person from a group thinks something is fine doesn't mean the rest do; one person from a racial group should not be asked to speak for all, nor should one person be allowed to stand for all. The Washington Redskins football team did conduct a poll about their mascot—of Redskins fans. Remember what we learned in Chapter 4 when we discussed the topic of racial identity development, and think for a minute about the connection to racial identity an American Indian person who roots for the Redskins might have. What stage would you guess they are in, and might that not account for their agreement with utilizing a racist team name and mascot in this way? People in any cultural group are diverse. Just because one person is not bothered by racism toward the group doesn't mean another won't be.

"I need a list of everything that is deemed cultural appropriation." We wish we had one too! This comment is often reflective of persons who would like to do the right thing and who are concerned that they may make a mistake and offend someone. Many of you (and we!) have been in a situation where you may have wished for something like this, but the reality is that there is no definitive list. There are some situations in which it is likely that most people might deem something appropriative, but there are others that might take you by surprise. Regardless of intentionality, the best response in our experience is that when someone says "Ouch," you should acknowledge it. It's OK to say that you didn't mean to offend, *and* say that you're sorry to have hurt them regardless. Cultural appropriation is something about which each person needs to make their own decision. You could be appropriately wearing a piece of culture that you have legitimate access to and still have someone comment on it in a negative way. This is one of the reasons we also caution our students not to "call people out" but to "call them in"—asking questions and getting to understand the perspectives of others is a very important part of interracial relationships overall.

"It's just a Halloween costume—I think it's funny to dress like this." Some students at the Ohio State University have worked to combat the type of cultural appropriation that often appears around the time of Halloween, when some may choose to dress up as members of a particular culture. Read about their group Students Teaching About Racism in Society (STARS) in Spotlight Feature 8.1.

SPOTLIGHT FEATURE 8.1

"STARS: Students Teaching About Racism in Society"

Students can make a difference. We know this, and yet perhaps no better illustration of how this might happen in the area of multicultural education is found in the example set by a group of students at Ohio University in Athens, Ohio. Students there formed a group called STARS, which stands for "students teaching about racism in society." Their mission statement, as posted on their website, is: "The purpose of STARS is to facilitate discussion about diversity and all isms (sexism, classism, heterosexism, ethnocentrism etc.) with an emphasis on racial issues. We aim to raise awareness about social justice, and promote racial harmony" (STARS, 2013)

Though the group was established in 1988 by Sheila Williams and Louise Annarino (STARS, 2013; Wang, 2016), it began to receive national attention for their campaign started in 2011 titled "We're a culture, not a costume" (Ng, 2011), which depicts photos of people dressed in Halloween costumes that appropriate from various cultural groups. Each poster includes someone of a non-White identity holding a photo of someone depicting their cultural group in a stereotypic and/or offensive way: "An Asian girl holds an image of someone dressed up as a geisha. A Mexican boy holds a photo of someone in a sombrero, colorful poncho, and exaggerated mustache riding a stuffed donkey" (Ng, 2011, para 2).

While the tagline "We're a culture, not a costume" has accompanied each iteration of the campaign, other statements have been featured each year, including, "When this is how the world sees you, it's just not funny," and "You wear the costume for one night, I wear the stigma for life" (Wang, 2016).

In the 2016 campaign, one of the posters depicted a couple dressed as a police officer and a person in black face with the tagline "My fight is not your costume" (Wang, 2016). The president of the group at the time gave the following statement to NBC

News: "We feel that culturally appropriative costumes alienate and exotify certain students on our campus, and [we] wanted to educate people on the harmful effects of enforcing negative stereotypes of minorities" (Wang, 2016, para 4).

STARS states that their guiding principle is "each one teach one," which is something you may be able to apply to your own life in thinking about these concepts. We encourage you to visit their website (www.ohio.edu/orgs/stars) to see their poster campaigns and to learn more about how to set up an organization at your own institution.

SPECIFIC ISSUES FOR SPECIFIC RACIAL AND ETHNIC MINORITY POPULATIONS

For the rest of this chapter, we have chosen a particular issue for each of four racial groups. We hope you will do more research on each of these specific issues, and we have laid out additional resources at the end of this chapter. These next sections can tell you more about being a person of color.

African Americans: The Struggle for True Freedom #Black Lives Matter

Four years ago, what is now known as the Black Lives Matter Global Network began to organize. It started out as a chapter-based, member-led organization whose mission was to build local power and to intervene when violence was inflicted on Black communities by the state and vigilantes.

In the years since, we've committed to struggling together and to imagining and creating a world free of anti-Blackness, where every Black person has the social, economic, and political power to thrive.

Black Lives Matter began as a call to action in response to state-sanctioned violence and anti-Black racism. Our intention from the very beginning was to connect Black people from all over the world who have a shared desire for justice to act together in their communities. The impetus for that commitment was, and still is, the rampant and deliberate violence inflicted on us by the state.

Enraged by the death of Trayvon Martin and the subsequent acquittal of his killer, George Zimmerman, and inspired by the 31-day takeover of the Florida State Capitol by POWER U and the Dream Defenders, we took to the streets. A year later, we set out together on the Black Lives Matter Freedom Ride to Ferguson in search of justice for Mike Brown and all of those who have been torn apart by state-sanctioned violence and anti-Black racism. Forever changed, we returned home and began building the infrastructure for the Black Lives Matter Global Network, which, even in its infancy, has become a political home for many.

We've accomplished a lot in four short years. Ferguson helped to catalyze a movement to which we've all helped give life. Organizers who call this network home have ousted anti-Black politicians, won critical legislation to benefit Black lives, and changed the terms of the debate on Blackness around the world. Through movement and relationship building, we have also helped catalyze other movements and shifted culture with an eye toward the dangerous impacts of anti-Blackness.

—Text on the official Black Lives Matter website
("What We Believe," n.d.)

In 2012, 17-year-old Trayvon Martin was walking in the neighborhood of his father's fiancée, headed to a convenience store to buy something to drink. He never made it there, as he was shot and killed by a neighborhood watch volunteer, George Zimmerman, after being thought to be "suspicious." Some said it had to do with anything but race. These voices argued that Trayvon's clothing (a hoodie and jeans) made him look dangerous; others commented that it couldn't be racism because the security guard who shot Trayvon wasn't White; still others said that he shouldn't have been out so late and that he had smoked marijuana in the past, and they questioned why he was walking alone at night. None of these reasons, of course, is a reason to shoot a 17-year-old kid. African American families and activists fought back against these reasons. Would these same reasons be used to justify this shooting if the boy shot had been White? Amidst the discussions of what had happened, some White Americans learned for the first time that Black Americans may not have the same relationship with the police that White Americans do. The shooting of Trayvon Martin opened a window into the lives of Black men and boys everywhere. George Zimmerman was acquitted of murdering Trayvon.

In 2014, John Crawford, age 22 and father of two, was walking through a Walmart in Ohio buying a few items for a family picnic. As he shopped, he picked up a toy gun sold at the store, intending to purchase it, and he is seen on a security camera holding it with his other purchases as he browses the aisles. After receiving a phone call that an African American man was "waving a gun around" in a store, police burst into the aisle Crawford was standing in and shot and killed him.

That same year, another unarmed African American teenager, Michael Brown, was killed by officer Darren Wilson in Ferguson, Missouri, outside of an apartment complex. Many witnesses noted that Michael had his hands up when he was shot, and it is clear that he was unarmed. Again, allegations that Michael had been in trouble with the law before and may have just stolen a pack of cigarettes from a nearby store began to circulate as reasons to justify the shooting. The grand jury in St. Louis declined to indict Wilson.

A few months later, Tamir Rice, age 12, was playing with a toy gun in a park in Ohio. After getting a phone call about a "Black man" pointing a gun at people in the park, officer Timothy Loehmann arrived on the scene and shot Rice within seconds of seeing him on the playground. Tamir died the next day. No indictment was brought against Loehmann or his partner.

And as this book goes to publication, we must add the name of George Floyd, who was killed during arrest when an officer knelt on his neck. And the name of Ahmaud Arbery, who was shot while jogging in his own neighborhood by two White men who mistakenly thought he was a burglar. And Breonna Taylor, and Rayshard Brooks, and so many more.

A second student effort to address racism, this time related to the Black Lives Matter movement, is shown in Spotlight Feature 8.2. This article was written by a student and is reprinted from *Monitor on Psychology,* a publication of the American Psychological Association.

You can do more research on these shootings and others including those of Eric Garner (killed by New York police officer Daniel Pantaleo after being put in a chokehold on the side of the road), Levar Jones (pulled over for a traffic violation and shot while reaching for his ID after being asked by an officer to do so), Alton Sterling (shot by police five times in the chest at close range outside a convenience store where he often sold CDs), and Sandra Bland (died in her jail cell of alleged suicide, though

SPOTLIGHT FEATURE 8.2

#BlackLivesMatter

Students Lead Anti-Racism Efforts

Graduate Students Are Organizing to Support the Black Lives Matter Movement

Hundreds of students and psychologists gathered at APA's 2016 Annual Convention in Denver for a march in solidarity with the Black Lives Matter movement. Their goal was to bring attention to racial discrimination and the police shootings of African-Americans and to encourage psychologists and APA to support the Black Lives Matter movement.

"We sincerely feel that while APA has done some great things to support research, programs and outreach that draw attention to discrimination, stress and police brutality, more can and still needs to be done," said a mission statement from the organizers, who are psychology graduate students at Arizona State University and the University of Kentucky.

Also at APA's convention, student activists held workshops and panels to discuss the movement and to plan future events. Students from the group Eradicate #BostonCollegeRacism, for example, presented a toolkit they developed to help those on other campuses start their own anti-racism groups (see the November 2015 gradPSYCH magazine (www.apa.org/gradpsych/2015/11) for more on Eradicate #BostonCollegeRacism).

The march and convention programming were among the most recent examples of how graduate students are leading support for the Black Lives Matter movement in psychology and on campuses. Earlier this year, on the anniversary of Martin Luther King Jr.'s assassination, psychology graduate students at 20 schools across the country staged die-in protests coordinated around the Twitter hashtag #psychologists4blacklives. At each event, they lay down in public places—university quads, libraries and dining halls and on city hall steps—for 16 minutes, one minute for each bullet that hit Chicago teen Laquan MacDonald, killed by a police officer in 2014.

In Chicago, more than 50 students protested in front of City Hall.

"It was a very emotional experience," says Kia Watkins, a graduate student at the Adler School of Professional Psychology who participated in the event. "It was a cold day. It started raining. Not all of the reaction we got [from passersby] was positive. But we reminded ourselves of the bigger picture and what it meant."

At the convention, the #psychologists4blacklives leaders discussed expanding a die-in protest to more schools next year.

"I believe social justice and advocating for our clients outside of the therapy room is a very logical and natural progression from the APA ethical requirement of advocating for our clients within therapy," says organizer Luciano Lima, a doctoral student at the Illinois School of Professional Psychology in Chicago. "We don't want to just heal the wounds of the patients we're seeing, but also help prevent the wounds from happening in the first place."

Source: Winerman (2016).

questions remain about her arrest and death). The common theme in each story (except for that of Sandra Bland, in which the reason for her death is suspicious, but unknown) is that police appeared to make quick decisions to shoot these Black men and boys in scenarios in which it seems that White boys and men would not be shot. Some of the Black boys and men were doing things that police told them to do, for example Philando Castile, a cafeteria worker at an elementary school who was driving with his girlfriend and her daughter in the car when he was pulled over and reportedly was trying to show his ID after being asked to do so by the officer. In other cases, such as that of 12-year-old Tamir Rice, police appear to shoot on sight without looking carefully at the situation. Many of the officers noted that they "feared for their lives" or that the person they shot seemed "dangerous" or "defensive." None of the men and boys described above had an actual gun in his hands or was aiming it at police, and many were unarmed. Police are held accountable for these deaths in very few of these cases.

As the African American community began to speak out against these injustices, the Black Lives Matter movement was founded. Three African American women, Patrisse Khan-Cullors, Alicia Garza, and Opal Tometi, founded a movement with the message "#BlackLivesMatter," and they devised a plan to create a global network of activists and supporters that addressed issues of intersectionality in the Black community and made the simple point that Black lives in our country have been seen as having less value than other lives for far too long. The movement was meant to highlight the message that the lives of Black people do not seem to matter as much as White lives in terms of the way they are treated on an everyday basis and by our legal system in general. It is important to note that this relationship between black men and boys and the police is not a new one. But the Black Lives Matter movement drew media attention to this long-standing issue and allowed a discussion to begin in our country on this relationship perhaps for the first time in the mainstream.

iStock/DJMcCoy

Organizers of this movement pointed to the shootings of Tamir Rice and others. If someone had seen a White boy playing with a toy gun in the park, would the police even have been called in the first place? Even if they had, would officers have arrived with guns drawn, shooting before they even made it a few steps out of the car? We think the answer is: No. The Black Lives Matter movement and its attempts to highlight this issue sparked other Americans to exercise their civil right to protest all across the country, and many African Americans and other Americans joined this wave.

In Ferguson, after the shooting of Michael Brown, protesters and police squared off against each other, leading to police in flak jackets and military gear aiming guns at protesters as they demanded that the protesters disperse. Pew Research Center conducted some polls at this time to ask questions about public viewpoints of the protests and police response, and large differences were found between White and Black individuals in their perspectives on this situation. To the question "Did the police response to protests go too far?" only 27% of Whites surveyed said "yes," and 36% believed the response was "about right." This differed sharply from the 50% of Blacks surveyed who said that the police protest had gone too far (Pew Research Center, 2014). A second question, "Did the protesters in Ferguson go too far?" also elicited different responses between White and Black respondents, with 67% of White people surveyed saying "yes," and only 15% saying that the response was "about right." This again contrasts with the responses of African American respondents, and while 43% of this group said that the protesters had gone too far, an almost equal amount (38%) said the response was "about right." Perhaps the most divided response was found to the question, "Was the shooting of Michael Brown justified?" Fifty-seven percent of African Americans surveyed said a resounding "no," whereas only 18% of Whites surveyed had this same answer.

In conducting the surveys above and others similar to them, the Pew Research Center has also given respondents the option of choosing "don't know" on some questions. An interesting pattern is found in making comparisons between White and Black respondents who answer this way. In the question above about whether the shooting of Michael Brown was justified, the majority of White people surveyed (67%) chose the answer "I don't know enough." In addition, in a question asking if Brown's shooting raises racial issues, the Whites surveyed appear to be divided. In answer to this question, 37% of White people surveyed chose the response, "This case raises important issues about race," but 47% said "Race is getting more attention than it deserves," and another 18% said "I don't know" (Pew Research Center, 2014). This contrasts with 60% of Black respondents saying that the case raised important issues about race, with a much smaller group of 18% saying that this attention was undeserved, and only 2% saying they didn't know (Pew Research, 2014). This difference may point to the fact that African American people experience racism in many ways on a daily basis, some resulting in deadly consequences, and therefore understand that race may be a factor in many of these circumstances.

There may be no way to definitively tell whether some of the police officers in the stories above were making racist assumptions when shooting these African American people. Research does show, however, that black boys are often viewed as "less child-like" than their White peers (APA, 2014). Goff, Jackson, Di Leone, Culotta, and DiTomasso (2014) found that these associations can be made for Black boys as young as 10 years old. In one portion of the study, Goff and colleagues found that African American boys between 10 and 17 years old were assumed on average to be 4.5 years older than they actually were. In a second part of this same study, researchers reviewed personnel records of White police officers and tested them on implicit biases regarding thinking of Black people as less human than White people. Goff and colleagues found "that those who dehumanized blacks were more likely to have used force against a black child in custody than officers who did not dehumanize blacks" (APA, 2014, para. 2).

Let's go back for a moment to what you learned in Chapter 5 about bias. You may recall that people may sometimes be aware of their biases and choose to act upon them or not, but in many cases, biases are unconscious or implicit and not readily available in our awareness. If a particular police officer, for example, carries a stereotype or bias that Black men and boys are more dangerous, or less human, than White men and boys, they may also misinterpret the behavior of Black men and boys to be more problematic or threatening than the same behavior observed in others, and they may approach a situation with a Black person differently than they would approach the same situation with a White person. This could then lead them to act with more deadly force. Many of the officers above noted they "felt threatened" or feared for their lives, though in retrospect this seems like an extreme assessment of many of the situations.

A 12-year-old boy playing in the park with a toy gun, for example, seems not particularly out of the realm of a normal activity, and yet the officer was shooting within minutes of exiting the car. The officer later noted that he thought Tamir was much older and commented on his height and weight. Was this an accurate perception, or was this perception colored at the time by the officer's implicit bias? Police officers must make split-second decisions all the time, and because of this may be more susceptible to following their biases if they do not feel they have time to assess a situation more thoroughly. This means that a child like Tamir Rice may have been viewed to be dangerous because of the police officer's implicit racist assumptions about African Americans, and this led to his death.

Statistics from the US Department of Justice, the US Sentencing Commission, and The Sentencing Project also support the idea that our country's legal system treats Black men (and sometimes women as well) very differently than their White counterparts. Here are some statistics and facts that show this injustice:

- African Americans constitute nearly 1 million of the total 2.3 million incarcerated, but make up approximately 14% of the population.

- Five times as many Whites are using drugs as African Americans, yet African Americans are sent to prison for drug offenses at 10 times the rate of Whites.

- Blacks and Hispanics are approximately 3 times more likely to be searched during a traffic stop than White motorists.

- African Americans are 2 times as likely to be arrested as Whites and almost 4 times as likely to experience use of force during encounters with the police.

- Once convicted, Black offenders receive longer sentences than White offenders (10% longer for the same crimes).

- Blacks use marijuana at 1.3 times the rate of Whites but are arrested for marijuana possession at 3.7 times the rate of Whites.

There is much more to be said about police violence against Black people as a population and about Black Lives Matter as a group in general. As we write these words, Americans are protesting in the streets over the treatment of Black people in our country. We will leave you with this thought for now, attributed to 16-year-old African American actress Amandla Stenberg, who was talking about the high amount of cultural appropriation of Black culture that exists in non-Black US society (hairstyles, music, clothing, etc.): "What if America loved Black people as much as they loved Black culture?"

Asian Americans: The Perpetual Foreigner and Model Minority Myths

"First time flying?" A portly businessman sitting next to me smiled. "Yes. I guess it shows," I responded. "I'm loving it, though. I think it's great." "Isn't it amazing," he chortled. "I flew a bomber in the Pacific during the war, and here I am still flying. This time on business. Progress in aeronautics is amazing." Then, without any indication of interest on my part, he proceeded to tell me how amazing he thought this progress had been. The man was a garrulous raconteur who rambled on and on to a captive audience tightly strapped in the seat. I kept an obliging but nervous smile on my face. I soon discovered that his favorite topic was his wartime air exploits. My smile froze in place, then slowly faded. He continued regaling me with his adventures. It was nerve-racking enough flying for the first time. Of all passengers on this full flight, why did I have to get for my seatmate an ex-bomber pilot who loved talking about bombarding Japanese? Then, out of the clear blue, he said, "I suppose you were in one of those Japanese camps here during the war." I gripped my armrest—gripped it hard to restrain my welling emotion. To him, I thought, I'm probably still the same as those enemies he fought in the war. I felt like ignoring him and looked out the window. Immediately, the memory of Mrs. Rugen, my fourth-grade teacher who called me Jap, came rushing back into my mind. No, I won't look away this time. I will confront him. With a tight smile, I turned to him slowly. As cool and as controlled as I could be, I answered, "Yes, I grew up in an internment camp in Arkansas. But, as a matter of fact, it was an American camp for American citizens of Japanese ancestry." I got it out. It felt good. He sighed and looked down, shaking his head. "A terrible thing. A terrible thing," he said, and sat there, silent for the first time, only shaking his head. I was puzzled. What did he think was terrible? "It was a terrible thing that was done," he began slowly. "You know, during a war people do crazy things. One of my neighbors in Denver is a Nisei—Jack Ishihara. Sweetest guy you could know. Veteran of the war in Europe. Fought for old Uncle Sam while his family was

behind barbed wire. Terrible thing. Terrible." He sat there, mutely shaking his head. He knew. He understood. He wasn't the man I had girded myself against. Suddenly, my unclenched muscles let loose a flood of emotions. I excused myself to go to the lavatory. I locked the door, and the pressure broke. Uncontrollably, the tears began to flow. There are people who know about us. There are people who understand. It took me some time to regain my composure. Then I washed my face and returned to my seat. The nerves had eased. I felt much lighter. Even the flight seemed smoother."

—George Takei

Excerpt from *To the Stars: The Autobiography of George Takei,* pp. 121–122.

Asian Americans are sometimes not the first group thought of in terms of those who experience racism and discrimination. At times it seems as though American society has allowed for continued stereotyping of this group in a way that seems somehow more "mainstream" than others. Consider this example. In 2012 the New York Knicks lost one of their starting five to an injury, and therefore they turned to their bench to select a fifth starter. The man chosen was Jeremy Lin, a Chinese American man that was newly recruited to the team and was the first player of Chinese American or Taiwanese descent in the NBA as a whole. Though he was a star in his college team, Lin hadn't played much in his first season in the NBA, mostly warming the bench. In the first game that Lin played, he racked up a whopping number of points and helped the Knicks to win the game. In the games that followed, he repeated that performance, shocking the audience and commentators in part because he was a new player and probably in part due to the fact that there are few Asian American players in the game. A few games later, Lin was not on point; he faltered during the game, and the team lost. On the next morning, ESPN posted the following headline, "Chink in the Armor." The term *chink,* as you might know, is a racist slur against Chinese Americans. ESPN is a major news organization with an immense editing staff, meaning that this headline and article likely went through several rounds of hands before making it to the page. The fact that a major news organization thought that using the word *chink* in a public news outlet was OK shows some of the ignorance that still exists surrounding the treatment of Asian Americans. In this section, we will focus on two stereotypes that affect many Asian Americans within the United States and their impact on the well-being of Asian Americans.

Perpetual Foreigner Stereotype

We chose the excerpt at the beginning of this chapter because of the emotion that is revealed between George Takei's words. Though the outcome at the end of this story is good, Takei did not expect it to be, based on his other experiences, and the amount of tension he felt is palpable in the lines as he tells the story. At the end, when he is mistaken about the man's views of him, his relief is so great to be seen as himself, an American who was wronged, that he is brought to tears. Many people of Asian descent deal with the stereotype that they are "foreigners" or were not born in the United States. This **perpetual foreigner stereotype** often persists despite the fact that many Asian American families may have been living in the United States for several generations (Wong, Owen, Tran, Collins, & Higgins, 2012). This stereotype is more common for Asian Americans and Latinx Americans than for other racial groups in the United States (Armenta et al., 2013). The Asian American population is a very diverse one, consisting of many different ethnic groups, including Japanese, Chinese, Burmese, Indian, Sri Lankan, Vietnamese, Korean, and many others (see Table 8.2 for detailed population numbers). Fifty-nine percent of Asians who live in the United States were born outside the United States, as Pew Research Center notes; however, this number belies the large numbers of US–born Asian Americans that come from groups who have had a place within US history for some time (Lopez, Ruiz, & Patten, 2017).

The Chinese were the first group to immigrate to the United States, coming over a century ago in the early 1800s to work on building railroads across the newly expanded United States and in the mines as well. Chinese immigrants often held the most dangerous jobs in this time period, including lighting the fuse of dynamite used to make tunnels for the railroads, and other such positions. In 1882, the Chinese Exclusion Act was enacted due to anti-Chinese sentiments that swirled around the false belief that the Chinese were taking jobs from White Americans. This act halted the immigration path from China and was not repealed until 1943 (Le, 2020). As the first immigrants were all men (Chinese women were forbidden from immigrating at

TABLE 8.2 ⬡ Asian American Population Diversity in the United States	
Ethnic Group	**Estimated Population**
Chinese	4,948,000
Indian	3,982,000
Filipino	3,899,000
Vietnamese	1,980,000
Korean	1,822,000
Japanese	1,411,000
Pakistani	519,000
Cambodian	330,000
Hmong	299,000
Thai	295,000
Laotian	271,000
Bangladeshi	188,000
Burmese	168,000
Nepalese	140,000
Indonesian	113,000
Sri Lankan	60,000
Malaysian	30,000
Bhutanese	24,000
Mongolian	21,000

Source: Lopez et al. (2017).

the time), and marriage to Whites was prohibited by law at the time, this left many from this first group of Chinese immigrants to make the decision to return to China (Wong et al., 2012).

Japanese immigrants were the next group to come to the United States with the Gentlemen's Agreement in 1907 ("Gentlemen's Agreement," n.d.). This brought a new wave of Asian immigrants to the United States, and unlike the Chinese immigrants, this wave included many families who were eager to put down roots in this new country. By the time that World War II had broken out, many of the Japanese individuals imprisoned in the Japanese internment camps were *nisei,* or second-generation Japanese, born in the United States. Again, anti-Asian (particularly anti-Japanese) sentiment was very high at this time due to World War II.

Today, the percentages of each group of Asian Americans born in the United States versus the immigrants born in the respective Asian countries are different, depending on the circumstances surrounding the original immigration story of their families. US–born Japanese Americans, the group that has now been here the longest in a consistent fashion (because the Chinese Exclusion Act prevented Chinese from living here consistently), make up 73% of the Japanese population in the United States, with only 27% being Japan-born (Lopez et al., 2017).

This differs sharply from the demographics of groups who have arrived in the United States more recently, such as the Burmese, 85% of whose group is foreign born, compared to only 15% being born in the United States (Lopez et al., 2017). Similarly, the percentages of Asian populations in the United States that speak English proficiently differ among the groups. Whereas 84% of Japanese populations within the United States, 80% of Filipinos, and 80% of Indians speak English proficiently, only 28% of Burmese in the United States are proficient English speakers (Lopez et al., 2017). Of the Asian American population (that is, those born in the United States), 94% speak English fluently. Thus, the notion of all Asians being foreigners or non–English speakers is a false one, despite the perpetual foreigner stereotypes that surround them. Nevertheless it is commonly believed that regardless of English proficiency, Asians are somehow "less American" than other ethnic groups. In a study by Devos and Ma in 2008, findings showed that participants found Lucy Liu (an Asian American actress with no accent) to be "less American" than Kate Winslet (a White actress from England) in an implicit association test. This is but one study showing that Asian Americans are often thought to be "foreign."

Several researchers have studied the impact of this stereotype upon Asian Americans in the United States. One of the major findings is that being labeled as such can often lead to the experience of depressive symptoms (Do, Wang, & Atwai, 2018; Kim, Wang, Deng, Alvarez, & Li, 2011). In a study designed to look at impacts on male and female

Executive Order 9066 sign

adolescents, Kim and colleagues (2011) noted that being branded as a perpetual foreigner is a significant contributor to the types of discriminatory treatment that many Asian Americans still face. Consider the execution of Executive Order 9066, which decreed that all Japanese living on the west coast of the United States be imprisoned in internment camps following the attack on Pearl Harbor by Japan on December 7, 1941. The reason the US government gave for this imprisonment was the notion that Japanese Americans (many of whom had never been to Japan and had been born in the United States) might assist Japan in its efforts to undermine the United States in the war. This is the most clear application, perhaps, of the perpetual foreigner stereotype (i.e., that even if a Japanese individual was born in America, they would still be loyal to "their" country) though not the only or most recent.

Lack of English proficiency is a clear predictor of this stereotype, but accented English that is proficient is also predictive of discrimination aimed at Asian people in the United States (Kim et al., 2011). The impact of this stereotype "may seem innocuous, but in reality, it constitutes a form of discrimination and therefore can be detrimental" (Kim et al., p. 291). Kim and colleagues found that exposure to the perpetual foreigner stereotype was predictive of perceived chronic daily discrimination in adolescent Asian girls and perceived discriminatory victimization in adolescent Asian boys. Both perceptions led to a higher level of depressive symptoms in both genders, though this finding was significant only in the female population.

Other studies have investigated the effects of this stereotype and others on Asian American men (i.e., those born in the United States) and have found them to be both negative and problematic for well-being in general. Wong and colleagues (2012) conducted a study in which they investigated the impact of knowledge of several stereotypes on the mental health of Asian American male college students. Stereotypes were clustered into (1) body-mind stereotypes (emphasizing lack of attractiveness of

Asian men), (2) nerd stereotypes (emphasizing greater intelligence and social awkwardness), and (3) outsider stereotypes (those that rely on the perpetual foreigner status). Of the three groups, only those participants most focused on the outsider stereotypes cluster showed significantly higher levels of depressive symptoms compared to the other two clusters.

Finally, Asian American individuals who were more aware of the perpetual foreigner stereotype had more racial identity conflict and a lower sense of belonging to American culture than comparable individuals who were *less* aware of the stereotype, as well as lower scores in life satisfaction and hope (Huynh, Devos, & Smalarz, 2011). In addition, Do and colleagues (2018) found that not only were depressive symptoms higher in Asian Americans who more strongly felt the perpetual foreigner stereotype was relevant to their experiences, but higher anxiety and lower self-esteem were also found than those who had less experience with this stereotype. Thus, Asian Americans are impacted by this seemingly "innocuous" stereotype, and education surrounding this stereotype is both warranted and essential for the mental health of many Asian Americans (Kim et al., 2011, p. 291).

Model Minority Myth

A second stereotype that often plagues the Asian population within the United States is that of the **model minority**. The model minority myth was coined during the 1960s and is the idea that among other racial and ethnic minority groups, Asian immigrants and their subsequent generations have succeeded and prospered, especially in comparison to African American and Latinx populations (Atkin, Yoo, Jager, & Yeh, 2018; Wong & Halgin, 2006). Two components of this myth exist: (1) The **model minority myth of achievement** focuses on the false idea that Asian Americans enjoy greater success because of their "stronger work ethics, perseverance, and drives to succeed"; and (2) the **model minority myth of unrestricted mobility** refers to the incorrect assumption that Asian American success is "associated with their stronger [in comparison to other racial minorities] belief in fairness of treatment and lack of perceived racism or barriers at school/work" (Parks & Yoo, 2016, p. 289).

This stereotype about Asian Americans is often touted to undermine accounts of racial inequality and to cast dispersion on African American and Latinx populations with reasoning such as, "If Asians are able to succeed in the United States, why can't Black and Latinx populations?" (Poon et al., 2016). Even at face value, this argument of "Why can't you be more like them?" is a racist one in the sense that it ignores the different immigration patterns of these different racial groups (e.g., African Americans being forcibly taken from their country as slaves and brutalized for over a century in these positions is a history that no other racial group in the United States has faced). It also casts Asian Americans in an odd role in between White and Black culture in particular that may cause strife between Black and Asian groups, particularly if Asian Americans internalize the model minority myth as "true" (Poon et al., 2016).

As we have already noted, the variety within the Asian population within the United States is a vast and diverse racial minority population including many different ethnic groups (Lopez et al., 2017). First, method and time of immigration is distinct for these different populations. While many Japanese, Chinese, and Indian immigrants came of their own volition and did not immigrate out of fear or strife in their home countries, this is not the case for many other Asian immigrant populations. Large numbers of Vietnamese, Cambodian, Burmese, and Bhutanese immigrants, for example, came to the United States with refugee status after being forced from their home countries by violence or other horrendous conditions (Lopez et al., 2017). You may recall from Chapter 4 that the process of fleeing one's country in such a fashion is often long and arduous, and can lead to posttraumatic stress and other mental health issues as well as physical health problems due to living in unsanitary or unsafe conditions in refugee camps and other lodgings along the way (Abe, Zane, & Chun, 1994).

Often touted as "proof" of the fact that Asian Americans are doing well economically in the United States are overall statistics that show that fewer Asians live below the poverty line (12.1% of Asians versus 15.1% of the US population in general; Lopez et al., 2017). In contrast to the myth of the model minority, however, the percentage of Burmese Americans in poverty (35%; Lopez et al., 2017) is more than double the percentage in the overall population and is higher than the percentages for both African American and Latinx populations (Fontenot, Semega, & Kollar, 2018). In addition, overall household income is often depicted as higher in Asian groups, with a median household annual income in homes headed by Asian Americans of $73,060 in comparison with $53,600 among US households in general (Lopez et al., 2017). This number belies, however, the fact that four groups of those listed in Table 8.2

show median incomes well below the median for all Americans (see Figure 8.2). Note in both of these examples (median household income and percentage living below the poverty line), the groups who immigrated here first and in non-refugee status circumstances (e.g., Japanese, Chinese, Indian, and Filipinos) are generally more successful. These groups also have the larger numbers within the general population, thus this success both offsets and hides the struggles faced by some of the other Asian populations living in the United States.

Trying to debunk the model minority myth is a sort of double-edged sword, as you may be noticing in reading the preceding text. On the one hand, it is not accurate to say that Asian Americans as a whole have succeeded in adapting to this country and to achieving status that is equal to that of White Americans in some areas. As we have noted here, this is not true for many ethnic groups within the Asian population. That said, in focusing on Asian American success completely within the model minority myth, researchers more often focus on the deficits of Asian American groups that are still struggling. Poon and colleagues (2016) note that focusing only on these groups sets up a sort of deficit-based understanding of Asian Americans, and this is problematic as well. Thus, we would like you to understand that the primary takeaway from this information is twofold: (1) The Asian population in the United States is a very diverse group and cannot be treated as a sole entity, and (2) some Asian Americans have been very successful in the United States, at times surpassing White Americans in some areas. It is important to note that this does not mean that

---

FIGURE 8.2 ◆ Income Diversity Within the US Asian Population

US Asians Have a Wide Range of Income Levels

Median annual household income, 2015

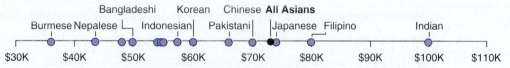

Note: It was not possible to reliably estimate the median annual household income for households headed by a Bhutanese, Malaysian, or Monogolian individual. Figure for all Asians based on mixed-race and mixed-group populations, regardless of Hispanic origin. Chinese includes those identifying as Taiwanese. Due to data limitations, figures for some groups are based on single-race population only, regardless of Hispanic origin. See methodology for more detail. The household population excludes persons living in institutions, college dormitories, and other group quarters. Households are classified by the race or detailed Asian group of the head.
Source: Pew Research Center analysis of 2013-2015 American Community Survey (IPUUMS).

Source: Lopez et al. (2017).

Asian Americans do not experience discrimination and racism (Kim et al., 2011; Museus & Park, 2015), and it is equally important to note that this is not due to some innate level of intelligence attributed to race or cultural beliefs (Sue & Okazaki, 1991). Regardless, it is important to see that groups other than White Americans are successful and intelligent, and this understanding will hopefully lead to other benefits White Americans enjoy being bestowed on other racial groups.

Other research has investigated the impact of the model minority myth on Asian Americans and found that internalization of this myth has been linked to many types of psychological distress (Atkin et al., 2018). Similar to other forms of internalized racism, internalization of the model minority myth may be manifested by Asian Americans endorsing the belief that racial inequality does not exist in the United States. This is obviously problematic, particularly for a population against whom racial inequality has been perpetuated over the history of our country. In addition, internalization of this myth may make Asian Americans less likely to engage in efforts to bring about sociopolitical change in their own group and in support of other racial and ethnic minority groups as well (Tran & Curtin, 2017). Some research has found that the problematic impact of internalization of this myth is in part moderated by the type of environment in which the Asian American person exists. Atkin and colleagues (2018) found that Asian American adolescents who went to schools that were predominantly non-Asian had a higher propensity to internalize the model minority myth, while those who went to schools that had more like peers (i.e., more Asian American students) were less likely to experience this internalization. Interestingly, those internalizing the myth in the context of the predominantly Asian schools reported more distress than those who experienced this within the mostly White context (Atkin et al., 2018).

Internalization of the model minority myth is not necessary for the existence of this stereotype to have a negative effect on Asian Americans, however. In a qualitative study by Museus and Park (2015), participants cited several reasons that it was difficult to have others believe in the model minority myth. One issue might be found in making career choices in the sense that some participants noted that they felt they often had to justify to others why they were not pursuing a science or medical degree. On the other hand, those who were pursuing medicine or pharmacy (often believed to be stereotypic to Asian individuals) felt like their true passion for their career field was dismissed in the sense that others said, "Oh, of course you're pursuing medicine—you're Asian," or assumed that parents were "forcing" them to choose this field. One Vietnamese American student noted that his peers sometimes delegitimized his good grades, saying "You're Asian. It's not fair" (Museus & Park, 2015, p. 563). Finally, some noted that others showed extreme surprise when they did need help with various school subjects. Another participant in Museus and Park's (2015) study noted that when she arrived at a free tutoring session, the others questioned why she would need help. She noted, "It felt discouraging. Like, 'Oh god, am I really that stupid?' . . . I feel like I don't belong there because this should come naturally to me and it doesn't" (Museus & Park, 2015, p. 564). As we have noted elsewhere, stereotyping is problematic even when the person engaging in it believes that stereotype to be "positive."

Finally, the model minority myth can also impact Asian Americans via others' views of them as well. Parks and Yoo (2016) conducted a study in which they investigated links between White college students' belief in the model minority myth and their subsequent feelings about Asian Americans in general. Results from this study showed that those who endorsed the model minority myth were more likely to also endorse the stereotype of Asians as perpetual foreigners (as defined previously) and more likely to hold negative views of Asian Americans in general. In addition, those who believed in the model minority myth were also more likely to have colorblind beliefs, which have been related to denial of the existence of racial inequalities (Parks & Yoo, 2016).

As we have noted in this and other chapters, stereotypes in any form are problematic both for the recipient (Parks & Yoo, 2016; Steele, 1997) and at times for the person holding the incorrect stereotype as well (Spanierman & Heppner, 2004). The two discussed here impact many Asian Americans in the United States. To assert that racial inequality has not been a factor in the lives of Asian populations living within the United States is incredibly inaccurate relative to the actual experiences of this population (Museus & Park, 2015; Tran & Curtin, 2017). Having a more clear understanding of the history of Asian Americans in our country is a key toward understanding their current positionality within the United States today.

American Indians: Psychological Invisibility and the Use of American Indian Mascots

Then the white kids began arriving for school. They surrounded me. Those kids weren't just white. They were translucent. I could see the blue veins running through their skin like rivers.

Most of the kids were my size or smaller, but there were ten or twelve monster dudes. Giant white guys. They looked like men, not boys. They had to be seniors. Some of them looked like they had to shave two or three times a day.

They stared at me, the Indian boy with the black eye and swollen nose, my going-away gifts from Rowdy. Those white kids couldn't believe their eyes. They stared at me like I was Bigfoot or a UFO. What was I doing at Reardan, whose mascot was an Indian, thereby making me the only other Indian in town? So what was I doing in racist Reardan, where more than half of every graduating class went to college? Nobody in my family had ever gone near a college.

Reardon was the opposite of the rez. It was the opposite of my family. It was the opposite of me.

—Sherman Alexie

Excerpt from *The Absolutely True Diary of a Part-Time Indian,* p. 56

Let's do a mental exercise for a minute. Picture a Native American or American Indian person in your head. Now, being very honest, how stereotypic was this picture in your mind? Did you think of someone who is from this century, or one from the past, like Crazy Horse, Sitting Bull, or Sacagawea? Did a cartoon character such as Pocahontas from the Disney film or a mascot from a sports team enter your mind, or did you think of a person you know who is American Indian? How many of you may have pictured someone who is not American Indian themselves, but has played on an Indian character, such as Johnny Depp as Tonto in *The Lone Ranger,* Rooney Mara in her role as Tiger Lily in the recent remake of *Peter Pan,* or Taylor Lautner as part of an Indian tribe that turns into werewolves in the *Twilight* movie series? Due to the fact that American Indians make up less than 1% of the US population today, these images likely occur more quickly to an average non–American Indian person in the United States than images of actual current American Indian persons.

Psychologist Dr. Stephanie Fryberg calls this absence of realistic and current portrayals of American Indians **psychological invisibility,** which is an "extreme form of colorblindness" (Fryberg & Stephens, 2010, p. 115). Mass media play an enormous role in the depiction of American Indians in the United States because of the very small living population of American Indians today. As Leavitt, Covarrubias, Perez, and Fryberg (2015) note, "Native Americans are rarely portrayed in mass media and, in the rare cases they appear, they are typically depicted in a stereotypical and historical fashion" (p. 39). This not only limits what others think about Native Americans but has also been shown to impact the way that Native Americans think of themselves (Covarrubias & Fryberg, 2015; Leavitt et al., 2015).

A lack of role models, for example, in school domains has been shown to lead to feelings of lack of belongingness in school and lower academic progress in other minority populations (Walton & Cohen, 2007). In an illuminating study conducted by Covarrubias and Fryberg (2015), Native American students were asked to read a passage about a student who is academically successful and then answer questions about themselves and about the student in the passage. The Native American students were divided into three groups, in this study, that differed only in terms of the description of the successful student. The successful student was (1) Native American as well (a self-relevant role model), (2) European American (a self-irrelevant role model), or (3) ethnically ambiguous (unknown ethnicity of role model). Results showed that the Native American students in the group with the self-relevant role model scored significantly higher on school belongingness than those who read about the self-irrelevant model or the ethically ambiguous role model.

Many other studies have examined the impact of using American Indian mascots in sports teams on both American Indians themselves and on non–American Indian individuals. Baca (2004) has asserted, as Chaney, Burke, and Burkley (2011) note, that "the mere presence of American Indian mascots in schools engenders racially hostile learning environments for American Indian people" (p. 43). This may occur in the form of shame, anger, or embarrassment at having their racial group be portrayed in a disrespectful way, but it may also impact American Indian individuals in ways of which some might not readily think. In the documentary *In Whose Honor* (Rosenstein, 1997), an interviewee describes students telling him of their experiences on their college campuses when their sports team is about to play a team with an American Indian mascot. These experiences include hearing cries of "scalp 'em!" and other racist terms in reference to beating the team with the Indian mascot and supporting their own team. Chaney and colleagues found that there is a significant relationship between a negative bias toward American Indian mascots and negative bias toward actual American Indian people. In addition, this study found that those who hold negative biases against American Indian people often also hold stereotype-consistent expectations of actual American Indian people.

Finally, in a multistep series of studies, Fryberg, Markus, Oyserman, and Stone (2008) found that exposure to stereotypic American Indian mascots and other images (e.g., the Cleveland Indians "Chief Wahoo" mascot, Disney's Pocahontas, etc.) resulted in a lower state of self-esteem and self-worth in the community. In addition, American Indian participants exposed to these images were found to develop fewer examples of possible selves related to high achievement. Thus, the authors conclude, "American Indian mascots are harmful because they remind American Indians of the limited ways others see them and, in this way, constrain how they can see themselves" (p. 208).

The results of these studies make a solid argument for decreasing stereotypic depictions of American Indians while at the same time increasing portrayal of realistic examples of American Indians in current times.

Our country has a bloody and discriminatory history with American Indians, the peoples native to the land we call "our country" today. Working to make reparations for the way Indigenous People have been treated since Christopher Columbus set foot on their soil might include paying more deliberate attention toward increasing positive representa-

iStock/FangXiaNuo

Modern-day American Indian woman

tions of American Indians in today's media and news. Portrayals might include more coverage of women such as Diane Humetewa, who became the first Native American woman confirmed as a federal judge in 2014, or other important figures such as Charles Trimble (an award-winning journalist), Sherman Alexie (a well-known American Indian author and poet), or Sharice Davids and Deb Haaland, who as of 2018 became the first Native American women ever elected to Congress (Reilly, 2018). In addition, getting rid of stereotypical and disrespectful caricatures, such as Chief Wahoo, may help the next generation to be less influenced by these negative images. This will not erase the past, but it may help our country as a whole, and American Indians in particular, to begin to heal from some of the devastation that has wracked this population.

Latinx Americans: Immigration, DACA, and Undocumented Individuals

I know what it's like to hide in plain sight. I've done it since I was 11 years old. I always knew that telling my story had consequences. The risks were very real, for myself and my family. So I kept quiet. I focused on being a kid. I tried to be the best student and athlete I could be.

Today I want to tell you my story. I'm a professional soccer player, but this is not a sports story—not really. It's not a "success" story or a sob story, either. It's just a story about my life, and it really means a lot to me that you're taking a few minutes of your day to read it. After you read it, you can decide for yourself who I am and what's right and wrong.

My journey doesn't have an ending yet, but I can tell you the beginning. It starts in the desert, on my eleventh birthday.

I woke up that day, August 30, 2004, on the Mexico side of the Chihuahuan Desert, which stretches from northern Mexico to parts of Texas and Arizona. A few days later I was in Sacramento. I've never been back to Mexico.

It's been 14 years since that day, and a lot has happened in my life. Sacramento became my new home, and I lived there through high school. Then I spent four years at the University of San Francisco, where I played D-I soccer and graduated with a degree in Finance. I married my college girlfriend a few months later. In the 2015 MLS draft, I was selected in the first round by D.C. United and made my MLS debut that year. In 2017, the L.A. Galaxy signed me to its reserve club. Today I'm a midfielder for the Galaxy II team.

But those are just the bullet points. My story is about what people couldn't see by watching me play soccer or looking at my résumé. A few months after I got to Sacramento, my temporary visa expired.

I was 11 years old, and I was undocumented.

I woke up that day to the promise of a Whopper.

My grandfather wished me happy birthday, and then he told me the news: We were going on a trip. A long trip—to visit my mother in a place called Sacramento, where she'd recently gone, also on a temporary visa. He promised to stop at Burger King on the way. So in my mind, the trip didn't sound like a big deal. My birthday was off to a pretty great start.

Actually, it wasn't my first time going across the border. Growing up, my mother had taken me, my brother and my sister across the El Paso–Juárez border—on temporary visas that allowed for short visits. Usually, they were day trips—to Wal-Mart or other chain stores. Man, I loved those trips. My mom would give me a couple dollars to spend and my favorite spot was a dollar store in El Paso. I'd go crazy in there, buying a squirt gun or a yo-yo or a mini soccer ball or a bag of Jolly Ranchers or some other toy.

What I knew about America was limited to what I saw on those trips: America was a collection of gigantic department stores, dollar stores and fast food places— connected by a confusing network of freeways. In my mind, America wasn't where people lived—it was where you went for a special occasion. Because that was my experience.

At the border, my grandpa showed our IDs to the American border-patrol agents. I remember them looking over our visas. They walked around the truck, inspecting the outside. Then they waved us through.

The drive was long. The desert went on forever. [M]y grandpa made good on his promise. I got that Whopper. I can't do it justice, though, so you'll just have to picture it—a skinny kid on his birthday, jammed into the middle seat of a pickup truck, with a burger in one hand and a chocolate milkshake in the other.

Then more driving. El Paso to Phoenix and into California. At some point on that long drive—maybe this is just how I remember it now—I think I started to put things together: This wasn't a vacation. I was going to remember my eleventh birthday for a long time.

On the outskirts of Juárez, pink crosses line the desert. Hundreds of wooden crosses, painted pink, are clustered in uneven rows. When I was a kid, I learned what they meant. Each cross was placed in memory of a woman who was raped, tortured or killed in the drug violence that's been going on in Juárez for years. [My mom] made a plan to get us out. She wanted a better life for us. She wanted us to have a future. We were going to leave the pink crosses behind.

Arriving in Sacramento in 2004, my first memory was how bright everything was. I'm not exaggerating when I say that it was almost like I saw color for the first time. I remember how the desert started to transition into green. The grass, the trees, the flowers, the perfect lawns. There was so much green.

—Miguel Aguilar, from the L.A. Galaxy Professional Soccer Team

Excerpt from "Undocumented" (2018).

Though Latinx individuals make up only part of people who are in the United States without documentation, they are the most focused upon in terms of the immigration debate. As a result, we have chosen to focus on the impact of this focus in this section. The words above from Miguel Aguilar are poignant and a very good example of what it might feel like to be undocumented in this country, without recourse to fully join the country, and for a decision that was not his own. Before turning to this topic more fully, however, we first would like to detail a short history of Latinx immigration to the United States. You may be surprised at how some of this history parallels what is happening in our country today.

Issues of immigration from the border of Mexico have been a topic of discussion for over a century. And at the same time, as we noted in Chapter 2, as California residents ourselves, we are aware of how inadequate this word *immigration* is in talking about the first Mexican residents of the United States. This is primarily because the land we sit upon now as we type these words was Mexico in the past, and thus no actual migration occurred for these first **Californios.** The land simply changed hands around them at the end of the Mexican American War in 1848. Some years later, in the early 1920s, the US government began to put more limits on immigration from Mexico. This was due to an anti-Mexican sentiment that arose out of the belief that Mexicans were taking jobs from US citizens. Whether this was true (like today, many of the jobs the Mexicans were taking were not jobs that White Americans were willing to do), this anti-Mexican sentiment came to a head as the Depression took hold of the United States. It is important to note that the Mexican individuals we are referencing here did not necessarily come to the United States illegally—many had come into the country in approved ways—but during this time of economic strife, talk ensued at the governmental level of deporting those Mexicans who were not US citizens back to Mexico. US government agents began to conduct raids of neighborhoods in which they expected to find Mexicans living and deported small numbers at first. This led to a wave of panic in the Mexican community. After some time, the government began instead to offer train tickets back to Mexico, and over 35,000 Mexican individuals decided to leave the United States voluntarily. As time went on, however, fewer of those who were left wanted to return—particularly as many Mexicans had started families and had children who were born in the United States. In the early 1930s, government agents from the welfare division visited homes of poor Mexicans and informed them that welfare would be cut off immediately and that their only recourse would be to accept the train ticket back to Mexico. Many felt they had no choice and packed their meager belongings, and often their US–born children, and headed back to a country that many of them no longer knew.

As World War II broke out, the United States again found themselves in need of cheap labor, as many of their workers were abroad fighting. At this time, they struck an agreement with the Mexican government to send temporary workers, called **braceros,** to work in the fields. Following the war, however, the anti-Mexican sentiment broke out again, and calls to deport Mexicans came again. In the mid-1950s, over 300,000 Mexicans—some who were Mexican American US citizens—were "repatriated" to

Mexico by forceful deportment in what the government called "Operation Wetback." As Kelly Lytel Hernandez, a UCLA historian noted, "It was lawless; it was arbitrary, it was based on a lot of xenophobia, and it resulted in sizeable large-scale violations of people's rights, including the forced deportation of U.S. citizens" (as quoted in Blakemore, 2019).

Fast forward to the early 2000s, when immigration reform was again a hot topic in the news and in everyday conversation. In 2001, the DREAM Act (Development, Relief, and Education for Alien Minors Act) was first proposed and offered a path toward citizenship for undocumented children who were brought to the United States as children. The plan included a series of steps that these children could undertake, including first obtaining conditional permanent residence and then obtaining a **green card** (signifying lawful permanent residence), and, after five years in the program in compliance, naturalization, that is, the ability to apply to become a US citizen, could occur. The DREAM Act was not voted into action by the Senate, however. In 2012, former president Barack Obama asked the Department of Homeland Security to enact a new plan for undocumented citizens brought as children called Deferred Action for Childhood Arrivals (DACA). This plan offered temporary escape from deportation for a period of two years, after which an application could be renewed. This did not provide permanent legal status, however, and there is currently no such pathway toward citizenship for undocumented immigrants today. President Trump, in office as we write this textbook, has sworn to end DACA at his first opportunity; however, the process of dismantling this program has thus far been thwarted by litigation. There are an 800,0000 estimated undocumented adult children, like Miguel Aguilar, waiting for a more permanent solution to their plight.

Regardless of your political beliefs, imagine for a moment what it must be like to be in the

iStock/vichinterlang

Dreamers marching

shoes of the undocumented adult children that live in the United States today. What fears might they hold of being sent "back" to a country that they do not remember and never really knew? Some do not speak the language of their home country and have been raised to be entirely "American" in terms of their cultural orientation. And yet what fears might they hold in staying in the United States, under threat of discovery? Now knowing the history of immigration and deportation, such as Operation Wetback, what fears might Mexican Americans who are *legal* citizens also hold, knowing that in the past people like them were sent "back" to a country to which they did not belong? Even if they themselves have citizenship, what might it be like to know that their parents could be deported at any time? Finally, regardless of citizenship, how might it feel to be Mexican American in a country that assumes they have a foreign status?

Similar to Asian Americans, many Latinx individuals also are treated as perpetual foreigners in the United States. In a study conducted by Forrest-Bank and Jenson (2015), Latinx individuals scored significantly higher than all other non-White groups except Asian Americans on the frequency of experiencing microaggressions related to being "exotic" (that is, not from the United States) and monolithic in terms of stereotypes about their racial group. In addition, Latinx individuals often similarly experience microaggressions about their prowess intellectually and educationally (Forrest-Bank & Jensen, 2015). These two stereotypes and the resulting impact occur for a variety of Latinx individuals, not only those who are immigrants, and yet are related to the current anti-immigrant and anti-Latinx sentiment in our country at present. In addition, White Americans' beliefs of stereotypes about Latinx and other non-White individuals are predictive of their general attitudes about immigration and the policies they support (Lu & Nicholson-Crotty, 2010). This may cause many day-to-day problems for Latinx individuals (regardless of immigrant or documentation status) but in addition causes problems for the culture at large. In another study, Ayón and Vigil (2018) found that Latinx parents are feeling particular pressure to transmit their culture to their children in terms of helping them to develop a healthy ethnic identity as opposed to being mired down in stereotypes about their culture. Other research has shown that a strong ethnic identity in non-White individuals can provide many benefits, including a buffer against the impact of racism and other discrimination (Romero, Edwards, Fryberg, & Orduña, 2014).

In addition, recent research is starting to evaluate the role of having particular statuses in terms of citizenship and documentation in the lives of Latinx individuals. Some studies have found that a perception of differential interpersonal treatment because of a lack of a visa is the strongest predictor of clinically significant distress (Garcini et al., 2019). Others have noted that the presence of DACA as a potential solution to fear of deportation has been positive for many undocumented children brought to the United States by their parents, though this varies somewhat depending on the age of the child at the time DACA status was granted (Gonzales Ellis, Rendón-Garcia, & Brant, 2018; Siemons, Raymond-Flesch, Auerswald, & Brindis, 2017). Further, those who were able to enroll in DACA increased in their well-being following actual enrollment as compared to prior to enrollment (Patler & Pirtle, 2018). Thus, having a pathway toward some sort of documented status, even if it does not include an actual path toward legal citizenship, is still better than having no path.

Finally, anti-immigrant sentiment that exists within the United States today, particularly against Latinx populations, has negative impacts in terms of acculturation opportunities. Many studies show that **acculturation** (striving to integrate a new culture into home culture practices as one adapts to the new culture) is beneficial in immigrants coming from other countries and for their families as well as across several domains (LaFromboise, Coleman, & Gerton, 1993). Note, this is not to say that pure assimilation (leaving behind a home culture in favor of adopting a White American culture) is necessarily beneficial. Acculturation, however, that allows individuals to begin to adapt to their new culture while still having access to facets of their old culture can be a benefit to many immigrants. In the current state of our country, however, fear and stereotypes are driving many Latinx people away from mainstream culture, because they fear their undocumented status will be revealed (if they are undocumented) or that others will assume they are undocumented even if they are US citizens or legal residents. This lack of acculturation is associated with depression in many studies (e.g., Calzada & Sales, 2018), but it may be difficult to overcome because of these fears and stereotypes.

In reading this portion of the chapter, especially the historical section, you may have felt a sense of déjà vu. We felt the same upon writing it. Poet and philosopher George Santayana is quoted as once saying, "Those who cannot remember the past are condemned to repeat it." We would ask you to take these words to heart and to thus learn more about episodes in history such as this type of anti-immigrant sentiment and where it has led our country in the past. We encourage you to look through the suggestions at the end of this chapter to find sources for descriptions of many historical events that might be different from the descriptions you learned long ago in elementary school. Having a full grasp of an unsanitized history is one of the few ways we know to avoid the condemnation of which Mr. Santayana speaks.

CONCLUSION

We hope you have a small glimpse into some issues related to being a person of color in the United States with the topics and stories we have recounted for you here. These can be viewed as snapshots of some of the issues that people of color might deal with in our current times. That said, it is important to remember that like any group, people of color are diverse, both within their home culture and in comparison to other cultural groups. Treating people as individuals first, but remembering that some of the experiences relayed here might also be their own, are important steps toward true understanding of each other.

ACT: Assess Your Knowledge, Critical Thinking, Take Part

Assess Your Knowledge

Think for a moment about your friendship group and about those around you. If you are a person of color, do you have friends from other non-White ethnic groups? If you are a White person, do you have friends who are people of color? Think for a moment: How is it different for you to interact with these folks in comparison to how it feels to interact with those from your same ethnic or racial group? Have you ever spoken to them about their families' histories in the United States, and what do they know about yours? Have you ever spoken to them about their experience as a member of the racial group to which they belong, and if not, how do you imagine it might be different from your own racial experiences?

Critical Thinking

Watch the YouTube video titled "How Microaggressions Are Like Mosquito Bites" (Fusion Comedy, 2016). What new information can you glean from this video? If you are a monoracial or biracial person of color, you have likely experienced some of these issues in the past. How does this video deepen your understanding of what is happening? How can you deal with these types of experiences in your life? If you are a White person, what new insights have you gained from this chapter or video? Have you made mistakes that you might now define as microaggressions and/or cultural appropriation? How might you work to make sure that you avoid these types of situations in the future? For a humorous flip on microaggressions, consider watching Ken Tanaka's "What Kind of Asian Are You?" video on YouTube (helpmefindparents, 2013). People of all races may be able to see the ridiculousness of using microaggressions as a way to interact with dissimilar others.

Note: Sometimes, upon thinking about past mistakes with regard to race, White people may want to approach the person of color involved and apologize or talk more about it. We caution you to think first about the impact of this and to ask yourself if you want to do this to relieve tension for yourself or to do something for the person of color. Remember that it may be painful for people of color to relive past experiences such as these, and that it is not their job to absolve you as a White person. It is often better to simply make the promise to yourself to try not to make this same mistake again.

Take Part

Participation: Select a novel to read that talks about someone from a different racial or ethnic group than your own. Choose another from that same ethnic or racial group, and read this as well. What similarities and differences do you see in these works in thinking about the experiences related to the characters' race and/or ethnicity? What new information did you gain?

Initiation: Look for courses or trainings you can take to have a better understanding of topics like microaggressions, bias, cultural appropriation, and other such topics. If you can't find these types of educational experiences in person, consider listening to podcasts such as "CodeSwitch" or developing a reading circle for books or articles on these topics. Try taking these with others in your life who are from your same racial background and following up with conversations about what you have learned.

Activism: If you are White, start coming up with strategies to talk to other White people about the harms that microaggressions and cultural appropriation can cause. How might you explain why this is problematic; what might you say? This type of education is often received differently when it is from another White person than when it is from a person of color. If you are a person of color or biracial, how might you cope with or decrease the effects of microaggressions or cultural appropriation? You could start a letter-writing campaign to companies that offer Halloween costumes of different ethnicities, or start a podcast yourself interviewing different people of color who have experienced microaggressions. Choose something that is doable for you, but partner with others as well.

SHADES OF GREY

Being a Biracial or Multiracial Person

LEARNING OBJECTIVES

- Know major definitions related to having more than one racial or ethnic identity
- Know the history related to issues relevant to biracial or multiracial people in the United States
- Understand the major models of biracial and multiracial identity development in the field of psychology
- Interpret the impact of a variety of factors (e.g., phenotype, family composition, etc.) on the development of biracial or multiracial identity
- Analyze the impact of common themes experienced in the lives of biracial and multiracial people
- Initiate or join an outside activity to learn more about biracial and multiracial individuals

My mom is White American and my dad is Japanese American, and so my brother and sister and I are hapa, *which signifies being "half" Japanese. My mom has a great story about when I first asked about race. I was about five, so it must have been about 1979. My mom was making dinner and I was playing with my sister in the kitchen when the question came up about what race meant. She answered by talking about the different groups, and the gist of her explanation was "There's many different races. There's the black race, the brown race, the white race, the red race, and the yellow race." I actually have a memory of picturing a racetrack in my head with people running around in different colored track suits. She says my sister and I just looked at her and then whispered together for a few minutes, and then she says I asked, "Ok, so what team are we on?"*

—Jennifer, age 45

This vignette is directly from one of the authors of this book (JTP) and describes her experience with learning about "being more than one thing" growing up. This is a common experience for many biracial and multiracial children. Race may be a difficult concept for children in general, but while most monoracial children are only learning about one racial identity, biracial and multiracial children are navigating more than one, as well as the potential identity that exists within the nexus of the combination as a whole. In addition, for most monoracial children, their parents share their race and usually their monoracial status. Biracial children often have parents who identify as monoracial, making the waters of exploration that much more uncharted. In this chapter we will discuss the history of biraciality and multiraciality in our country and how we experience it today. Next, we'll discuss some racial identity development models that seek to explain this process in biracial and multiracial individuals. Finally, we will discuss some common themes experienced by people who come from more than one racial background.

DEFINITIONS

We'd like to start with a few definitions to make sure the terms we are learning are understood. First, the term **biracial** means a person who has racial heritage from two races, while **multiracial** individuals have more than two racial heritages. For this chapter, it may become clumsy to continue using "biracial or multiracial" throughout the text, and so we will use the term "biracial" to encompass the multi-racial experience as well. The main reason we do this is that much of the literature that we will discuss in this chapter deals with biracial people. The population of individuals in the United States who have more than two racial heritages is growing but is still relatively small, with only 10% of the multiracial population noting "3 or more races" on the last iteration of the US Census (See Figure 9.1). We will, however, discuss a few issues unique to multiracial individuals and will use the term correctly there. Finally, **monoracial** refers to a person who has only one racial heritage or background.

Sometimes people confuse the meaning of *biracial* with **biethnic,** which refers instead to a person who has family heritage from more than one ethnicity. A person who has family that originally came from Portugal and Sweden, for example, is biethnic, but as both ethnicities come from Europe, the person is still classified as 100% White and thus monoracial. A second example is the family of one of our authors (JTP)—Dr. Teramoto Pedrotti is biracial (half Asian [Japanese American] and half White [Irish and German]), while her husband is monoracial (all White, but biethnic [Irish and Italian]). Their children then are still biracial

FIGURE 9.1 ● Census Data on Multiracial Children and Adults

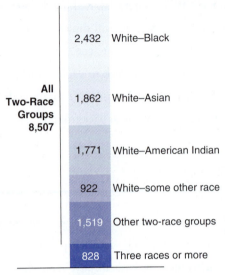

In thousands

All Two-Race Groups 8,507

2,432	White–Black
1,862	White–Asian
1,771	White–American Indian
922	White–some other race
1,519	Other two-race groups
828	Three races or more

9,335 All Two Races or More

Note: Two-race groups shown are the four largest ones. American Indian category includes Alaska Natives. Totals calculated before rounding. All subgroups include Hispanics.

Source: Parker, Horowitz, Morin, & Lopez (2015).

(Asian and White) but also **multiethnic** (Japanese, Irish, German, and Italian). If you are wondering if you accidentally signed up for a math class at this stage in the paragraph, we understand why! The bottom line is that ethnicity and race are separate entities, even though some talk about them interchangeably, and this is particularly important for our discussion here.

Finally, the terms **bicultural** and **multicultural** should also be defined here. Both of these terms refer not to personal heritage in terms of where a family originated but instead to cultural experiences. A European American family who lives for a significant amount of time in China, for example, may be bicultural in that they understand the culture of China and are intimately familiar with it, knowing language and customs common to China as well as those that originate from their own home country of the United States. It is important to note that bicultural distinctions are only given to individuals who have a truly intimate knowledge of another culture of which they are not originally members. Traveling to another country for a brief time (e.g., a study abroad or mission experience) and getting to know something about it does not make one bicultural. The person must be immersed within the culture for a significant period of time and be able to move comfortably in both cultures. The most common examples of people who are bicultural that you may see on a regular basis are people who have immigrated to the United States and have found ways to acculturate to the rituals, customs, and norms here.

Finally, some people may become bicultural or multicultural due to a high level of exposure to certain racial groups within their neighborhoods, schools, or other parts of their daily lives. Some researchers have posited that all non-White individuals in the United States (regardless of whether they were born in the United States) can be described as bicultural, because they may know about their home cultures as, for example, Mexican Americans or Hmong Americans, but they must also understand White American norms, values, and rules in order to survive and succeed in the United States, as it is these cultural values that the institution as a whole is currently based upon (Kulis, Robbins, Baker, Denetsosie, & Parkhurst, 2016; LaFromboise, Coleman, & Gerton, 1993). Biculturality and multiculturality are strengths and are desirable in terms of multicultural knowledge and in terms of the ability to build relationships with people from cultures that are different from your own.

HISTORY OF EXPERIENCE OF BIRACIAL PEOPLE IN THE UNITED STATES

In 1937, American sociologist Everett V. Stonequist wrote his book *The Marginal Man: A Study in Personality and Culture Conflict.* This tome was focused on both the experiences of people with multiple racial heritages and those that various monoracial individuals might have when moving from one culture to another, but it became the basis of many thoughts about biracial individuals and their experiences. In 1937, marriage between a White person and people of Asian, African American, American Indian, and Latinx descent was against the law in most states (Viñas-Nelson, 2017), and therefore there were few people who openly admitted being someone of more than one race. Of course, it must be pointed out that due to slavery, the occupation of colonial settlers, and other atrocities that included the sexual abuse of racial minority women, the children of these rapes were biracial in terms of their parentage, though they may have often been raised as monoracial due to the experiences surrounding their births (Viñas-Nelson). In 1948, a seminal court case, *Perez v. Sharp,* was decided in the California Supreme Court, making California the first state to declare that banning interracial marriage violated the state constitution of California (Viñas-Nelson, 2017). It would take 20 years from that time for this question to be put to the US Supreme Court.

In addition to marriage between White people and people of other races being illegal in the United States, there was also much enforced physical separation of groups due to housing restrictions, ghettoizing, and segregation in schools and in many public places, particularly in the South. You may have heard the term **antimiscegenation,** which refers to a position against the mixing of the races. Debates about the necessity to keep racial groups apart (namely to keep all other racial groups away from White people) included arguments from the Bible but also from research like Stonequist's (1937) that appeared to point to problems and difficulties for children who arose out of these unions. Some of these feelings may still exist in some people in the United States today, and you may still hear covert racism expressed against interracial marriage that includes the reason: "But it will be so difficult for the children!" In the past, many felt it would be too confusing for children to not know which race they should choose when the number of options was more than one.

In the mid-1960s, Virginia and 15 other states still had laws on their books against interracial marriage, but this all came to change in 1967 with the landmark case involving an interracial couple with the apt surname Loving. *Loving v. Virginia* involved Mildred (African American and Native American) and Richard (White), who were married in 1958 in Washington DC, as their home state of Virginia did not allow interracial marriage. After a local sheriff burst into their bedroom in the middle of the night, they were arrested and given a choice of spending one year in prison or leaving Virginia and not returning for 25 years. The couple chose the second and moved to Washington DC, but they missed their families and wanted to return.

Some accounts of this story state that Mildred wrote a letter to Robert F. Kennedy (US attorney general at the time) about their situation, and it was referred to the American Civil Liberties Union (ACLU), while others say she wrote directly to the ACLU. Though the Lovings were rather ambivalent about the public notoriety they were sure to gain in fighting the constitutionality of Virginia's antimiscegenation law, they agreed to participate in the lawsuit, and nine years later, the Supreme Court ruled that any antimiscegenation law was unconstitutional. A poll analyzed by National Opinion Research Center (NORC) at the University of Chicago showed that the percentage of individuals against interracial marriage had fallen from 36% in 1972 to just 11% in the year 2002 (Livingston & Brown, 2017). A report based on a slightly more recent set of data from YouGov (2018) puts the percentage of people

Francis Miller/Contributor/Getty Images

Richard and Mildred Loving

who viewed interracial marriage as "morally wrong" at closer to 17%, with virtually no differences in responses from different racial groups, genders, age groups, or regions. (See Figure 9.2 for another poll regarding interracial marriage.) Some small differences existed between groups with different political ideologies, with only 6% of people identifying as "liberal" reporting opposition to interracial marriage, while 15% of those identifying as "moderate" and 25% of those identifying as "conservative" reported the view that interracial marriage was morally wrong (YouGov, 2018).

Today, more than nine million individuals check more than one box on the US Census after being allowed to do so for the first time in the year 2000 (US Census Bureau, 2000; Jones & Bullock, 2012). Other research notes that one in six new marriages include people of different races (Livingston & Brown, 2017), and some research predicts that by the year 2050, one in five people in the United States will have heritage from more than one racial group. This is thus a group worth studying, as it includes so many people in the United States.

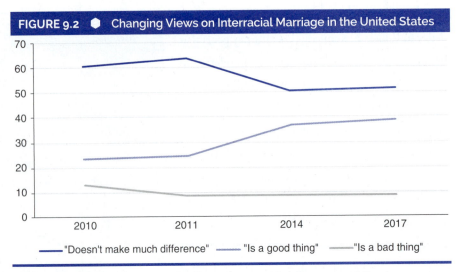

FIGURE 9.2 ● Changing Views on Interracial Marriage in the United States

Source: Author created using data from Pew Research source: https://www.pewsocialtrends .org/2017/05/18/2-public-views-on-intermarriage/pst_2017-05-15-intermarriage-02-03/.

BIRACIAL IDENTITY DEVELOPMENT MODELS

Like individuals in other, monoracial groups, biracial individuals go through a process of forming racial identity as well. This process is often more nuanced for biracial individuals, as it involves more than one racial group. Though researchers at first attempted to study biracial individuals using monoracial identity models, psychologists soon realized that additional models were needed. Poston (1990) noted four main issues in using monoracial models to talk about biracial identity development, including (1) implications that biracial individuals would need to choose one race over another in order to follow the models, (2) the fact that the models involve a rejection first of their minority racial identity and then a rejection of the dominant racial group (biracial individuals may belong to both of these groups, while monoracial people of color have only a racial minority identity), (3) there is no integration of identities in the models set up for use with monoracial individuals, and finally, (4) monoracial models usually end in an individual's acceptance of their racial group, and this may not occur for biracial individuals. Here we delineate several models that have been developed, in chronological order.

Jacobs's Biracial Identity Development Model

One of the first known models that incorporated biracial children into a racial identity development process was developed by James H. Jacobs, a psychologist and parent to two biracial children himself. As you may remember from Chapter 4, Dr. William Cross had recently created his model of nigrescence at the time Jacobs was developing his model, and Jacobs was heavily influenced by Cross's work. Jacobs (1978) delineated three main stages through which biracial children were thought to progress that were linked to developmental stages. First, Pre–Color Constancy described the stage of children from birth to age 4.5 and involved a recognition of skin tone and color but not an actual sociocultural association with race. Additionally, similar to the idea of gender constancy from developmental psychology, in which children may identify themselves as able to change gender by certain outward features (e.g., short hair means the child is a boy, wearing a dress turns the child into a girl; see the work of Jean Piaget for an overview of this concept), Jacobs felt children in this stage were not yet sure that their race and skin color were constant or permanent. Children in this first stage, according to Jacobs, may think of themselves as "tan" or "pink" and are just beginning to notice these differences.

The second stage in Jacobs' (1978) model is Post–Color Constancy (ages 4.5 to 8) and encompasses the stage in which biracial children now understand that their race (color) will not actually change when they grow up, but children in this stage are still experimenting with identifying with the different pieces of their racial heritage. Some parents may introduce the term *biracial* to the child at this point, but others may not. Interestingly, research has shown that even when parents don't offer this option to their children, most biracial children still describe themselves in this way (though they may not use the actual term) and often assert that they are not monoracial, even when parents refer to them in this way (Parker et al., 2015).

Finally, Jacobs (1978) defines the third stage as occurring from ages 8 to 12 and involving moving from the idea of being a particular color to having a particular heritage. This is consistent with other research that states that children in this age range are beginning to develop a better understanding of race as a sociocultural (not biological) concept (Tatum, 2003). Note that Jacobs's model stops at this point developmentally and assumes the biracial child, having mastered this identity, is finished with this process (see Table 9.1).

TABLE 9.1 ⬢ Jacobs's 1978 Biracial Identity Development Model		
Stage	**Approximate Age**	**Description**
Pre–Color Constancy	Birth to 4.5 years old	Play and experimentation with *color* of skin
Post–Color Constancy	4.5 to 8 years old	Biracial label and racial ambivalence
Biracial Identity	8 to 12 years old	Moving from "color" toward "heritage"

Source: Jacobs (1978).

Poston's New and Positive Model

Poston recognized the limitations of some of the other racial identity models that existed in 1990 and decided to create a more fleshed-out model that attended to some of the same stages of racial identity development that Cross (1971), Morten and Atkinson (1983), and others had developed for monoracial populations. As mentioned previously, Poston noted that there were problems with simply applying use of monoracial models to biracial populations, and he set out to correct the problem that most research prior to the development of his model incorporates a rather negative cast of the life and experiences of biracial people in general. Stonequist's (1937) description of biracial individuals as "marginal" and as living in the margins of society, but never a part of any racial heritage group, fueled the idea that biracial development must be difficult and fraught with challenge. It was due to this idea that many lay people advocated for biracial children to make choices about their heritage instead of trying to live as both.

Poston's (1990) "new and positive model" (Poston, 1990, p. 153) was therefore intentionally positive in nature and offered positive outcomes for biracial individuals for the first time (see Table 9.2). The first stage in this model is termed Personal Identity and, similar to Jacobs's (1978) first stage, it places the age of this first stage as very young. In this stage, sense of self is not necessarily entwined with racial identity yet, according to Poston, and though children may have some understanding of the concept of race, their sense of identity is tied heavily to their personal traits and competencies.

The second stage, Choice of Group Categorization, was thought to occur when children are a bit older and being pushed to make a choice to be one race (thereby needing to choose one parent over the other) or to be multiple races (for which they may have no model; Hall, 1980). Poston (1990) describes this stage as potentially "a time of

TABLE 9.2 ● Poston's New and Positive Theory of Biracial Identity Development

Stage	Descriptive Statement Common to Stage
Personal Identity	"I am Me."
Choice of Group Categorization	"I am Black" or "I am Latino,"
Enmeshment/Denial	"I guess I am Black, but I am also White—I am not really either."
Appreciation	"I want to know more about being Black and about being White."
Integration	"I am both" or "I am all of the above."

Source: Poston (1990).

crisis and alienation" (p. 153) for biracial children and notes that the decision is made based on a multitude of factors, including physical appearance, support received for their choice in a particular direction, the demographics of their surroundings, status of their parents' racial groups, and other cultural knowledge. Poston notes that it is unlikely that children will choose a multiracial identity at this stage, and instead are most often choosing between the two races that represent their heritage.

The third stage in Poston's (1990) model is called Enmeshment/Denial and involves "confusion and guilt at having to choose one identity that is not fully expressive of one's background" (p. 154). Biracial individuals experiencing this stage are often also feeling a lack of acceptance from one or both monoracial groups to which they could potentially belong. Eventually, some resolution of this confusion, guilt, and anger occurs, and many start to appreciate both cultural groups at this time.

This leads into Poston's (1990) fourth stage, Appreciation, which involves starting to accept and appreciate the benefits of multiple identities. Poston does note, however, that in this stage, biracial individuals are still likely to identify more with one group or the other, though they may appreciate both.

Finally, Integration is the fifth and final stage of Poston's (1990) model and represents a time in which biracial individuals have fully integrated both cultures into their identity. Poston notes that in this stage biracial people "tend to recognize and value all of their ethnic identities" (p. 154).

Note on Poston, Jacobs, and Other Stage Models

At this point, before moving on to more models of biracial identity development, we would like to note that similar to the monoracial identity development models of Cross (1971), Morten and Atkinson (1983), and others, the models for Jacobs (1978) and Poston (1990) represent a rather linear progression from confusion to integration of multiple racial identities. The process is seen as going in one direction, and though there are some mentions of environmental influences (e.g., support, rejection, etc.) the process is primarily internal and intrapersonal. In addition, these models each end with a positive endpoint that results in integration of racial groups. Keeping one identity dominant or choosing to identify with only one racial group is not a positive option in these models (Pedrotti, Edwards, & Lopez, 2008). We next turn to the ecological racial identity model of Maria P. P. Root (1999), which is distinctly different from these models and addresses some of the limitations put forth by the previous models.

Root's Ecological Model of Multiracial Identity Development

Root's ecological model is a different breed of model, based on her own research, that interacts with Bronfenbrenner's (1979) ecological systems model (e.g., microsystem, mesosystem, etc.; see Chapter 3 for more description). Root's (1999) model emphasizes the context in which the biracial individual lives and breathes and depicts identity development in a more multifaceted way. Instead of a linear model, Root offers five different identity outcomes, all of which are deemed potentially healthy and positive to the biracial individual.

The first of these is Acceptance of Ascribed Identity, in which individuals allow others to assign race to them as the others see fit. An example would be an African American/White biracial individual who is comfortable with others identifying her as solely African American if they so choose, or as White or biracial depending on how they view her. A second outcome is Identification With Both Racial Groups, which is fairly self-explanatory; an individual here may simply identify as "Asian and White" or "Latino and African American." Root (2003) describes a third identity outcome for biracial individuals as Identification With a Single Racial Group. Distinct from others whose outcome is the acceptance of ascribed identity, these individuals make a conscious choice to adopt one particular racial group as their identity. A person whose parentage includes Latino and American Indian roots, for example, deciding to identify solely as American Indian, might fit within this outcome status. Fourth, some biracial individuals may choose Identification With a New Group, for example, identifying as "biracial" as opposed to identifying with their distinct racial groups. Finally, Root (2003) offers a final outcome in which biracial individuals may choose Adoption of a Symbolic Race. Individuals who fall within this last outcome group are often, according to Root (2003), individuals who look and identify as White to the outside world even though their heritage may include more than one racial group. Root (2003) has noted that individuals who fall into this group often take pride in their particular racial makeup but perhaps do not have a very strong attachment to it. (See Table 9.3 for statements that can be associated with these outcomes.)

It is also worth repeating that Root considers each of the five identity outcomes for biracial people to be positive. This was a very new concept at the time that Root developed her model, as most other models prior to this delineated a natural progression toward one position outcome: integration of the races. Root makes the point that different coping responses related to making the decision to actively identify as more than one race are required in some cases, and these may be different for people of different phenotypes or other characteristics. At times our students have a difficult time understanding all five as positive, particularly the outcome of ascribed identity. Typically, in Western society, having ownership over one's identity is very important, and so it may be difficult for some to think of reasons why people would allow

TABLE 9.3 ● Root's Ecological Systems Model: Example Statements	
Stage	**Example Statement**
Acceptance of Ascribed Identity	"I am what you say I am."
Identification With Both Racial Groups	"I am Asian and White."
Identification With a Single Racial Group	"I am Black" (or another single race).
Identification With a New Group	"I am biracial" or "I am multiracial."
Adoption of a Symbolic Race	"I am White" (though I am also other races).

Source: Root (2003).

others to ascribe an identity to them. Consider the following vignette from one of the authors of this textbook (JTP) on an experience she had in the Midwest during graduate school.

> *I was raised in the Bay Area in California, and so there are many people who look like me there. Most people there were able to guess that I was biracial Asian/White—it was a pretty common mix. Sometimes people would think I was just Japanese or just White, but I always corrected them, because both of my races are important to me.*
>
> *When I got to the Midwest, though, almost no one looked anything like me, and so people asked me all the time "What are you?" with regard to my racial heritage. They seemed confused when I would say "Oh, I'm biracial." I don't think they'd ever heard that term except maybe to describe people who were Black/White. So I spent a lot of time explaining what I meant, and enduring more and more questions about my ethnicity and my nation of origin and my language ability, and all of these things were often being asked by someone I didn't really even know! I got to the point where if someone said, "What are you?" I just said "Japanese," because I knew that was the part of me they were wondering about. If they asked, "Are you Asian?" I would just say, "Yes," and let it go at that, unless it was a friend of mine asking or someone I knew. No one thought I was monoracial White there, but if they had, I would have just gone with that as well.*
>
> *I'm pretty tied into my biracial heritage and to both my Japanese and White sides, so it was odd for me to think of letting someone else take one of those races away from me in identifying me sometimes, but honestly it was just easier a lot of times. I didn't want to have such in-depth conversations with people I didn't even know. When I got back to California again, I switched back to saying I was biracial again.*
>
> —Jennifer, age 45

As you can note above, in this situation, ascribed identity required fewer coping skills and so was a positive outcome for the author in that environment.

It is Root's model (and the models of others who discuss environment as a part of biracial identity development) that is most current and most accepted today in the field, and therefore we would like to spend some time here talking about why this emphasis on context and environment is indeed important in learning about and studying the experiences of biracial individuals.

CONTEXTUAL AND ENVIRONMENTAL INFLUENCES OF IDENTITY DEVELOPMENT

Root (2003) notes that there are many, many factors that might influence the type of identity the biracial individual develops and also states that biracial identity may change from context to context. She defines it as a "spiraling and circular process . . . by which one resolves tensions and accomplishes identity" (Root, 1999, p. 77). Take a look at Figure 9.3 to see the myriad ways that identity development of the biracial individual is impacted according to Root.

Inherited influences, personal traits, and interactions with the community in terms of social relationships all may intersect to create different outcomes with regard to racial identity development. Consider the two individuals represented in Table 9.4, who have the same racial makeup (Japanese father, African American mother) but have differences along various inherited influences, traits, and social interactions.

In looking at the details about Jamal and Kenji in Table 9.4, one might be able to see some of the influences on their identity. Jamal has less interaction with the Japanese side of his heritage, as his father is not involved in his life. Compounded by his dark skin and hair, name, and the nondiverse makeup of his region, it may be obvious why he often chooses to identify as African American or Black. The lack of diversity in his region may mean that there are fewer people that look like him or who have interacted with other non-White people. Thus, it may be easier at times to allow them to ascribe identity to him as opposed to asserting his biracial status and then having to explain it. Kenji, on the other hand, with his Japanese first name, access to both parents and communities, and experience growing up in Los Angeles, may have been able to explore his dual cultural identity a bit more and so is more comfortable identifying as biracial

FIGURE 9.3 ● Factors Affecting Identity Development of Biracial Individuals

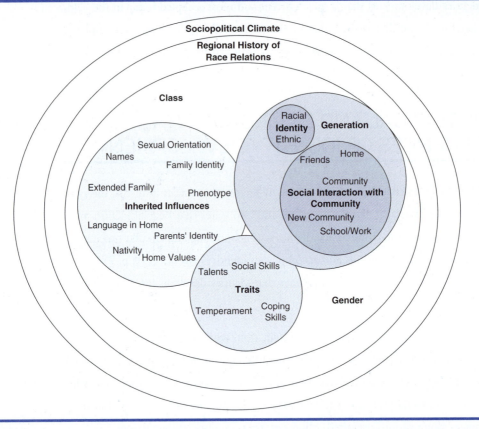

Source: Root (1999).

TABLE 9.4 ● Comparison of Two African American/Japanese Biracial Individuals		
	Jamal	**Kenji**
Languages	English spoken at home	English and some Japanese spoken at home
Phenotype	Dark skin and hair	Dark skin and hair
Parents	Raised by mother, little interaction with father	Raised by both parents
Extended family	None	Both sides accessible
Talents	Athletics, singing	Athletics, music
Makeup of region	Midwest—mostly White	Los Angeles—diverse
Identity	Ascribed, or single racial group (Black)	Biracial in some contexts, Black in others

in most contexts. That said, his dark skin and hair may lead others to identify him as African American, and so he may have experiences that are consistent with those of other monoracial African American individuals when interacting with the police, teachers, or other entities; this is common for many Black/White biracial individuals (Museus, Sariñana, Yee, & Robinson, 2016; Parker et al., 2015). Note also, in Figure 9.3, that Root (1999) considers regional racial history, gender, and class as part of the dynamic creation of identity in the biracial person. Being part of a class that has more access to education may mean that one's parents have had an opportunity to think more abstractly about identity and to consider more options than parents from a class that does not provide this type of opportunity in college or other schooling.

Other researchers have also spoken about reasons that biracial individuals might be drawn toward identifying as a member of one or another of their potential racial identity groups. If an American Indian/White individual grows up with access to and community with her tribe, there may be more pull toward the American Indian side of her heritage than for a comparable individual who does not know much about that side of her culture. Physical characteristics, as noted in the comparison of Jamal and Kenji above, might also influence this process with regard to the effort it takes the individual to claim one of Root's positive outcomes or another. African Americans who are very light skinned may have a much more difficult time asserting a monoracial African American identity than a biracial or White identity. On the other side, dark-skinned African Americans may have difficultly claiming a sole identity of White. One important point: This does not mean that any of the outcomes Root notes are *not* options for any of these individuals. Any biracial person can claim the identity outcome that best fits. However, different coping resources (e.g., dealing with questions, dealing with rejection of that identity from others, etc.) may be needed to assert various identity choices.

Rockquemore and Brunsma (2004) call this process that biracial persons go through to make decisions about the identity that best fits for them "the pushes and pulls of validation" (p. 93). These pushes and pulls may come in many forms. Identification with members of one's family from a particular side might "pull" biracial individuals toward that side of their heritage. Rejection from a particular side (e.g., others not accepting an identity choice made) might "push" them from that side (Rockquemore & Brunsma). Parents might also impact this process. As one might infer from looking at the various

models and number of variables present in identity for biracial or multiracial individuals, their identity development is often more nuanced and could be categorized as more complicated than for a monoracial individual. Compounding this difficulty is that biracial children may not have a role model for moving through this process, or even one who understands it, as their parents are often monoracial themselves. Parents may instead identify a child in a way that they feel might suit the child best, but perhaps not have a full understanding of the myriad choices available. In situations where biracial children are being parented by biracial parents, there may be more opportunities to pass along cultural information about how to navigate the process or how one might cope with various comments, rejections, or questions.

Often biracial siblings develop identity partially based on their comparisons to each other (Root, 1998, 2003) or to other members of the family. Take a look at Cate's thoughts:

In my immediate family I have the darkest skin of all the kids. My sister is much lighter in skin, hair, and eyes than I am, and my brother is a little darker than she is, but not very much. They both have more characteristics of the White side of our family. I have darker hair and brown eyes, and my skin is at least two shades darker than theirs. All three of us knew that we were biracial and what our race makeup was, but I think it was harder for my siblings to say they were Latinx without getting a lot of questions. When I identified like this, no one questioned me at all. It was strange later when we all grew up, because our identities changed a little. My brother married a woman who is Dutch, and so she is much lighter in skin, hair, and eyes than he is, and his children look quite a bit like her. In his new family he is the most Latino looking, and I can see that it changed how he thinks of himself in terms of identity too.

—Cate, age 34

Changing with age or with other alterations to physical appearance may also cause differences in identification or others' acceptance of identity choice. Cate continues:

It's always changing for each of us depending on who else is around us, where we live, sometimes even the clothes we wear or whether we are wearing makeup or not. I used to have lighter highlights put in my hair, and people commented on my biracial status more than when I went back to dark hair again. Who knows what will happen when my hair turns grey? It's always changing.

Other researchers note that categorization of a biracial person often depends on who is doing the categorizing. Lewis (2016) conducted a study in which he showed participants photos of racially ambiguous faces (i.e., photos blended from White and Black parent faces) and asked them to categorize whether the photo was of someone who was Black or someone who was White. Other research has shown that this scenario usually results in faces with racial ambiguity being classified as Black more often than White (Parker et al., 2015). This may be at least in part due to our complicated history with the **one drop rule** (also known as **hypodescent**), which was used in times of slavery to classify any person with "a drop" of African American blood as non-White (Viñas-Nelson, 2017; see Chapter 2 regarding this term and its history). But Lewis added another dimension to his research in this area, dividing his participants into two groups: those who had greater experience with White faces, and those who had greater experience with Black faces. In his research, the findings changed somewhat, showing that the categorization of "Black" was given much more often by the group who had less experience with Black faces, in comparison to the group who had more experience here. This finding suggests that when we have more experience with a particular race, it might change the way we see someone from that group. As Lewis notes in his findings, "Racial categorization of a mixed-race face, therefore, depends on who is doing the categorizing" (p. 505).

COMMON THEMES IN THE LIVES OF BIRACIAL INDIVIDUALS

Thus far in this chapter we have tried to give you several different ways of thinking about biracial identity development and the biracial or multiracial experience. It is important to note that though biracial individuals are a very diverse group, they may share some commonalities in terms of experiences in their lives, similar to how similarities may be found in terms of monoracial ethnic group experiences, even if they don't share the same racial makeup. We would like to detail a few of these here for you to consider.

Being Asked "What Are You?"

This particular question is one that biracial and multiracial individuals hear quite often. One of the authors (JTP) has a running joke with a group of other biracial friends in which they try to top one another with the oddest place they have been asked that question (JTP: "Mine was at a Giants/Dodgers game in the restroom—the woman seemed confused when I said, 'Dodger fan!'"). Depending on features and other physiognomy, a biracial person may not be easily identifiable as a member of one race or another, and so the guessing game often begins. This may be a negative experience for some biracial and multiracial individuals, as Bradshaw (1992) notes: "Though this question is often innocently intended . . . underlying this question is the assumption of the multiracial person's foreignness or nonbelonging" (p. 77). Part of the reason this question may be thought of in this way may be the way in which this question is asked: *What* are you? Many biracial people note that the use of *what* in this question connotes a strangeness to their being that can be experienced as depersonalizing. The question isn't "*Who* are you?" or "*What race* are you?" which both might be experienced differently. Though people differ in the way this question affects them, many biracial people would prefer that others not ask the question in this way. See Janie's experiences that follow:

> *I don't like when people say, "What are you?" in general—it makes me feel like some kind of oddity—like someone just can't figure what I could possibly be. But I really don't like it when someone who doesn't know me asks that question. I've been asked this question by random people when I'm taking the bus, by checkers at the grocery store, and by people waiting in line at the post office. I think that's odd. It's just because they're curious. You wouldn't say to someone "So, are you gay or straight?" or "Are your parents divorced?" or some other kind of question when you didn't know someone. It feels personal to me—race is a sensitive topic sometimes, and I don't usually want to talk about race with people I don't know. What if they have a prejudice against African Americans but didn't know I was part Black until I tell them, or something similar? I'm not ashamed of my biracial heritage—I'm happy to explain it if I'm asked by a friend or someone I know is trying to get to know me better. In those cases, it's OK because I understand their motivation is positive and it's not just idle curiosity.*

—Janie, age 22

Historically, biracial people have often been treated as a curiosity or an "other" and therefore it may be the "what" that is the particularly bothersome part of this question. In addition, however, is the fact that, as Janie notes above, race can be a personal topic and may not be something people want to discuss with people they do not know well. This does not mean that biracial identity development is a topic not to be discussed. Friends may begin to ask one another more personal information as they get to know one another, and this may be a more appropriate time to ask questions of a biracial friend if you are interested. Again, "*What* are you?" is not usually the best way of phrasing this question.

Focus on Physical Features and Attributes

This is another common occurrence that sometimes stems from the question "What are you?" Throughout history, biracial individuals have often been viewed as either fascinating and exotic or as other and different. In her chapter "Beauty and the Beast: On Racial Ambiguity," Carol Bradshaw (1992) discussed the role that physical appearance plays in the life of many biracial individuals. Bradshaw talks about the political, social, interpersonal, and intrapersonal roles that physical attributes can play within the life of the biracial individual. Politically, it has often been considered beneficial to "look White" as a person of color, and though racist in its ideology, we can also understand that this was true to some extent in terms of safety of a person of color. Nella Larsen, the well-known author of the book *Passing* (1929), details the experience of one of her main characters, Irene Redfield, a very light-skinned African American woman who occasionally "passes" for White in social circles. In the passage reproduced here, the setting is a very hot day in which Irene decides to go to the White-only restaurant at the top of a building in New York to have a glass of iced tea to cool herself down while shopping. Larsen writes in Irene's voice:

> Feeling her colour heighten under the continued inspection, she slid her eyes down. What, she wondered, could be the reason for such persistent attention? Had she in her haste in the taxi, put her hat on backwards . . . . What was it? Again she looked up, and for a moment her brown eyes politely returned the stare of the other's black ones, which never for an instant fell or wavered. Irene made a little mental shrug. Oh well let her look! . . . And gradually in Irene there rose a small inner disturbance,

odious and hatefully familiar. She laughed softly, but her eyes flashed. Did that woman, could that woman, somehow know that here before her very eyes on the roof of the Drayton sat a Negro? (Larsen, 1929, p. 150)

Irene, fearful of being kicked out of the Whites-only restaurant, hopes only that no one can see her "negro-ness" (p. 150). This was perhaps a common experience for many light-skinned people of color at this time, as shedding one's color might result in better treatment.

Today, however, there are still many issues surrounding physical appearance that are experienced by the biracial individual. Though some research has found that physical appearance does not correlate strongly with identification of a particular race (Hall, 1980), it may be that physical appearance still correlates strongly with *ascribed* identity, and this can influence one's views of oneself. There is often much fixation on the physical attributes of biracial individuals in terms of which pieces seem to be from which culture. Shelby, who is half Asian and half White, details her experience below.

> When I was little I had this encounter with a little girl in my class who said, "Well, what part of you is Chinese then?" I found myself at age 8 trying to dissect my body to help her to understand, "Well, my hair is Asian I guess because it's black. My skin is both—it's lighter than my dad's. My eyes are hazel—that's both I guess?" It was like the super hard version of one of those Punnett squares they talk to you about in biology class. Your mom has blue eyes and your dad has brown, so there's this much percentage of chance that you'll have blue eyes or something. But the math doesn't work out. When you're biracial, you're sometimes just this spectacle, this strange conglomeration of features, and no one can quite figure you out. And God forbid you say what you think you look like, because someone will disagree with you. "Really? You call yourself a person of color? I think you look White." It's confusing. You're trying to be authentic, but so many ideas are being thrust upon you.
>
> —Shelby, age 40

Because of the White beauty standard that exists within the global community (not only within the United States), there are many accounts of various cultures bleaching skin to appear more white, dying hair to blonde, and assuming other affectations that try to align with Whiteness (Harper & Choma, 2018). Biracial individuals, therefore, may be praised for the overlay of Whiteness that exists on their non-White cultural appearance. You may have seen the exoticization of the combination of dark skin and blue eyes for example. Consider the experience of Jamisa:

Biracial woman with light eyes

I'm biracial Black/White, and I have medium brown skin, brown hair, and blue eyes. People can tell I'm African American usually, but my eyes throw them off. People always comment on how beautiful my eyes are, and it's because they are blue. This is not only White people. I remember my grandmother on my African American side bragging about my eyes to her Black friends—"Look—we've never had blue eyes before. She's the most beautiful baby we've ever had." But I couldn't help thinking that if I'd had brown eyes she wouldn't have thought that. She thought I was better looking because I was more White. That's upsetting when you think about it. She had dark black eyes and beautiful black hair well into her 50s, and rich brown skin. She was a beautiful woman, but she thought I was prettier than she was because I looked Whiter.

—Jamisa, age 25

We have discussed this in other chapters (see Chapter 5), but this is a prime example of internalized racism—the belief that White is superior in every way. In addition, many biracial individuals report that their appearance seemed to invite superficial attention and attraction, rather than genuine interest, although women were more likely to report exoticization as a significant part of their experience (Museus et al., 2016, p. 692). Specifically, biracial individuals who include Asian or Pacific Islander may experience this more often regardless of gender (Museus et al., 2016). In summary, there is much focus on the physical features of the biracial individual, and many have the experience of being asked to "prove" their connection to their races (Bradshaw, 1992).

Being Asked to Choose Just One Race

This is a very common experience for many biracial and multiracial individuals. As we have noted in other chapters, our culture and society are often focused on efficiency in terms of categorization. In the life of biracial individuals, this often manifests as people asking for them to choose the race with which they most strongly identify. The best example of this exists within the use of categorization of race as a part of many data collection procedures, from standardized testing to the categorization of race on birth certificates of biracial children, to the US Census prior to the year 2000.

> *I remember being in fourth grade and having to take some standardized state test. In the first section you had to put your name, your age, and then also your race. And there were these instructions on that part that said, "Choose one option"; basically it would mess up the computer if you chose more than one. I remember asking my teacher what I should put down, because I was more than one thing and it said pick only one. She wasn't sure either—maybe she hadn't had that question yet—and I was only 9, so I was sure she'd know what I should do. She finally said, "I guess pick the one you identify with most." I remember thinking, "Do I identify with my mom or my dad more?" I picked one—I can't even remember which one I picked—but I felt like I got the first question wrong on that test. I wasn't sure if it would affect my score, but I worried about it while I was taking the test. I talked to my mom about it when I got home, sure that she would know the right answer, but she seemed stumped as well and said, "I don't see why you can't choose both." Next time I took that kind of test, I just checked both, but I could see those bolded instructions "Choose only one." And I knew I'd gotten the first one wrong again. When the US Census changed in 2000 and I was "allowed" to pick two, I can't even tell you my relief. Not elation or pride really, just relief. I'd gotten that one right for sure.*
>
> —Steve, age 47

In addition to these anecdotal accounts regarding feelings of annoyance or lack of belonging when multiple options are prevented, quantitative research has been conducted with biracial individuals as well. Townsend, Markus, and Bergsieker (2009) conducted a study in which some biracial participants were permitted to choose multiple races on a demographic form, and then they were compared on a variety of measures to a second group of biracial participants who were compelled to choose only one race. Findings showed that the group who was forced to choose only one race scored lower on measures of self-esteem and motivation to complete a subsequent task. In addition, other studies have found that compelling biracial individuals to define themselves in a way that does not fit with their actual self-identification leads to negative affect and increased effort to identify themselves correctly (Cheryan & Monin, 2005; Museus et al., 2016). The type of invalidation that many biracial individuals feel when they are forced to choose just one racial identity category is well documented (Franco, Katz, & O'Brien, 2016; Museus, Sariñana, Yee, Robinson, 2011).

Checking boxes on demographic forms is not the only example of this type of common experience for biracial people. Many may experience pressure to choose one race based on physical characteristics or other such contextual features (Evans & Ramsay, 2015; Hall, 1992; Rockquemore, Brunsma, & Delgado, 2009). A Latina/White biracial woman with light hair, eyes, and skin may be told that she "cannot" assert her identity as a Latina. Similarly, a dark skinned, dark haired Asian/Black man may be told he is solely black. This denies biracial persons the right to define themselves if they so desire, and it may also negate other experiences that they have had in their lives. Telling a lighter skinned Black/White biracial person, for example, that she cannot claim African American heritage based on her looks may belie the experience her family had during the Jim Crow years that continues to define her family's socioeconomic status. Additionally there are some situations in which biracial individuals may be pressured to choose one race based on political objectives:

> At my university, we just switched over to allowing people to choose more than one race, which, for me as a biracial person, was a good thing. But I was in a meeting later where one of the White administrators was complaining that doing this made the other non-White population percentages go down, because prior to this, some people who were actually biracial were checking just Black or just Asian, et cetera. I'm not sure that's a good justification for forcing people to choose something that doesn't fit for them in terms of identity, but I'd never heard an argument for the "check one box" for such a political reason—he wanted us to appear more diverse. I've mostly heard people argue "It doesn't matter—just choose one!" or "It's too hard to classify for research." I mentioned this to a friend of mine who is non-White but monoracial, and he said, "Well, it also dilutes the resources that go to us as minority groups. If it looks like there aren't as many minorities, they may not have as many services for our specific groups." It's interesting that these two differ-

ent (but both monoracial) people were arguing the same thing for very different reasons, but both were willing to deny biracial people an opportunity to identify themselves correctly for political reasons.

—Suzanne, age 38

Finally on this topic, it is important to note that not all people have access to the term *biracial* growing up; this is especially evident in looking generationally at different biracial individuals across several age groups. Root (2003) discusses the demographics of biracial people as occurring in three different waves (see Table 9.5). First is the Exotic wave, which includes those that were born before the late 1960s. Since there were laws against people of color marrying White people up until the late 1960s in many states, many individuals at this time may have hidden their biracial heritage or may have had some special circumstances surrounding their birth (e.g., a birth due to a White father being in Japan or another non-European country during World War II). The Exotic group had only two options for identity, according to Root (2003): to accept the identity that society assigned them, or to assert a monoracial identity.

Second was the Vanguard wave, which Root describes as those born in the late 1960s to late 1970s. This group, had an additional option of identifying as multiple races, perhaps. Root asserts that this does not mean that they had access to the term *biracial* or that they could identify themselves as this new group as a

TABLE 9.5 ⬡ Waves of Biracial People in the United States					
	Accept Identity Society Assigns	Monoracial Identity	Multiple Races	New Race	Symbolic Race
Exotic (born before late 1960s)	Yes	Yes	No	No	No
Vanguard (born late 1960s to late 1970s)	Yes	Yes	Yes	No	No
Biracial Boomer (born after 1980)	Yes	Yes	Yes	Yes	Yes

Source: Root (2003).

comprehensive identity, but instead they were able to talk about being "half and half" or to discuss the components of their racial heritage.

Finally, there is the Biracial Boomer wave, which Root describes as those born after 1980. This is the group that the option to adopt all five of Root's (1999) positive identity outcomes, and it has had access to both the term *biracial* and other identity nomenclature. It is also relevant to note that identity options and their accessibility may also be limited or increased by access to psychological literature and/or by education of the biracial person's parents or community. This is noted as one of the factors in Root's (1999) ecological model.

Being Thought of as Damaged

As we mentioned in the very beginning of this chapter, one of the first academic tomes to be written about biracial people, *The Marginal Man* (Stonequist, 1939), focused strongly on the deficits and problems biracial people were sure to have based on their complex identity. More than one psychological source at this time discussed the experience of the "tragic mulatto" or defined biracial individuals as "doomed to walk in the margins of society, never fully belonging anywhere." As noted previously, this argument was often used as a reason why miscegenation (or mixing of races) should not be allowed. Even today you may hear the whispered racist comment, "Well, I'm not against interracial marriage, but what about the children? It's too difficult for them."

Current research rather strongly disputes this long-held belief that there is some trauma associated with being multiracial or biracial. Margaret Shih and Diana Sanchez, both academic researchers in the field of biracial identity, conducted a review in 2005 of the psychological literature on biracial individuals. This review found that mental health and psychological adjustment are effectively the same across many different types of indices (Shih & Sanchez, 2005). Miville (2005) found similar results in her content analysis looking at psychological health of multiracial populations. Indeed, studies that have found problems with psychological adjustment in biracial individuals most often reveal that these have to do with some prevention of allowing biracial people to identify as such (Townsend et al., 2009). Some studies have shown that there are unique strengths that biracial people may possess more frequently than their monoracial counterparts. Phinney and Alipuria (1996), for example, found that biracial people score higher on measures of openness to experience and are more adaptable overall. More recently, Soliz, Cronan, Bergquist, Nuru, and Rittenour (2017) found that perceived benefits of being biracial may also include a stronger sense of self and more pluralistic worldviews (e.g., being more open minded). Others have found that biracial individuals have more tolerance with ambiguity as well (Miville). Thus, contrary to historical belief, being biracial may have distinct benefits both physically and psychologically.

Interestingly, studies have also found that being more open to thinking of oneself as part of multiple races may be a source of positive health effects for biracial individuals. In one study, multiracial individuals who used multiple racial categories to define them-selves as opposed to using just one were found to have fewer health issues in comparison to those multiracial or biracial individuals who used just one category to define them-selves (Tabb, 2016). This same study found that this group was also more healthy than the monoracial individuals overall. In another study looking at biracial individuals who were Asian/White, the group identifying more strongly as "Asian-White integrated" (i.e., those who identify with both White and Asian sides of their heritage equally) also had the highest level of psychological adjustment (Chong & Kuo, 2015) compared to biracial Asian/White individuals who identified more strongly as "Asian Dominant" or "White Dominant." Thus, being able to identify oneself in a multifaceted (and accurate) way may be beneficial for one's physical and psychological health as well.

This said, it is important to note that biracial individuals do report experiencing discrimination in levels that mirror those in monoracial minority populations (Ho, Sidanius, Levin, & Banaji, 2011; Museus et al., 2016). Other studies have shown the prominence of hypodescence (originally the one drop rule), or the tendency for White majority individuals to classify Black/White biracial people solely as Black (Ho et al., 2011; Lewis, 2016; Sanchez, Good, & Chavez, 2011). Former president Barack Obama was once asked why he identified as Black more often than as bira-cial, particularly as he was primarily raised by his White mother. Obama discussed this in a number of interviews, but spoke often about his everyday racial experience in the United States. In an interview for the Public Broadcasting Service, he is quoted as saying, "If I'm outside your building trying to catch a cab, they're not saying 'Oh, there's a mixed-race guy.'" Discrimination is not a pathology of bira-cial individuals, and in fact, like all discrimination, it occurs outside the person as opposed to being the result of something internal. But we do want to note that the biracial population is not one that is necessarily protected from discrimination, even if one of the racial heritages a person possesses is White.

CONCLUSION

In this chapter we have tried to give you an overview of what kinds of different experiences exist for people who "check more than one box" each day. As noted in the beginning of this chapter, over 9 million people in the United States classify themselves as biracial, and there are predictions for 2050 that up to 20% of the population may be biracial or multiracial by this time. At times people have talked about the increase of biracial numbers as a herald that we are becoming **postracial**. It may be that, as people from non-White races grow in numbers, all people will be more in contact with people from races different than their own. However, it is likely that this will make them *more* (not less) aware of race, though in more positive ways. Studies have shown that getting to know people who are different from us in some way broadens our own horizons, and subsequently we show increases in awareness, knowledge, and skills in interacting with dissimilar others (Pedrotti, 2017; Wang et al., 2001). Developing ethnocultural empathy means paying attention to race in positive ways and being sensitive to others' experiences. Biracial and multiracial people are a part of our racial landscape and represent their own group within the diverse tapestry that is the United States.

ACT: Assess Your Knowledge, Critical Thinking, Take Part

Assess Your Knowledge

- For a better understanding of the feelings of many biracial people today, watch the 2009 documentary *Biracial Not Black Damn It!* (Battle-Cochrane, 2009) or the 1995 documentary *None of the Above* (Anderson, Seurat, & Wilson, 1995).

- Take some time to reflect and write about your reactions to these films. What questions are you still left with? Were any of your assumptions challenged by these new views?

Critical Thinking

- Think about ways that you may have unintentionally contributed to the discomfort of biracial people in the past—were you a "What are you?" asker in the past?

- Try this small experiment:

  o   Write down three of your most important identities on separate index cards or pieces of paper—these are things you'd like everyone to know about you and that are important to who you are as a person.

  o   Put the cards or papers face down and mix them up.

  o   Choose one at random and rip it up.

  o   Look to see which two are left. What if you were no longer able to claim the identity on the card you ripped up? Which identity was taken from you?

  o   Now look closely at the remaining two identities. Make a decision about which of the two you will take away yourself—you can choose only one for this exercise.

  o   Take some time to reflect on this exercise. What did it feel like to know that the one identity was taken from you? How did you make your choice about the others? Can you connect this to how biracial people might feel when someone asks them to "just choose one"?

Take Part

Participation: Consider attending the one-woman show by Fanshen Cox Giovanni, *One Drop of Love* (www.onedropoflove.org/about) or browsing through her website, https://mixedrootsstories.com. The site tells stories of many biracial and multiracial people in the United States. Take some time to listen to others who have a biracial identity development.

Initiation: Do some research on this topic designed to challenge various views of biracial and multiracial people as "damaged" or as "living in the margins." Create a list of these stereotypical views, and find studies to demonstrate these views are not supported by facts. Share your work with colleagues or classmates as part of a presentation.

Activism: Organize a viewing and discussion of *Loving* (Nichols, 2016), the biopic produced in 2016 as a major motion picture. Consider hosting a panel discussion made up of biracial individuals and/or experts from this area of the field.

MOVING AHEAD

Emerging Issues and Goals

SECTION IV

iStock/pixelfusion3d

10

MULTICULTURAL PSYCHOLOGY IN DIFFERENT SETTINGS

LEARNING OBJECTIVES

- Illustrate the importance of including multicultural understanding and education in schools, the workplace, and therapy settings

- Analyze the impact of stereotype threat in the lives of African American students and other minoritized students in the United States

- Understand the positive impact early learning can have on development of nonracist views of people of color

- Evaluate the impact inequality has had on non-White and nonmale individuals in the workplace with regard to their current statuses

- Understand the benefits of diversity management in the workplace

- Explain the concepts of *cultural competence* and *cultural humility* in developing awareness, knowledge, and skills in working with people of all cultures in the therapy room

- Assess the diversity that exists in the environments in which you spend most of your time (e.g., neighborhoods, school, workplace, etc.). and determine at least one way multiculturalism might take more priority in those spaces

Multicultural psychology and multiculturalism in general are relevant in many different settings. Many different researchers have applied the tenets and concepts of multicultural psychology to a variety of different fields and domains. Some of the reasons for this have to do with the truth that any social construct that deals with people must also attend to their cultural context. As you have read in the other chapters of this book, culture is all around us, and our social, behavioral, and personal development are impacted by it daily. In this chapter, we address multicultural psychology and its concepts in three different settings: school, work, and therapy.

MULTICULTURALISM IN SCHOOLS

In thinking about this section of the chapter, we thought it might be useful to start off with some specific issues that impact students related to race, ethnicity, gender, and other cultural facets. We'll then talk about the recent trends that have begun to increase multicultural education in the classroom and finish up by talking about the kinds of training teachers might find useful to teach in today's culturally diverse environment.

Demographics and Gaps

Looking at the most recent reports of the National Center for Education Statistics (NCES, 2016) can give us a breakdown of demographics in elementary and secondary education. As of this report, 50% of the student population is White, with Latinx students next at 25%, then African American (16%), Asian (5%), biracial

(3%), and finally American Indian (1%). These numbers have changed to become somewhat more diverse in comparison to totals found in earlier decades. The NCES (2016) predicts that by 2024, the White population will likely have fallen to 46%, making a minority majority across the country.

However, students from different racial groups are not graduating high school at the same rates. Often this disparity is referred to as the **achievement gap**, reflecting the lower rates of graduation achievement of non-White students in the United States. Today, some have begun referring to this as the **opportunity gap** or **equity gap** instead, as we know from our other chapters that differences exist in terms of access

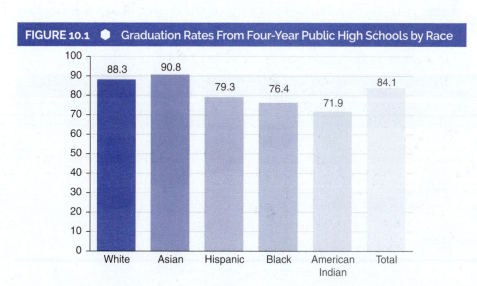

FIGURE 10.1 ● Graduation Rates From Four-Year Public High Schools by Race

White 88.3	Asian 90.8	Hispanic 79.3	Black 76.4	American Indian 71.9	Total 84.1

iStock/FatCamera

to resources, cultural capital, and other extracurricular variables that may influence one's ability to graduate high school. Racial disparity is stark in looking at these gaps: Black and Latinx students from all 50 states graduate at lower rates than White and Asian students (NCES, 2017; see Figure 10.1). These results are further magnified when looking at data for students moving into postsecondary education. Many studies have looked at differences among these groups and made hypotheses about the reasons for them. Many have found correlations between lower socioeconomic status (SES) and lower graduation rates, and though we know that race does not always align with SES, it is also true that there are higher percentages of racial and ethnic minorities in the lower-SES groups as compared with those that are White (Macartney, 2011). Being a child in a lower-SES home may not only mean having less money overall in one's household but may also correlate with less-nutritious food, potentially less parental supervision (due to having to work more hours to stay afloat financially), less time for schoolwork (due to additional responsibilities for the home), less housing security, and more overall stress, all of which might obviously impact ability to stay on track in school (Wang & Finch, 2018). In addition to these more obvious reasons, however, additional studies have looked at other issues for racial and ethnic minority students that might impact achievement and success in school.

One such factor that may impact students' success in racial and ethnic minority populations is the demographics of the teaching workforce, which does not mirror the student racial diversity discussed previously in this chapter, though numbers have changed slightly in some racial groups (see Table 10.1).

TABLE 10.1 ⬢ Percentages of Teachers by Race: 1987 Versus 2011		
	1987–1988 School Year	**2011–2012 School Year**
White teachers	87	82
Latinx teachers	3	8
African American teachers	8	7
Asian teachers	1	2
American Indian teachers	1	0.5

Source: NCES, 2016.

White teachers still make up 82% of the elementary and postsecondary educational workforce, with all other racial groups making up less than 10% each of the workforce. Latinx teachers are the next largest, making up 8% of the educational workforce, with African American making up 7%, Asians accounting for 2%, and American Indian teachers at 0.5% (NCES, 2016). Thus, the demographics of educators do not align with the students they are teaching. Moore, MacGregor, and Cornelius-White (2017) conducted a study in which they looked at racial congruence between teaching staff and students and then looked at the gaps in achievement among racial groups as a function of this congruence. Results showed that elementary students whose teachers' race matched their own had significantly higher reading scores (after controlling for economic disadvantage, Moore et al., 2017). Moore and colleagues noted that increases in African American and Latinx teacher numbers could potentially narrow the gaps that have been found to date.

Stereotype Threat

Another potential source of gaps found in achievement may be related to a concept (conceived of by Dr. Claude Steele (1997), a psychology professor from Stanford), known as **stereotype threat**. As you know from Chapter 1, there is a history of stereotypes with regard to intelligence and its potential connections to race, gender, and other factors. Recall also that despite trying to confirm some of these stereotypes (for example regarding women and brain size), science was not able to find connections between gender or race and intelligence. Nevertheless, differences are often found in achievement on IQ tests when comparing races. Many social scientists and psychologists have formed hypotheses around why this difference exists. Some, such as the authors of *The Bell Curve* (Herrnstein & Murray, 1994), have posited that race and intelligence are actually biologically linked. In this book, Herrnstein and Murray stated that their research found evidence that African Americans do not have the same capacity for intelligence as White Americans have.

This book met with much scorn for its lack of scientific rigor and many rebuttals to the sort of "science" that was used to "provide evidence" for such ideas. Stephen Jay Gould (1996), in his *The Mismeasure of Man: The Definitive Refutation to the Argument of* The Bell Curve, provides page after page of evidence showing why the conclusions made by Herrnstein and Murray are not only flawed but also false. Gould gives a step-by-step critique of the research methods employed, but key among these is a tendency to look only for results that support the authors' hypotheses, and, in Gould's words, "In violation of all statistical norms that I've ever learned, they plot *only* the regression curve and do not show the scatter of variation around the curve, so their graphs show nothing about the *strength* of the relationship [between IQ and other cultural facets]" (1996, p. 375). Put simply, Herrnstein and Murray (1994) found *a relationship,* but a weak one at best, between IQ and other cultural factors. As you may know and remember from statistics courses you have likely taken, if there is any connection between two variables at all, you may call that a "relationship"; however the statistical calculations performed using the data that shows that relationship tell you how likely it is that you would find that relationship in another sample. In the *Bell Curve* research, Herrnstein and Murray admit that their correlations are weak, but then contend that this does not matter. Despite the frivolity of these claims, many across the United States and beyond read *The Bell Curve* and had their own stereotypes confirmed by its faulty pseudoscience.

One of the main refutations to the type of hypotheses made in *The Bell Curve* calls into question the *direct* relationship between IQ and race. Many have said that it is not race but socioeconomic status that makes the difference between African American and White performances on IQ tests. Some studies have found a consistent 15-point difference between these races on IQ tests (Steele, 1997) and have made the claim that this difference is due to higher percentages of African Americans living in poverty and thus having less access to good schools, good nutrition, and other benefits that may impact IQ. While this idea that economic advantage is linked to ability to do well on a test has been supported many times (e.g., Wang & Finch, 2018), there are other studies that show that even when socioeconomic status and income level are held constant between African Americans and Whites (i.e., comparing low-SES African Americans to low-SES White Americans), the same 15-point difference is found (Steele, 1997). This suggests that something other than these socioeconomic differences must be at play.

In the 1990s, Steele was conducting research surrounding knowledge of the existence of stereotypes and what this might mean to those who were being stereotyped in negative ways. Dr. Steele reviewed research by Ogbu (1988) and others that charted differences in IQ found in different populations in other nations, and began to see a pattern that surrounded potential stigma. In India, Ogbu noted that measurements of IQ between people of higher castes and those of lower castes seemed to show an approximately 15-point difference, and in Japan a similar difference existed in IQ test scores between those of the *buraku* (a stigmatized social group in Japan) and those from the majority population in Japan. Interestingly, in a study of buraku Japanese children who immigrated to the United States, the point difference in IQ tests disappeared when they were tested in the United States and compared to other nonstigmatized Japanese immigrant children (Ito, 1967). When these groups (e.g., the buraku or individuals from stigmatized castes) immigrate to the United States, these social differences are erased in the sense that people within the United States are unlikely to know about the social meaning behind their caste or group. Ogbu cited the erasure of the point difference in IQ scores as attributable to the fact that the buraku Japanese immigrants and nonstigmatized Japanese immigrants are both treated the same when in the United States. Notably, based on stereotypes about Asian individuals and academic achievement, they are likely not stigmatized at all in terms of beliefs about their academic achievement in the United States. Steele (1997) began to investigate the possibility that the sociopolitical stigma attached to some groups might impact their performance on IQ tests (though potentially not their net intelligence).

In 1997, Dr. Steele wrote a paper titled "A Threat in the Air," in which he detailed his theory of stereotype threat. Steele posited that when individuals from a population that is often stereotyped in negative ways are aware of these stereotypes (regardless of their belief in them), they may work hard to avoid confirming them with their behavior. Though much data and research abound to disconfirm the idea that race, gender, and intelligence are inextricably linked, these stereotypes still exist in popular culture and everyday thought.

Steele decided to test the impact of knowledge of the stereotypical assumption that men are better at math than women.

In order to test this impact, Steele cultivated a sample of both men and women who were exceptionally good at math. Sampling from Stanford University's math majors, he chose only students who identified strongly as excellent math students and who had the skills to back up this belief. Because Steele wanted to study differences in reactions to a stereotype in men versus women, he made sure to hold other variables constant, including ensuring that SAT scores were very close, grades in math classes were similar (and very high), and other factors such as socioeconomic status and other facets were similar. He then separated this population into two groups and gave both the exact same, very difficult math test. Just before giving the test to the first group, he told them, "This test has found differences between men and women in their scores in the past. This research is to find out more information about that." For the second group he gave a different prompt, telling them, "This test has been specially created to be unbiased and has never found differences between men and women on their scores." He then proceeded to give the test to both.

The results from this study are found in Figure 10.2. Before looking at these results, recall that the students in this study were all matched on socioeconomic status, GPA, and SAT scores—they were essentially the same except for a difference in gender, and so one would assume that they should perform the same on this test. As you can see from the results, however, this is not the case. In the group that was told that the

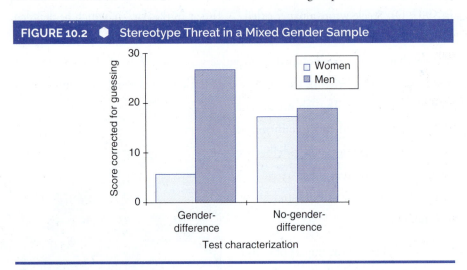

FIGURE 10.2 ● Stereotype Threat in a Mixed Gender Sample

Source: Steele, C. M. (1997). "A threat in the air: How stereotypes shape intellectual identity and performance." *American Psychologist, 52*, 613–629.

test had been found to be biased in the past, women were significantly outscored by their male counterparts. In the group that was told the test was specially designed to be unbiased, however, there was no significant difference in the scores. The results provide evidence for the idea that when women in the first condition were told that bias might occur, they were put in a position of potentially confirming a stereotype about themselves as women doing math if they did not perform strongly. This *threat* appeared to have impacted their ability to do well on their test. In the second group, however, women did not have to contend with the threat of confirming a stereotype, as they were told the test was unbiased. Therefore, their performance was not impacted by extra anxiety over trying to avoid stereotype confirmation.

Some questioned the interpretations made by Steele with regard to the fact that the stereotype influenced the results, because the test-taking situation (specifically the noting of expected bias prior to taking the test) was somewhat different than an actual administration of an IQ test. Critics noted that there would not be such an overt reminder of stereotypes or bias directly before an IQ test. Steele, however, conducted other studies in which this overt reminder was not present. In a second study, Steele (1997) decided to look at race instead of gender, and he again matched the participants very closely on all aspects other than race. For this study, a very difficult verbal test was used; the idea was to use a test that "threatened" African Americans with the risk of confirming stereotypes that they would do poorly on it in comparison to their White counterparts. In actuality, though, the participants were chosen based on their exceptional aptitude for language arts and other verbal skills. At the beginning of Steele's study, the participants were separated into two groups. In attempts to mirror the actual testing situation of most standardized tests, in this study Steele had one group fill out a demographic questionnaire that included questions about race prior to the administration of the test, and he did not ask the other group to fill out anything beforehand. Results can be seen in Figure 10.3, and they show that in the group in which participants were asked to indicate their race prior to the administration of the test, the African American students scored significantly lower than their White counterparts in that condition. In the condition where race was not asked about prior to the administration, however, there was no significant difference between scores in terms of race.

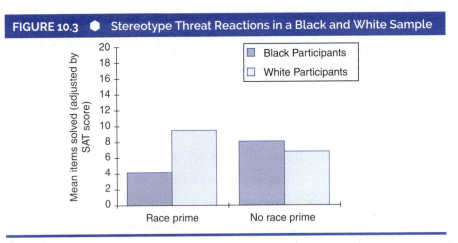

FIGURE 10.3 ● Stereotype Threat Reactions in a Black and White Sample

Source: Steele, C. M. (1997). A threat in the air: How stereotypes shape intellectual identity and performance. *American Psychologist, 52,* 613–629.

You might notice something else that is interesting about the patterns of scores found in the previous figures. For groups that were told they might have more success (i.e., the men in the condition where they are told that the test was biased, or the White students in the condition where they were asked to indicate their race prior to the taking of the test), scores were higher than scores for groups in the conditions in which they were not primed in this way. This phenomenon is referred to as **stereotype lift** and refers to the increased scores one often may find when a group is reminded of their powerful status (i.e., not stereotyped in a negative way) prior to taking a test. This is another important part of the puzzle. When people are primed by norms and culture to know that they are expected to do well, an increase in score is found (Walton & Cohen, 2003).

One final study is important to describe here. Aronson and colleagues (1999) attempted to induce stereotype threat in White male college students. As in the other studies noted above, students were chosen from a pool of very high-achieving math students who identified strongly with being good math students. In this study, participants were randomly assigned to one of two groups: (1) the stereotype condition, in which students were given two minutes to read quickly through a packet of articles that detailed the superior achievement in math of Asians, and then told by the researcher that "in math, it seems to be the case that Asians outperform whites" (Aronson et al., 2000, p. 33), and (2) a control condition in which no mention of Asian math superiority was mentioned.

Results mirrored those found in the studies we have just reviewed, with one important difference: White students in the group told about the "Asian superiority" in math performed significantly more poorly than those who were not told about this stereotype before taking their test. Thus, even White men can be susceptible to a "threat" when one mentions a stereotype just before the men take a test related to that ability.

The implications of this collective research point toward a clear call that stereotypes harm students about whom they are made. As more negative stereotypes exist with regard to Latinx, African American, and American Indian racial groups, these groups are likely to be the most impacted. Reducing stereotypes and exposing all children to positive models of non-White individuals is essential for decreasing the equity gaps that currently exist in our society.

Multicultural Education and Social Justice

You already know from information you have learned from other chapters in this book that stereotypes often arise from a lack of knowledge about people who are from groups that are different from one's own (see Chapter 5). In addition to addressing directly issues that impact racial and ethnic minority students' achievement in school, one way we can fill in the gaps in knowledge about any underrepresented group is to make sure that curricula approved for all grades include all groups. In recent years some states have begun to mandate the inclusion of a variety of cultural groups in the curriculum. In California, for example, the FAIR Education Act was approved in 2011 and requires that accomplishments of a variety of cultural groups, including LGBTQ+ groups and those with disabilities, be included in the social studies curriculum (see Spotlight Feature 10.1).

 SPOTLIGHT FEATURE 10.1

With California in the Lead, LGBTQ+ History Gets Boost in School Curriculum

California is the home of some of the nation's earliest and most influential "out" gay leaders. It's no surprise then that California has paved the way for teaching gay history in our K–12 schools and that other states are beginning to follow suit.

(Continued)

(Continued)

The 2011 passage of California's FAIR Education Act mandated that LGBTQ (Lesbian, Gay, Bisexual, Transgender, Queer) accomplishments be taught in our history and social studies classrooms in an age-appropriate manner. This law doesn't teach morality; it teaches our students that gay Americans have been an integral part of our society and continue to shape our current world.

What does teaching gay history look like? In elementary schools, this might be reading a book where a character has two moms or two dads. In secondary education, it can be learning about California's own Harvey Milk or the gay liberation movement. For teachers, these shifts can seem minimal—after all, more and more teachers are being trained on culturally responsive pedagogy.

However, for students, the impact could be, quite literally, the difference between life and death. Nearly 7 percent of US millennials identify as a member of the gay community. Though there has been social progress in recent history, disparities in how often LGBTQ youth are victimized have not improved since the 1990s. In fact, there has been an uptick in hate crimes in our schools.

One study suggests that each episode of LGBT victimization, such as physical or verbal harassment or abuse, increases the likelihood of self-harming behavior by 2.5 times on average. Student suicides among sexual and gender minorities are still frequent headlines, with gay youth five times as likely to have attempted suicide than their straight peers.

This bullying is impacting both their physical safety and their schoolwork. Academically, higher rates of truancy and lower GPAs have been documented among LGBT students. With lives at stake, it is no wonder that at least two other states have followed California's lead to ensure that LGBTQ students feel less excluded and LGBTQ history and contributions are part of the school curriculum.

In April of this year, Massachusetts created optional LGBTQ history lessons that may be taught in schools. Additionally, this year, the Illinois State Senate took a historic vote to mandate LGBTQ history be taught in schools through the passage of SB 3249, a bill similar in scope to the FAIR Education Act.

The California FAIR Education Act and Illinois' SB 3249 won't solve every problem for our gay youth, but they work to ensure that students have an understanding that our gay students are not alone and build tolerance among their straight peers.

Representation matters. Seeing that there have been gay people throughout American history is an important first step to letting our current students know that they can and will achieve greatness, just as others have done before them.

• • •

James Hilton Harrell is a transformational support specialist with WestEd, a non-profit research, development, and service agency and, prior to that, served as a teacher and director of instruction at Oakland Unified School District.

Source: Harrell (2018).

Though California education code already had some requirements for teachers to be inclusive of groups other than White Americans, the FAIR Act added the bolded language below to bolster the original intent:

> A study of the role and contributions of both men and women, Native Americans, African Americans, Mexican **Americans**, Asian **Americans**, Pacific Islanders, **European Americans, lesbian, gay, bisexual, and transgender Americans, persons with disabilities**, and members of other ethnic **and cultural** groups, to the economic, political, and social development of California and the United States of America, with particular emphasis on portraying the role of these groups in contemporary society. (Senate Bill 48, California Education Code, section 51204.5)

By sharing information about the different groups who built the United States from the ground up—whether in legislative roles, in physically building the railroad, through working in fields and farms, or teaching in the classroom—we allow continuing generations to have a more clear understanding of what has transpired in our country's history. This allows our young people to both take pride in the contributions of their own groups and others, and to mark mistakes made so as not to repeat them again. Some of these decisions have brought controversy, and it is important to acknowledge that it may be hard to learn that the history one thought was correct may have left out some of the darker parts of history. That said, we can learn from the past and use it to craft a better future for our country. Consider the viewpoint and realizations of a parent who learned a more sanitized version of American history than her son is learning now:

> *My child came home today and told me about some of the things he learned in his fourth-grade classroom today, and it was really different from what I learned in school. At first I felt pretty defensive—it seemed like they were changing history! But one of the things that he said they learned was that Christopher Columbus didn't really "discover" America, since the Native Americans were already living there. I never really thought about that before. Our family loves camping, and we've gone to this one spot in Big Basin almost every year since the kids were babies. It's our favorite spot—we know*

everything about it. My child said it was like if someone just heard about Big Basin and said, "Look what I discovered!" and changed the name and said it was theirs now and we couldn't camp there anymore. He said if someone did that our family would feel really bad about that and would feel like that was unfair, and we might try to fight back or get angry.

I started thinking of some of the other things I'd learned and asked him some questions about the Pilgrims and the Indians. I remember learning that the Indians were very primitive and set in their ways, and that it was good that the White people showed them how to do a lot of things that made them more "modern," but I didn't think about it from their perspective at the time. I don't know many people who are Native American, and so when I think about them, I remember those teachings: They're primitive; they didn't like the White people; they fought them. My son doesn't think those things about them. He thinks that they liked the way they were living just like any of us might, and when they tried to keep their way of life going, Columbus and others didn't really let them, and that makes him feel empathy for them. He also told me that in the United States, Native Americans only make up 1% of the population. He said he thinks they must be a very strong culture because they fought back for their culture and are still here even though they had to put up with so many things. I felt so great that when he meets people who are Native American in his life, those will be the things he thinks about their culture, and now I will too.

—Annabelle, age 35

Another way that multiculturalism can be brought into the classroom is via direct programs and curricula dealing with diversity and inclusion. Okoye-Johnson (2011) conducted a thorough meta-analysis, in which many studies using a multicultural education curriculum were assessed. Results of this meta-analysis showed that use of multicultural education "was found to be effective in improving racial attitudes of students in prekindergarten through 12th grade" (p. 1266). The impact of this education was more effective as children got older, as one might expect, but Okoye-Johnson recommends that starting multicultural education intervention early in school can lay a foundation to be built upon in later years.

This type of education is not used only in the United States with positive impact. A study conducted with adolescents in the Netherlands showed that students' understanding and knowledge about other cultures increased, and created "the establishment of anti-racism norms within the classroom," as a result of multicultural education tactics (Verkuyten & Thijs, 2013, p. 179). Other research has supported this same finding, showing that use of curriculum to teach antiracism and multicultural responsiveness had a beneficial effect on achievement in students in academic, cultural, and social domains (Wiggan & Watson, 2016). Thus, using multicultural education can have a direct impact on the way in which children and adolescents think about cultures other than their own, and can lead them toward more antiracist attitudes overall. Many researchers today call for more training to be offered for teachers in terms of how to impart this information to their students.

Teacher Preparedness

In order for the types of topics discussed above to be included in our curricula, we must also think about how to prepare elementary and secondary teachers to be able to address these topics in their classrooms. One way of doing this is to offer multicultural education for teachers as a part of their preservice education. Some suggest that this can be best accomplished by changing the way in which teachers are trained for a single-subject certificate, such that diverse perceptions and content are included in all areas of study (Ambe, 2006). In addition, others note that helping teachers to be more aware of their own attitudes about culture and race (awareness about both their own race and that of others) can be a beneficial step toward having more knowledge and skills at teaching in culturally competent ways (Geerlings & Thijs, 2017; Gibson, 2004). Given the information already shared about the demographics of the teaching workforce in the United States today, it is often the case that White teachers may find themselves learning in non–racially diverse classrooms as they obtain their education, but then teaching in very racially diverse classrooms upon beginning their actual jobs. Qualitative data suggests that teachers may find themselves feeling frustrated by their lack of preparation in working with students whose backgrounds are so different from their own (Gibson, 2004).

For this reason, some programs are beginning to emerge that give specific information to preservice teachers in order to better equip them to provide multicultural education to their students. Rogers-Sirin and Sirin (2009) detail a program called the Racial and Ethical Sensitivity Training KIT (REST-KIT), which is "designed to (a) increase preservice teachers' ability to recognize ethical dilemmas related to intolerance in schools and (b) provide preservice teachers with techniques and skills for handling these dilemmas" (p. 19). The REST-KIT uses a model based on ethical principles that align with school professional codes of ethics and combines this with basic cultural competence skills. Following the training involved in utilizing the REST-KIT, preservice teachers in Rogers-Sirin and Sirin's (2009) study were asked how they would rate the experience. Many had positive comments about the style of the workshops and lectures associated with the training, with praise such as "I loved the atmosphere generated. It felt conducive of open discussion on how to deal with real-life situations instead of the usual hypotheticals that we don't see in schools" (p. 25).

Some websites have been developed that offer lesson plans and other curricular resources that can assist teachers in developing more multicultural competence in their daily work. You might take the time to look up the website for an organization called *Teaching Tolerance* at www.tolerance.org for more ideas and information. In sum, more research is needed in this area, but developing teacher competence and confidence in being able to use inclusive teaching strategies to work with students who are different from them, and imparting important multicultural educational material, could make change in what our youngest learners gain as they move through the school system.

MULTICULTURALISM IN THE WORKPLACE

In 2018, data from the US Bureau of Labor Statistics showed that 78% of the workforce then employed listed their race as White. Next largest in terms of racial group were Latinx workers at 17% of the workforce, African American or Black workers at 13%, and Asian workers at 6%.[1] These numbers show that White Americans are represented at higher numbers in the workforce than they are in the population (approximately 67% of the US population identified themselves as White on the last

---

[1] These percentages do not add up to 100, as some workers of Hispanic or Latinx ethnicity also chose White, Black, or Asian as their race; someone of Hispanic ethnicity can be from any racial group.

census; Humes, Jones, & Ramirez, 2011), though numbers are roughly similar. Some population estimates, however, predict that non-White populations will become the majority (when counted together) in the United States by 2042 (Grieco & Trevelyan, 2010). This is already true in some states, like California (Schevitz, 2000). Therefore, knowing how to work together with people different from themselves becomes very important to all workers within the United States. Taking a multicultural psychology course will get anyone part of the way toward this goal, but understanding differences that are specific to the workplace environment are becoming more and more important.

Segregation of Racial Groups Within the Workforce

We know, from any US history book, that workers from different groups have historically been separated in the workforce. In the past, women tell stories of not being hired for certain types of jobs or being asked to leave work if they became pregnant, and women were kept out of many fields in the past within our country. We know today that women and non-White minority groups continue to be underrepresented in STEM fields and other more lucrative fields (National Girls Collaborative, 2018). Even the military was segregated until 1948. Much of this segregation has been intentionally enforced; examples include the strategy employed that you have already learned about regarding indentured White servants being separated from non-White servants and slaves (see Chapter 6 for a refresher on the social construction of Whiteness) as well as laws that prevented particular groups from holding certain jobs. Economic separation confounded with race also kept certain racial groups from obtaining the type of education needed to access higher-level jobs.

As of 1964, because of the Civil Rights Act, employers were no longer allowed to racially discriminate against certain races (namely African American at this time), and therefore some workforces began to become a bit more diverse (Bouie, 2011). Many employers, however, were not particularly proactive at increasing the diversity in their pools of applicants or in those who were hired at this time. In 1972, however, with the passage of the Equal Employment Opportunity Act, many employers were mandated to use affirmative action practices to begin to make access to a variety of jobs more common (Bouie, 2011). Today, affirmative action mandates have decreased in some states. In California, for example, affirmative action was declared unconstitutional in 1996, and these practices were abolished. Debate points exist on both sides (pro–affirmative action and against), but the loss of affirmative action policies within the California State University (CSU) and University of California (UC) resulted in a decrease in racial and ethnic diversity for several years after the policies were dropped (Perez, 2012). At present, only eight states have bans that prohibit affirmative action regarding employment (Desilver, 2014). In addition, federal law protects employees from being fired solely because of race.

In the past few years, a new push to increase racial and gender equity in all levels of positions has begun to resurface. Many companies, including Google, Apple, and Yahoo, have begun to create positions for diversity and inclusion vice presidents or those with similar titles to renew efforts toward having more diverse workforces within their companies. In addition, diversity training has become more common; for example, implicit bias workshops have been offered in which employers learn about unconscious biases that may impact diversity in the workforce (and other arenas). In addition, some groups have hired diversity consultants who work to help companies to ensure that they are in compliance with federal guidelines (Bouie, 2011). Others have begun groups, such as a firm based in Portland, Oregon, called White Men as Full Diversity Partners, in which White men who are well versed in diversity and inclusion topics and theory work with other White men to "enhance their understanding of diversity and to emphasize the extent to which 'whiteness' is as much a category as being black or Hispanic" (Bouie, 2011, para 7). This particular strategy has been helpful as it relies on majority culture individuals to take responsibility for teaching about diversity as opposed to asking minority individuals to be completely responsible for these endeavors. This type of ally work is important to success in spreading awareness about the importance of culture.

Value of Work in Different Cultural Groups

Some research notes that different racial groups employ different value systems in terms of the way they approach work. As others have noted, "Workers whose personal work values are consistent with their job facets/rewards have reported higher levels of job satisfaction" (Kashefi, 2011, p. 639). These values may be personal values, such as wanting to be in a field that serves others (e.g., a nonprofit) because one believes in personal service as a duty, but they may also be based on racial characteristics. In the late 1960s and into the 1970s, some studies found that extrinsic rewards were more important to African American workers (e.g., good pay, job security, etc.) whereas White workers were more invested in the intrinsic value of a job (e.g., a sense of accomplishment; Bloom & Barry, 1967; Kashefi, 2011). Interestingly, other studies have found that these racial preferences and values may exist as differences even when other factors, such as socioeconomic status, are kept consistent (Martin & Tuch, 1993). This said, however, it is easy to think of instances in which race might have been related to another factor, and thus this value manifested in a particular racial group for more external reasons. If jobs were harder to come by for African American workers, for example, they may as a group have valued things like higher pay or job security because they were rare; this type of scarcity may not have been experienced by White workers in the same way at this time.

In addition, other research has found that the way in which people think of themselves individually and in relation to the group also influences endorsement of particular values. Gahan and Abeysekera (2009) found that self-construal mediates the relationship that exists between national culture and particular intrinsic work values. Those who live in a collectivist nation for example, but have more individualist personal values have a different work-value profile than those who have different national and personal culture. Gahan and Abeysekera (2009) called for more research "assessing the impacts of work values on behaviours and interactions in the workplace, particularly where these values might diverge among work team members and between superiors and subordinates" (p. 140). This point is particularly important as our workforce grows more diverse and as different levels of leadership are being diversified as well.

Finally, different gender groups may have different values for different types of work as well. Flexible work arrangements, strong work-life balance, and having a family-supportive culture have long been values that many female-identified workers have held, and to some extent this is still found today, though other genders are becoming more desirous of work cultures with these types of values as well (Wayne & Casper, 2016). We next turn to ways in which diversity might manifest itself, and the increasing need for emphasis and awareness of differences within today's workplace.

Diversity Management in the Workplace

Today, as Youssef-Morgan and Hardy (2014) state, "Large scale changes in the demographic makeup of the United States have led its labor force to being the most diverse in history" (p. 220). The concept of **diversity management** was created circa the 1990s by Dr. R. Roosevelt Thomas, Jr., an organizational behaviorist trained at Harvard University, and is described as utilizing the attributes and benefits of having a diverse workforce toward other positive outcomes for businesses across the country (Thomas, 2005). Many researchers have found that having diversity in the workforce is correlated with other desirable work-related results. Cunningham (2009), for example, found that in looking at athletic departments within the National Collegiate Athletic Association (NCAA) across the United States, overall performance and racial diversity in employment were positively associated. These results, however, were strongest in those athletic programs in which **proactive diversity management** was used. Some of the tenets of proactive diversity management included viewing diversity as a broad and multifaceted concept (e.g., including social identity facets such as race, ethnicity, gender, socioeconomic status, nationality, etc.) and making sure that value for diversity was institutionalized (e.g., using it in mission and value statements and including it in overarching goals for the department). In addition, the most successful programs also made sure that there were a variety of individuals responsible for decision making as opposed to an isolated leader (Cunningham, 2009). These findings are similar to another research finding that the most successful diversity management strategies involve engagement with diversity from the top level of management down (Howarth & Andreouli, 2016). In addition, diversity in a workforce has been associated with higher levels of group satisfaction for all groups, including those who identify as White, and better performance overall, again across multiple groups (Pitts, 2009).

Some research in the area of diversity and performance has conflicted with the above accounts, however, and this "cancelling out" has led some overall meta-analyses of studies of diversity and the workforce to find little impact of diversity on performance overall (Bowers, Pharmer, & Salas, 2000). Some more recent analyses, however, have broken these studies down more carefully to look at contextual factors that may explain the conflicting results sometimes found in this area of the field. In 2010, Stahl and colleagues conducted a massive meta-analysis using a total of 112 studies that focused on issues relevant to this topic (Stahl, Maznevski, Voigt, & Jonsen, 2010). Stahl and colleagues analyzed these studies using a conceptual model that hypothesized that factors such as task complexity, team size and tenure (i.e., length of time working together), and proximity to one another in working might impact team performance. A number of other factors that may have affected the impact of these team details on performance included creativity, conflict, communication effectiveness, satisfaction, and social integration.

To simplify, let us use an example. Stahl and colleagues would expect, for instance, that a diverse team that had been working together for quite some time, was relatively small, and had a task that was not complex might have more satisfaction and better communication than teams that did not have these facets. Through a series of complicated hypotheses, Stahl and colleagues (2010) developed a model to help explicate the impact of cultural diversity on team performance. Overall, they found that cultural diversity tended to decrease convergence ("processes that align a team along common objectives, commitment, or conclusions,") and increase divergence ("processes . . . that bring different values and ideas into the team and juxtapose them with each other," p. 692). Both convergence and divergence have assets and deficits. For example, a positive consequence of divergence is creativity; multiple perspectives at the table lead to multiple ideas. A negative consequence of divergence is conflict, however; multiple perspectives can also lead to fighting within the group. Cultural diversity seems related to divergence, according to this analysis, but it is less clear whether it is related to convergence. The following specific findings were discovered:

- Cultural diversity increased conflict within teams at times, but also resulted in greater creativity in many circumstances.

- More conflict in a culturally diverse team arose if a task was more complex, if they had been working together longer, and if they were located in the same office,

- Culturally diverse teams had higher satisfaction than nondiverse teams, and they did not have less effective communication. (This second finding is contrary to what was hypothesized.)

- In larger culturally diverse teams, there was a lower amount of satisfaction.

These findings point to the presence of both positive and negative factors of culturally diverse teams, but also suggest that some of the negatives can be resolved with other solutions. For example, Stahl and colleagues (2010) posited that perhaps the dispersion of the teams made the members "more attentive to cultural diversity, and [thus] more inclined to resolve conflicts constructively" (p. 704). Perhaps increasing attention to cultural diversity in settings in which members are colocated can mitigate the results regarding more conflict. The finding that higher satisfaction was found in culturally diverse teams was also significant and valuable. At times, participants of culturally diverse groups may have expectations that conflict will be high. If they are also aware that satisfaction will be high, this may counteract this negative expectation. Time spent at work is a large amount of time for most adults in the US workforce. As diversity in our country increases, most workplaces will be more culturally diverse overall. Therefore, it is beneficial to think of ways in which we can make diversity both productive (in terms of creativity and outcome) and satisfactory (in terms of interaction and decreasing conflict). More research is needed in areas of diversity management and other such strategies that can help to make progress toward these goals. As some conflict and other negative divergence may come from workers having little experience with diversity, it is a possibility that some of these goals will be achieved as people grow more multiculturally competent via positive interactions with diverse others.

MULTICULTURALISM IN PSYCHOLOGY: MULTICULTURAL COUNSELING IN THERAPY

In 1977, counseling psychologist Derald Wing Sue wrote the introduction for a special issue of the *Personnel and Guidance Journal* that was one of the first attempts at discussing how culture might make its way into the therapy room. In this introduction he cited a compilation of studies he had just conducted with colleagues detailing rates of early termination for counseling sessions for racial and ethnic minorities versus majority culture clients (e.g., Sue, Allen, & Conway, 1978; Sue & McKinney, 1975; Sue, McKinney, Allen, & Hall, 1974). In these studies the researchers found that "Asian Americans, Blacks, Chicanos, and Native Americans terminated counseling at a rate of approximately 50 percent after the first interview. This was in sharp contrast to a 30 percent rate for Anglo clients" (Sue, 1977, p. 422). To Sue, and others at the time, this signified an overarching issue in the field: Non–majority culture clients were not having the same experiences in counseling as their majority culture counterparts. Sue (1977) noted, "[They] find the values of counseling to be inconsistent with their life experiences" (p. 422). Counseling theories at the time were created and implemented by an overwhelmingly White population within the field of psychology, and the most accepted theories were those that matched with majority-culture, Western values of independence, openness, and expressiveness. While these values have been shown to be positively interpreted by White cultural groups, they are not preferred by all cultures. Thus, psychologists sought to make changes at the time to make their field more culturally inclusive.

Fast forward several decades, and the American Psychological Association (APA) has developed a number of different initiatives and guidelines that integrate multicultural tenets into counseling and therapy across many different orientations. In 1990, the *Guidelines for Providers of Psychological Services to Ethnic, Linguistic, and Culturally Diverse Populations* (APA, 1990) were developed by the Task Force on the Delivery of Services to Ethnic Minority Populations as part of the APA. This set of guidelines was developed as an aspirational set of ideas that counselors and psychologists should follow regarding counseling ethnic minority populations, and it gave examples and descriptions of positive work in this area. In 2002, the *Guidelines on Multicultural Education, Training, Research, Practice, and Organizational Change for Psychologists* (APA, 2002) were created to speak "to the profession's recognition of the important role that diversity and multiculturalism plays, both in terms of how individuals and groups define themselves, and how they approach others within the United States and globally" (APA, 2017, para 1). These guidelines expanded the original work focused primarily on therapy services into education, research, and other areas within the field of psychology. Today, these guidelines have been revised and renamed as *Multicultural Guidelines:*

iStock/fizkes

Multicultural therapy interaction

An Ecological Approach to Context, Identity, and Intersectionality and "are conceptualized from a need to reconsider diversity and multicultural practice within professional psychology at a different period in time, with intersectionality as its primary purview" (APA, 2017, para 2).

The attention given to cultural context and multiculturalism in therapy practice by the American Psychological Association shows a great evolution from the first studies cited by Sue in the 1970s and represents a deep commitment to culturally competent therapy practice in the field. As our population in the country becomes more and more diverse, however, cultural competence in the therapy realm is also needed in terms of development of awareness of one's own racial identity and biases, knowledge in working with clients that are culturally different from oneself, and skills in working with clients from all cultural groups (APA, 2002, 2017). Finally, the idea of **cultural humility** is valued and beneficial to therapists. This refers to the idea that one can never be "done" with cultural training or know all the information there is to know about this vast topic. Instead, striving to remember that there is always more to learn is an important part of culturally competent training for therapists.

We would next like to turn to a few specific issues that are important to address in this particular setting. We'll first discuss the importance of racial or ethnic match between clients and counselors, talk briefly about population-specific treatments, and finish by discussing how racism, sexism, heterosexism, and other forms of bias might impact therapists themselves.

As Derald Wing Sue and others were first discussing the importance of attending to clients' culture as a part of the therapy process, a question was raised about the need for counselors to be thoughtful about the fact that the life experiences of racial and ethnic minorities might differ from those of White individuals. One question that arose at the time was whether having a therapist that matched the client culturally might address some of these issues. Some research has found that perceived or real similarities and differences between clients and their therapists with regard to race and gender appear to have no impact on the length of time spent in therapy or view of the therapeutic relationship (Maramba & Nagayama Hall, 2002; Vera, Speight, Mildner, & Carlson, 1999). Others show that some ethnicities might appreciate ethnic match between therapist and client more than others.

In a study looking at several different racial and ethnic groups, findings showed that Asian Americans attended more sessions, dropped out of therapy less frequently, and had better treatment outcomes when they were matched either linguistically, ethnically, or both (Sue, 1998). Mexican American clients in this same study appeared to mirror these results, though with slightly less dramatic effects. For African Americans and White Americans in this study, treatment outcomes were not significantly different when they were matched racially with a therapist, although individuals from both groups attended more sessions when they had the same racial background as their therapist (Sue, 1998). Finally, while African Americans did not show an increase in premature termination of therapy, White Americans did prematurely end therapy more often at a significant rate when they were not racially matched to their therapist.

More research is needed in this particular area, but one point must be made. At present, though diversity has increased in recent years, the field of psychology is still predominantly White in terms of race (Lin, Stamm, & Christidis, 2018), similar to the teacher workforce as noted previously in this chapter. If racial or ethnic match is important to some clients, it is essential that the counselor workforce become adequately diverse to best serve the current population.

Some research has also been conducted on treatments for specific populations in terms of race, ethnicity, gender, and other cultural facets. Hall, Hong, Zane, and Meyer (2011) noted that mindfulness-based psychotherapies appeared to be particularly effective for Asian and Asian American populations. These modalities appear to fit well with traditional Eastern values and therefore may promote health in these populations (Leong, & Kalibatseva, 2011). Lilian Comas-Diaz, a Latina psychologist who has studied cultural competence in therapeutic practices for many years, argued in a 2006 article about the need to adapt more majority-culture-driven psychological practices to Latinx populations. She offers many examples of "Latino ethnic psychology," including incorporating *cuento*, *dichos*, and spirituality into treatment for Latinx clients. In addition, she and others note that discussing and promoting **cultural resilience** as a part of the therapy process can be beneficial for multiple non-White populations (Comas-Diaz, 2006). Recently, more attention has been devoted to serving transgender and gender nonconforming populations. This research notes the high rates of suicide as well as the increased risk for violence that many trans individuals face, and as a result, these researchers discuss therapy recommendations that investigate ways in which the trans and gender nonconforming community may develop resilience and coping strategies related to these issues (Burnes & Stanley, 2017; Singh & Chun, 2012). dickey, Singh, Chang, and Rehrig (2017) address the need for guidelines specific to psychological practice with this growing population.

In addition, understanding that cultural values that differ from majority values are not signs of inferiority (Sue & Sue 2016), showing value for biculturalism in therapy with racial and ethnic minorities (LaFromboise, Coleman, & Gerton, 1983), and having a view that racism, sexism, heterosexism, and other types of bias exist *outside* of the individual (Edwards & Pedrotti, 2004) are essential for culturally responsive therapy and treatment. To this last point, experts in this area of the field note that racism is not a "person of color problem," or heterosexism a "LGBTQ+ problem" but instead these are problems for all of us to tackle and try to decrease, regardless of our racial background, sexual orientation, or gender.

In conclusion to this section, we would like to speak briefly about the impact racism, sexism, heterosexism, or other biases might have on the *therapist*, as opposed to looking solely from the perspective of the client. As a part of psychological training of therapists, the therapist is often counseled to "keep your values out of the therapy room" and to make sure the focus is on the client as opposed to drawing attention to one's own views or personal perspective. While this is appropriate in thinking about the client (not counselor) as central to the counseling focus, it is important to note that counselors may experience some forms of bias at the hands of the client.

Ali and colleagues (2005) compiled a series of experiences from non-White therapists in training in their chapter, "When Racism Is Reversed: Therapists of Color Speak About Their Experiences with Racism." In this compilation, the various therapists talk about times that racism has occurred in the therapy room or process in some form. Many note being unsure of how to handle this, or that questions such as, "They know I am not White, they know I'm a person of color, why do they think that they can say something like that and not offend me?" (p. 120) arise for them during the session. This can be both disconcerting and anger inducing—neither feeling is one that is comfortable for a therapist of color in this situation. Race and ethnicity are not the only types of discrimination a therapist may feel. Some female therapists also note feeling uncomfortable or afraid in dealing with clients who exhibit sexism or misogyny (Rastogi & Wieling, 2005).

It is also important for those who are supervising therapists in training to be cognizant of these issues. Consider the following experience of an Asian American psychologist with her supervisor in graduate school:

> *I was a first year practicum student in my program, and I was placed at a Veterans Affairs (VA) hospital. I knew I'd be working with a lot of Vietnam vets, and I was concerned because I thought some of them might have a negative reaction to my being Asian American. I remember talking to the White professor who supervised my practicum just before. We'd been taught not to share much personal information with the client, but I was pretty sure some of them might want to know my heritage and whether or not I was Vietnamese. I asked my supervisor what I should say if someone asked me that. He told me that this likely wouldn't happen, and that even though he could see that I was focused on my race, that was a personal issue I'd have to get over myself. He said I'd have to get rid of that "internalized racism" that made me assume that people would be bothered by a non-White therapist. I felt some shame over this admonition, especially being a brand new graduate student, and so I agreed and went into my new site the next week.*
>
> *My first client (and my second, third, and fourth) asked me my ethnicity almost immediately upon starting the therapy sessions. One asked to switch therapists*

right off the bat. I could tell he felt a little bad about it, but he just didn't think he could talk to me about his experiences in the war. In group therapy at the VA, I listened to people use ethnic slurs for people like me, describe ways in which they hated the look of Asian people, and discuss why they still felt Asians were "less human" than White people. I understood why they felt like this—they were traumatized by war and struggling in so many ways—but it was very, very hard to stay in therapeutic mode sometimes when they would talk about those things. I wished I had someone to talk to about how I felt when that happened or someone to give me some advice about how to cope with it. But I also felt guilty—therapy shouldn't be about me, right?

—Kate, age 37

Herein lies the rub for therapists of color in this circumstance. Therapy is not about the therapist, it is about the client, and in some cases clients may not be willing to discuss the foundations of their beliefs or tolerate working to change them. This said, supervisors or trusted colleagues of therapists who report these unsettling experiences must be ready to validate the fear and anger some of these situations might bring up in a therapist of color or from some other marginalized background (Ali et al., 2005). The supervisor above diminished the situation and invalidated the therapist in training, compounding the situation and giving her no place to discuss these feelings. More research is needed on this topic, but therapists who experience "–isms" in the therapy room need to know that this experience is not internal to themselves.

MULTICULTURALISM CAN BE BROUGHT TO ALL CONTEXTS

In this chapter, we sought to explain ways in which multiculturalism and multicultural psychology may be applied to three different contexts: school, work, and therapy. It must be noted, however, that multiculturalism can be brought to almost any context one might encounter. Multiculturalism in the home as a part of parenting has been discussed in other chapters in this book (see Chapter 5), and it may also be a part of relationships between friends. Multicultural issues are experienced in governmental and legal contexts as well. Put plainly, understanding cultural context in general will help you in any domain in which you find yourself. The result in attending to cultural context in this way is to create a more inclusive space, regardless of your environment or domain.

ACT: Assess Your Knowledge, Critical Thinking, Take Part

Assess Your Knowledge

Think for a minute of the contexts in which you reside currently. Are you a student? If so, your major, your college, and your university are all contexts in which you participate. What does diversity look like in these contexts? If you have children, are their schools racially or ethnically diverse? Do you work? Do you play sports or take classes such as yoga? What does your neighborhood grocery store look like? Does it carry foods from all ethnic groups? How about the television stations you receive—are a variety of cultures represented? Take a minute to reflect on the ways in which multiculturalism is brought to these contexts. Have you ever thought about this before? Why or why not? What is one context in which you would feel comfortable trying something new to increase multiculturalism?

Critical Thinking

After assessing the above, next, think about who resides in these spaces. Is the clientele or student body diverse in terms of race and ethnicity? How do the amount of diversity and the way multiculturalism is integrated in the space correlate with one another? What ideas do you have for why it is diverse or why it is not?

Take Part

Participation: Choose a context from those you thought about above. Do some research online into what is usually found within these contexts. (For example, is it hard for some ethnic groups to find foods they enjoy across all states and cities, or just in yours? Do television stations across the country generally focus on majority populations, or is this the case just your area?) Share what you find with someone you know and see what they think as well.

Initiation: Think of a way that you could make a change in one area in which you currently reside. For example, does your local library provide children's literature from all racial or ethnic groups? If not, think of ways you might be able to increase the diversity of its children's literature collection. Write a letter to the library board to ask them to consider increasing these offerings. Start a book drive to increase donations of this type of literature. Work with others to make a difference in this one area. What kind of plan can you develop? If you are reading this book as a university student, ask your multicultural psychology teacher if developing a plan such as this might be an assignment that could be developed for your class.

Activism: In what contexts do you have some influence? If you are an officer in a club, a manager at work, or even a student intern at a local organization, you can exert some influence over policies and procedures used in these various contexts. Take a moment to think about control that you might have. For example, a manager often has control over hiring. If your organization is not particularly diverse in terms of its employees, why might this be the case? Look into implicit bias training for groups who participate in interviewing, think about recruiting from more diverse locations, and look over hiring policies that might inadvertently be keeping your workforce less diverse. Even if you are a student and don't feel you have power or influence, you do have this over your own work. For example, if a professor or teacher allows students to pick topics for oral presentations or reports, try to focus on a topic that relates to multiculturalism, or to choose to include sections on culture, race, or ethnicity in relevant ways. You can make change from any level of influence, even if it is only on yourself.

11

LOOKING TO THE FUTURE

Becoming an Ally, Social Justice Work, and Emerging Issues

LEARNING OBJECTIVES

- Define allyship, and provide examples of and generate new possibilities for allies in social justice work
- Design strategies to work toward being an ally
- Differentiate between allyship, advocacy, and charity
- Apply the Ally Action Continuum to your own life, and understand how to develop skills and actions that further the tenets of social justice
- Understand the role of media and family influences on the messages you have received toward the goal of stripping away these lenses to look at things clearly
- Use wholistic cultural reflexivity to make changes in your own life toward becoming a more culturally competent and culturally humble person
- Analyze your own development at the beginning of this book, and compare it to your awareness, knowledge, and skills as you finish this book

We have covered many different topics in this textbook and have guided you through a number of different exercises in our ACT sections at the end of each chapter. We hope you have tried some of these small exercises and searches for additional information and education. In this, our last chapter, we now turn our thoughts to more explicit action that you may be able to take. Before we cover these important topics, we'd like to address how you are feeling at this point in your journey through this material. Sometimes after several class sessions on racism, discrimination, privilege, oppression, and other topics, we find that our students become a bit overwhelmed. "It's just too pervasive!" we've heard students say. "How could I possibly change it all?" The answer we give to students in this moment involves reminding them of an important fact: *You don't have to change everything. But you can change something.* This chapter is designed to show you some things *you* can do right this moment to impact change.

We will begin by talking about what it means to be an ally, and then talk more about social justice as a movement and as a value system. Finally, we will address some emerging issues at the end of this chapter. As we write this last chapter introduction, we find ourselves hopeful for your future and for ours as well—you have taken the time and made the choice to educate yourself about the important topics in this book.

That knowledge will serve you well, likely better than you can imagine, in your future within our ever-changing multicultural world.

ALLYSHIP

The term **ally** was first used in connection with individuals who identified as heterosexual but who wanted to help support the LGBTQ+ movement. The term has burgeoned to include supporting marginalized communities of all kinds. An ally is someone from a privileged group who is willing to work alongside someone from a group that has been disenfranchised both historically and currently. For example, a White ally is a person who identifies as being White but is willing to stand beside people of color in the fight to end discrimination and racism. Some famous White allies are described in Figure 11.1. We encourage you to learn more about these White

FIGURE 11.1 ● White Allies		
James Peck	**Margaret Gunderson**	**Tim Wise**
A member of the Congress of Racial Equality (CORE), James Peck planned and led the first Freedom Rides with fellow African American civil rights activist James Farmer and others. Though beaten badly in the riots that surrounded the challenging of Jim Crow laws, he continued to fight for the rights of the African American community.	Margaret Gunderson was a high school history teacher in the 1940s when World War II broke out, and she moved to Tule Lake Relocation Center to teach in the Japanese Internment Camps. Her former Japanese American students remember her telling them that it wasn't right that they were being interned, and they credit her with giving them self-worth in a terrible time of turmoil.	A White anti-racist author and educator, Tim Wise has traveled the country giving talks on how to dismantle racism in the United States. Wise has written several books such as *White Like Me: Reflections on Race from a Privileged Son*, which focus on explicating social justice and the ways in which White people can join the fight against racism.
Robin DiAngelo	**Myles Horton**	**Viola Liuzzo**
Robin DiAngelo is the author of the book *White Fragility* and other works that explicate the White experience and its relation to the sustenance of racism in the United States. Known for her ability to discuss hard facts in ways that lead White people to a greater understanding of themselves and non-White people, DiAngelo strives to create additional White allies as well.	Co-founder of the Highlander Folk School (now the Highlander Research and Education Center), Myles Horton worked hard to champion educational and other rights for African Americans in the segregated South. Today, his center is a training school for social justice leadership.	Mother and civil rights worker, Viola Liuzzo lost her life for her role in defending the rights of African Americans during the civil rights movements in the 1960s. A member of the NAACP, Liuzzo was murdered by KKK members after the marches from Selma to Montgomery in Alabama.

allies and others and about the work they did either in the past, or continue to do today. An important point to note is that allies work alongside their disenfranchised counterparts or sometimes behind them—they let the stakeholder group determine the course of action but work to lend the privilege they carry to this group as well.

A second point we'd like to address in introducing this topic is that allies often take risks in supporting various groups. They do this because they know that the group itself has risks to face every day, and they seek to help them to fight back against these types of discrimination and at times even violence, both emotional and physical.

One example from history that you may already know about took place in the 1960s surrounding the civil rights movement. A mixed group of people (both Black and White) from a group called the Congress on Racial Equality (CORE) decided to enact a plan to challenge the southern states' refusal to adhere to a federal decision made in 1960 regarding segregation of interstate facilities such as bus terminals, lunch counters, and restrooms. *Boynton v. Virginia* resulted in the decision that this segregation (e.g., separate seating for White and Black people in the terminal) was unconstitutional, yet many southern states did not change their policies and still maintained segregated spaces in violation of the law. The individuals in CORE, including now congressman John Lewis, decided to travel to the South to test these laws by attempting to use lunch counters, waiting rooms, and restrooms for people of the opposite race. Importantly, the group was trained in nonviolent confrontation, something for which Dr. Martin Luther King Jr. also advocated, which involved refusing to fight back if violence broke out. The original group of **Freedom Riders**, as they were called, included seven African American riders and six White riders who traveled on Greyhound and Trailways busses together to these southern states. As sources report, things started off fairly smoothly in Virginia and North Carolina, but when the riders reached South Carolina and Alabama, violence ensued. John Lewis and a White ally Freedom Rider named Albert Bigelow were violently attacked as they entered a Whites-only bus terminal waiting area together. Shortly after this event, the riders made their way to Anniston, Alabama, where again violence broke out, resulting in someone from an angry White mob throwing a bomb into the bus and barring the doors with the Freedom Riders inside. Though no one was killed, the riders were beaten severely and barely made it out of the bus alive.

Following these harrowing incidents, the Freedom Riders could not find a bus driver who was willing to drive them to complete their journey to further their cause, but college students from Fisk University, led by Diane Nash from the Student Nonviolent Coordinating Committee (SNCC), organized groups of students to continue the rides in vans and other vehicles throughout the South. In addition to more violent attacks, riders were also arrested for using Whites-only bathrooms and other facilities,

Congressman John Lewis next to mugshots taken when he was part of the Freedom Riders

Rick Diamond/Staff/Getty Images

and many were sent to Parchman Prison. Through the next several months, the riders continued. Where one fell, another replaced them, both White and Black riders continuing the fight through the summer and into that fall. At this time, President John F. Kennedy and Attorney General Robert F. Kennedy became involved in pressuring the Interstate Commerce Commission to prohibit segregation in all states, forcing even the South to adhere to the already established law. You can learn more about the Freedom Riders by watching a documentary made by *The American Experience* aired in 2011.

Why do we tell you this story to start our description of allies? The main takeaway we would like you to get from this story is that being an ally is not for the faint of heart. This message is not meant to discourage you, by any means, but it is important to understand that becoming an ally involves serious dedication, and you cannot call yourself by this term lightly. In the Freedom Rides, for example, White members who stood alongside the African American members of CORE, SNCC, and other groups showed their support by accepting the same treatment as the folks at the center of this battle. For the White Americans involved in the Freedom Rides, the outcome of prohibiting segregation had no effect on their freedom, their ability to travel, or their safety, but they made it their issue as well by standing with their African American brothers and sisters in this fight. Some might ask, "How do you know if you are actually an ally?" The answer to this question is simple: The group you are allied with is the one that makes this decision. If no one has called you an ally, you shouldn't use this term lightly. Regardless, becoming an ally is not a box to be checked; it is a lifelong process of learning and engaging.

In recent years, many White people have looked to find ways to better educate themselves about topics that are related to race. This same statement might be applied to other groups in terms of their self-education about sexual orientation and the LGBTQ+ community; about gender, particularly in terms of how the world is experienced by women, transgender, and nonbinary folks; and about different religious groups that lack privilege in the United States. It is important to note that people who would like to be allies to any of these groups must first think about their own capacity to help and then decide what course of action they can take. This begins with taking some time to do some self-exploration. Think about a group for whom you could be an ally—what makes you want to help this group? Some answers might include, "Because it is the right thing to do!" or "I know someone from this group, and I care about them." Other, sometimes buried, answers might be, "I don't want people to think I'm racist," or "I want to be part of a movement to show others my values." These second two reasons are actually very common underlying ones for joining movements—and yet, they are more about the person making the statement than about the group they are wanting to help. Thinking long and hard about your motivations for getting involved is a very important step that sometimes people miss. Consider the following vignette:

> I know I can help fight racism as a White person. I have much more privilege—I've learned about this in my multicultural psychology class—so I know I can help. I also want to make sure others know that not all White people are racist. I made sure to say this at the activism meeting I went to last week where a group is organizing to do a march supporting the American Indians at Standing Rock. I was so excited to get to march with everyone and show everyone that White people can be on the right side too. But then I found out that they were only going to have the American Indian students in the march and that the White students would support them from the sidelines. I don't think this is fair. We should all be able to stand together and fight this kind of thing. I'm an ally and so I want to be a part of the march too, not just watch.
>
> —Rebecca, age 20

In the words above, what kind of motivation do you hear from Rebecca? Though her heart may be in the right place in terms of wanting to help, she may need a bit more self-reflection before she begins to truly work toward allyship. Being an ally means understanding your own racial identity development and acknowledging the history associated with it. Though Rebecca may be working on understanding ideas like White privilege, her motivation appears to be focused on her image as a White woman, not so much on the issues at hand. Becoming an ally is a process that starts with better understanding of oneself. Skipping this step is like being excited to learn to fly a plane and deciding to just try it as opposed to taking lessons: you may end up unintentionally hurting a lot of people.

Another thing to take into consideration is the difference that exists between being an ally and being an **advocate**. Advocates might often step in front of the person for whom they are trying to advocate. An example might be a teacher stepping up for a student who needs help talking to their parents about a difficult issue. An advocate takes the lead and sometimes also makes decisions about what is best for the person for whom they are advocating. We often act as advocates for our students when they need help with some other entity on campus. We've called the registrar at times to see if a fee hold can be lifted for a particular student so that they don't lose their financial aid, and we've intervened with a professor when a student is dealing with a mental health concern. Though taking on the role of an advocate at times is not necessarily unhelpful, this role is different than that of an ally. Allies, instead, allow the person who is most involved to take the lead. One of us (JTP) has a White friend and colleague who has consistently acted as an ally for her in doing diversity work on campus.

My friend, Carrie, is a wonderful ally in working to make change in areas of diversity, equity, and inclusion. When we began working together on these issues, I was the chair of our department diversity committee, and I noticed she would often come to see me ahead of a meeting where we would be presenting a new idea related to diversity to ask me how she could best support my effort. We would strategize a bit, and she would ask my preference on her role, which might be as supporter of an idea or as initiator if that was more comfortable for me, or as someone who could speak to our White colleagues separately to see about garnering support for an idea related to race. Today, she coleads our "Working Toward White Allyship" faculty group and helps educate and involve that group in working toward positive change in equity issues on our campus. Carrie helps the cause for diversity, equity, and inclusion in so many ways, and she is devoted toward using her White privilege to help with this process. Sometimes she will be able to get farther than I can with certain changes because of her status as a White person. Sometimes I'm able to get farther myself because it's clear I have her support, that is, the support of a White person. Carrie doesn't expect me to feel grateful for her support—she acts the ways she does because bringing positive change is important to her. But I can't tell you how grateful I am to have her support in whatever way I, as a person of color, need it.

—JTP, age 45

As shown in this example, allies might often work behind the scenes or lend their power to others who have less. Allowing stakeholders to lead doesn't mean allowing them to do all the work. Instead it often means taking on a less visible but still very important role. In 1971, Dorothy Pittman Hughes and Gloria Steinem were partners in talking about feminism and racism and together founded *Ms. Magazine*. You can do an internet search of their first cover together (try *Ms. Magazine, Gloria,* and *Dorothy* as keywords). In viewing the image you will see the two women standing together, fists raised to demonstrate solidarity in the fight for equality. Notice the placement of the women in the picture. Steinem, a White ally for racial justice and a staunch feminist, is standing just behind Pittman Hughes, who is an African American feminist and advocate for child welfare—Steinem is effectively *backing* Pittman Hughes in the fight for equality. Recently, the two women did a follow-up photo recreating the original image, which might have also appeared when you did your search. As it was then, it is still important for White people involved in antiracist activism to use their privilege and power to support people of color in ways that are visible, and yet sometimes standing just behind them as is depicted in this iconic image.

One of the first steps toward becoming an ally is to work to change your own behavior. Being accurate about your knowledge base (and where it is lacking) and thinking about your own identity can be first steps. This may involve some discomfort at first. Making change, even when it is on yourself, can be hard at first. Some examples of ways to make change might be to read more on various topics, to work to interact with a more diverse friendship circle, or to work to be intentional about your own language usage. See Tom's efforts that follow:

When I was in high school, I remember that many of us used the term gay *sort of offhand. We weren't talking about gay people even, more like "That kid's shirt is so gay!" But when I got to college I realized that even though I am not thinking about gay people when I say that, it still could be hurtful to gay people. So, I thought about what I really mean when I use that phrase, and I usually said it when I was talking about something I didn't like or that I thought was weird or stupid. That's not what I think about* gay *people, and I'm just perpetuating those ideas if I keep using the word* gay *in that way. Now I don't use that word anymore in that way. My next step is to try to get my friends to stop doing it too. I started with my friend Zander who usually gets this kind of thing, and he is stopping too. We're trying to question it when people we know use* gay *in that way. It's just a small change, but it's not very hard once you get started.*

—Tom, age 19

You can see that Tom chose an action that he could control himself and started to work on it, and he is now thinking about broadening it to include others he knows. Oftentimes when individuals realize that something they are doing can cause hurt for others, they begin to work to change it—this self-realization and action to make change is a first step.

One way of looking at things that you might do about inclusion or social justice is to use the continuum in Figure 11.2 (Wijeyesinghe, Griffin, & Love, 1997). Start by looking at the continuum as a whole. The goal is to move from having more actions that work against inclusion and social justice toward more actions that are for diversity and social justice. On the left, you see Actively Participating as the furthermost point. People who engage in this status may tell racist, sexist, heterosexist, or other derogatory jokes and may also be involved in actively avoiding or discriminating against people in marginalized groups. Before you dismiss this as "not me," consider that this also includes laughing at these so-called "jokes" or brushing them off as "comedy" and so not serious. Second is Denying, which refers to behavior that doesn't purposefully discriminate or target oppressed individuals, but denies that this is problematic or even exists. This status involves colluding with oppressive behavior, even if you are not the one to start it. Third is the status Recognizing, No Action. In this status people are often struggling with fear or worry about what to do and how

FIGURE 11.2 ◆ Ally Action Continuum

Actively Participating	Denying	Recognizing, No Action	Recognizing, Action	Educating Self	Educating Others	Supporting and Encouraging	Initiating and Preventing
Telling derogatory jokes, putting down people from targeted groups, intentionally avoiding targeted group members, discriminating against targeted group members, verbally or physically harassing targeted group members.	Enabling discrimination and injustice by denying that targeted group members are oppressed. Not actively discriminating or oppressing, but by denying that oppression exists, colluding with oppression.	Being aware of oppressive actions by self or others and their harmful effects, but taking no action to stop this behavior due to fear, lack of information, or confusion about what to do. Experiencing discomfort at the contradiction between awareness and action.	Being aware of oppression and injustices, recognizing oppressive actions of self and others, and taking action to stop them.	Taking action to learn more about oppression and privilege and the life experiences affected by unjust social relations by reading; attending workshops, seminars, and cultural events; and participating in discussions and other educational and change events.	Moving beyond only educating self to questions and dialogue with others too. Rather than only stopping oppressive comments or behaviors, also engaging people in discussion to share reasons for objection to a comment or action.	Supporting others who speak out against injustices or who are working to be more inclusive of targeted group members by backing up others who speak out, forming an allies' group, joining a coalition group.	Working to change individual and institutional actions and policies that discriminate against targeted group members, planning educational programs, working for passage of legislation that protects excluded groups from discrimination, explicitly involving members of historically marginalized groups as full participants in organizations.

Source: Adapted from Wijeyesinghe, Griffin, & Love (1997).

to assist in the fight against oppression and discrimination. People in this status often don't speak up when they witness these types of behaviors, though they feel bad about their inaction.

Fourth is the status Recognizing, Action, in which people begin to try to take action to stop oppression of others. This can take many forms. Next is Educating Self. In this status, action is taken by reaching out to learn more about oppression, privilege, and other topics of this sort, and sometimes joining other groups who are learning about how to take action together. Next, Educating Others, is part of moving beyond just self-education to reach out to others in your immediate environment. Some call this your **sphere of influence** and think of it as the group you can impact the most. This is the first part of the continuum that begins to take action outside oneself. Next is Supporting and Encouraging, which may take many forms. Examples might include being a support for someone who is taking an even more active role in speaking up for others or backing someone who takes a stand against oppression. Forming an allies group and working with others are other examples. Finally, the status Initiating and Preventing describes actions taken that are meaningful and broad in promoting diversity and social justice. Working to change and challenge both individual and institutional –isms marks this far end of the continuum. It is important to note that a single person could have actions or behaviors that fit in more than one place on the continuum. For example, individuals might be starting to recognize that oppression exists but still catch themselves laughing when a friend tells a racist "joke" from time to time. The important part is to continue working on moving to the right side of the continuum.

In thinking about your own ally work, start with small doable goals to avoid feeling too overwhelmed. Challenging or asking questions about a policy at school or work that seems to limit inclusivity, or learning more about a group you don't know much about, might be first steps. Joining a group at your campus multicultural center, or being part of a committee to help plan an event that celebrates a particular group, might be good starts. Taking classes on topics that you know little about that relate to gender, race, sexual orientation or other social identities may also be a possibility. You can also practice by talking to people who you know share your views first. This can help you to build confidence and work up to sharing these ideas with others who may disagree. Another benefit of working with someone else is that you can use this "buddy system" to support each other when encountering resistance to your "new self." Sometimes when we change a behavior in our personal lives, others close to us are not happy with the change.

> *I'm working on being a better male ally to women. I know in the past I haven't been as good at this, but I realize sometimes how much sexism affects my friends who are women, and I just know that I need to do a better job of using my privilege as a man to stand against that. This hasn't been as easy as I thought, though. One of my friends is pretty crude in the way he talks about women, and so the other day when he was doing this I said, "Sometimes it makes me uncomfortable to hear how you talk about women. It's like you don't have much respect for them." He laughed in my face and said I was getting so "sensitive" and asked me why I cared about that, since there weren't any women around anyway right then. I just tried to stay firm and told him that I don't think it matters if there are women here or not, I don't think anyone should talk about them that way. He tried to just make a joke about it, but I notice he sort of stopped doing this around me. I felt glad I said something, even though it's only a small step.*
>
> —David, age 26

The preceding vignette is a small example of what can happen sometimes when people share new views with a friend they've had for a while. Sometimes this leads to a change in friends as well, so this is important to realize, but doing nothing may feel worse the farther you get along the continuum. If David had a buddy who felt similarly to him in this scenario, you can see that it might have been even more effective. It's hard to speak up in these cases, but you may find that deciding to make these changes leads to richer and more authentic friendship choices as well.

One thing that allies can agree to do is to remain a part of the conversation. If you are from a privileged group, one privilege you might enjoy (whether you know it or not) is the privilege of not becoming involved with a particular social identity issue, and at the same time not being particularly affected one way or another regardless of the outcome. As an example, think about some of the recent debates about bathroom use in relation to transgender populations. In California, former governor Jerry Brown signed a law into effect that required public buildings to have gender-neutral restrooms in any single-stall facility (Associated Press, 2016). Some protested this move, and people in other parts of the country vowed to prevent similar changes from happening in their states. At the end of the day, however, having gender-neutral single stalls rarely impacts anyone except transgender folks! If someone who is not transgender wants to use a non-gender-neutral restroom, it is not particularly hard to find a multistall single-gender restroom. For someone who is transgender, however, being able to avoid the stress of being called out for using the "wrong" bathroom (i.e., the one others might choose for them) is likely life changing in a positive way.

A second example may be found in thinking about same-sex marriage. In what way does allowing same-sex marriage impact the marriage of heterosexual couples? This is an easy one: It doesn't. Heterosexual couples still have all the same rights that they did before this law changed, and now same-sex couples can enjoy these rights as well. Thinking hard about where our privilege lies, and then making good decisions about how to use that privilege, is a good basis for starting steps toward becoming an ally.

One final note on this topic before we move to focusing more explicitly on social justice: The status of "ally" is not something that one can confer on oneself. Instead, allies are identified by members of the stakeholder group. A person of color might bestow this status on a White friend, for example, or people from the LGBTQ+ community might give this label to a heterosexual person who works with them. For this reason, it is often a good idea to label oneself as "working toward allyship" or "standing in solidarity with" a group as opposed to calling oneself an ally before another has noted this in you. We all want to be seen as being on the "right side of history," but it is important to give the power of naming allies to the groups who are most affected by their presence.

SOCIAL JUSTICE

"Never forget that justice is what love looks like in public."

We begin this section with a quote from Cornel West (2015) from his seminal book *Black Prophetic Fire*. West goes on to say, "It is a beautiful thing to be on fire for justice . . . there is no greater joy than inspiring and empowering others—especially the least of these, the precious and priceless wretched of the earth!" (West, 2015, p. 5). Not a helping hand, not charity, not voluntourism; social justice is an ethos, commitment, and movement to assure equitable access to resources and opportunities; it combats oppressions, values all of humanity, and strives for liberation and restorative justice. Where charity assumes inequality—someone with resources assisting someone with less, solidarity is predicated on an equitable relationship, a reciprocal partnership with shared goals. Scot Nakagawa in "On Solidarity, 'Centering Anti-Blackness,' and Asian Americans," writes,

> Harmony is our goal. Not amalgamation or appropriation or imitation. We need to use the political space and cultural opportunity that the Movement for Black Lives has created for us and use it for this purpose, picking up the diverse threads of our lives and weaving them into a powerful, prophetic cry for justice. This after all, is the true self-interest we all share in the cause of Black liberation. Black liberation has always been the teacher, the prophet, the true hope for the liberation of us all. (2016, p. 643)

Nakagawa's focus on anti-Blackness here isn't signaling a disregard for other populations of people, but is designed to focus on the form that racism and racialized social policies have taken in our society. At its conceptual core, race in the United States has been constructed around the Black/White binary, and in order to break down any system, we must go to its source. A study of how to combat this anti-Blackness can then be used to develop strategies to aid in the fight against people from any group that experiences oppression. At times you may hear people trying to rank these oppressions in a sort of hierarchy. This is sometimes called "oppression Olympics" in a tongue-in-cheek sort of way. The reality is, however, that oppression is awful in all forms and results in some folks in our country not being able to reach their potential. Giving freedom to some but not all keeps us all in servitude to oppression. By this we mean that when any group experiences oppression, we must all live with the fact that oppression is being kept in place, and unless we are fighting against it, we are all responsible for keeping it in place. A quote from Nelson Mandela sums up this point: "For to be free is not merely to cast off one's chains, but to live in a way that respects and enhances the freedom of others" (Mandela, 1994, pp. 624–625) If we are to take on the pursuit of taking on a culturally sustaining, social justice stance as practitioners, we must start with ourselves.

CRITICAL REFLECTIVE PRACTICE

In your preparation to serve as therapists, academics, researchers, counselors, or social workers, or in positions outside of the field of psychology such as business, the medical profession, or K–12 education, it is easy to make the mistake of focusing all of your assessment tools and professional skills on the individuals you will serve. To do so with a multicultural psychology frame is to infuse that process with *critical reflective practice.* Critical theory applies the tools of social science and the humanities to critically analyzing society's sociohistorical context and power relations and structures, with an aim to liberate those who have been constrained and to give voice to those who have not been heard. Critical theory is the concept behind the development in law of critical race theory (Crenshaw, Gotanda, Peller, & Thomas, 1995; Bell, 1995) and in counseling psychology of critical disability theory (Ingham, 2018), as well as the development of the field of critical psychology more broadly (Painter, 2015). Critical reflective practice calls for the casting of that lens on ourselves and not only on those with whom we work or serve.

To draw from the language of Whiteness studies, we should make ourselves "strange"— make our history, thoughts, behaviors, and emotions the site for critical analysis. Who are we? How did we arrive at this moment? What are the meanings behind our choices? It can at times be difficult to see ourselves as clearly as we see others, and this failure to see may be a problem for which psychology can get an assist from sociocultural anthropology and its research method, autoethnography. In an autoethnographic study, researchers are the subjects of their own analyses, and they use sets of prompts to gather their own personal data. Some examples (from Chang, 2016, pp. 71–81):

- Considering your research focus, select and chronologically list major events or experiences from your life. Include the date and brief account of each item. Select one event/experience from your timeline that led to significant cultural self-discovery. Describe its circumstances and explain why it is important in your life.

- Select a time cycle—annual, seasonal, weekly, or daily—that you want to focus on. List chronologically activities and/or events in which you participate regularly within this time cycle. Identify each item with the time framework. Briefly describe the context of such routines. Select one and describe it in detail.

- List five proverbs, in order of importance that you heard repeatedly in your family, extended community, and/or society and that have had an impact on your life. Describe briefly the context in which each of them was used. Select the one most important to you and explain how it influenced your thought, belief, and behavior.

- List five personal, familial, or social rituals, in order of importance, in which you have participated. Briefly describe the context of each ritual. Select the most important one and describe it in detail in terms of who, when, where, what, and how. Explain why it is important in your life.

- List five artifacts, in order of importance, that represent your culture and briefly describe what each artifact represents. Select one and expound on the cultural meaning of this article to your life.

- Select a place of significance that helped you gain an understanding of yourself and your relationship to others. Draw the place, putting in as many details as possible. You may outline the place or do a realistic drawing. Identify objects and persons in the drawing when necessary. Expand this exercise to additional places. Describe the place and explain why this place is significant to you.

- Select a specific behavioral or cognitive topic on which you want to observe yourself. Select a manageable time frame for self-observation and identify a recording method (narrative, structured format, or hybrid). Conduct systematic self-observation and record your observation including context information such as time, duration, location, people, occasion, and mood.

- Form a group of two to four people who share similar experiences with you that you want to investigate further. Meet regularly to discuss your experiences. Take notes of your exchanges. Compare and contrast your experiences with theirs. Reflect on how others' contributions to the discussion stimulate your recall of the experiences.

- List five values, in order of importance, that you consider important in your life. Give a brief definition of each in your own terms. Select the most important one and explain why it is important.

Part of that critical reflection of the self must engage the messages and social narratives that inform our views of ourselves, others, and the world around us. Here we discuss a few of the sources of these messages and ask you to allow yourself to contemplate how they have impacted your own understanding of people from all different groups and how they might impact your own desire or feelings of competence in working toward social justice.

MEDIA

As discussed in Chapter 7, media is one of the primary message delivery systems we confront. You may not even be aware of some of the media you are consuming on an almost minute-to-minute basis. Consider a television show you like to watch. Think about the main characters and their cultural backgrounds, the characteristics they portray as a part of their role—what patterns do you see? Who is the comic relief? Who is in charge? How do these portrayals affect our understanding of what "that kind" of character is like? Do you have real-world examples of people who might be similar to the groups these characters are meant to represent?

If you are, like many in the United States, consuming media without awareness, you may be missing some of the more inherent messages media provides. According to the Center for Media Literacy (CML, 2019), "Media literacy is the ability to access, analyze, evaluate and create media in a variety of forms." Over the last couple of decades, what we have known as "media" has expanded to include a variety of message centers from social media to the pervasiveness of advertising. In response, the CML has, in turn, expanded its definition:

> Media literacy is a 21st century approach to education. It provides a framework to access, analyze, evaluate, create and participate with messages in a variety of forms—from print to video to the internet. Media Literacy builds an understanding of the role of media in society as well as essential skills of inquiry and self-expression necessary for citizens of a democracy.

A critical engagement with messages, sources disempowers their impact on our psyches, as well as assisting us in recognizing their role in the attitudes and beliefs of our clients and others with whom we work and interact in our day-to-day lives.

Think now about other types of media—print, social media, platforms like Twitter, and news sources from all perspectives. In the past, many news outlets strove to be more neutral, but in present times, so many sources of news are available at the touch of a button that we are able to effectively curate our own sources, such that the "news" we hear is a perfect reflection of our own beliefs. Living in this type of an echo chamber, where we hear our own views over and over, is foolish at best but dangerous at worst. This chamber may also start to form ideas of "roles" that groups play in society at large. Who are the "heroes," and who are those who need to be "saved" or "rescued"? Without media literacy, creation of these roles via our limited perspectives may impact our beliefs about justice in a broad sense, and may cause us to think that some groups deserve their own plight or to ignore critical historical evidence that speaks to the contrary.

We encourage you to keep developing your own media literacy and to look at all sources as coming from a particular lens that has been formed by all sorts of cultural aspects: race, gender, ability status, socioeconomic background, sexual orientation, age, and more. Being responsible about the way in which we consume media is a step toward challenging our own beliefs and making sure that we are also considering the beliefs of others. This may be especially important for you during your undergraduate career. Approximately 31% of the population over the age of 25 holds a college degree in the United States today (US Census Bureau, 2017). Access to education means greater access to skills like Piaget's **dialectical reasoning**, which you may have learned about in your developmental psychology course. Dialectical reasoning means having the ability to see how another thinks or arrives at a particular perspective despite potentially not agreeing with that perspective (Riegel, 1973). This is a very common skill utilized in almost every class in college as different texts and philosophies are unpacked and compared and contrasted, but perhaps not practiced in the same way by those who haven't gone to college. Thus, you and your fellow classmates, who also have access to this skill, may have similar abilities in being able to talk about a variety of topics. When this group is surrounding you every day, you may begin to believe that this is "what *people* think" instead of it being "what *some people* think." Again, stepping outside one's usual zone to consider that all may not think the way you do is a critical step toward becoming a more multiculturally competent person.

PRIMARY AND SECONDARY EDUCATION

We have spoken elsewhere about the importance of explaining the historical differential experiences of different groups within our country to children at a young age. When listening to teachers and parents, we often hear a refrain of "It's too scary and hard to process," or "We don't want them to get the wrong idea about our country" when referring to diving deeper into topics like African American slavery, the oppression of women, or the genocide of American Indians. Certainly there is a way to present difficult material to children that does not traumatize them, as evidenced by the many children's books that tackle difficult issues. In addition, there are many ways to "lift up" other populations that have been ignored in recounting positive history of inventions, in science, of humanitarianism.

We would like for a minute, however, to ask you to consider the impact of *not* imparting this type of education. What kinds of messages did you learn in your elementary school years that you have come to realize did not represent the whole story? Pretending as though we should still think of Christopher Columbus as a hero to be celebrated for his invasion of American Indian lands, or focusing only on Martin Luther King, Jr.'s messages of kindness while effectively glossing over the difficulties and violence faced by him and other activists as they tried to dismantle Jim Crow laws potentially teaches our children that none of these incidences was all that bad. Thus, the possibility exists for children to feel as though things like racism do not really exist today, or to lack understanding for why people of color and other disenfranchised groups are still fighting for equity. To keep our children in the dark, so to speak, may lessen the desire that our youth have to spend time making progress toward social justice, primarily because they may not think it is necessary.

Think of some of the new material you learned in this class. It is likely that many of you learned new information that changed your view on something you learned in elementary school. Think about the members of your class. Do you remember that some may have rejected some of these new ideas outright because of these old messages? Mightn't it have been better for all of us to learn these facts earlier on and to then build on them as we grew? The bottom line we would like to impart here is that giving a sanitized version of history, or a narrow view of who was involved in forming this country. Though we often only hear of the "founding fathers" and their work in forming this country's government, talking about these White men as the only ones who were involved in the formation of the country prevents students from learning about those who also contributed to its formation through service, or keeping the home fires burning, or through their very sweat and blood as they toiled in agricultural fields or on battlefields. Presenting a sanitized history may lead to a false understanding of just who the founders included and what was sacrificed by many Americans who do not look like those we are shown in paintings of the time. Using a critical lens that includes understanding and analysis of the impact of social identities like race, gender, and other identities is the only way to undo this reliance on a single perspective and to instead see our world in its reality. Without this understanding of the past and present, it is unlikely that anyone would move toward change. Working to make our world more socially just requires a realistic understanding of the past.

FAMILY MESSAGES

We have discussed elsewhere the importance of family in imparting messages about race, gender, sexual orientation, nationality, and other cultural identities. In the spirit of turning the lens on yourself, we ask you to consider what messages you received about race in your family growing up. Think back to when you first learned about race and what that meant. How was it explained to you, and what were you told about those of other races? As you have learned in other chapters, if you are a person of color, you may have learned about race at an earlier age than your White classmates. If you are biracial or multiracial, you may have had more complex discussions about these combinations than your friends and colleagues who are monoracial. Regardless of your personal identity, your family is often a source of your first messages about race and other issues. Sometimes it can be painful to think of the messages your family gave you if they conflict with what you think or know today. That said, it's important to recognize that your family comes from a particular context too, and generation, the region a person spent time in growing up, and other factors may have influenced your family members as well. Separating a bad message from a good person might be an important first step in these cases. Without this separation, working toward social change might be viewed as a denouncement of one's family. Instead, thinking more carefully about the influence of family may cause you to make different choices about how you choose to make change and what you impart to your own family either now or in the future.

THINKING ABOUT YOUR FUTURE IN YOUR FIELD

As professionals, that critical reflective lens can also be cast on our practice, regardless of the field you choose. Beyond a critical assessing of our environs, critical theory also seeks to make seen those who have been hidden and bring voice to the voiceless. To that end, critical reflective practice calls for a "counselor as researcher" model (also sometimes called a **scholar-practitioner**). In this approach, we as professionals chronicle our interactions, not simply for notation and client relations, but to look for patterns and emerging ideas as a part of our **working hypothesis**, particularly for clients from underserved populations or from those backgrounds that are different from our own. What are we seeing in the words and lives of women, transgender youth, recent immigrants, and others who come to receive services? Who does not come and why?

As you read in Chapter 10, these were the types of questions asked first by Dr. Sue in 1978 as he began to investigate why clients of color had a much higher therapy dropout rate after the first session in comparison with White clients. The patterns we discover could help raise the voices of those who have not had the ability to speak for themselves in the past, and to introduce conversations that deepen our professional discourse around the issues these populations face, and could ultimately inform future empirical research on these topics. Taken together, the individual and professional practice of critical reflection establishes a foundation on which we can live consciously, see and understand our relationship to the context from which we emerge, and use that same lens to more fully understand others. It is a foundation for activism and antiracism that can inform our use of our identity and our identity privilege as tools for inclusivity, equity, and social justice.

WHOLISTIC CULTURAL REFLEXIVITY

In this next section, we would like to take you into what we see as the future of multicultural psychology. An example might be found in the field of education. In the 1980s, culturally responsive pedagogy (Cazden & Leggett, 1981) was one way of thinking about incorporation of culture in teaching. It asserted that students of color struggle, in part, because we have put White American culture into the content, expectations, and norms of schooling, as opposed to putting education into a student's culture. Next in the progression came culturally relevant pedagogy (Ladson-Billings, 1992), which moved toward empowering communities through cultural consciousness. And most recently, the idea emerged of culturally sustaining pedagogy (Paris, 2012), a theoretical frame aimed at supporting and sustaining an inclusive cultural stance toward schooling and a disruption of oppressive power relations in school and beyond. We have also seen a progression in social science more broadly from cultural tolerance to cultural competence to cultural humility. We are arguing in this text for another move forward, an approach that draws from those theoretical foundations and applies them to the practice of multicultural psychology.

Employing the critical lens described previously, we submit the next stage should be termed *wholistic cultural reflexivity* to describe the relationship between the critical work practitioners conduct on themselves and their engagement with others. This includes seeing themselves in a critical culturally/socially situated frame, seeing others via their matrixed context (historical, social, familial, individual, etc.) and social location (unique identity), and understanding the implications of those intersections on and in the therapeutic relationship (see Figure 11.3). Therapists then can utilize the information gleaned from those reflections to better understand, validate, and empower the complex sociocultural identity of their clients. This is a perpetual cycle that continues to build new understandings as new relationships and interactions emerge, requiring the participants to be reflexive in this continual revising. In this

FIGURE 11.3 ● **Wholistic Cultural Reflexivity**

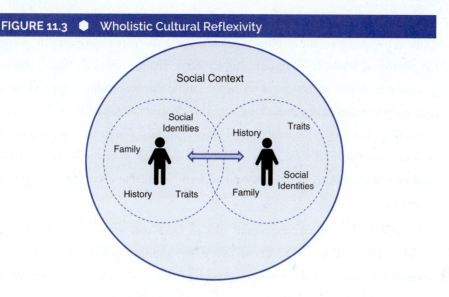

way, we can move to higher and deeper levels of understanding of race, culture, ourselves, and others, all at the same time.

Another way of thinking about your progress in the process of learning about multiculturalism is to consider this a sort of "fluency." At the National Conference on Race and Ethnicity (NCORE) in higher education, one of us (JTP) was lucky enough to hear an analogy offered by Lasana Hotep in his presentation with Katrina Pantig on designing professional development opportunities for faculty, staff, and administrators at universities surrounding multicultural competence and development. After talking for a moment about the importance of thinking of learning about multiculturalism as a process, Hotep (2019) compared this process to learning a new language.

A quick Google search of the phrase "how to learn a new language" takes us to multiple websites with tips and ideas to get fluent quickly. In one from the staff at TED (Aparta, 2014), seven tips are given from TED translators to help anyone who wants to learn a language. In looking at these suggestions, you may be already able to see the parallels that likely lead to Hotep's analogy. For each of the tips given for language fluency, a corresponding tip could be given for cultural fluency. For the first tip, Aparta (2014) offers, "Get real. Decide on a simple, attainable goal to start with so that you don't feel overwhelmed" (para 1). This is also a good first step toward cultural fluency; choosing something that is doable can help a beginner to try out new skills in becoming an ally or other type of fledgling diversity proponent. The second tip offered is, "Make language-learning a lifestyle change" (para 2). Again, this has an easily accessible equivalent to learning cultural fluency. Making sure that being culturally reflexive is not something you only do every now and then, but instead something that is of value to you consistently, can help you to be culturally fluent. You can see Figure 11.4 for the rest of the suggestions from the TED translators and some comparisons we think can be drawn to learning about multiculturalism in general.

Before closing this book, we would like to leave you with a thought that we envision as the future of multicultural psychology and that each of our social justice–oriented roles can embody in the progression of this part of the field. In the 1990s,

FIGURE 11.4 ● Parallels Between Language Fluency and Cultural Fluency	
How to Attain Language Fluency:	**How to Attain Cultural Fluency:**
1. *Get real. Decide on a simple, attainable goal to start with so that you don't feel overwhelmed.*	1. Get real. Similar to making a goal in attaining language fluency, making goals in attaining cultural fluency is a good plan. Start with something small, like committing to read a particular book or joining a club focused on cultural competence.
2. *Make language learning a lifestyle change. Find a language habit that you can follow even when you're tired, sick, or madly in love.*	2. Make cultural competence a lifestyle change. Developing new habits in your life and sticking to them can help you in your progress. One example: Try a simple exercise of examining your own internal biases without making excuses. Write these down, and try to avoid jumping to these conclusions when you meet people from the groups you may be biased against. Reflect in a journal on a regular basis to see if you are working toward acting on some of these biases.
3. *Play house with language. The more you invite a foreign language into your daily life, the more your brain will consider it something useful and worth caring about.*	3. Bring cultural competence into your house. Encourage yourself to bring books, art, commentary, and music into your house from a variety of cultures. The more you think about cultural competence and striving toward developing it, the better.

4. *Let technology help you out. Changing the language on your phone or browser can help you to learn new words right away. Or you can seek out more structured learning opportunities online.*	4. Technology can help you here as well. Though you can't set a phone or browser to "nonracist" language, you can rid your own language of words or phrases that demean other groups. Technology can help you to learn the origins of some of these. And of course online structured learning opportunities are available for cultural fluency as well.
5. *Think about language learning as a gateway to new experiences. New languages open up new opportunities like watching undubbed versions of your favorite movies, or visiting different festivals.*	5. Becoming culturally fluent can also allow you to have many new experiences. Knowing more about people who are different from you culturally can allow you to feel more comfortable getting close to them, and to engage in opportunities where you know there will be a diverse crowd. Decreasing racism in your life also decreases anxiety about saying or doing the wrong thing.
6. *Make new friends. Interacting in the new language is key—it will teach you to intuitively express your thoughts, instead of mentally translating each sentence before you say it.*	6. When we say, "Make new friends," we do not mean this in a tokenistic way in which someone might seek out an African American or Asian American friend. However, when you open yourself up to exploring cultural fluency, you may naturally find that you are in groups of more racially diverse people on a regular basis. This allows for friendships with people who are different from you to occur organically. Instead of feeling nervous around folks who are different from you, increasing your cultural fluency will allow you to speak more naturally about your thoughts.
7. *Do not worry about making mistakes. One of the most common barriers to conversing in a new language is the fear of making mistakes. The more you speak, the closer you'll get to fluency.*	7. This is a big one for cultural fluency as well. Many well-intentioned people state that they are anxious they'll do the wrong thing and that this keeps them from engaging in discussions of diversity or multiculturalism. Removing this excuse from your language can help you to become closer to cultural fluency. You will make mistakes—we all do—but trying, and acknowledging your failures if necessary, is so much better than doing nothing at all.

Adapted from Aparta (2014).

Afrofuturism emerged as a concept that built a new future that valued humanity and shed light on an overlooked past filled with incredible innovations by people of African descent. Depictions of Black people in the future were a major prong in the platform of answers. Music was a liberator. Organic food and holistic living were answers, too. This seamless relationship between art, history, music, mysticism, and science appeared to be the key to unlocking the destinies of lives in need of a refresh. This idea of a "refresh" is encountered in other places within the field of psychology. In working with clients from all backgrounds who may have suffered in the past, the field of counseling psychology often touts the benefit of clients imagining a future in which they are strong, perhaps embattled, but resilient, and as persons who can be happy and live a good life. Often this approach is used in narrative therapy as put forth by White and Epston (1990), and it involves taking time to flesh out these future visions of positivity as growing from the past and yet moving on from it. Afrofuturism provides this same sort of process. The forces described here, such as art, music, history, and now psychology, can fuel a new vision of the future for African American people—one that includes positive outcomes and solid educational futures for all Black children.

This of course is not something that only African American populations can use to envision a different future for themselves (eg.. Indigenous futurism). Other populations who have been historically disenfranchised or are currently oppressed can also use this framework. But we would like to suggest that this is also something that *you* as a psychology student can use to envision a field that takes race and culture into account in different ways than it has in the past, a field that compels its practitioners to be reflexive in thinking about how history and social structures impact our daily lives and how change can occur, and to envision a future that is positive for all people, as opposed to only those who have been privileged. You can also use this process to envision and project a future in which you are a culturally fluent person and a part of making change in the greater landscape of social justice work. As noted previously, activism and social justice can take many different types of forms—striving to educate those around you, joining forces with those who need your allyship, or fighting alongside others in your cultural group who have experienced oppression as you have. These are big thoughts and big goals, but because of what we see in our current students, we know you can do this. This is your task in the greater scheme of the current zeitgeist in which we find ourselves—you, as budding multiculturalists, can be the group to make a socially just future a reality.

ACT: Assess Your Knowledge, Critical Thinking, Take Part

Assess Your Knowledge

Think back to the first day you opened this book or started taking a class that is using this textbook to guide it. Where were you then? What changes have occurred in your thinking, your actions, and your ideas? What new facts have you learned that have led to these changes, and what questions do you still have? What new awareness, knowledge, and skills have you gained?

Critical Thinking

Take a few moments to answer the following questions in written form. Sometimes writing our answers down and looking at them in black and white helps us to fully embrace them.

- Who are you? Which pieces of your identity are most salient to you today?

- What are your spheres of influence? Which positions or roles do you hold in your microsystem (including self-control, family, and friends) and mesosystem (work, school, etc.) that might assist you in making change in the macrosystem throughout your life? (See Chapter 4 for an overview of these terms from Bronfenbrenner's ecological theory if necessary.)

- Who is with you on this journey toward cultural fluency and wholistic cultural reflexivity? Are there classmates that can continue this journey with you? Friends, family, significant others?

- What are you ready to do? What can you promise, what can you set as a goal, and what *actions* can you take?

Take Part

In each of the previous chapters, we have separated this section into three levels of action: participation, initiation, and activism. Here, in this last chapter, we will abandon this separation for the simple reason that none who are reading this book are still in these beginning stages. All of you who have read this far in this text are capable of ACTing in ways that will assist social justice in all its forms. We ask you to remain aware. We are hoping that we have assisted in opening your eyes to new issues and ideas, potentially waking you up to the real-ity of how race and ethnicity, alongside other social identities, impact everyday life for us all. We implore you: Do not go back to sleep. Instead, we challenge you to use the following exercise, developed by Dr. Teramoto Pedrotti as a part of her multicultural psychology course at California Polytechnic State University, San Luis Obispo, to make a promise for your future. Once you are finished, consider printing this out in large font on a piece of paper and hanging it somewhere you might see it daily. You might use some of the thoughts from the "Assess Your Knowledge" and "Critical Thinking" sections above to help you develop your ideas.

The Multicultural Mission Statement

Instructions: Throughout this class, you have learned new knowledge about groups that are different from you, but I am also hoping that you have learned some new pieces of information about yourself. In this vein, this assignment has the goal of helping you to crystallize some of this new self-concept in the form of a formal mission statement.

For this assignment, please write your mission statement with regard to your commitment to multicultural competence. It does not have to be long and may use bullet points or other short statements (as the following examples show), but the end product must state in some way what you stand for with regard to multiculturalism. Points will be based on your effort and attention to detail, *not* on any of your personal ideas or commitments.

Examples of Personal Mission Statements

(Note: These are life mission statements, not necessarily statements about multiculturalism, but they may be used as models for your multicultural mission statement.)

Let the first act every morning be to make the following result for the day:

I shall not fear anyone on earth.

I shall fear only God.

I shall not bear ill will toward anyone.

I shall not submit to injustice from anyone.

I shall conquer untruth by truth.

And in resisting untruth, I shall put up with all suffering.

—Gandhi

I stand for honesty, equality, kindness, compassion, treating people the way you want to be treated, and helping those in need. To me those are traditional values.

—Ellen DeGeneres

We come now to create our album of life . . . Throughout our individual and collective journeys—sometimes through pain and conflict—we have discovered the true meaning of family. As we accomplish ultimate togetherness, we become healers of ourselves and the countless who embrace us and our message. We have learned and we understand. Now we must share.

—Metallica

Rule the world.

Get lots of cookies.

Eat the cookies.

Get more cookies.

Eat those too.

—The Cookie Monster

Source: All examples are quoted from Searight & Searight (2011).

GLOSSARY

Acculturation: striving to integrate a new culture into home culture practices as one adapts to the new culture.

Achievement Gap: the lower rates of graduation achievement of non-White students in the United States.

Advocate: an individual from a privileged group or position who takes the lead in helping a less privileged individual; distinct from an *ally* in that an advocate may make decisions for the less-privileged individual.

Affective Costs of Racism: refers to emotional costs that exist for White people when they hold racist views toward non-White people.

Afrofuturism: a concept that emerged in the 1990s regarding the imagining of a new future for African Americans that includes positive outcomes.

Allocentric: a collectivist-oriented individual.

Ally: someone from a privileged group who is willing to work alongside someone from a group that has been disenfranchised both historically and currently.

American Dream: a belief that in the United States, all have an equal chance at gaining success through hard work.

Antimiscegenation: a view that the practice of mixing races is wrong.

Arab Spring: A period in the early 2010s when anti-government protests/uprisings occurred in several Muslim countries.

Assimilate: to adhere closely to cultural norms (as set forth by the dominant culture in the context), which also involves leaving behind a home culture in favor of adopting a White American culture; also *assimilation*.

Aversive Racism: a subtle, often unintentional form of bias that characterizes many White Americans who possess strong egalitarian views and believe they are nonprejudiced.

Back Translation: a process in which a bilingual translator makes sure that the items in a translated measure mirror the meaning they had in the original language.

Behavioral Costs of Racism: White people may have the desire to avoid situations in which they will come into contact with people of another race when they hold racist beliefs.

Bias: a preference for or an avoidance of a particular group based on a belief.

Bicultural: a person who has an intimate understanding of two different cultural contexts (still may be monoracial).

Biethnic: a person who has family heritage from two ethnicities.

Biracial: a person who has family heritage from two racial groups.

Black Fishing: adjusting appearance on social media to look Black or mixed race.

Braceros: temporary workers from Mexico.

Californios: a term used to describe people of Mexican heritage that are native to the land that is now California.

Chicanx/Latinx: nonbinary/gender-neutral term for people of Latin American decent.

Cisgender: having a match between the way one identifies their gender internally and the way others identify them externally.

Cognitive Costs of Racism: the distortion that occurs for White people in terms of thinking about themselves as well as those who are not White when they hold racist beliefs.

Cognitive Dissonance: a psychological term that describes the mental discomfort that occurs when a new idea challenges one's long-held belief.

Collectivism: a value system adhered to by many non-Western groups that focuses on the group as a whole and encourages cooperation and dependence.

Color Conscious: talking about race and differences in skin color.

Color Mute: staying silent about race.

Colorblind: a tendency to act as though race does not matter or that one does not "notice" race.

Conceptual Equivalence: refers to a psychological construct having the same meaning in two distinct cultural contexts.

Confirmation Bias: the tendency for humans to look for evidence that confirms things they already believe at the expense of seeing evidence that counteracts this view.

Confirmatory Bias: paying attention to a result only if it fits a stereotype one already holds.

Counter Narrative: a narrative that goes against a common narrative.

Countercultural: a term used to describe people whose personal value system does not mesh with their culture's primary value system.

Covert Racism: actions, beliefs, or emotions that are predicated on stereotypes or other types of discrimination that are hard to see and often unintentional.

Cross-Cultural: comparisons of differences between groups in distinct contexts.

Cultural Appropriation: an adoption of various objects, cultural content, and/or voice of a culture to which one does not belong.

Cultural Humility: the idea that one can never be "done" with cultural training or know all the information there is to know about this vast topic.

Cultural Racism: the pseudoscientific (and faulty) idea that racial inequality can be explained exclusively by the behavior of people of color.

Cultural Resilience: defined by Elsass (1992) as "the set of strengths, values, and practices that promote coping mechanisms and adaptive reactions to traumatic oppression."

Culturally Responsive Counseling: therapist's understanding, and use of, a client's culture, beliefs, values.

Culture: "a shared pattern of beliefs, attitudes, norms, role perceptions, and values" (Triandis, 1995, p. 3).

Deficit Model: refers to the fact that theories usually favor the cultural group from which they originate.

Dependent Variable: during the experimental process, the variable that is being measured.

Dialectical Reasoning: term coined by Riegel (1973) and used by Piaget to describe the cognitive ability to think about things from more than one perspective (e.g., yours and someone else's) at the same time.

Discrimination: treatment that stems from prejudice or bias about another group.

Diversity: differences, variation.

Diversity Management: utilizing the attributes and benefits of having a diverse workforce toward other positive outcomes for businesses across the country.

Equivalence: equality between measures or scales; four subtypes (conceptual, linguistic, metric, and functional).

Ethnic Enclaves: a term used to describe living areas populated almost exclusively by people of one racial or ethnic identity; many of these neighborhoods were created because of laws that prohibited people of color from living in certain areas. See *Redlining.*

Ethnicity: "groups that are characterized in terms of a common nationality, culture, or language" (Betancourt & López, 1993, p. 631).

Ethnocultural Empathy: empathy or understanding of the feelings of an individual who is different culturally from oneself.

Evaluative Beliefs: part of Rokeach's (1973) values model; encompasses beliefs about who is good and who is bad.

Existential Beliefs: part of Rokeach's (1973) values model; involves beliefs about what is true and what is false.

Exosystem: part of Bronfenbrenner's (1979) ecological systems theory; refers to inclusion of surrounding institutions that impact the child indirectly, such as the legal system or media.

Familial Ethnic/Race Socialization: the way in which families teach their children about race and its social meaning and consequences.

Freedom Riders: a group of activists (many of whom were college students) who fought to force southern states to adhere to the federal law against segregation in bus terminals, lunch counters, and restrooms.

Functional Equivalence: refers to the use and function of a particular construct in daily life as being the same in different cultural groups.

Gender Constancy: a developmental stage noted by Kohlberg (1966) in which children gain understanding that gender is a constant, as opposed to being able to change moment to moment due to outside factors (e.g., a boy with long hair does not become a girl because of the hairstyle).

Green Card: a form of identification given to someone from another country who has lawful permanent residence in a new country.

Heterosexism: discrimination based on sexual orientation, favoring heterosexuality.

Hypodescent (One Drop Rule): an old belief that "one drop" of Black blood meant that a person was culturally Black; was used to justify enslaving biracial Black/White children of masters; follows the faulty idea that race is biological.

Ideologies: system of ideas.

Idiocentric: an individualist-oriented individual.

Implicit Bias: favoritism or avoidance of something in a seemingly unconscious way.

Imposed Ethics: a practice of imposing one's own norms, values, and worldviews onto another; often occurs to disenfranchised groups by dominant cultural groups.

Independent Variable: during the experimental process, the variable that is being manipulated.

Individualism: a value system adhered to by many Western cultural groups that value the individual above the group in most cases.

Institutionalized Racism: differential access to the goods, services, and opportunities of society by race. See also *structural racism*.

Internalized Racism: acceptance by members of stigmatized (non-White) races of negative messages about their own abilities and intrinsic worth.

Intersectionality: a term coined originally by Kimberlé Crenshaw (1989) that is meant to describe the way in which our multiple social identity facets (e.g., race, ethnicity, gender, sexual orientation, etc.) intersect to create our identity as a whole.

Jim Crow: racial caste system most known for segregation enforced by law and racial violence.

Linguistic Equivalence: refers to equivalence in meaning of items on a measure or scale when they are translated into a different language.

Locus of Control: one dimension of Sue's (1987) worldview model; defines the level of control individuals perceive they have over their own lives.

Locus of Responsibility: one dimension of Sue's (1987) worldview model; defines the level of responsibility individuals perceive they have for their own life circumstances.

Macrosystem: part of Bronfenbrenner's (1979) ecological systems theory; the societal and cultural values that impact the child.

Mesosystem: part of Bronfenbrenner's (1979) ecological systems theory; the connections such as neighborhood, school, and parents' workplace that interact with the child's personal environment.

Metric Equivalence: refers to equivalence in the way response items are used in different cultural groups.

Microaggressions: "brief and commonplace daily verbal and behavioral indignities that communicate hostile, derogatory, or negative racial slights and insults" (Sue, Capodilupo, & Holder, 2008, p. 329).

Microassaults: intentional acts of racism that are intended at a particular group.

Microinsults: comments, actions, and behaviors that are generally unintentional but appear to rely on stereotypes, communicate surprise at the accomplishments of people who are not part of the dominant culture, or exhibit rudeness in discussing these groups.

Microinvalidation: situations in which a dominant culture person invalidates the experience of another involving a microinsult or other action.

Microsystem: part of Bronfenbrenner's (1979) ecological systems theory; describes children's experience in their personal environment.

Model Minority: the idea that among other racial and ethnic minority groups, Asian immigrants and their subsequent generations have succeeded and prospered, especially in comparison to African American and Latinx populations.

Model Minority Myth of Achievement: the incorrect assumption that Asian Americans enjoy greater success because of their stronger work ethics, perseverance, and drive to succeed.

Model Minority Myth of Unrestricted Mobility: the incorrect assumption that Asian American success is "associated with their stronger [in comparison to other racial minorities] belief in fairness of treatment and lack of perceived racism or barriers at school/work" (Parks & Yoo, 2016, p. 289).

Monoracial: a person whose family heritage comes from a single racial group.

Multicultural: a person who has an intimate understanding of more than two different cultural contexts (still may be monoracial).

Multicultural Competence: the possession of awareness (of both your beliefs and others'), knowledge (of history, practices, commonly held values), and skills to work and interact with people who are different from you culturally.

Multicultural Psychology: the study of differences with regard to cultural context and cultural identities.

Multiethnic: a person who has family heritage from two ethnic groups.

Multiracial: a person who has family heritage from more than two racial groups.

Narrative Frame: central organizing idea or concept.

New Deal: series of work and financial programs and projects enacted by Franklin D. Roosevelt, starting in 1933, designed to move the country out of the Great Depression.

One Drop Rule: used in times of slavery to classify any person with "a drop" of African American blood as non-White. See also *hypodescent*.

Opportunity Gap (Equity Gap): the lower rates of opportunities that exist for non-White students in the United States (sometimes used instead of *achievement gap* to denote that gaps in graduation are often related to social inequities).

Oppression: when a group in power exerts that power over another group in such a way as to benefit themselves, and exploit and abuse the other.

Overt Racism: actions, beliefs, or emotions that are predicated on stereotypes and other types of discrimination and prejudice that are intentional and sometimes violent.

Pathologized: attributing abnormality or unhealthy characteristics to a person or thing.

Perpetual Foreigner Stereotype: a stereotype that exists for some racial groups (namely Asian) that views them as immigrants for all generations regardless of their birthplace.

Personal Racism (Personally Mediated Racism): racism that occurs in an interpersonal context; some believe this is better described as prejudice when it refers to actions of nonprivileged groups.

Polygenism: the pseudoscientific belief that different races may have emerged from different genetic pools; used as an argument that racial differences were completely biological in the past.

Postracial: the idea that race has no meaning in society any longer.

Predictive Algorithms: the use of data and machine learning to predict future outcomes.

Proactive Diversity Management: a method used to maintain diversity among the employees within an organization that includes viewing diversity as a broad concept that includes multiple social identity facets; it ensures that value for diversity is institutionalized within the organization.

Proscriptive/Prescriptive Beliefs: part of Rokeach's (1973) values model; encompasses beliefs about what individuals should do (prescriptive) and what they should not do (proscriptive).

Psychological Invisibility: extreme form of colorblindness.

Race: a sociocultural construct that groups individuals together by both physical and social characteristics.

Racial Segregation: laws that were held at state and federal levels that prevented interaction between races; see *Jim Crow*.

Racial Wealth Gap: disparity in median household wealth.

Racist: using race to make decisions about people and how to treat them that may result in different outcomes for different racial groups.

Redlining: a color-coded, race-based mapping system that identified neighborhoods that the Federal Housing Authority set up to determine where (and to whom) banks could give mortgage loans.

Reparative Therapies: nonlegitimate "therapies" that purport to change a person's sexual orientation from nonheterosexual to heterosexual; banned by the American Psychological Association for any licensed therapist to practice.

Reverse Racism: perceived discrimination against people who are White.

Scapegoating: blaming a disenfranchised group for its own plight; sometimes used when dominant cultural groups are trying to make sense of inequities between their group and others.

Scholar-Practitioner: a model often used within clinical and counseling psychology to refer to the fact that therapists must use the scientific method to determine diagnosis and course of treatment.

Scientific Racism: refers to the fact that pseudoscience (based on the White standard) was often used to pathologize non-White individuals.

Social Darwinism: a view held by Darwin that different racial groups might be evolving differently such that they were becoming different species; used as an argument that non-White people were incapable of being as intelligent as Whites.

Social Narrative: a commonly held shared belief or idea (though not necessarily a true one).

Socioeconomic Status: social class of an individual or group based on a combination of education, income, and occupation.

Sphere of Influence: refers to the individuals in domains around you over which you have some influence or control (e.g., friendship circle, employees at work, etc.).

Status-Based Identity Uncertainty: a phenomenon described by Destin and colleagues (2017) that may bring about psychological distress when one changes socioeconomic status.

Stereotype: a belief that one holds and applies to all members of a group.

Stereotype Lift: the increased test scores one often may find when a group is reminded of their powerful status.

Stereotype Threat: a theory developed by psychologist Claude Steele (1997) that attempts to explain the reason African American individuals' achievement may be impacted by their fear of confirming negative stereotypes about their racial group with regard to intelligence and achievement.

Structural Racism: See *institutionalized racism*.

"The Other": based on opposing identities, "the other" refers to those who are not considered part of the dominant group.

Transgender: describes persons whose personal gender identity does not match their biological birth sex.

Unidimensional: viewing a person by way of a single piece of information about a group to which the person belongs (often the basis of stereotypes).

White Privilege: a set of unearned and inherent advantages ascribed to those seen as racially White; may include better treatment, more benefit of the doubt, and lack of negative stereotyping.

White Space: physical space dominated by Whites.

White Standard: the fact that most theories have come from White/European points of view and thus favor this point of view as the "standard" or "normal."

Whiteness: constantly shifting, constructed racial identity.

Working Hypothesis: a term used in clinical and counseling psychology that refers to patterns and emerging ideas about diagnosis of a client but allows for changes to be made as more data is collected.

Worldview: the way in which we see the world through the varying lenses of our culture, our identities, and our experiences.

REFERENCES

Abe, J., Zane, N., & Chun, K. (1994). Differential responses to trauma: Migration-related discriminants of post-traumatic stress disorder among Southeast Asian refugees. *Journal of Community Psychology, 22,* 121–135.

Aboud, F. E., Mendelson, M. J., & Purdy, K. T. (2003). Cross-race peer relations and friendship quality. *International Journal of Behavioral Development, 27,* 165–173.

Adelman, L. (Executive producer). (2003). *Race, the power of an illusion, Part 3: The house we live in* [Video program]. San Francisco: California Newsreel. Retrieved from https://vimeo.com/133506632

Aguilar, M. (2018, September 17). Undocumented. *The Players Tribune.* Retrieved from https://www.theplayerstribune.com/en-us/articles/miguel-aguilar-undocumented-galaxy

Ajibade, A., Hook, J. N., Utsey, S. O., Davis, D. E., & Von Tongeren, D. R. (2016). Racial/ethnic identity, religious commitment, and well-being in African Americans. *Journal of Black Psychology, 42,* 244–258.

Alexie, S. (2007). *The absolutely true diary of a part-time Indian.* New York: Little, Brown.

Ali, S. R., Flojo, J. R., Chronister, K. M., Hayashino, D., Smiling, Q. R., Torres, D., & McWhirter, E. H. (2005). When racism is reversed: Therapists of color speak about their experiences with racism from clients, supervisees, and supervisors. In M. Rastogi & E. Wieling (Eds.), *Voices of color: First-person accounts of ethnic minority therapists* (pp. 117–133). Thousand Oaks, CA: Sage.

Allport, G. W. (1954). The nature of prejudice. In C. Stangor (Ed.), *Stereotypes and prejudice: Essential readings* (pp. 20–48). New York: Psychology Press.

Alvarez, A. N., Liang, C. T. H., & Neville, H. A. (2016). *The cost of racism for people of color: Contextualizing experiences of discrimination.* Washington, DC: American Psychological Association.

Ambe, E. B. (2006). Fostering multicultural appreciation in pre-service teachers through multicultural curricular transformation. *Teaching and Teacher Education, 22,* 690–699.

American Psychiatric Association. (1968). *Diagnostic and statistical manual of mental disorders* (2nd ed.). Washington, DC: Author.

American Psychiatric Association. (1980). *Diagnostic and statistical manual of mental disorders* (3rd ed.). Washington, DC: Author.

American Psychiatric Association. (1987). *Diagnostic and statistical manual of mental disorders* (3rd ed., Rev.) Washington, DC: Author.

American Psychiatric Association. (2013). *Diagnostic and statistical manual of mental disorders* (5th ed.). Arlington, VA: Author.

American Psychological Association. (2017, August). *Multicultural guidelines: An ecological approach to context, identity, and intersectionality.* Retrieved from https://www.apa.org/about/policy/multicultural-guidelines

American Psychological Association, Task Force on Appropriate Therapeutic Responses to Sexual Orientation. (2009). *Report of the American Psychological Association, task force on appropriate therapeutic responses to sexual orientation, on appropriate therapeutic responses to sexual orientation.* Retrieved from http://www.apa.org/pi/lgbc/publications/therapeutic-resp.html

American Psychological Association. (1990). *Guidelines for providers of psychological services to ethnic, linguistic, and culturally diversity populations.* Retrieved from https://www.apa.org/pi/oema/resources/policy/provider-guidelines

American Psychological Association. (2002). *Guidelines on multicultural education, training, research, practice, and organizational change for psychologists.* Washington, DC: Author.

American Psychological Association. (2007, March 13). *APA task force on appropriate therapeutic responses to sexual orientation.* Retrieved from https://www.apa .org/news/press/releases/2007/03/lgbc-task -force.aspx

American Psychological Association. (2008). *Report of the task force on the implementation of the multicultural guidelines.* Washington, DC: Author.

American Psychological Association. (2014, March 6). *Black boys viewed as older, less innocent than Whites, research finds.* Retrieved from https://www.apa.org/ news/press/releases/2014/03/black-boys-older

American Psychological Association. (2015). *Demographics of the U.S. psychology workforce: Findings from the American Community Survey.* Washington, DC: Author.

Andersen, E. S., & Wilson, B. (1995). *None of the above.* New York: Filmmakers Library.

Anderson, M., & Jiang, J. (2018, May 31). *Teens, social media, & technology 2018.* Pew Research Center. Retrieved from https://www.pewinternet .org/2018/05/31/teens-social-media-technology-2018/

Anderson, M., Toor, S., Rainie, L., & Smith, A. (2018, July 11). *Activism in the social media age.* Pew Research Center. Retrieved from https://www.pewresearch .org/internet/2018/07/11/activism-in-the -social-media-age/

Anderson, M., Toor, S., Rainie, L., & Smith, A. (2018, July 11). *Activism in the social media age.* Pew Research Center. Retrieved from https://www.pewinternet .org/2018/07/11/activism-in-the-social-media-age/

Anti-Defamation League. (2020). *ADL hate crime map.* Retrieved from https://www.adl.org/adl-hate -crime-map

Aparta, K. (2014, November 4). How to learn a new language: 7 secrets from TED translators. *TED Blog.* Retrieved from https://blog.ted.com/how-to-learn-a -new-language-7-secrets-from-ted-translators/

Armenta, B. E., Lee, R. M., Pituc, S. T., Jung, K-R., Park, I. J. K., Soto, J. A., Kim, S. Y., & Schwartz, S. J. (2013). Where are you from? A validation of the Foreigner Objectification Scale and the psychological correlates of foreigner objectification among Asians Americans and Latinos. *Cultural Diversity and Ethnic Minority Psychology, 19,* 131–142.

Arnesen, E. (Oct. 2001). Whiteness and the historians' imagination. *International Labor and Working Class History, 60,* 3–32.

Aronson, J., Lustina, M. J., Good, C., Keough, K., Steele, C. M., & Brown, J. (1999). When White men can't do math: Necessary and sufficient factors in stereotype threat. *Journal of Experimental Social Psychology, 35,* 29–46.

Associated Press. (2016, September 29). *Governor Jerry Brown approves gender neutral bathroom bill.* Retrieved from https://abc7news.com/politics/ governor-jerry-brown-approves-gender-neutral -bathroom-bill-/1532857/

Atkin, A. L. Yoo, H. C., Jager, J., & Yeh, C. J. (2018). Internalization of the model minority myth, school racial composition, and psychological distress among Asian American adolescents. *Asian American Journal of Psychology, 9,* 108–116.

Awareness of implicit biases. (2017). Retrieved from https://poorvucenter.yale.edu/ImplicitBiasAwareness

Ayón, C., & Vigil, A. Q. (2018). Promoting Mexican immigrant families' well-being: Learning from parents what is needed to have a strong family. *Families in Society, 94,* 194–202.

Baldwin, J. (1962, January 14). As much truth as one can bear. *The New York Times,* pp. 1–2.

Barnshaw, J. (2008). Race. In R. T. Schaefer (Ed.), *Encyclopedia of race, ethnicity, and society* (pp. 1178–1093). Thousand Oaks, CA: Sage.

Battle-Cochrane, C. (Director). *Biracial not black damn it!* [Motion picture]. (2009). Winston-Salem, NC: Battlecatt Productions.

Bell, D. A. (1995). Who's afraid of critical race theory? *University of Illinois Law Review, 1995,* 893–910.

Benedikoviová, J., & Ardelt, M. (2008). The three-dimensional wisdom scale in cross-cultural context:

A comparison between American and Slovak college students. *Studia Psychologica, 50,* 179–190.

Berensen, T. (2015, October 29). Here's how China's one-child policy started in the first place. *Time Magazine.* Retrieved from: http://time.com/4092689/china-one-child-policy-history/

Berry, J. (1990). Psychology of acculturation: Understanding individuals moving between cultures. In R. Brislin (Ed.), *Applied cross-cultural psychology* (pp. 232–253). Newbury Park, CA: Sage.

Betancourt, H., & López, S. R. (1993). The study of culture, ethnicity, and race in American psychology. *American Psychologist, 48,* 629–637.

Bhopal, R. (2007). The beautiful skull and Blumenbach's errors: The birth of the scientific concept of race. *The BMJ, 335,* 1308–1309.

Bigler, R. S. (1995). The role of classification skill in moderating environmental influences on children's gender stereotyping: A study of the functional use of gender in the classroom. *Child Development, 66,* 1072–1087.

Bigler, R. S. (1997). Conceptual and methodological issues in the measurement of children's sex typing. *Psychology of Women Quarterly, 21,* 53–69.

Bigler, R. S., & Liben, L. S. (2007). Developmental intergroup theory: Explaining and reducing children's social stereotyping and prejudice. *Current Directions in Psychological Science, 16,* 162–166.

Bilodeau, B. L. (2005). Beyond the gender binary: A case study of two transgender students at a midwestern university. *Journal of Gay and Lesbian Issues in Education, 3,* 29–44.

Biolsi, T. (2007). Cultural appropriation. In T. Biolsi (Ed.), *A companion to the anthropology of American Indians* (pp. 383–397). Oxford, UK: Blackwell.

Blakemore, E. (2019, June 18). *The largest mass deportation in American history.* The History Channel. Retrieved from https://www.history.com/news/operation-wetback-eisenhower-1954-deportation

Blakeslee, G. H. (1915/2017). *The Journal of Race Development, 1910–1911.* Baltimore: MD: Waverly Press. (Original work published 1915)

Bloom, R., & Barry, J. R. (1967). Determinants of work attitudes among Negroes. *Journal of Applied Psychology, 51,* 291–294.

Blume, A. W., Lovato, L. V., Thyken, B. N., & Denny, N. (2012). The relationship of microaggressions with alcohol use and anxiety among ethnic minority college students in a historically White institution. *Cultural Diversity and Ethnic Minority Psychology, 18,* 45–54.

Bonifacio, L., Gushue, G. V., & Mejia-Smith, B. X. (2018). Microaggressions and ethnic identity in the career development of Latina college students. *The Counseling Psychologist, 46,* 505–529.

Bonilla-Silva, E. (2018). *Racism without racists: Color-blind racism and the persistence of racial inequality in America.* Lanham, MD: Rowman & Littlefield.

Bouie, J. (2011, March 30). The segregated workplace. *Slate.* Retrieved from https://prospect.org/article/segregated-workplace.

Bouie, J. (2014, August 22). The two very different worlds of Ferguson. *Slate.* Retrieved from https://slate.com/news-and-politics/2014/08/fergusons-white-and-black-communities-they-see-the-citys-problems-very-differently.html

Bowers, C. A., Pharmer, J. A., & Salas, E. (2000). When member homogeneity is needed in work teams: A meta-analysis. *Small Group Research, 31,* 305–327.

Bradshaw, C. K. (1992). Beauty and the beast: On racial ambiguity. In M. P. P. Root (Ed.), *Racially mixed people in America* (pp. 77–90). Thousand Oaks, CA: Sage.

Brewer, L. C., & Cooper, L. A. (2014). Race, discrimination, and cardiovascular disease. *The Virtual Mentor, 16,* 455–460. doi:10.1001/virtualmentor.2014.16.6.stas2-1406

Brody, G. H., Yu, T., Miller, G. E., Ehrlich, K. B., & Chen, E. (2018). John Henryism coping and metabolic syndrome among young black adults. *Psychosomatic Medicine, 80,* 216–221.

Bronfenbrenner, U., & Morris, P. A. (2006). The bio-ecological model of human development. In W. Damon (Series Ed.) & R. M. Lerner (Vol. Ed.), Handbook of child psychology; Vol. 1: Theoretical models of human development (pp. 793–828). New York: Wiley.

Bronfenbrenner, U. (1979). *The ecology of human development: Experiments by nature and by design.* Cambridge, MA: Harvard University Press.

Brown v. Board of Education, 347 U.S. 483 (1953).

Brown, T. N., Tanner-Smith, E. E., Lesane-Brown, C. L., & Ezell, M. E. (2007). Child, parent, and situational correlates of familial ethnic/race socialization. *Journal of Marriage and Family, 69,* 14–25.

Buck, P. D. (2016). Constructing race, creating white privilege. In P. S. Rothenberg (Ed.), *Race, class, and gender in the United States* (pp. 21–26). New York: Worth.

Burnes, T. R., & Stanley, J. L. (Eds., 2017). *Teaching LGBTQ psychology: Queering innovative pedagogy and practice.* Washington, DC: American Psychological Association.

Calzada, E. J., & Sales, A. (2019). Depression among Mexican-origin mothers: Exploring the immigrant paradox. *Cultural Diversity and Ethnic Minority Psychology, 25,* 288–298.

Capodilupo, C. M., & Sue, D. W. (2013). Microaggressions in counseling and psychotherapy. In D. W. Sue & D. Sue (Eds.), *Counseling the culturally diverse* (pp. 147–174). Hoboken, NJ: John Wiley & Sons.

Carter, R. T. (1991). Racial identity attitudes and psychological functioning. *Journal of Multicultural Counseling and Development, 19,* 105–114.

Carter, R. T. (2007). Racism and psychological and emotional injury: Recognizing and assessing race-based traumatic stress. *The Counseling Psychologist, 35,* 13–105.

Carter, R. T., Mazzula, S., Victoria, R., Vazquez, R., Hall, S., Smith, S., Sant-Barket, S., . . . & Williams, B. (2013). Initial development of the Race-Based Traumatic Stress Symptom Scale: Assessing the emotional impact of racism. *Psychological Trauma: Theory, Research, Practice, and Policy, 5,* 1–9.

Cass, V. C. (1979). Homosexual identity formation: Testing a theoretical model. *Journal of Sex Research, 20,* 143–167.

Cass, V. C. (2015). *A quick guide to the case theory of lesbian & gay identity formation.* Bentley, DC, Australia: Brightfire Press.

Castelli, L., De Dea, C., & Nesdale, D. (2008). Learning social attitudes: Children's sensitivity to the nonverbal behaviors of adult models during interracial interactions. *Personality and Social Psychology Bulletin, 34,* 1504–1513.

Cazden, C. B., & Leggett, E. L. (1976). *Culturally responsive education: A response to LAU Remedies II.* Retrieved from https://eric.ed.gov/?id=ED135241

Center for Media Literacy. (2019). *Media literacy: A definition and more.* Retrieved from https://www.medialit.org/media-literacy-definition-and-more

Chaney, J., Burke, A., & Burkley, E. (2011). Do American Indian mascots = American Indian people? Examining implicit bias towards American Indian people and American Indian mascots. *American Indian and Alaska Native Mental Health Research, 18,* 42–62.

Chang, H. (2016). *Autoethnography as method.* New York: Routledge.

Chasmar, J. (2017, June 13). Katy Perry apologizes for cultural appropriation during 4-day livestream. *The Washington Times.* Retrieved from https://www.washingtontimes.com/news/2017/jun/13/katy-perry-apologizes-for-cultural-appropriation-d/

Cherng, H. (Sept. 2017). The ties that bind: Teacher relationships, academic expectations, and racial/ethnic and generational inequality. *American Journal of Education, 124*(1), 67–100.

Cheryan, S., & Monin, B. (2005). Where are you *really* from?:Asian Americans and identity denial. *Journal of Personality and Social Psychology, 89,* 717–730.

Chester, R. (2017, February 13). Sex and intimacy 101: Refrain from touching your phone. *The Daily Telegraph.* Retrieved from https://www.dailytelegraph.com.au/rendezview/sex-and-intimacy-101-refrain-from-touching-your-phone/news-story/a5cf4137fe74d0544d1d58e4d38e91d9

Cheung, W.-Y., Maio, G. R., Rees, K. J., Kamble, S., & Mane, S. (2016). Cultural differences in values as self-guides. *Personality and Social Psychology Bulletin, 42,* 769–781.

Chong, V., & Kuo, B. C. H. (2015). Racial identity profiles of Asian-White biracial young adults: Testing a theoretical model with cultural and psychological correlates. *American Journal of Psychology, 6,* 203–212.

Clark, K. B., & Clark, M. P. (1947). Racial identification and preference in Negro children. In E. L. Hartley (Ed.), *Readings in Social Psychology* (pp. 169–178). New York: Holt, Rinehart, and Winston.

Clark, R., Anderson, N. B., Clark, V. R., & Williams, D. R. (1999). Racism as a stressor for African Americans: A biopsychosocial model. *American Psychologist, 54,* 805–816.

Coelho, P. (1993). *The alchemist.* New York: HarperCollins.

College Board. (2017). *Trends in college pricing.* Retrieved from https://research.collegeboard.org/trends/college-pricing/resource-library

Collins, J. W., Rankin, K. M., & David, R. J. (2015). Downward economic mobility and preterm birth: An exploratory study of Chicago-born upper class White mothers. *Maternal and Child Health Journal, 19,* 1601–1607.

Collins, P. H. (2000). *Black feminist thought: Knowledge, consciousness, and the politics of empowerment* (2nd ed.). New York: Routledge.

Comas-Diaz, L. (2006). Latino healing: The integration of ethnic psychology into psychotherapy. *Psychotherapy: Theory, Research, Practice, Training, 43,* 436–453.

Covarrubias, R., & Fryberg, S. A. (2015). The impact of self-relevant representations on school belonging for Native American students. *Cultural Diversity and Ethnic Minority Psychology, 21,* 10–18.

Crandall, C. S., Bahns, A. J., Warner, R., & Schaller, M. (2011). Stereotypes as justifications of prejudice. *Personality and Social Psychology Bulletin, 37,* 1488–1498.

Crayton, L. (2018). *Everything you need to know about cultural appropriation.* New York: Rosen Young Adult.

Crenshaw, K. (1994). *Mapping the margins: Intersectionality, identity politics, and violence against women of color.* Auckland, New Zealand: Pearson Education New Zealand.

Crenshaw, K. (2016). *The urgency of intersectionality.* TEDWomen. Retrieved from https://www.ted.com/talks/kimberle_crenshaw_the_urgency_of_intersectionality?language=en

Crenshaw, K. W. (1989). Demarginalizing the intersection of race and sex: A Black feminist critique of antidiscrimination doctrine, feminist theory and anti-racist politics. *University of Chicago Legal Forum, 1989,* 139–167.

Crenshaw, K., Gotanda, N., Peller, G., & Thomas, K. (Eds.). (1995). *Critical race theory.* New York: The New Press.

Crocker, J., Major, B., & Steele, C. (1998). Social stigma. In D. T. Gilbert, S. T. Fiske, & L. Gardner (Eds.), *The handbook of social psychology* (pp. 504–553). New York: McGraw-Hill.

Cross, Jr. W. E. (1991) *Shades of black: Diversity in African American identity.* Philadelphia: Temple University Press.

Cross, W. E. (1971). The Negro-to-Black conversion experience. *Black World, 20,* 13–27.

Cudd, A. E. (2013). Oppression. In B. Kaldis (Ed.), *Encyclopedia of Philosophy and the Social Sciences* (pp. 698–699). Thousand Oaks, CA: Sage.

Cunningham, G. B. (2009). The moderating effect of diversity strategy on the relationship between racial diversity and organizational performance. *Journal of Applied Social Psychology, 39,* 1445–1460.

Davis, K. (2005) *A girl like me.* United States. Reel Works Teen Filmmaking,

de Souza, L. E. C., Pereira, C. R., Camino, L., de Lima, T. S. S., & Torres, A. R. R. (2016). The legitimizing role of accent on discrimination against immigrants. *European Journal of Social Psychology, 46,* 609–620.

De Walt, P. S. (2013). Discourse on African American/Black identity: From nigrescence theory to a lived diasporic consciousness. *SpringerPlus, 2,* 233.

design in counseling (4th ed.). Boston, MA: Cengage Learning.

Desilver, D. (2014, April 22). *Supreme Court says states can ban affirmative action; 8 already have.*

Pew Research Center. Retrieved from https://www.pewresearch.org/fact-tank/2014/04/22/supreme-court-says-states-can-ban-affirmative-action-8-already-have/

Destin, M., Rheinschmidt-Same, M., & Richeson, J. A. (2017). Status-based identity: A conceptual approach integrating the social psychological study of socioeconomic status and identity. *Perspectives on Psychological Science, 12,* 270–289.

Devos, T., & Ma, D. S. (2008). Is Kate Winslet more American than Lucy Liu? The impact of construal processes on the implicit ascription of a national identity. *British Journal of Social Psychology, 47,* 191–215.

DiAngelo, R. (2018). *White fragility: Why it is so hard for white people to talk about racism.* Boston: Beacon Press.

Diaz, T., & Bui, N. H. (2017). Subjective well-being in Mexican and Mexican American women: The role of acculturation, ethnic identity, gender roles, and perceived social support. *Journal of Happiness Studies, An Interdisciplinary Forum on Subjective Well-Being, 18,* 607–624,

dickey, l. m., Singh, A. A., Chang, S. C., & Rehrig, M. (2017). Advocacy and social justice: The next generation of counseling and psychological practice with transgender and gender-nonconforming clients. In A. Singh, & l. m. dickey (Eds.), *Affirmative counseling and psychological practice with transgender and non-conforming clients* (pp. 247–262). Washington DC: American Psychological Association.

Do, K. A., Wang, C., & Atwal, K. (2019). Peer victimization and the perpetual foreigner stereotype on Sikh American adolescents' mental health outcomes: The moderating effects of coping and behavioral enculturation. *Asian American Journal of Psychology, 10,* 131–140.

Dobrow, J. R., & Gidney, C. L. (1998). The good, the bad, and the foreign: The use of dialect in children's animated television. *The Annals of the American Academy of Political and Social Science, 557,* 105–119.

Dovidio, J. F. (1999). On the nature of contemporary prejudice: Outcomes and process. *Proceedings of the 3rd Biennial EO/EEO Research Symposium.* Cocoa Beach, FL: Defense Equal Opportunity Management Institute.

Dovidio, J. F. (2001). On the nature of contemporary prejudice: The third wave. *Journal of Social Issues, 57,* 829–849.

Dovidio, J. F., Gaertner, S. E., Kawakami, K., & Hodson, G. (2002). Why can't we just get along? Interpersonal biases and interracial distrust. *Cultural Diversity and Ethnic Minority Psychology, 8,* 88–102.

Dovidio, J. F., Kawakami, K., & Gaertner, S. E. (2002). Implicit and explicit prejudice and interracial interaction. *Journal of Personality and Social Psychology, 82,* 62–68.

Drake, B. (2014, November 26). *Ferguson highlights deep divisions between blacks and whites in America.* Pew Research Center. Retrieved from https://www.pewresearch.org/fact-tank/2014/11/26/ferguson-highlights-deep-divisions-between-blacks-and-whites-in-america/

Drescher, J. (2015). Queer diagnoses revisited: The past and future of homosexuality and gender diagnoses in DSM and ICD. *International Review of Psychiatry, 27,* 386–395.

Duchscherer, K. M., & Dovidio, J. F. (2016). When memes are mean: Appraisals of and objections to stereotypic memes. *Translational Issues in Psychological Science, 2,* 335.

Dunbar-Ortiz, R. (2015). *An indigenous peoples' history of the United States.* New York: Beacon Press.

Dubois, W. E. B. (1935, 1998). *Black reconstruction in America 1860–1880.* New York: The Free Press.

Dyer, R. (1997, 2017). *White.* New York: Routledge.

Dyer, R. (2016). The matter of Whiteness. In P. S. Rothenberg (Ed.), *White privilege: Essential readings on the other side of racism* (9–14). New York: Worth.

Edwards, L. M., & Pedrotti, J. T. (2004). Utilizing the strengths of our cultures: Therapy with biracial women and girls. *Women and Therapy, 27,* 33–43.

Elsass, P. (1992). *Strategies for survival: The psychology of cultural resilience in ethnic minorities* (F. Hopenwasser, Trans.). New York: NYU Press.

Ethnic diversity in the Senate. (n.d.) Retrieved February 27, 2020, from https://www.senate.gov/senators/EthnicDiversityintheSenate.htm

Evans, A. M., & Ramsay, K. (2015). Multiracial and biracial individuals: A content analysis of counseling journals, 1991–2013. *Journal of Multicultural Counseling and Development, 43,* 262–274.

Feagin, J. R. (2013). *The white racial frame: Centuries of racial framing and counter-framing.* New York: Routledge.

Feeney, N. (2013, November 25). Katy Perry's "geisha-style" performance needs to be called out. *The Atlantic.* Retrieved from https://www.theatlantic.com/entertainment/archive/2013/11/katy-perrys-geisha-style-performance-needs-to-be-called-out/281805/

Fingerhut, A. W., & Maisel, N. C. (2010). Relationship formalization and individual and relationship well-being among same-sex couples. *Journal of Social and Personal Relationships, 27,* 956–969.

Fontenot, K., Semega, J., & Kollar, M. (2018). *Income and poverty in the United States: 2017.* U.S. Census Bureau, Current Population Reports. Retrieved from https://www.census.gov/content/dam/Census/library/publications/2018/demo/p60-263.pdf

Forber-Pratt, A. J., & Zape, M. P. (2017). Disability identity development model: Voices from the ADA-generation. *Disability and Health Journal, 19,* 350–355.

Forrest-Bank, S. S., & Cuellar, M. J. (2018). The mediating effects of ethnic identity on the relationships between racial microaggression and psychological well-being. *Social Work Research, 42,* 44–56.

Forrest-Bank, S., & Jenson, J. (2015). Differences in experiences of racial and ethnic microaggression among Asian, Latino/Hispanic, Black, and White young adults. *Journal of Sociology and Social Welfare, 42,* 141–161.

Franco, M. G., Katz, R., & O'Brien, K. M. (2016). Forbidden identities: A qualitative examination of racial identity invalidation for Black/White biracial individuals. *International Journal of Intercultural Relations, 50,* 96–109.

Fryberg, S. A., & Stephens, N, M. (2010). When the world is colorblind, American Indians are invisible: A diversity science approach. *Psychological Inquiry, 21,* 115–119.

Fryberg, S. A., Markus, H, R., Oyserman, D., & Stone, J. M. (2008). Of warrior chiefs and Indian princesses: The psychological consequences of American Indian mascots. *Basic and Applied Social Psychology, 30,* 208–218.

Frye, M. (1983). Oppression. *The politics of reality: Essays in feminist theory* (pp. 1–16). Trumansburg, NY: The Crossing Press.

Fusion Comedy. (2016, October 5). *How microaggressions are like mosquito bites* [Video file]. Retrieved from https://www.easybib.com/guides/citation-guides/apa-format/youtube-video/

Gahan, P., & Abeysekera, L. (2009). What shapes an individual's work values? An integrated model of the relationship between work values, national culture and self-construal. *The International Journal of Human Resource Management, 20,* 126–147.

Garcini, L. M., Galvan, T., Peña, J. M., Klonoff, E. A., Parra-Medina, D., Ziauddin, K., & Fagundes, C. P. (2019). "A high price paid": Migration-related loss and distress among undocumented Mexican immigrants. *Journal of Latinx Psychology, 7,* 245–255.

Gay and Lesbian Alliance Against Defamation (GLAAD). (2019). *GLAAD About.* Retrieved from https://www.glaad.org/about

Geena Davis Institute on Gender in the Media. (2018). *Gender representations in the top 100 family films of 2017.* Retrieved from https://seejane.org/

Geerlings, J., Thijs, J., & Verkuyten, M. (2019). Preaching and practicing multicultural education: Predicting students' outgroup attitudes from perceived teacher norms and perceived teacher–classmate relations. *Journal of school psychology, 75,* 89–103.

Gentlemen's agreement. (n.d.). In *Encyclopaedia Britannica.* Retrieved March 5, 2020, from https://www.britannica.com/event/Gentlemens-Agreement

Ghandnoosh, N. (2014, September 3). Race and punishment: *Racial perceptions of crime and support for punitive policies.* Retrieved from https://www.sentencingproject.org/staff/nazgol-ghandnoosh/

Gibson, C. (2004). Multicultural pre-service education: Promising multicultural pre-service teacher education initiatives. *Racial Pedagogy, 6,* Retrieved from http://rad icalpedagogy.icaap.org/content/issue6_1/gibson.html

Gluszek, A., & Dovidio, J. F. (2010). The way they speak: A social psychological perspective on the stigma of nonnative accents in communication. *Personality and Social Psychology Review, 14,* 214–237.

Goff, P. A., Jackson, M. C., Di Leone, B. A. L., Culotta, C. M., & DiTomasso, N. A. (2014). The essence of innocence: Consequences of dehumanizing Black children. *Journal of Personality and Social Psychology, 106,* 526–545.

Gonzales, R. G., Ellis, B., Rendón-García, S. A., & Brant, K. (2018). (Un) authorized transitions: Illegality, DACA, and the life course. *Research in Human Development, 15,* 345–359.

Gould, S. J. (1996). *The mismeasure of man: The definitive refutation to the argument of* The Bell Curve. New York: Norton.

Grieco, E. M., & Trevelyan, E. N. (2010). *Place of birth of the foreign-born population: 2009.* Retrieved from http:// www.census.gov/prod/2010pubs/acsbr09-15.pdf

Gruenewald, T. L., Karlamangla, A. S., Hu, P., Stein-Merkin, S., Crandall, C., Koretz, G., & Seeman, T.E. (2012). History of socioeconomic disadvantage and allostatic load in later life. *Social Science & Medicine, 74,* 75–83.

Gutierrez, I. A., & Park, C. L. (2015). Emerging adulthood, evolving worldviews: How life events impact college students' developing belief systems. *Emerging Adulthood, 3,* 85–97.

Hadden, B. R., Tolliver, W., Snowden, F., & Brown-Manning, R. (2016). An authentic discourse: Recentering race and racism as factors that contribute to police violence against unarmed Black or African American men. *Journal of Human Behavior in the Social Environment, 26,* 336–349.

Haidt, J. (2017). The unwisest idea on campus: Commentary on Lilienfeld (2017). *Perspectives on Psychological Science, 12,* 176–177.

Hall, C. C. I. (1980). *The ethnic identity of racially mixed people: A study of Black-Japanese.* Unpublished doctoral dissertation, University of California, Los Angeles.

Hall, C. C. I. (1992). Please choose one: Ethnic identity choices for biracial individuals. In M. P. P. Root (Ed.), *Racially mixed people in America* (pp. 250–264). Thousand Oaks, CA: Sage.

Hall, E. T. (1978). *Beyond culture.* New York: Random House.

Hall, G. C. N., Hong, J. J., Zane, N. W. S., & Meyer, O. L. (2011). *Clinical psychology: Science and practice, 18,* 215–231.

Hansen, E. (2017, November 13). *The forgotten minority in police shootings.* Cable News Network. Retrieved from https://www.cnn.com/2017/11/10/us/native-lives -matter/index.html

Harper, K., & Choma, B. L. (2018). Internalised white ideal, skin tone surveillance, and hair surveillance predict skin and hair dissatisfaction and skin bleaching among African American and Indian women. *Sex Roles: A Journal of Research, 80,* 735–744.

Harrell, J. H. (2018, June 26). With California in the lead, LGBTQ history gets boost in school curriculum. *EdSource.* Retrieved from https://edsource.org/2018/ with-california-in-the-lead-lgbtq-history-gets-boost -in-school-curriculum/599626

Harrell, S. P. (2000). A multidimensional conceptualization of racism-related stress: Implications for the well-being of people of color. *American Journal of Orthopsychiatry, 70,* 42–57.

Hays, P. A. (2016). *Addressing cultural complexities in practice: Assessment, diagnosis, and therapy* (3rd ed.). Washington, DC: American Psychological Association.

Helms, J. (2017). The challenge of making Whiteness visible: Reactions to four Whiteness articles. *The Counseling Psychologist, 45,* 717–726.

Helms, J. E. (1984). Toward a theoretical explanation of the effects of race on counseling: A Black and White model. *The Counseling Psychologist, 12,* 153–165.

Helms, J. E. (1990). *Black and white racial identity: Theory, research, and practice.* New York: Greenwood Press.

Helms, J. E. (1992/2008). *A race is a nice thing to have: A guide to being a White person or understanding the White persons in your life.* Alexandria, VA: Microtraining Associates.

Helms, J. E. (1995). An update of Helms's White and people of color racial identity models. In J. G. Ponterotto, J. M. Casas, L. A. Suzuki, & C. M. Alexander (Eds.), *Handbook of multicultural counseling* (pp. 181–198). Thousand Oaks, CA: Sage.

Helms, J. E., Jernigan, M., & Mascher, J. (2005). The meaning of race in psychology and how to change it: A methodological perspective. *American Psychologist, 60,* 27–36.

helpmefindparents. (2013, May 23). *What kind of Asian are you?* [Video file]. Retrieved from https://www.youtube.com/watch?v=DWynJkN5HbQ

Heppner, P. P., Wampold, B. E., Owen, J., Wang, K. T., & Thompson, M N. (2008). *Research design in counseling.* Boston: Cengage Learning.

Heppner, P. P., Wampold, B. E., Owen, J., Wang, K. T., & Thompson, M. N. (2015). *Research*

Herrnstein, R. J., & Murray, C. (1994). *The bell curve: Intelligence and class structure in American life.* New York: Free Press.

Ho, A. K., Sidanius, J., Levin, D. T., & Banaji, M. R. (2011). Evidence for hypodescent and racial hierarchy in the categorization and perception of biracial individuals. *Journal of Personality and Social Psychology, 100,* 492–506.

Ho, M. K. (1987). *Family therapy with ethnic minorities.* Newbury Park, CA: Sage.

Ho, S. M. Y., Rochelle, T. L., Law, L. S. C., Duan, W., Bai, Y, & Shih, S-M. (2014). Methodological issues in positive psychology research with diverse populations: Exploring strengths among Chinese adults. In J. T. Pedrotti & L. M. Edwards (Eds.), *Perspectives on the intersection of multiculturalism and positive psychology* (pp. 45–57). New York: Springer Science + Business Media.

Hotep, L. (2019, May). *What's race got to do with it?: Transformative professional development for faculty, staff, and administrators.* Symposium presented at the annual National Conference on Race and Ethnicity in Higher Education. Portland, OR.

Howarth, C., & Andreouli, E. (2016). "Nobody wants to be an outsider": From diversity management to diversity engagement. *Political Psychology, 37,* 327–340.

Huguley, J. P., Wang, M-T., Vasquez, A. C., & Guo, J. (2019). Parental ethnic-racial socialization practices and the construction of children of color's ethnic-racial identity: A research synthesis and meta-analysis. *Psychological Bulletin, 145,* 437–458.

Humes, K. R., Jones, N. A., & Ramirez, R. R. (2011, March). *Overview of race and Hispanic origin: 2010.* 2010 Census Briefs. Retrieved from https://www.census.gov/prod/cen2010/briefs/c2010br-02.pdf

Hutchinson, Y. (2016, August 23). MIT technology review. *Biased by design: Exclusion hurts tech companies more than they know.* Retrieved from https://www.technologyreview.com/s/602154/biased-by-design/

Huynh, Q-L., Devos, T., & Smalarz, L. (2011). Perpetual foreigner in one's own land: Potential implications for identity and psychological adjustment. *Journal of Social and Clinical Psychology, 30,* 133–162.

Hvistendahl, M. (2017, October 18). Analysis of China's one-child policy sparks uproar. *Science.* Retrieved from sciencemag.org/news/2017/10/analysis-china-s-one-child-policy-sparks-uproar

Ingham, E. (2018). Attitudes toward disability in society viewed through the lens of critical disability theory: An analysis of *Me Before You. Counseling Psychology Review, 33,* 2–12.

Institute for Policy Studies. (2019). Dreams deferred: How enriching the 1% widens the racial wealth gap. Retrieved from https://ips-dc.org/racial-wealth-divide-2019/

Ito, H. (1967). Japan's outcastes in the United States. In G. A. DeVos & H. Wagatsuma (Eds.), *Japan's invisible race: Caste in culture and personality* (pp. 200–221). Berkeley: University of California Press.

Jacobs, J. H. (1978). *Black/White interracial families: Marital process and identity development in young children.* Retrieved from Dissertation Abstracts International, 38, 5023.

Jacobson, E. (2009, September). I have a dream house. *Harper's Magazine*. Retrieved from https://harpers.org/archive/2009/09/i-have-a-dream-house/

James, S. E., Herman, J. L., Rankin, S., Keisling, M., Mottet, L., & Anafi, M. (2016). *The Report of the 2015 U.S. Transgender Survey*. Washington, DC: National Center for Transgender Equality.

Jones, C. P. (2000). A gardener's tale: Levels of racism: A theoretic framework and a gardener's tale. *American Journal of Public Health, 90,* 1212–1215.

Jones, N. A., & Bullock, J. (2012, September). *The two or more races population: 2010.* 2010 Census Briefs. Retrieved from https://www.census.gov/prod/cen2010/briefs/c2010br-13.pdf

Jung, J. Y., McCormick, J., & Gross, M. U. M. (2012). The forced choice dilemma: A model incorporating idiocentric/allocentric cultural orientation. *Gifted Child Quarterly, 56,* 15–24.

Kaholokula, J. K. (2016). Racism and physical health disparities. In A. N. Alvarez, C. T. H. Liang, & H. A. Neville (Eds.).*The cost of racism for people of color: Contextualizing experiences of discrimination* (pp. 163–188). Washington, DC: American Psychological Association.

Kashdan, T. B., Mishra, A., Breen, W. E., & Froh, J. J. (2009). Gender differences in gratitude: Examining appraisals, narratives, the willingness to express emotions, and changes in psychological needs. *Journal of Personality, 77,* 691–730.

Kashefi, M. (2011). Structure and/or culture: Explaining racial differences in work values. *Journal of Black Studies, 42,* 638–664.

Kashima, T. (1997). *Personal justice denied: Report of the Commission on Wartime Relocation and Internment of Civilians.* Seattle, London: University of Washington Press.

Katz, P. A. (2003). Racists or tolerant multiculturalists? How do they begin? *American Psychologist, 58,* 897–909.

Katz, P. A., & Kofkin, J. A. (1997). Race, gender, and young children. In S. S. Luthar, J. A. Burack, D. Cicchetti, & J. R. Weisz (Eds.), *Developmental psychopathology: Perspectives on adjustment, risk, and disorder* (pp. 51–74). New York: Cambridge University Press.

Keel, T. D. (2013). Religion, polygenism and the early science of human origins. *History of the Human Sciences, 26,* 3–32.

Kenney, T. (2016, September 5). Number of Black-owned businesses grow, but still lags behind growth of other groups. *Atlanta Black Star.* Retrieved from https://atlantablackstar.com/2016/09/05/number-of-black-owned-businesses-grow-but-still-lags-behind-growth-of-other-groups/

Kiang, L., Supple, A. J., & Stein, G. L. (2018). Latent profiles of discrimination and socialization predicting ethnic identity and well-being among Asian American adolescents. *Journal of Research on Adolescence, 29,* 523–538.

Kill the Indian, and save the man: Capt. Richard H. Pratt on the education of Native Americans. (n.d.). History Matters. Retrieved from http://historymatters.gmu.edu/d/4929

Kim, D., Pan, Y., & Park, H. S. (1998). High- versus low-context culture: A comparison of Chinese, Korean, and American cultures. *Psychology & Marketing, 15,* 507–521.

Kim, J. (1981). *The process of Asian American identity development: A study of Japanese American women's perceptions of their struggle to achieve personal identities of Americans of Asian ancestry.* Dissertation Abstracts International, *42,* 155 1A (University Microfilms No. 81–18080).

Kim, S. Y., Wang, Y., Deng, S., Alvarez, R., & Li, J. (2011). Accent, perpetual foreigner stereotype, and perceived discrimination as indirect links between English proficiency and depressive symptoms in Chinese American adolescents. *Developmental Psychology, 47,* 289–301.

Klein, A. V. (2014, April 11). Katy Perry responds to her AMAs geisha costume controversy. *Fashionista.* Retrieved from https://fashionista.com/2014/01/katy-perry-repsonds-to-that-geisha-costume-controversy-in-february-gq

Kluckhohn, C. (1954). Southwestern studies of culture and personality. *American Anthropologist, 56,* 685–697.

Kluckhohn, F. R., & Strodtbeck, F. L. (1961). *Variations in value orientations.* Evanston, IL: Row, Patterson.

Kohlberg, L. (1966). Moral education in the schools: A developmental view. *The School Review, 74,* 1–30.

Koltko-Rivera. M. E. (2004). The psychology of world-views, *Review of General Psychology, 8*, 3–58.

Kovel, J. (1970). *White racism: A psychohistory.* New York: Pantheon Books.

Kulis, S. S, Robbins, D. E., Baker, T. M., Denetsosie, S., & Parkhurst, N. D. (2016). A latent class analysis of urban American Indian youth identities. *Cultural Diversity and Ethnic Minority Psychology, 22*, 215–228.

Kyere, E., & Huguley, J. P. (2018). Exploring the process by which positive racial identity develops and influences academic performance in Black youth: Implications for social work. *Journal of Ethnic & Cultural Diversity in Social Work: Innovation in Theory, Research & Practice*, 1–29.

Ladson-Billings, G. (1992). Culturally relevant teaching: The key to making multicultural education. In C. A. Grant (Ed.), *Research in multicultural education: From the margins to the mainstream* (pp. 107–121). Bristol, PA: The Falmer Press, Taylor & Francis.

LaFromboise, T., Coleman, H. L. K., & Gerton, J. (1983). Psychological impact of biculturalism: Evidence and theory. In N. R. Goldberger & J. B. Veroff (Eds.), *The culture and psychology reader* (pp. 489–535). New York: NYU Press.

Larsen, N. (1929). *Passing.* New York: Penguin Classics.

Le, C. N. (2020, March 1). The first Asian Americans. *Asian Nation: The Landscape of Asian America.* Retrieved from http://www.asian-nation.org/first .shtml#sthash.7yi6yRLF.dpbs

Leavitt, P. A., Covarrubias, R., Perez, Y. A., & Fryberg, S. A. (2015). "Frozen in time": The impact of Native American media representations on identity and self-understanding. *Journal of Social Issues, 71*, 39–53.

Lee, K. M., Lindquist, K. A., & Payne, B. K. (2018). Constructing bias: Conceptualization breaks the link between implicit bias and fear of Black Americans. *Emotion, 18*, 855–871.

Lee, R. (1999). *Orientals: Asian Americans in popular culture.* Philadelphia: Temple University Press.

Leong, F. T. L., & Kalibatseva, Z. (2011). Effective psychotherapy for Asian Americans: From cultural accommodation to cultural congruence. *Clinical Psychology: Science and Practice, 18*, 242–245.

Leong, F. T. L., Leach, M. M., Marsella, A. J., & Pickren, W. E. (2012). Internationalizing the psychology curriculum in the USA: Meeting the challenges and opportunities of a global era. In F. T. L. Leong, W. E. Pickren, M. M. Leach, & A. J. Marsella (Eds.), *Internationalizing the psychology curriculum in in the United States* (pp. 1–9). New York: Springer Science + Business Media.

Lewis, M. B. (2016). Arguing that Black is White: Racial categorization of mixed-race faces. *Perception, 45*, 505–514.

Lilienfeld, S. O. (2017). Microaggressions: Strong claims, inadequate evidence. *Perspectives on Psychological Science, 12*, 138–169.

Lin, L., Stamm, K., & Christidis, P. (2018, February). How diverse is the psychology workforce? *Monitor on Psychology: Datapoint.* Retrieved from https://www .apa.org/monitor/2018/02/datapoint

Livingston, G., & Brown, A. (2017, May 18). *Intermarriage in the U.S. 50 years after Loving v. Virginia.* Pew Research Center. Retrieved from https://www.pews ocialtrends.org/2017/05/18/intermarriage-in-the-u -s-50-years-after-loving-v-virginia/

Logan, T. K., & Walker, R. (2017). The gender safety gap: Examining the impact of victimization history, perceived risk, and personal control. *Journal of Interpersonal Violence.*

Lopez, G., Ruiz, N. G., & Patten, E. (2017, September 8). Key facts about Asian Americans, a diverse and growing population. *Fact Tank: News in the Numbers.* Retrieved from https://www.pewre search.org/fact-tank/2017/09/08/key-facts-about -asian-americans/

Lopez, S. J., Pedrotti, J. T., & Snyder, C. R. (2019). *Positive psychology: The scientific and practical explorations of human strengths* (4th ed.). Thousand Oaks, CA: Sage.

Lu, L., & Nicholson-Crotty, S. (2010). Reassessing the impact of Hispanic stereotypes on White Americans' immigration preferences. *Social Science Quarterly, 91*, 1312–1328.

Macartney, S. (2011, November). *Child poverty in the United States 2009 and 2010: Selected race groups and Hispanic origin.* Report Number ACSBR/10-05.

Retrieved from https://www.census.gov/library/publications/2011/acs/acsbr10-05.html

Mandela, N. (1994). *Long walk to freedom: The autobiography of Nelson Mandela.* New York: Little, Brown.

Manduca, R. (2018). Income inequality and the persistence of racial economic disparities. *Sociological Science, 5,* 182–205.

Maramba, G. G., & Nagayama Hall, G. C. (2002). Meta-analyses of ethnic match as a predictor of dropout, utilization, and level of functioning. *Cultural Diversity and Ethnic Minority Psychology, 8,* 290–297.

Martin, K. M., & Tuch, S. (1993). Black-White differences in the value of job rewards revisited. *Social Science Quarterly, 74,* 884–901.

Matsumoto, D., & Juang, L. (2017). *Culture and psychology.* Boston, MA: Cengage Learning.

McCarthy, J. (2018, November 12). In year two of #MeToo, fears about sexual assault remain. *Politics.* Retrieved from https://news.gallup.com/poll/244724/year-two-metoo-fears-sexual-assault-remain.aspx

McCormick, M. P., Cappella, E., Hughes, D. L., & Gallagher, E. K. (2014). Feasible, rigorous, and relevant validation of a measure of friendship homophily for diverse classrooms. *The Journal of Early Adolescence, 35,* 817–851.

McGarty, C., Yzerbyt, V. Y., & Spears, R. (Eds.) (2002). *Stereotypes as explanations: The formation of meaningful beliefs about social groups.* New York: Cambridge University Press.

McGirt, E. (2018, March 1). raceAhead: Only three Black CEOs in the Fortune 500. *Fortune.* Retrieved from https://fortune.com/2018/03/01/raceahead-three-black-ceos/

McIntosh, P. (1988). White privilege and male privilege: A personal account of coming to see correspondences through work in women's studies. In M. L. Anders, & P. H. Collins (Eds.), *Race, class, and gender: An anthology* (pp. 76–87). Belmont, CA: Wadsworth.

McIntosh, P. (2017). White privilege: Unpacking the invisible knapsack. In P. S. Rothenberg (Ed.), *White privilege: Essential readings on the other side of racism* (pp. 176–180). New York: Worth.

Mercer, S. H., Zeigler-Hill, V., Wallace, M., & Hayes, D. M. (2011). Development and initial validation of the Inventory of Microaggressions Against Black Individuals. *Journal of Counseling Psychology, 58,* 457–469.

Miehls, D. (2010). Racism and its effects. In N. R. Heller, & A. Gitterman (Eds.) *Mental health and social problems: A social work perspective* (pp. 62–85). London: Routledge.

Mio, J. S., Barker, L. A., & Domenech-Rodríguez, M. (2015). *Multicultural psychology: Understanding our diverse communities.* New York: Oxford University Press.

Miville, M. L. (2005). Psychological functioning and identity development of biracial people: A review of current theory and research. In R. T. Carter (Ed.), *Handbook of racial-cultural psychology and counseling: Theory and research* (vol. 1, pp. 295–319). Hoboken, NJ: John Wiley and Sons.

Moore, A. B., MacGregor, C., & Cornelius-White, J. (2017). School personnel-student racial congruence and the achievement gap. *Journal of Multicultural Education, 11,* 264–274.

Moradi, B., & Grzanka, P. R. (2017). Using intersectionality responsibly: Toward critical epistemology, structural analysis, and social justice activism. *Journal of Counseling Psychology, 64,* 500–513.

Morten, G., & Atkinson, D. R. (1983). Minority identity development and preference for counselor race. *Journal of Negro Education, 52,* 156–161.

Moses, J. O., Villodas, M. T., & Villodas, F. (2020). Black and proud: The role of ethnic-racial identity in the development of future expectations among at-risk adolescents. *Cultural Diversity and Ethnic Minority Psychology, 26,* 112–123.

Mossakowski, K. N. (2008). Dissecting the influence of race, ethnicity, and socioeconomic status on mental health in young adulthood. *Research on Aging, 30,* 649–671.

Murthy, D. (2018). *Introduction to social media, activism, and organizations.* Social Media+ Society, 4.

Retrieved from https://journals.sagepub.com/doi/pdf/10.1177/2056305117750716

Museus, S. D., & Park, J. J. (2015). The continuing significance of racism in the lives of Asian American college students. *Journal of College Student Development, 56,* 551–569.

Museus, S. D., Sariñana, S. A. L., Yee, A. L., & Robinson, T. E. (2011). A qualitative analysis of multiracial students' experiences with prejudice and discrimination in college. *Journal of College Student Development, 57,* 680–697.

Mushonga, D. W., & Henneburger, A. K. (2019). Protective factors associated with positive mental health in traditional and nontraditional Black students. *American Journal of Orthopsychiatry.*

Nadal, K. L., Wong, Y., Griffin, K. E., Davidoff, K., & Sriken, J. (2014). Racial microaggressions and Asian Americans: An exploratory study on within-group differences and mental health. *Asian American Journal of Psychology, 6,* 136–144.

Nakagawa, S. (2016). On solidarity, "centering anti-Blackness," and Asian Americans. In P. S. Rothenberg (Ed.), *Race, class, and gender in the United States* (pp. 642–644). New York: Worth.

National Center for Education Statistics (NCES). (2016). *Characteristics of public school teachers by race/ethnicity.* Retrieved from https://nces.ed.gov/programs/raceindicators/spotlight_a.asp.

National Girls Collaborative. (2018). *Statistics.* Retrieved from https://ngcproject.org/statistics

Newport, C. (2019). *Digital minimalism: Choosing a focused life in a noisy world.* New York: Portfolio

Ng, C. (2011, October 25). *Ohio U. students hit "racist" Halloween costumes.* Retrieved from https://abcnews.go.com/blogs/headlines/2011/10/ohio-university-students-hit-racist-halloween-costumes

Nichols, J. (Director). (2016). *Loving* [Motion picture]. New York: Big Beach.

Nisbett, R. E. (2003). *The geography of thought: How Asians and westerners think differently . . . and why.* New York: The Free Press.

Noble, S. U. (2018). *Algorithms of oppression: How search engines reinforce racism.* New York: NYU Press.

Norton, M. I., & Sommers, S. R. (2011). Whites see racism as a zero-sum game that they are now losing. *Perspectives on Psychological Science, 6,* 215–218.

Norton, M. I., Sommers, S. R., Apfelbaum, E. P., Pura, N., & Ariely, D. (2006). Color blindness and interracial interaction: Playing the political correctness game. *Psychological Science, 17,* 949–953.

Ochoa, G. L. (2013). *Academic profiling: Latinos, Asian Americans, and the achievement gap.* Minneapolis: University of Minnesota Press.

Ogbu, J. U. (1988). Culture, development and education. In A. D. Pellegrini (Ed.), *Psychological bases for early education.* (pp. 245–273). Oxford, England: John Wiley & Sons.

Okoye-Johnson, O. (2011). Does multicultural education improve students' racial attitudes? Implications for closing the achievement gap. *Journal of Black Studies, 42,* 1252–1274,

Omi, M., & Winant, H. (2015). *Racial formation in the United States.* New York: Routledge.

Ong, A. D., Cerrada, C., Lee, R. A., & Williams, D. R. (2017). Stigma consciousness, racial microaggressions, and sleep disturbance among Asian Americans. *Asian American Journal of Psychology, 8,* 72.

Order of Argument in the Case, Brown v. Board of Education. (2016). Retrieved from https://www.archives.gov/education/lessons/brown-case-order

Orfield, G., Ee, J., Frankenberg, E., & Siegel-Hawley, G. (2016). *Brown at 62: School segregation by race, poverty, and state.* UCLA Civil Rights Project. Retrieved from https://civilrightsproject.ucla.edu/research/k-12-education/integration-and-diversity/brown-at-62-school-segregation-by-race-poverty-and-state/Brown-at-62-final-corrected-2.pdf

Otterbacher, J. (2016, October 20). New evidence shows search engines reinforce social stereotypes. *Harvard Business Review.* https://hbr.org/2016/10/new-evidence-shows-search-engines-reinforce-social-stereotypes

Overton, S., & Sotto, J. (2016, August 7). *Reducing long lines to vote.* The Joint Center for Political and Economic Studies. Retrieved from https://jointcenter .org/content/how-reduce-long-lines-vote%E2%80% 94joint-center-policy-brief-0

Painter, D. (2015). Post colonial theory: Towards a worlding of critical psychology. In I. Parker (Ed.), *Handbook of critical psychology* (pp. 366–375). New York: Routledge/Taylor & Francis.

Palomar-Lever, J. (2007). Class identification and psychological variables related to well-being and social mobility. *Applied Research in Quality of Life, 2,* 165–188.

Paone, T. R., Malott, K. M., & Barr, J. J. (2015). Assessing the impact of a race-based course on counseling students: A quantitative study. *Journal of Multicultural Counseling and Development, 43,* 206–220.

Paris, D. (2012). Culturally sustaining pedagogy: A needed change in stance, terminology, and practice. *Educational Researcher, 41,* 93–97.

Park, B., & Hastie, R. (1987). Perception of variability in category development: Instance- versus abstraction-based stereotypes. *Journal of Personality and Social Psychology, 53,* 621–635.

Park, P. (2013, November 26). Why all the fuss over Katy Perry's geisha performance at the AMAs? *The Guardian.* Retrieved from https://www.theguardian .com/commentisfree/2013/nov/26/katy-perry-geisha performance-american-music-awards-fuss

Parker, K., Horowitz, J. M., Morin, R., & Lopez, M. H. (2015). *Multiracial in America: Proud, diverse and growing in numbers.* Pew Research Center. Retrieved from https://www.pewsocialtrends.org/2015/06/11/ multiracial-in-america/

Parks, S. J., & Yoo, H. C. (2016). Does endorsement of the model minority myth relate to anti- Asian sentiments among White college students? The role of a color-blind racial attitude. *Asian American Journal of Psychology, 7,* 287–294.

Patler, C., & Laster Pirtle, W. (2018). From undocumented to lawfully present: Do changes to legal status impact psychological well-being among Latino immigrant young adults? *Social Science & Medicine, 199,* 39–48.

Patton, T. O., & Snyder-Yuly, J. (2007). Any four black men will do: Rape, race, and the ultimate scapegoat. *Journal of Black Studies, 37,* 859–895.

Pedersen, P. (1990). *Multiculturalism as a fourth force.* Philadelphia: Brunner/Mazel.

Pedrotti, J. T. (2013). Positive psychology, social class, and counseling. In W. M. Liu (Ed.), *Handbook of social class in counseling* (pp. 131–143) New York: Oxford University Press.

Pedrotti, J. T. (2017, August). *Effective multicultural education: Intergroup dialogues as a 4-unit general education class.* Poster presented at the annual meeting of the American Psychological Association Convention, Washington, DC.

Pedrotti, J. T., Edwards, L. M., & Lopez, S. J. (2008). Promoting hope: Suggestions for school counselors. *Professional School Counseling, 12,* 100–107.

Pei, M. L. (2005). *Old horse knows the way.* Retrieved from http://www.chinapae.com/story/oldhorse.html

Perez, E. (2012, Feb 24). Despite diversity efforts, UC minority enrollment down significantly since Prop. 209, *KQED News, California Watch.* Retrieved from https://www.kqed.org/news/57464/ despite-diversity-efforts-uc-minority-enrol lment-down-since-prop-209

Perez v. Sharp (1948). L. A. No. 20305 32 Cal.2d 711.

Pew Research Center. (2014, August 18). *Stark racial divisions in reactions to Ferguson police shootings.* Retrieved from https://www.people-press .org/2014/08/18/stark-racial-divisions-in-reac tions-to-ferguson-police-shooting/

Pew Research Center. (2017, May 15). *Public views on intermarriage.* Retrieved from https://www .pewsocialtrends.org/2017/05/18/2-public-views-on -intermarriage/pst_2017-05-15-intermarriage-02-03

Pew Research Center. (2019). *Use of different online platforms by demographic groups.* Retrieved from https:// www.pewresearch.org/wp-content/uploads/2019/04/ FT_19.04.10_SocialMedia2019_Useofdifferent.png? resize=930,1024

Pew Research Center. (2019, June 12). *Social media fact sheet.* Retrieved from https://www.pewinternet.org/fact-sheet/social-media/

Phinney, J. S., & Alipuria, L. L. (1996). At the interface of cultures: Multiethnic/multiracial high school and college students. *The Journal of Social Psychology, 136,* 139–158.

Pierce, C. (1978). *Television and education.* Beverly Hills, CA: Sage.

Piña-Watson, B., Martinez, A. J., Cruz, L. N., Llamas, J. D., & López, B. G. (2018). Ethnic identity affirmation as a strength for Mexican descent academic outcomes: Psychological functioning and academic attitudes as mediators. *Psychology in the Schools, 55* (10), 1155–1170.

Pitts, D. (2009). Diversity management, job satisfaction, and performance: Evidence for U.S. federal agencies. *Public Administration Review, 69,* 328–338.

Plenke, M. (2015, September 9). The reason this "racist soap dispenser" doesn't work on black skin. *Mic.* Retrieved from https://www.mic.com/articles/124899/the-reason-this-racist-soap-dispenser-doesn-t-work-on-black-skin

Poon, O., Squire, D., Kdoama, C., Byrd, A., Chan, J., Manzano, L., Furr, S., & Bishundat, D. (2016). A critical review of the model minority myth in selected literature on Asian Americans and Pacific Islanders in higher education. *Review of Educational Research, 86,* 469–502.

Poston, W. C. (1990). The biracial identity development model: A needed addition. *Journal of Counseling & Development, 69,* 152–155.

Primack, B. A., Bisbey, M. A., Shensa, A., Bowman, N. D., Karim, S. A., Knight, J. M., & Sidani, J. E. (2018). The association between valence of social media experiences and depressive symptoms. *Depression and Anxiety, 35,* 784–794.

Quillian, L., Pager, D., Midtboen, A., Hexel, O. (2017, October 11). Hiring discrimination against black Americans hasn't declined in 25 years. *Harvard Business Review, 11.* Retrieved from https://hbr.org/2017/10/hiring-discrimination-against-black-americans-hasnt-declined-in-25-years

Rastogi, M., & Wieling, E. (2005). (Eds.). *Voices of color: First-person accounts of ethnic minority therapists.* Thousand Oaks, CA: Sage.

Reilly, K. (2018, November 7). Democrats in Kansas, New Mexico become first Native American women elected to congress. *Time.* Retrieved from https://time.com/5446593/sharice-davids-deb-haaland-first-native-american-woman-congress/

Ridley, C. R. (1989). Racism in counseling as an adversive behavioral process. In P. B. Pedersen, J. G. Draguns, W. J. Lonner, & J. E. Trimble (Eds.), *Counseling across cultures* (pp. 55–77). Honolulu: University of Hawaii Press.

Riegel, K. F. (1973). Dialectic operations: The final period of cognitive development. *Human Development, 16,* 346–370.

Rios, D., Stewart, A. J., & Winter, D. G. (2010). "Thinking she could be the next president:" Why identifying with the curriculum matters. *Psychology of Women Quarterly, 34,* 328–338.

Rockquemore, K. A., & Brunsma, D. L. (2004). Negotiating racial identity: Biracial women and interactional validation. *Women & Therapy, 27,* 85–102.

Rockquemore, K. A., Brunsma, D. L., & Delgado, D. J. (2009). Racing to theory or retheorizing race? Understanding the struggle to build a multiracial identity theory. *Journal of Social Issues, 65,* 13–34.

Rodriguez, J. (2006). Color-blind ideology and the cultural appropriation of hip-hop. *Journal of Contemporary Ethnography, 35,* 645–668.

Rogers, R. A. (2006). From cultural exchange to transculturation: A review and reconceptualization of cultural appropriation. *Communication Theory, 16,* 474–503.

Rogers-Sirin, L., & Sirin, S. R. (2009). Cultural competence as an ethical requirement: Introducing a new educational model. *Journal of Diversity in Higher Education, 2,* 19–29.

Rokeach, M. (1973). *The nature of human values.* New York: Free Press.

Romero, A. J., Edwards, L. M., Fryberg, S. A., & Orduña, M. (2014). Resilience to discrimination stress across ethnic identity stages of development. *Journal of Applied Social Psychology, 44,* 1–11.

Root, M. P. P. (1992). (Ed). *Racially mixed people in America.* Newbury Park, CA: Sage.

Root, M. P. P. (1998). Experiences and processes affecting racial identity development: Preliminary results from the Biracial Sibling Project. *Cultural Diversity and Mental Health, 4,* 237–247.

Root, M. P. P. (1999). The biracial baby boom: Understanding ecological constructions of racial identity in the 21st century. In R. Sheets & E. Hollins (Eds.), *Racial and ethnic identity in school practices: Aspects of human development* (pp. 67–89). Mahwah, NJ: Erlbaum.

Root, M. P. P. (2003). Multiracial families and children. In J. A. Banks & C. A. McGee Banks (Eds.), *Handbook of research on multicultural education* (pp. 110–124). San Francisco: Jossey-Bass.

Rosenstein, J. (Filmmaker). (1997). *In whose honor* [Motion picture]. United States: New Day Films. Available at https://www.newday.com/film/whose-honor

Rosette, A. S., Leonardelli, G. J., & Phillips, K. W. (2008). The White standard: Racial bias in leader categorization. *Journal of Applied Psychology, 93,* 758–777.

Rothenberg, P. S. (Ed.) (2016). *Race, class, and gender in the United States.* New York: Worth.

Rothstein, R. (2017). *The color of law: A forgotten history of how our government segregated America.* New York: Liveright.

Ruiz, A. A. (1990). Ethnic identity: Crisis and resolution. *Journal of Multicultural Counseling and Development, 18,* 29–40.

Salim, S. (2019, January 4). *How much time do you spend on social media? Research says 142 minutes a day.* Digital Information World. Retrieved from https://www.digitalinformationworld.com/2019/01/how-much-time-do-people-spend-social-media-infographic.html

Sanchez, D. T., Good, J. J., & Chavez, G. (2011). Blood quantum and perceptions of Black-White biracial targets: The Black ancestry prototype model of affirmative action. *Personality and Social Psychology Bulletin, 37,* 3–14.

Santayana, G. (1905). *The life of reason, or the phases of human progress.* New York: C. Scribner's Sons.

Schachner, M. K., Brenick, A., Noack, P., van de Vijever, F. J. R., & Heizmann, B. (2015). Structural and normative conditions for interethnic friendships in multiethnic classrooms. *International Journal of Intercultural Relations, 47,* 1–12.

Schevitz, T. (2000, August 30). California minorities become majority: Census reflects surge among Latinos, Asians. *SF Gate.* Retrieved from https://www.sfgate.com/news/article/California-Minorities-Become-Majority-Census-3238512.php

Schneider, M. E., Major, B., Luhtanen, R., & Crocker, J. (1996). Social stigma and potential costs of assumptive help. *Personality and Social Psychology Bulletin, 22,* 201–209.

Searight, B. K., & Searight, H. R. (2011). The value of a personal mission statement for university undergraduates. *Creative Education, 2,* 313–315.

Shih, M., & Sanchez, D. T. (2005). Perspectives and research on the positive and negative implications of having multiple racial identities. *Psychological Bulletin, 131,* 569–591.

Siemons, R., Raymond-Flesch, M., Auerswald, C. L., & Brindis, C. D. (2017). Coming of age on the margins: Mental health and well-being among Latino immigrant young adults eligible for Deferred Action for Childhood Arrivals (DACA). *Journal of Immigrant and Minority Health, 19,* 543–551.

Simonite, T. (2017, March 29). How coders are fighting bias in facial recognition software. *Wired.* Retrieved from https://www.wired.com/story/how-coders-are-fighting-bias-in-facial-recognition-software/

Singh, A., & Chun, K. Y. S. (2012). Multiracial/multiethnic queer and transgender clients: Intersections of identity and resilience. In S. H. Dworkin & M. Pope (Eds.), *Casebook for counseling lesbian, gay, bisexual, and transgendered persons and their families* (pp. 197–209). Alexandria, VA: American Counseling Association.

Slaughter-Acey, J. C., Talley, L. M., Stevenson, H. C., & Misra, D. P. (2018). Personal versus group experiences of racism and risk of delivering a small-for-gestational age infant in African American women: A life course perspective. *Journal of Urban Health, 967,* 181–192.

Smithsonian National Museum of the American Indian. (2014). *Nation-to- nation: Treaties between the United States and American Indian nations*. Exhibition script. Washington, DC.

Soliz, J., Cronan, G., Bergquist, G., Nuru, A. K., & Rittenour, C. E. (2017). Perceived benefits and challenges of a multiethnic-racial identity: Insight from adults with mixed heritage. *Identity: An International Journal of Theory and Research, 17,* 267–281.

Song, S. Y., & Pyon, S. M. (2008). Cultural deficit model. In N. J. Salkind (Ed.), *Encyclopedia of educational psychology* (vol. 1, pp. 216–217). Thousand Oaks, CA: Sage.

Spanierman, L., & Heppner, M. (2004). Psychosocial Cost of Racism to Whites Scale (PCRW): Construction and initial validation. *Journal of Counseling Psychology, 51,* 249–262.

Stahl, G. K., Maznevski, M. L., Voigt, A., & Jonsen, K. (2010). Unraveling the effects of cultural diversity in teams: A meta-analysis of research on multicultural work groups. *Journal of International Business Studies, 41,* 690–709.

Steele, C. M. (1997). A threat in the air: How stereotypes shape intellectual identity and performance. *American Psychologist, 52,* 613–629.

Stenberg, A. (2015, July 15). *Don't cashcrop on my cornrows* [Video file]. Retrieved from www.youtube.com/watch? v=O1KJRRSB_XA

Stephens, M. (2013, May 10). Geography of hate: Mapping the origins of online hate speech. *Humboldt State Now*. Retrieved from http://now.humboldt.edu/news/geography-of-hate-mapping-the-origins-of-online-hate-speech

Stonequist, E. V. (1937). *The marginal man: A study in personality and culture conflict*. New York: Wiley.

Students Teaching Against Racism in Society (STARS). (2013). *Mission statement*. Retrieved from https://www.ohio.edu/orgs/stars/Home.html

Study: White and black children biased toward lighter skin. (2010, May 14). Cable News Network. Retrieved from https://www.cnn.com/2010/US/05/13/doll.study/index.html

Sue, D. W. (1977). Counseling the culturally different: A conceptual analysis. *Personnel and Guidance Journal, 55,* 422–426.

Sue, D. W. (1978). Eliminating cultural oppression in counseling: Toward a general theory. *Journal of Counseling Psychology, 25,* 419–428.

Sue, D. W. (2001). Multidimensional facets of cultural competence. *The Counseling Psychologist, 29,* 790–821.

Sue, D. W., & Sue, D. (1990). *Counseling the culturally different: Theory and practice*. New York: Wiley.

Sue, D. W., & Sue, D. (2016). *Counseling the culturally diverse: Theory and practice* (7th ed.). New York: Wiley.

Sue, D. W., Allen, D. B., & Conway, L. (1978). The responsiveness and equality of mental health care to Chicanos and Native Americans. *American Journal of Community Psychology, 6,* 137–146.

Sue, D. W., Capodilupo, C. M., & Holder, A. M. B. (2007). Racial microaggressions in the life experience of Black Americans. *Professional Psychology: Research and Practice, 39,* 329–336.

Sue, S. (1998). In search of cultural competence in psychotherapy and counseling. *American Psychologist, 53,* 440–448.

Sue, S., & McKinney, H. (1975). Asian Americans in the community mental health care system. *American Journal of Orthopsychiatry, 45,* 111–118.

Sue, S., & Okazaki, S. (1991). Explanations for Asian-American achievements: A reply. *American Psychologist, 46,* 878–880.

Sue, S., McKinney, H., Allen, D., & Hall, J. (1974). Delivery of community mental health services to black and white clients. *Journal of Consulting and Clinical Psychology, 42,* 794–801.

Tabb, K. M. (2016). Changes in racial categorization over time and health status: An examination of multiracial young adults in the USA. *Ethnicity and Health, 21,* 146–157.

Takaki, R. (2008). *A different mirror: A history of multicultural America*. New York: Back Bay Books.

Takei, G. (1994). *To the stars: The autobiography of George Takei, Star Trek's Mr. Sulu.* New York: Pocket Books.

Tao, K. W., Owen, J., & Drinane, J. M. (2017). Was that racist? An experimental study of microaggression ambiguity and emotional reactions for racial-ethnic minority and white individuals. *Race and Social Problems, 9,* 262–271.

Tatum, B. D. (1997/2017). "Why are all the Black kids sitting together in the cafeteria?" and other conversations about race. New York: Basic Books.

Taylor, K-Y. (2016). *From #Blacklivesmatter to Black liberation.* Chicago: Haymarket Books.

Thomas, A., & Sillen, S. (1972). *Racism and psychiatry.* New York: Brunner/ Mazel.

Thomas, Jr. R. R. (2005). *Building on the promise of diversity: How we can move to the next level in our workplaces, our communities, and our society.* New York: AMACOM.

Time flies: U.S. adults now spend nearly half a day interacting with media. (2018, July 31). Retrieved from https://www.nielsen.com/us/en/insights/article/2018/time-flies-us-adults-now-spend-nearly-half-a-day-interacting-with-media/

Townsend, S. S. M., Markus, H., R., & Bergsieker, H. B. (2009). My choice, your categories: The denial of multiracial identities. *Journal of Social Issues, 65,* 185–204.

Tran, J., & Curtin, N. (2017). Not your model minority: Own-group activism among Asian Americans. *Cultural Diversity and Ethnic Minority Psychology, 23,* 499–507.

Treviño, J. G. (1996). Worldview and change in cross-cultural counseling. *The Counseling Psychologist, 24,* 198–215.

Triandis, H. C. (1995). A theoretical framework for the study of diversity. In M. M. Chemers, S. Oskamp, & M. a. Costanzo (Eds.), *Diversity in organizations: New perspectives for a changing workplace* (pp. 11–36). Thousand Oaks, CA: Sage.

Triandis, H. C. (2002). Subjective culture. *Online Readings in Psychology and Culture, 2.* doi:10.9707/2307-0919.1021

Triandis, H. C. (2006). Cultural intelligence in organizations. *Group & Organization Management, 31,* 20–26.

Tull, A. G. T., Scott, P. B., & Smith, B. (1982) (Eds.). *All the women Are White, all the Blacks are men, but some of us are brave.* New York: The Feminist Press.

Tyson, T. B. (2017). *The blood of Emmett Till.* New York: Simon & Schuster.

US Census Bureau. (2000). *Census 2000 data for the United States.* Retrieved from https://www.census.gov/census2000/states/us.html

US Census Bureau. (2017). *Educational attainment of the population 18 years and over, by age, sex, race, and Hispanic origin.* Retrieved from https://www.census.gov/data/tables/2017/demo/education-attainment/cps-detailed-tables.html5

US Census Bureau. (2020). *Quick facts.* Retrieved from https://www.census.gov/quickfacts/fact/table/US/PST045219

US Senate. (2018). *Ethnic diversity in the senate.* Retrieved from: https://www.senate.gov/senators/EthnicDiversityintheSenate.htm

Vannucci, A., & Ohannessian, C. M. (2019). Social media use subgroups differentially predict psychosocial well-being during early adolescence. *Journal of youth and adolescence, 48,* 1469–1493.

Vera, E. M., Speight, S. L., Mildner, C., & Carlson, H. (1999). Clients' perceptions and evaluations of similarities to and differences from their counselors. *Journal of Counseling Psychology, 46,* 277–283.

Vera, H., & Gordon, A. (2003). *Screen saviors: Hollywood fictions of Whiteness.* Lanham, MD: Rowman & Littlefield.

Verkuyten, M., & Thijs, J. (2013). Multicultural education and inter-ethnic attitudes: An intergroup perspective. *European Psychologist, 18,* 179–190.

Viñas-Nelson, J. (2017). Interracial marriage in "post-racial" America. *Origins: current events in historical perspective, 10.* Retrieved from http://origins.osu.edu/article/interracial-marriage-post-racial-america

Vittrup, B. (2018). Color blind or color conscious? White American mothers' approaches to racial socialization. *Journal of Family Issues, 39,* 668–692.

Vittrup, B., & Holden, G. W. (2010). Children's assessments of corporal punishment and other disciplinary practices: The role of age, race, SES and exposure to spanking. *Journal of Applied Developmental Psychology, 31,* 211–220.

Wallace, M. E., Green, C., Richards, L., Theall, K., & Crear-Perry, J. (2017). "Look at the whole me": A mixed-methods examination of black infant mortality in the US through women's lived experiences and community context. *International Journal of Environmental Research and Public Health, 14,* 727.

Walton, G. M., & Cohen, G. L. (2003). Stereotype life. *Journal of Experimental Social Psychology, 39,* 456–467.

Walton, G. M., & Cohen, G. L. (2007). A question of belonging: Race, social fit, and achievement. *Journal of Personality and Social Psychology, 92,* 82–96.

Wang, F. K-H. (2016, October 27). *Student campaign fights "culturally appropriative" Halloween costumes.* National Broadcasting Company. Retrieved from https://www.nbcnews.com/news/asian-america/student-campaign-fights-against-culturally-appropriative-halloween-costumes-n673546

Wang, L., & Finch, H. (2018). Motivation variables mediate the relationship between socioeconomic status and academic achievement. *Psychology and Education: An Interdisciplinary Journal, 55,* 123–136.

Wang, Y-W., Davidson, M. M., Yakushko, O. F., Savoy, H. B., Tan, J. A., & Bleier, J. K. (2001). The Scale of Ethnocultural Empathy: Development, validation, and reliability. *Journal of Counseling Psychology, 50,* 221–234.

Wayne, J. H., & Casper, W. J. (2016). Why having a family-supportive culture, not just policies, matters to male and female job seekers: An examination of work-family conflict, values, and self-interest. *Sex Roles: A Journal of Research, 75,* 459–475.

Weldon Cooper Center for Public Service. (2013). *Racial dot map.* Retrieved from https://demographics.coopercenter.org/Racial-Dot-Map/?q=demographics/Racial-Dot-Map

West, C., & Buschendorf, C. (2015). *Black prophetic fire.* Boston, MA: Beacon Press.

What we believe. (n.d.). Black Lives Matter. Retrieved from https://blacklivesmatter.com/what-we-believe/

White, F. A., Wootton, B., Man, J. D., Diaz, H., Rasiah, J., Swift, E., & Wilkinson, A. (2009). Adolescent racial prejudice development: The role of friendship quality and interracial contact. *International Journal of Intercultural Relations, 33,* 524–534.

White, M., & Epston, D. (1990). *Narrative means to therapeutic ends.* New York: W. W. Norton.

Whitman, S. (n.d.). *The opposite of colorblind: Why it's essential to talk to children about race.* Retrieved February 10, 2020, from https://www.leeandlow.com/imprints/tu-books/articles/the-opposite-of-colorblind-why-it-s-essential-to-talk-to-children-about-race

Wiggan, G., & Watson, M. J. (2016). Teaching the whole child: The importance of cultural responsiveness, community engagement, and character development in high achieving African American students. *The Urban Review, 48,* 766–798.

Wijeyesinghe, C. I., Griffin, P., & Love, B. (1997). Racism-curriculum dialogue. In M. Adams, L. A. Bell, & P. Griffin (Eds.), *Teaching for diversity and social justice: A sourcebook.* (pp. 82–109). New York: Routledge.

Williams, J. L., Anderson, R. E., Francois, A. G., Hussain, S., & Tolan, P. H. (2014). Ethnic identity and positive youth development in adolescent males: A culturally integrated approach. *Applied Developmental Science, 18,* 110–122.

Williams Institute, UCLA. (2019, March). *LGBT people in the United States not protected by state non-discrimination statuses.* Retrieved from https://williamsinstitute.law.ucla.edu/wp-content/uploads/Equality-Act-March-2019.pdf

Winerman, L. (2016). Students lead anti-racism efforts: Graduate students are organizing to support the Black Lives Matter movement. *Monitor on Psychology, 47*(9), 16.

Wise, T. (2011). *White like me: Reflections on race from a privileged son.* Berkeley, CA: Soft Skull Press.

Wong, F., & Halgin, R. (2006). The "model minority": Bane or blessing for Asian Americans? *Journal of Multicultural Counseling and Development, 34,* 38–49.

Wong, Y. J., Owen, J., Tran, K. K., Collins, D. L., & Higgins, C. E. (2012). Asian American male college students' perceptions of people's stereotypes about Asian American men. *Psychology of Men & Masculinity, 13,* 75–88.

Wong-Padoongpatt, G., Zane, N., Okazaki, S., & Saw, A. (2017). Decreases in implicit self-esteem explain the racial impact of microaggressions among Asian Americans. *Journal of Counseling Psychology, 64,* 574–583.

Yang, S. (2008). Real-life contextual manifestations of wisdom. *International Journal of Aging and Human Development, 67,* 273–303.

Yoo, H. C., & Lee, R. M. (2008). Does ethnic identity buffer or exacerbate the effects of frequent racial discrimination on situational well-being of Asian Americans? *Journal of Counseling Psychology, 55,* 63–74.

YouGov. (2018, May 20–22). *The Economist/YouGov poll.* Retrieved from https://d25d2506sfb94s.cloudfront.net/cumulus_uploads/document/o61zinhwe1/econTopl ines.pdf

Young, S. G., Hugenberg, K., Bernstein, M. J., & Sacco, D. F. (2012). Perception and motivation in face recognition: A critical review of theories of the cross-race effect. *Personality and Social Psychology Review, 16,* 116–142.

Youssef-Morgan, C. M., & Hardy, J. (2014). A positive approach to multiculturalism and diversity management in the workplace. In J. T. Pedrotti & L. M. Edwards (Eds.), *Perspectives on the intersection of multiculturalism and positive psychology* (pp. 219–233). New York: Springer Science + Business Media.

Zaharna, R. S. (2000). Intercultural communication and international public relations: Exploring parallels. *Communication Quarterly, 48,* 85–100.

APPENDIX: MULTICULTURAL NOVELS

American Indian

Lakota Woman by Mary Crow Dog

Solar Storms and Power by Linda Hogan

Where the Dead Sit Talking by Brandon Hobson

Ceremony and Gardens in the Dunes by Leslie Marmon Silko

Tracks and Future Home of the Living God by Louise Erdrich

House Made of Dawn by N. Scott Momaday

There, There by Tommy Orange

African American

The Color Purple by Alice Walker

The Bluest Eye by Toni Morrison

A Lesson Before Dying by Ernest J. Gaines

Passing by Nella Larsen

Mama Day by Gloria Naylor

Latinx

The House on Mango Street by Sandra Cisneros

Bless Me Ultima by Rudolfo Anaya

How the Garcia Girls Lost Their Accents by Julia Alvarez

Asian

The Woman Warrior by Maxine Hong Kingston

Everything I Never Told You by Celeste Ng

The Best We Could Do by Thi Bui

Dogeaters by Jessica Hagedorn

Interpreters of Maladies by Jhumpa Lahiri

Middle Eastern

The Kite Runner by Khaled Hossani

INDEX